ECONOMIC SOVEREIGNTY

Prosperity in a Free Society
(Alvarism Book 1)

THOMAS E. KUREK

© 2016 by Alvarian Press
Reston, VA 20194

Editor: Jennifer Serrano
Foreword: Steven Yeh
Photo of Thomas Kurek walking in snow: Jennifer Serrano
Photo of Thomas Kurek speech in Senate: Charlene Brosius
Cover design & graphic art: Thomas E. Kurek

Alvarian Press publications are offered at special discounts for bulk purchases. For more information, please message the Alvarian Press at: **https://alvarism.com/contact/**

Visit **https://alvarism.com** for events, updates, supplemental resources, and opportunities.

A CIP catalog record for this book is available from the Library of Congress.

LCCN: 2016909719

ISBN: 978-0-9976978-0-3 (paperback)

ISBN: 978-0-9976978-1-0 (e-book)

Table of Contents

Table of Contents

Thomas E. Kurek

Table of Photos

Table of Equations

Table of Figures

Table of Figures

Thomas E. Kurek

Dedication

Without blessings, passion, love, good, evil, strife, and suffering, this work would not have been possible. All Alvarism books are dedicated to those, who in any way, inspired this research and contemplation (alphabetical listing of names for the groupings):

Above all, the eternal, Holy Trinity. The Kurek family: Aunt Sophie, Carol, Dan, Helen, Janice, Kathleen, Kelly, Mary, Michael, and Thomas. August, Claire, Concetta, and Mark Kupco. Andrew, Anthony, and Johanna Cipolla. Eileen, Edwin Zwetsch, and their children. Charlene, Todd Brosius and their children. Ashleigh, Emily, Heather, Jennifer, Katie, Mary, Megan, Natalie, Renee, Sarah, Vanissa, Victoria. Anthony and Jamee Abbruscato, Barbara Krajewski, Barbara Pendergrass, Bevlee Watford, Colin Hawley, Corey Wise, Dmitry Shiryaev, Erin Anderson, Erin deRenouard, Eugene Ruffner, Jack and Julia Warden, Jason Storch, Jennifer Serrano, John Brandon, John Domm, Lance Luttschwagger, Lee Rider, Phuc Vuong, Richard Burkholder, Scott Struber, Sevil Kalayci, Shannon Kirkpatrick, Steven Yeh, Suzanne Bullen, Osmund and Linda Chan, Joseph Hanbury, Robert Mascatello

Pedagogues: Adam Smith, Aristotle, Bruce Johnson, Bruce Thornton, Carl E. Olson, Charles Dickens, Dr. Daniel J. Schneck, Dr. Luther Glenn Kraige, Denise Wingfield, Edmund Burke, Edward Bernays, Eldon Taylor, F.A. Hayek, Gail Martin, J. R .R. Tolkein, JoAnn Harvill (bogtrotter), John Locke, Karl Popper, Kent Clizbe, Kurt Bryan Engel, Ludwig von Mises, Marcus Aurelius, Maryann Skrzycki, Milton Friedman, Montesquieu, Niccolo Machiavelli, Norman Dowling, Pamela Burns, Phil Rosenthal, Pope John Paul II, Pope St. Gregory I, Rick Reeves, St. Thomas Aquinas, Sun Tzu, Susan Cooper, The USA Forefathers, Thomas Sowell, Thomas Walker, Victor Davis Hanson, Walter Lippmann, William R. Johnson, William Shakespeare

Acknowledgements

I wish to personally thank the following people for their direct or indirect support for this research:

- Alma Jackson
- Charla Quimby
- Daniel Egtvedt
- Erin Anderson
- Geraldine Davie
- Jennifer Serrano
- John Brandon
- Jim, Carol, Claire, and Molly Wallwork
- Kathy Mallard
- Mark Fitzgibbons
- Patricia Shockey
- Peggy Nienaber
- Sevil Kalayci
- Stephanie Reis
- Steven Yeh
- Suzanne Spikes
- Tom and Linda Cranmer

Lastly, my thanks to all of the tireless and devoted researchers, organizations, and professors that are cited in the data analysis or bibliography. These philanthropic not-for-profit endeavors are impossible without your good will and inspiration.

Thomas E. Kurek

Foreword

A GIFT and a LABOR of love.

Not since Allan Bloom's *The Closing of the American Mind (1987)* has such an important compendium of information been assembled. In *Economic Sovereignty*, Thomas Kurek has written an important and information-packed work, which demystifies the complex interplay between politics, economics, prosperity, poverty, jobs, and *perceived* wealth. Imagine an economic and political cloak-and-dagger detective navigating his way through the morass of dark alleys to find vital clues buried in data, interestingly in plain sight, to understand what has happened. In the end, there is no cliffhanger; it is just disconcerting to realize that the morass is Main Street, USA and the body count of collateral damage is just beginning.

In July of 1997 in Salon, Camille Paglia called *The Closing of the American Mind*, "the first shot in the culture wars." *Economic Sovereignty* demonstrates in no uncertain terms why, in the ensuing twenty-five years, the nation and its people lost those culture wars to the detriment of our posterity. Kurek's work details the end result of the education system's focus on teaching, "what to think," rather than, "how to think," which has been devastating to the foundation of societal thought, resulting in a population that is now growing in functional illiteracy. Compared with illiteracy (the inability to read or write simple sentences), functional illiteracy is the inability to comprehend and assimilate information beyond a basic level. A functionally illiterate society cannot comprehend or even sense that to which it is being subjected to, molding it into something that few would recognize until it is too late.

At the same time, as the percentage of the functionally illiterate increases, the norm of the leadership pool which affects our ability to compete globally, decreases. Kurek's sociological research is compelling, logical, and a basis for change. Any problem requires one to address the root issue, not just the symptoms, in order to reverse and undo the effects. *Economic Sovereignty* is that first step. It is a first step and the clarion call for a proper dialogue to address the economic problems in our society. It will take nothing less than a well-organized national crusade, if this country is to be saved as a free society, where the efforts of one's toils become personal wealth instead of being spirited away in the middle of the night by theft, taxes, regulations, and waste.

For those who have not become the victims of functional illiteracy, whether bureaucrat, psychologist, sociologist, economist, teacher, pastor, and others in people-oriented professions, understanding emotions and perspectives can only enhance the chance of successful outcomes. From the small local businessman to the corporate lead, understanding the employee and their expectations, whether realistic or not, can only help to improve performance, the bottom line and sometimes just avoid hassles and issues. The social and economic concepts presented in *Economic Sovereignty* provide a crucial understanding for harmonious connectivity.

Our country has lost untold wealth, irrecoverable to the sands of time. There is no effort that can undo the inefficient utilization of resources in the past. Let us imagine this nation as an onion, and peel back the layers, one by one. *Economic Sovereignty* allows us to understand that while we would expect to see onion at each new level, the reality is that we find hidden rot. Left unchecked that rot will destroy everything. The timidity of those unwilling to speak out is no longer a luxury we can afford. Knowledge is power and an educated citizen is society's greatest asset. This work will be criticized and dismissed, but that is just "business as usual" for brutally honest works that induce us to take a hard look at ourselves, with conclusions that are validated by reliable data. It is never easy to hear the truth, particularly when it is disturbing.

I promise you that the few precious hours you will spend with this book are not a waste. I encourage you to create avenues of discussion that must be opened and debated publicly. Dare I say, you will never look at the world the same way again.

Steven Yeh
Threat Assessment Policy Director
Integrated Threat Assessment Solutions Consortium America
(ITASCA), Former Congressional Candidate

Thomas E. Kurek

Preface

At Virginia Tech's College of Engineering, I shared classrooms with some of the brightest students in America. On the first day of class, our Engineering Fundamentals professor said, "You are among the best performing students in the nation, but don't get too prideful. Look to your left, and look to your right. By the beginning of next year, the people sitting next to you will no longer be in this program. Our attrition rate is over fifty percent. You must succeed this year, if you want to be accepted by one of our specific engineering programs."

I was appalled. I had just surpassed ninety-five percent of my peers to get where I was, and the first thing my new mentor tells me is that I need to compete for another program, and to humble myself? In truth, eighteen-year-olds need doses of humility like infants need caged playpens. Clearly, this engineering professor had not been teaching at retirement homes – he knew how to design such benevolent cages for brash young'uns. He continued to demonstrate his expert command of youthful psychology:

"The good news is that for those of you who succeed, you will have one of the best careers you can get in America. You will always have employers competing for your knowledge and skills, because there aren't many people who can do what you're capable of. You will have challenging, exciting work. You will be tasked with raising the poor from poverty, healing disease, taming the hostile forces of nature, and sheltering the bare bones of science with technologies that make life better for everyone. You will be the engine of the real progress of humanity. And you will have a very comfortable compensation. A number of my students last year received Corvettes as part of their signing bonus."

Corvettes? Now he was talking! My peers glanced at each other and smiled at the thought. A year later, they looked at my Engineering Physics (ESM) classmates like a child looks at a drunken adult. The other engineers had to take courses from our ESM department to gain their foundation in applied physics – vibration and control, finite element analysis, fluid mechanics, dynamics, statics, and mechanics of deformable bodies. They despised the complexity of our courses; but, while our peers offered loathing, the academic community offered respect. US News and World Report ranked Virginia Tech ESM as fifth in the nation alongside Stanford. Absent from the report was the department's student-blessed nickname: Engineering Sado-Masochism. Sometimes I noticed chains and leather in the Deforms lab,

Photo 1: Stress Testing Bovine Pericardium for Cardiomend's Intraoperative Autologous Tissue Tester (LTR: Dr. Scott L. Hendricks, Rebecca, Thomas Kurek)

and professors did wear black most of the time. They also cracked some students' spirits with a hard-boiled attitude when three-fourths of the vibrations class failed the first major exam. Still, I could never relate to the ESM joke. I thought Calculus of Variations and programming Finite Element Method software from scratch was kind of fun. Let me assure you that these sentiments do not implicate my romantic proclivities in any way, although I'm a big fan of leather and black clothes. Coincidence?

After graduation, we would need the humility that our mentors and rigorous coursework inculcated. The effects of the dot-com collapse and the September 11th attacks were manifesting. Engineers were no longer receiving Corvettes. In fact, entry-level engineers, lawyers, and computer programmers were having a hard time finding work. For liberal arts graduates, the job market was even worse. Most of my college-educated peers had to live with their parents and take jobs that did not even need a college education.

Still, my transition to the working world was less dramatic than my foray into college. Even during the recession, I obtained a degree-related job within three months. I began programming enterprise databases and web applications for the U.S. State Department. One system was a collaboration with the National Federation of the Blind, and another helped poor Africans to get their products onto the global market. It was good work, but not as challenging as my previous work in college, improving the reliability of bioprosthetic heart valves, and preventing life-threatening hip fractures with kinematic analysis.

Despite such great medical projects, I was unprepared to face my heartbroken friends who sprained their hopes and dreams by tripping over the gamed economy. The resounding sentiment of my peers was disillusionment. They felt lied to, and as if their productivity was not rewarded. They felt that their degrees were a waste. They felt that their responsible choices were irrelevant. Many lived off of their parents, peers, loans, or the government. Even the statistics indicated a great exodus from independence. Pew Research showed that young adults (18-31) living alone or married declined from 59% to 30% from 1968 to 2012. Those who were cohabitating with parents, kin, or peers increased from 41% to 70% during the same interval.[1] Sallie Mae recently estimated that two-thirds of parents expect to financially support their children for up to five years after they graduate from college.[2]

Photo 2: Karen Roland and Thomas Kurek Partner on USAID's South African Trade Hub

Early adulthood in America looked more codependent than ever. Liberated and prosperous young adults are supposed to stake their own claim, live alone, or make independent families as they used to in the 1960s, throughout history, and even in modern third-world countries. These modern first-world lifestyles went against nature, the globe, and humanity itself. The metropolis was a *robotic nurse*, ready to mechanically dispense whatever injection the patient needed to run away from their irksome disappointments. Many twenty-first century cohabitating adults were jaded – compelled to escape reality with narcotics, alcohol, entertainment-obsession, over-socialization, religious fanaticism, wanderlust, promiscuity, or anthropomorphism (ascribing human features to animals). They

---

[1] (Pew Research Center, 2013)
[2] (Clabaugh, 2015)

were transforming financial parasitism into instant gratification, luxury, and vice – emulating the rise of Weimar Germany.

Discontent to let the grass grow under their feet, live within their means, provide for themselves, and build a life where they stood, they scattered to the winds every night, turning life into Dante's second circle of hell – always wandering, always seeking to take in more stimuli, but never able to obtain peace and satisfaction. Reminiscent of some dystopian movie like Fight Club,[3] they were like psychological vagabonds who returned to the same home every night. By the time the vagabonds woke up from their escapism in their thirties, their vanity fair would leave irreversible consequences. Lost time can never be found again.

This toxic social dynamic could not be separated from the economic atmosphere. Economic freedom preserves personal freedom. The housing, public transportation, cars, education, government, and healthcare were not worth what we paid. Price signals were distorted by taxation, government spending, regulations, subsidies, private cartels, and monetary policy. Instead of increasing productivity and competition, reducing prices across the board, the power and size of institutions increased, and the codependency of the debt-serfs rose in turn. Net worth was consumed by this voracious spending cycle and malinvestment. Young adults emerged in their thirties without a dime in their pockets, and shackled by the debts they had chosen, including their wasted time. They needed a dose of humility to accept their obstructed independence. I could kindly support my floundering friends, but despite my technical expertise, I couldn't cure their hearts or reprogram the *robotic nurse* they lived in.

My situation was different than my vagabond peers, but humility would strike me from a different angle. Even with my career off to a great start, social misfortunes force-fed me my pride. With American, Eastern European, and Italian blood flowing through my veins, I expected it to taste like hot dogs and kielbasa over spaghetti. It actually tasted more like genuine liberation from my impulse to exhort and control, which has a similar level of indigestion during the idealistic arrogance of young adulthood.

---

[3] (Fincher, 1999)

Thomas E. Kurek

As my economic and business knowledge unveiled the illusions of progress and prosperity around me, I was perturbed by the phony smiles of the *poverty-hustling* entertainers, politicians, educators, clergy, and journalists. Their disingenuous platitudes masked their seething wrath and envy. Fear, aggression, and the self-loathing animosity of classism dripped from their lips in every speech, however cleverly disguised as *positive* and *loving* at times. My economic research would do something much more than disprove these class warriors. It would reveal facts that nobody has discussed before regarding our economy, prosperity, and the way we improve our lives. The truth of our economy is not somewhere between the perceptions of socialists or capitalists – but on an alternate plane altogether.

But how could such impersonal abstractions motivate me to invest so much of my own hard-won earnings and energy into such a tedious pursuit of truth? Was I really motivated by the outrageous tax and economic policies of inept politicians? Pure altruism is a four-leaf clover. Most often, there is a deeply personal motivation underlying altruism, even if subconscious. I reflected upon my life to discover my own experiences with classism that went beyond the great depression ghettos of my family, and looked past the mountains of unmerited income in the *institutionalist* economy. After much introspection, I realized that my motivation was deeply personal – to willingly spend months of my free time crunching data, researching, making spreadsheets and charts, and reading heady economic analyses from leading economists in the world.

Underlying my motivation was an aggregation of every injustice inflicted upon friends and family by ubiquitous government usurpation of the sweat from their brow, and the Orwellian destruction of merit, liberty, honor, and self-reliance that robbed their spirits. Policies inspired by classism darkened their souls with dishonesty and codependence, so that they were more apt to lose their identity to some collectivist interest group, in which other self-abdicating, self-loathing people could commiserate and plan attacks on their scapegoats. The social malaise from this psychological robbery was awful enough. But my most profound experience with classism was during a romance that Charles Dickens may have greatly expected.[4]

In light of my own deeply personal experience, what of the people who speak of *the rich* and *the poor* who don't even know what it means for classism to go beyond material concerns, and forge a blade right into the heart? What of those who can't even conceive of how classism can destroy true love? I know firsthand that the darkest side of classism is its moral and social consequences. That was the burning fire in my soul that gave me the willpower to spend hundreds of hours of my time buried in spreadsheets and data for economic analysis.

Ultimately, economy and society are massive forces that are beyond the control of any one individual. As much as I could not prevent classism from destroying romance, I could not prevent the housing collapse, even though I predicted it. Neither could I compel my peers to do productive things with their energy, and stop running away from their social and economic setbacks. I could only do the right thing for my own life; responsibility for "the world" is just a fanciful abstraction. But that abstraction can be comprehended analytically. Something much deeper instigated class conflict in our illusory economy, and for all of these deeply personal reasons, I was compelled to investigate.

President Obama called income inequality "the defining challenge of our times." *Occupy Wall Street* rallied against *the rich* for years. The *TEA Party* said that Americans were Taxed Enough Already (TEA). American unemployment shifted to declining labor force participation at an astonishing rate. Prices were increasing, while they claimed that there was no inflation. Real estate was still massively overpriced. Trillions in deficit spending by the government sacrificed our future to the present. Severe warnings of economic calamity began to circle the wagons. A French economist preaching about income inequality was paraded around the media and political forums like a prophet of global salvation. All around us, the drums of class warfare were beating stronger by the minute, instigating deep resentments.

---

[4] (Dickens, 1861)

Thomas E. Kurek

Underneath all the fanfare, what was the true story of the American economy? How did we get here? How have things changed for us? Are the rich getting richer? Are the poor getting poorer? What principles do we need in order to deter classism and increase cooperation? What knowledge do we need to vote wisely, and pursue the right economic decisions for our families and our nation? How can we increase American prosperity?

The answers to these questions are crucial to every American. For me, the research conveyed in this book has been a great adventure in both enlightenment and humility. It is the most principled and comprehensive public analysis of the American economy to date, decorated by social implications. I know that it will be highly valuable to citizens, academics, journalists, analysts, and our elected officials. They will discover fundamental concepts for discerning their own place in the economy, and new evidence from my charts and figures for their own specific interests. They will gain an understanding of the American economy that is rare, and contrary to many popular misconceptions.

I know that this research struck a chord because one of my childhood heroes, Buzz Aldrin, chose to come to two of my speeches in the U.S. Senate for briefings on the preliminary results. I could not have been more honored! The audience was comprised of gracious, wise, and great Americans with whom I am delighted to collaborate. Regrettably, I could not even have a word with COL(R) Aldrin when we shook hands, because we were shuffled out of the room so quickly. Nonetheless, it is an experience I will never forget. Men like COL(R) Aldrin inspired me as a child to pursue scientific and technological dreams.

Photo 3: COL(R) Buzz Aldrin attends Thomas Kurek's first research briefing in the U.S. Senate on October 27th, 2014

Despite my passion for science and technology and the inspiration of such heroes, I found that this technical research must be complemented with social considerations. Whether it is animosity towards *the poor*, or wrath against *the rich*, classism is a social disease. On a personal level, I don't resent those who have fallen by the wayside or done me wrong. I only welcome them to a new life of prosperity, understanding, and cooperation. If I can find this mercy and kindness in my heart for those who have personally injured me, then can't we more easily find mercy for strangers whom we can only make assumptions about?

Even if these massive economic forces are far beyond our individual control, and humbling beyond words, I think the American people have been humbled enough for the past generation. Let this final dose of humility resonate, and let us realize what must be done to restore a vibrantly productive nation. Only with *economic sovereignty* will we be able to short-circuit the *robotic nurse* that tranquilizes the jaded, and hypnotizes the class warriors who create the jaded.

Thomas E. Kurek

Introduction

America is not at a crossroads. It already stumbled onto the wrong path, and descends its dismal trail deeper into economic despair. Unfortunately for the people who ignore economics, our concurrent social and political chaos cannot be decoupled from this ill-fated financial journey. It will continue to reach into their homes with increasing ferocity. The things that seem positive are illusions, and what seems awful is actually much worse.

In slightly under two-hundred pages, all of this uncommon knowledge is presented to the reader with flowing text, reduced to the most concise and easy-to-read presentation possible without losing substance. The computed reading grade level for the entire book is thirteen, meaning that any college freshman, advanced placement high school student, or college graduate will comprehend the writing flawlessly. Authoritative sources of data and information were selected for analysis from the most well-respected organizations, thinkers, and professors from ancient through the contemporary times.

Drawing from that treasure trove, the evidence of our economic perdition is written into over a hundred pages of charts and citations, conveniently removed to the back of the book. The most curious and diligent readers will be thrilled with the opportunity to dig even deeper into the references and charts. Perhaps they will make observations that are more relevant to their specific interests, but outside of the scope of this book. They may also find something profound that escaped the attention of this author. Since the source material is encyclopedic in scope, it should open a new conversation, rather than end all debate.

The book begins with a creative short narrative based upon true stories. It sets the tone for the personal impact imposed by our economic illusions, and many people will relate to the heartrending experiences. The rest of the first chapter is a concise evaluation of American economic history, and global competitiveness, along with a rebuttal of deceptions surrounding poverty and welfare in America. People who have followed print and television news will be shocked at the amount of economic misinformation they have consumed from many journalists and politicians. Those who work at the highest levels of economic analysis and research may not be as jolted, but they will be impressed with some unique perspectives.

The second chapter obliterates the left/right, Democrat/Republican political paradigm and presents a vision-based model for ideology. This accurate ideological paradigm is derived from Thomas Sowell's *A Conflict of Visions*,[5] and is crucial to understand how legal and institutional influence has corrupted our economy. Common economic fallacies in the education, energy, environment, and labor markets are dispelled. Anyone who is curious about the impact of discrimination, affirmative action, and diversity programs on labor markets will be thrilled with the end of *Chapter 2: The Institutionalist Creed.*

Chapter three presents very practical knowledge of income, wealth, and prosperity that should interest any working person in the modern world. Without an understanding of prosperity, citizens are apt to be haplessly acted upon by manipulative organizations. The knowledge of prosperity is a cornerstone of liberty, since economic freedom preserves personal freedom. Concepts of wealth vs. income, "fair shares," "level playing fields," unaccounted resources, financial moments in time versus lifetimes, and intangibles are elaborated.

Next, the false fears of income inequality are thoroughly debunked, as income inequality for experience (age), industry, and real income contradicts the lamentations of egregious inequality from *poverty hustlers* and the vote-pandering politicians who gallivant themselves upon the broken dreams of our most vulnerable neighbors. In fact, the exact opposite is shown – that America has been living under a socialistic and oppressively imposed equality that has damaged labor markets and demotivated productive careers. Section three of the third chapter unveils a large unspoken inflator of our healthcare costs, and also shows how a public school teacher earns the same total compensation as an average CEO over the course of her career – which is much higher than lawyers, engineers, technologists, scientists, and economists. Five new

---

[5] (Sowell, A Conflict of Visions, 1987)

Thomas E. Kurek

income-based socioeconomic classes emerge and the fabled "rich" class is evaluated by the numbers.

Finally, a novel model for *Lifetime Prosperity* is presented, addressing all forms of taxation, wealth, income, and access to resources. It is the culmination of all the principles used in this *prosperity analysis*, with powerful application in personal finance, financial planning, debt reduction, tax policy, and socioeconomic propositions. There is nowhere for *poverty hustlers* to hide from this model, since their claims must account for all of its factors. They prey on the uninformed, and no reader of this book will ever again become a victim of the *poverty hustlers'* manipulations.

Chapter four begins with a summary of the findings, and ends with serious proposals needed to recover *economic sovereignty*, including voting laws, tax filing, welfare reform, government transparency, government spending limits, bureaucratic accountability, and a coordinated clandestine tax revolt as a last resort. The pattern of *vorardennes* – the oppression of the upper-middle class – is shown through historical accounts of Nazi Germany, Communist Russia, China, and French Revolutionary atmospheres. Modern *vorardennes* in social democracies is perpetrated with sophisticated taxation and cultural tricks instead of violence.

The ultimate outcome is to compress all middle class people into a powerless mob, with *vorardennes* acting on the top of the middle class, while welfare, subsidies, and minimum wage laws work on the bottom. All normal citizens – the ones who survive by their own merits – are rendered irrelevant to the civic process. By defeating the upper-middle class, those privileged citizens with favor from the ruling elites turn the most productive workers of society into beasts of burden. Plans by the Democrats to increase taxes on successful middle class workers for the few years of their life when they attain high income is the last nail in the coffin of the American dream. Meanwhile, truly destitute people are suffering while phony "poor" people encumber exhausted middle class workers. There is no compassion for real poverty in this arrangement, and everyone is poorer with their necks under its boot.

It might be said that this kind of precision and formulation is somewhat devoid of humanity. On the contrary, there is always the inspiration of those like Galileo, Sir Isaac Newton, Hypatia, Benjamin Franklin, Thomas Edison, and the Wright brothers. Without analytics, the incredible system-based wizardry that expresses our greatest human needs and desires would have been impossible. Math, reason, and philosophy are great powers; but, all power comes with a price. The metropolitan *robotic nurse* that we live in is a grey, concrete parasite. It also operates mechanically, but its precision keeps its jaded children as "safe" as they are hypnotized. There is nothing more devoid of humanity than this system of control and parasitism. With enlightenment, we will defeat it and recover *economic sovereignty* for all citizens.

Part 1: Demystifying the American Economy

*Photo 4: The Aghileen Pinnacles in Alaska,
Clouded in Mist, Penetrated by the Sun*

Chapter 1: American Socioeconomic Indications & Warnings

§ 1.1 Redistribution of Blood, Sweat, and Merit

"Everything that deceives may be said to enchant." –
Plato [6]

A young man named Cato was graduating from an American high school with merit scholarships, top grades, and unprecedented coursework. The glistening sweat on his olive skin in the summer heat and his calloused baker's fingers separated him from his mollycoddled peers. In contrast, their skin was soft and pale from ceaseless hours of TV, video games, intoxication, and socializing in modern caves made of white drywall.

Cato could appreciate the occasional drywall-cave gathering, but his passions and ambitions were found elsewhere. He was an academic prodigy, a musical prodigy, and in great shape from his sports and exercise activity. He held a job as a baker to earn a car and college tuition, getting up every weekend at 4:00 AM to stand in front of a hot oven for ten hours. With a less-than-ideal family situation, he turned outwards for guidance and inspiration, finding spectacular role models in Christianity, Western history, music, classic literature, and select movies.

The story of his personal journey would help anyone to understand how merit and productivity do not yield personal gains in the interventionist economy. In the 21st century, the redistribution of blood, sweat, and merit is ubiquitous, and the corrupt habits of the rich and poor alike motivate their entitled quests of *something-for-nothing*. A wealthy realtor made a fortune from manipulated housing markets. The low-income, subsidized-housing recipient suckled upon the same housing that cost a neighboring public school teacher fifty-percent of her earnings. The public school teacher was forced to pay the welfare recipient through her taxes, and the wealthy realtor through artificial price inflation. Nobody was footing the bill for the public school teacher. The

---

[6] (Plato, 380 BC)

Thomas E. Kurek

housing interventions robbed from her, and redistributed to both the rich and poor. The meritorious middle-class earners joined the school teacher as part of a great host body from which the rich and poor were sucking dry. It required knowledge of economics and liberty from institutional interests to perceive the invisible robbery.

Like most Americans, Cato lacked that knowledge as he wandered through the illusory economy. By the time he reached adulthood, he could relate to the public school teacher's burden, and he felt that something was not right, even if he did not understand it. As a child, his environment varied. He spent summertime and winter in a declining American inner city, hollowed out from decades of high taxes, welfare, and economic intervention policies. His grandparents' house was a depression-era bungalow that stood out beautifully because of the devoted personal touch of his grandfather's war-torn hands, within a neighborhood of assembly-line housing. Narrow alleys painted gaps between the bungalows. From the bathroom, Cato could see the windows of the house next door, as if the neighbors were welcome parties to his personal care and hygiene.

Organized criminals generally left the family alone, except for imposing an occasional intimidating attitude. Poverty in the neighborhood was much higher before the Vietnam War, but crime used to be rare. The worst crime Cato's family could recall during the old days, was a peeping tom. Cato's grandfather organized the men of the neighborhood to form a watch. They hid in the bushes at night, and eventually caught the pervert without the help of the police.

Increased ghetto prosperity from welfare and government housing intervention was counterintuitively accompanied by an increase in violent crime that the old cultures never had. Even with much greater poverty, the old neighborhood was content to work without government assistance, redistributed healthcare, or handouts. Cato's family members worked as waitresses, hairdressers, construction workers, enlisted soldiers, gas station attendants, stationary engineers, and secretaries. They did not earn much, but they earned enough to live and love.

After the welfare, government healthcare, and gangs moved in, some street smarts were necessary. When a person is living off of redistributed tax dollars and illicit spoils, they have a lot of time on their hands. Organized criminals would loiter about, daring anyone to look at them the wrong way. On one evening, Cato carelessly followed a car navigation system down a one-way street, and found his vehicle blocked by a white van and criminals. His mother was in the passenger seat. He knew that the criminals were deciding what to do with him as the seconds crawled off his watch into some jealous keeper's hands.

Eventually, the mob cleared out of the way, and Cato slowly passed by. A car length away, the piercing blast of a gunshot ripped through the night. He dug the accelerator through the floor and swerved like a drunken fish to make his mother a harder target. After safely dropping off his mother at the bungalow, he vowed to never go past that house again. Ostensibly, that was the desired effect of the criminals' warning shot. A few months later, they murdered someone in the same place. The compassionate and brave government officials responded to this slaughter by changing directions on the one-way street and putting a surveillance camera on the corner. Aggressive and effective law enforcement was too old-fashioned for such a "progressive" city.

A few blocks away, Cato's grandmother sent him into a convenience store to collect two dollars for a winning lottery ticket. He noticed criminals sitting in a parked car. One was loading a handgun magazine. The byzantine gun control laws of the progressive city failed to keep guns out of the hands of criminals who were intent on doing what they pleased. Would they rob the store? Would they threaten his grandmother like the deranged man on Elmwood Avenue once did? Would they try to assault Cato because of his white skin, like the black men who yelled racial epithets while chasing after him and his cousin a few years ago? Returning to the car with two dollars in hand, he passed it to his grandmother and told her about the gun. She didn't believe it. Denial and passivity were survival mechanisms, but they also paved the path for the degeneration of the neighborhood. Neither Walt Kowalski, his Gran Torino,[7] nor Clint Eastwood graced the block to confront these gangs.

---

[7] (Eastwood, 2008)

During Cato's school year, life was not as adventurous. A small townhouse was Cato's ticket to a top public school system, but the school was a minefield. There were exemplary and horrible teachers. One teacher was living a double life in a marriage while secretly performing in homosexual pornography. He would pat the young men on their buttocks during football practice. Cato was one of those young men. His jovial boss at the bakery got a lot of comedic mileage out of that story, "Cato, that gay porno teacher was one of your coaches, right? Did he come into the shower with you guys? Did he pat your buns when you ran by, real nice?"

Another young teacher got off on kissing young men acting in her plays, absent child molestation charges. Down the hall from her was a youthful hippie teacher sauntering around the classroom with bare feet and a hipster attitude. She took pleasure in selecting biased progressive content with which to indoctrinate her students, before they knew a thing about the world around them. Her students did not even know Homer, Virgil, Cicero or Harriet Beecher Stowe, and she was feeding them Toni Morrison.

A few doors down from her hippie commune, there was a seasoned old woman, well-past retirement age, who offered her World Literature and Advanced Composition class out of sheer love for the students. In her classroom, there was only the smell of books, chalk dust, and a subtle jasmine fragrance – a welcome contrast to the odor of dirty bare feet, indignation, and activist intoxicants. Cato imagined that this noble old woman would be working until her bones could no longer hold her gentle presence above the ground. Cato selected the old woman's course instead of jumping into the melodrama of the progressive commune.

A vulnerable student's selection of which mentors to identify with could make an enormous difference in their life. Cato selected the exemplary ones, based on values that Christianity and his elderly family members instilled. Students with opposing values identified with the fun and easy teachers who acted like friends instead of mentors. They enjoyed the emotional progressive commune atmosphere. They sought a therapeutic environment instead of an annealing one. Cato enjoyed the traditional, disciplined, and efficient classroom.

In school, the capacity of young adults was bare naked. It had yet to acquire all of the irrelevant credentials, cronyism, paid-dues, masks, illusions, and deceptions of people in the adult world. In school, you could either beat the opposing team, or lose. You could either fly through the coursework, or struggle with it. You could outperform your peers with your musical instrument, or practice infrequently and squeak along. You could get top scores on your tests, or you could bomb them and blame some scapegoat. You could sit at attention and take things seriously, or you could chew bubblegum in the back of the class, pass notes, and fiddle around with social interests. Cato remembered how things were back then. Holistically, he was always ahead of his peers, which made for very interesting experiences when reconnecting with some of them, later in life.

His peers did not change much over the years. The bad ones were just as bad, and the good ones were just as good. Rarely, he would find someone who had truly changed for the better or worse. One thing that changed dramatically were the masks that his peers wore. The bare naked capacity of youth was covered up! Their authentic selves were masked by money they had spent, but not earned, loans they had taken but could not afford, friendships they had used but not developed, and irrelevant credentials they had pasted on their walls, but not merited.

Mostly, they had gained the ability to generate a basic repetitive result, but not the ability to think critically or independently, adapt, and discover. Their journalists, entertainers, and leisure buddies influenced their minds more than the great thinkers of history. Many had transformed all of their insecurities into victimhood, self-abdication, and self-pity, choosing cowardice over strength, surrendering the measurement of their identity to commiserating grievance-mongers.

To the mollycoddled citizen, it felt good to disown personal responsibility. There was always a scapegoat – to the atheist it was religion, to the Christian it was the devil, to the feminist it was the man, to the homosexual it was the Bible, to the racial minority it was the white-skinned majority, to the poor it was the rich, to the rich it was the poor, to the school it was the parents, to the parents it was the school, to the citizen it was the government, and to the government it was the opposition party. Half-baked stories of history and society oozed into the visions of the mollycoddled, like mutant bread loaves seeping through the cracks of an oven. It did not matter which collectiva they identified with – rich, poor, feminist, homosexual, atheist – if they disowned responsibility, and confused happenchance with *fait accompli*, they would feel entitled to *something-for-nothing*. They would call it *social justice*.

Irrespective of race, gender, or class, it took time to discern the self-reliant from the mollycoddled. On the surface, Cato could not tell who was successful, because of ubiquitous wealth redistribution, regulations, cronyism, socialism, and a profoundly intuitive concept – the measure of success in life is not prosperity. No reasonable person would claim that a wealthy prostitute, thief, corrupt businessman, or drug dealer was successful in life. The distinctions between lawful careers were more ambiguous. The most brilliant, productive, or merited people did not always have the material wealth that their abilities would command in a truly free market.

Cato couldn't tell if the guy next to him was doing well, deeply in taxpayer-bailed-out debt, or if he really earned everything he owned with lawful productivity. As he was stopped in traffic on the way to work, he looked around at the other cars. The guy in the Mercedes Benz was $800,000 in debt after his mortgage, car, and student loans. The guy next to him in the Porsche was a drug dealer, one step away from prison. The guy behind him in the Corvette sold his no-interest-loan house for a fortune, stealing from his neighbors through the government bailouts, banking policies, and subsidies that bubbled the prices up. The woman beside him in the Lexus was unemployed, and drawing $70,000 per year from welfare and subsidies while her children crawled around barefoot. The woman at the front of the line in the luxury SUV spent her days as a government bureaucrat barely doing four hours of work a day; she filled the rest of her "work hours" with trivial video games on her smart phone, surfing the internet, perusing social networks, and texting friends and family.

Lawyers and engineers ate in the same restaurants as welfare recipients. They shopped at the same stores. They visited the same doctors. In casual settings, a stripper wore the same designer clothes as a trendy female heart surgeon. In the casino, a wealthy businessman played poker with an unemployed ex-wife spending her ill-gotten alimony. Mooching from peers, ex-spouses, parents, government, inheritance, and criminal subsidies of lifestyle were more common than total lifelong financial independence. Very rarely, Cato would meet a person who was not in debt, and had paid for their own college, their own meals, their own furnishings, their own home, and their own cars, without ever mooching from government, parents, or peers, or "ethically" leeching from government market interventions and regulations.

Some of the most unintelligent and immoral people found themselves in great wealth with luck, connections, or underhanded deeds in their careers. Some had acquired material wealth by marrying, inheriting, or by coercing it out of a law suit. Blue-collar workers were paid much more than some of their college-educated peers. Government workers, soldiers, teachers, and union members were receiving much of their compensation in benefits such as pensions, supplemental retirement healthcare accounts, and time off of work. They claimed to be paid poorly, but the enormous cost of their benefits contradicted that complaint. Some of Cato's peers got lucky with their investments, others rode inflated real estate prices to sales-commission heaven, while others enjoyed third-party-payer-inflated pharmaceutical sales. Some had collected welfare and government handouts, giving them advantages over others who paid their own way for everything in life.

Due to economic intervention of all sorts, there was a lot of wealth slushing around through hands that were not at all associated with productivity. In the interventionist economy, a person's perceptible ability, merits, and successes were just illusions. Somewhere under the veil was the bare naked student from high school, with the same tendencies and capacities, but now decorated with a series of costumes, and illusory credentials. The conformity-inducing, identity-eroding large institutions of government, nonprofits, academia, and business demanded that its worker bees look good on paper, and look good on reports of their work. They valued appearances and processes over production and results. Everyone was pursuing a checkbox on an application, statuses, recognition, and authority, instead of the wonder of creation and industry. The certification and credential factory of professional training picked up where the American higher education goliath left off.

Those heroes who did produce in real terms were shackled. Their results and achievements were collectivized and redistributed. Some bureaucrat would take credit for what a genius consultant slaved away to produce. They would make jokes in meetings about the high number of middle-managers, and how few people were capable of generating real work. Yet nobody cared to reform the organizations, because these phony jobs would be lost. Consequently, large numeric values on government and corporate reports would turn ugly, and illusions would be dispelled. Production and mission-orientation were disposable in the interventionist economy. Appearances, status, and imagination became the assets of economic exchange.

Cato's head was spinning from the radical egalitarianism that was drowning America in disillusionment. The crusade to manufacture equal outcomes for everyone was a race to mediocrity. People felt it everywhere around them. Freedom of opportunity was sacrificed on the altar of equal outcome. It buried the productivity of the ambitious and diligent. It directed human energy towards the most wasteful activities imaginable. In short, the material outcomes of people were not good indicators of merit, productivity, or ability, due to the corruption of valuation at all levels of the interventionist and socialist societies.

This destructive feedback loop between society and economy gradually imbued inferior motivations into communities. Values and desires cannot be easily changed. They are programmed into people early on, and personally chosen. The slow pace at which the malaise set in, would be the slow pace at which society could rediscover superior values. Whether rich, poor, criminal, opportunistic, or mooching, the underlying value that drove this radical egalitarianism was the normalized pursuit of *something-for-nothing*. That quest runs in the opposite direction of the sincere pursuit of happiness – a raison d'être of the U.S. Constitution. As Cato considered how equal everyone was in material outcome, whether they deserved to be or not, he became cynical.

Along came an army of journalists, politicians, preachers, entertainers, and professors who were claiming the exact opposite.

They said that income inequality was higher than ever. They said the rich were getting richer and the poor were getting poorer. They claimed that everything was unfair and that only more control, more redistribution, and more *something-for-nothing* at all levels could fix the inequities. How could that be? Any semi-vigilant person living in a metropolis could reflect the intuitive observations Cato had made. The pervasive egalitarianism was a painful vice, squeezing an aggressively compressed middle class. Americans had become a nearly indistinguishable mass, leaving a political and cultural elite dominating government, culture, businesses, and institutions.

With annual taxation exceeding six trillion dollars, regulations exceeding two trillion, and nonprofits exceeding two trillion, law and order was two-thirds of the weight of America's production. The cacophony of classism from cultural leaders sought to turn American minds against their own intuition and eyes. While other nations advanced their economies with peace and cooperation, America turned the poor against the rich, the middle class against itself, and imposed social and political barriers to accurate price alignment. The feud became more visceral by the moment.

The contradictions between classist visions and reality must be understood by the population in order to make choices that will prevent catastrophes like the French and Bolshevik revolutions. Although America is the modern specimen for this analysis, the concepts elaborated here are crucial to any nation, in any time of history. This economic knowledge will liberate Americans like the Pillars of Hercules liberated Atlas. If Americans continue to listen to the classist antagonists, Atlas will shrug, and our society will be brought to its knees in chaos.

Cato was not the only one whose intuition detected fraud and illusion in every market and community that he encountered daily. In the tale of two economies, the illusory tale leads to Napoleon, and the true story leads to salvation. The nation has become completely enchanted since the end of World War 2, and commensurately deceived; Plato's ancient admonition quoted at the beginning of this section is lost on modern America. The deception is now as ubiquitous as our leisure and luxury. We have yet to discover whether America will abandon its imaginative and illusory economic tale to embrace the true story.

§ 1.2 Prosperity, Poverty, and Destitution

"Industry pays debts, while despair increases them."
–Benjamin Franklin, Way to Wealth, 1758

When Cato visited his family in the ghetto, he could buy four people dinner for the same price that it cost two people in the expensive metropolis. When he was struggling through college in debt, he was considered *impoverished* by the statistics. When he was living with three other young professionals, he was considered *rich* by the statistics. The poverty activists who promote belief in American income inequality and widespread poverty exclude so many relevant distinctions from their statistics that their conclusions are meaningless, and the people who trust these experts are pumping their fists in the air over illusions in their head. We must begin by understanding the language of class warfare that mystifies the topic.

Surveying poverty activists reveals the following key phrases:

1. Income inequality
2. Social justice
3. Wealth distribution
4. The 1%, the 99%, (or any uneven division of the total population)
5. The corporate class
6. The billionaire class
7. The rich people
8. The working poor
9. The rich get richer and everybody else gets poorer
10. Jobs and the economy
11. Poverty
12. The underserved
13. Plutocracy
14. Redistribution
15. Socialism
16. Capitalism
17. The western economic system
18. Level playing field
19. Inclusion
20. Corporate malfeasance
21. May Day

22. Mobility
23. Justice
24. Class warfare
25. Disparity between the *top* and *bottom*
26. Disposable poor
27. Property owners
28. Idolatry of money
29. Marketplace autonomy
30. Financial speculation
31. Free markets
32. Haves versus the have-nots
33. Fair share

When these terms appear in discourse, the participants are inducing us to form beliefs about *prosperity incidence*. Most often they have no clue what they are talking about, because they fixate upon some individual parameter, and lack the economic knowledge in this book that they would need to approach their concerns intelligently. We will refer to these terms as the *buzzwords of poverty hustling*. As time goes on, the terminology of this propaganda will change, but the concepts will remain the same.

According to multiple measures Americans in all socioeconomic classes are more prosperous than ever. Very few Americans are actually poor. Before we justify this fact with the data, it is important to get our definitions correct. Prosperity is success in material terms alone, but not necessarily general success in life. In this book, that literal definition is always assumed and poetic uses of the term are never implied.

Many discussions on poverty and prosperity are derailed to the point of absurdity, when people use the poetic meanings. They talk about poverty of *spirit, family, morality,* or *love*. What they mean is that people are deficient and dysfunctional in these social areas, which is a much different concern than having food, clothing, and shelter. Whether or not mountains of money can have positive impacts on social deficiencies is another story. Poetic poverty hustlers forget eternal truths such as:

> *"Semper inops quicumque cupit" (whoever desires is always poor)* –*Claudius Claudianus circa 400 A.D.*

Thomas E. Kurek

That wisdom leads to more specific observations like: money cannot buy love, morals, or perfect parents to replace bad ones. Money can only temporarily emulate those intrinsic goods. It is up to the willpower of the individual to enrich themselves with superior cultural wealth. By filling the heads of the "poor" with desires that go beyond satisfactory human needs, and false visions of wealth and poverty, they inculcate envy and wrath in the hearts of the most vulnerable citizens. As the tempting devil is to the sinner, the tempting *poverty hustler* is to the bloodbaths of the French, Bolshevik, and socialist revolutions.

Moreover, redistributed money can pour oil on the fire of real poverty. If we pay for the housing, food, and education of a person who uses every bit of extra money to buy drugs, alcohol, gambling bets, or other entertainment – we are not really subsidizing their human needs, we are indirectly subsidizing their bad habits that keep them poor. *Poverty hustlers* would like people to believe that social deficiencies are consequences of poverty, instead of precursors. For those government, religious, academic, and entertainment leaders who profit from poverty hustling, keeping people poor is a matter of career survival, so they tend to recoil at the mere mention of these realities.

Social factors aside, we require much more than a measurement of income to discern *prosperity incidence*. There are retirees living off of fortunes in savings and investments, in fully-paid housing, who have very low income. They are wealthy, but will show up as "poor" in the income statistics. There are single mothers obtaining more government subsidies than most people can earn with decent jobs, and those subsidies do not fully register as income in the statistics. There are workers like school teachers, soldiers, and union members who receive so much compensation in benefits and subsidies, that their incomes must be lower because their employer is paying for those expensive benefits. Income is just one factor that contributes to prosperity. There are many prosperous people with low incomes at some point in their lives.

The antithesis of prosperity is *destitution*. A destitute person does not have adequate shelter, food, or clothing. According to the same government sources that promote beliefs in poverty, there is very little destitution in America. Ninety-nine percent of Americans said that they always had enough food to eat, and 98.2% of Americans went to the doctor when they needed to without being deterred by the cost.[8] In a future publication, the popular statistic claiming that dozens of millions of Americans lacked health insurance will be debunked. When those dozens of millions of people are looked at more closely, the truth is that only 1-4% of them have lacked sufficient medical care since the 1980s. Homelessness is most often transitional. A full 99.5% of Americans had no chance of being homeless, or in a shelter, for even a single night in 2009.[9] With these facts in mind, it is clear that only 0.5 – 1% of Americans live in *real* poverty (destitution).

Why do some government agencies, professors, churches, and nonprofits inflate these numbers? They are duped by the income fallacy. A consistent annual monetary income is not the sole determinant of prosperity, as they presume. The U.S. Census Bureau claimed that over 14% of Americans were in poverty in 2013. Based on our correct definition of *destitution*, they are exaggerating by 14 to 28 times. They use a before-tax income threshold, which excludes the value of public housing, Medicaid, food stamps, and other subsidies. They also exclude capital gains, and they do not consider whether the person is living in a paid-off house. Although they adjust for inflation, they do not adjust for geography. The cost of living can significantly vary from city to city.

For households that are not destitute, but considered "poor" by the government, what is life like? The Heritage Foundation analyzed data from the U.S. Department of Energy to make that determination:

> *The average poor person, as defined by the government, has a living standard far higher than the public imagines.*
>
> *As scholar James Q. Wilson has stated, "The poorest Americans today live a better life than all but the richest persons a hundred years ago." In 2005, the typical household defined as poor by the government had a car and air conditioning. For entertainment,*

---

[8] (U.S. Census Bureau, 2016)
[9] (U.S. Department of Housing and Urban Development, 2010)

Thomas E. Kurek

the household had two color televisions, cable or satellite TV, a DVD player, and a VCR. If there were children, especially boys, in the home, the family had a game system, such as an Xbox or a PlayStation. In the kitchen, the household had a refrigerator, an oven and stove, and a microwave. Other household conveniences included a clothes washer, clothes dryer, ceiling fans, a cordless phone, and a coffee maker.

The home of the typical poor family was not overcrowded and was in good repair. In fact, the typical poor American had more living space than the average European. The typical poor American family was also able to obtain medical care when needed. By its own report, the typical family was not hungry and had sufficient funds during the past year to meet all essential needs.[10]

It seems that the term "poverty" no longer refers to destitution. This loose definition of poverty now refers to people who do not have the best of everything and are sometimes inconvenienced or constrained by limited discretionary spending choices. Fake poverty and the *buzzwords of poverty hustling* create a contagion of envy and false indignation, but they do not enlighten us. Even worse, there are misguided educators, entertainers, politicians, and activists who are promoting these false beliefs with good intentions. The false poverty activism is harmful, because the 0.5 – 1% of America that actually is destitute would benefit from targeted, truthful programs. Social justice advocates are therefore a vile detriment to people who are truly poor, and to those hard workers who are diligently holding on to their self-sufficiency.

As it stands, there are many Americans who are not destitute, but still suckling upon trillions of redistributed dollars from taxpayers and nonprofits. Today, the *something-for-nothing,* fake "poor" class represents 13 – 13.5% of America. Moreover, we must multiply the statistical income of the "poor" by 2.6 – that is the

---

[10] (Rector & Sheffield, Air Conditioning, Cable TV, and an Xbox: What is Poverty in the United States Today?, 2011)

money they actually spend, from uncounted resources available to them.[11] A "poor" person who has an income of $15,000 is actually spending $39,000 when all of the uncounted benefits are considered, while their neighbors are actually earning that money to purchase the same things. Since one-in-three Americans have received welfare benefits, there is another 20% of America that took *something-for-nothing* while possessing middle class income.

Many would consider this level of redistribution to be a deeply socialist economic atmosphere. Good citizens should learn to distinguish the difference between the poverty hustlers' *statistical poverty* and real *destitution*. There are a handful of truly destitute Americans who need us to reform this phony slush fund for immoral citizens and their corruptly indignant advocates.

---

[11] (Rector & Sheffield, The War on Poverty After 50 Years, 2014)

§ 1.3 American Prosperity by the Numbers

"Magnas inter opes inops." (A pauper in the midst of wealth) –Horace, Odes Book III, 23 B.C.

Driven by an insatiable desire for social validation, leisure, and material niceties, many citizens of the interventionist nation felt like paupers in the midst of historically unprecedented wealth. When Claudianus said "whoever desires is always poor," as he traversed amongst the plebeians of Rome, he may have anticipated 21st century profligacy. Even the poorest citizen lived like an aristocrat of the last century. Despite this unfathomable prosperity for all Americans, the more their physiological and security needs improved, the poorer they felt as their psychological satisfaction atrophied.

Food, shelter, and medical care were abundant in 2009. Americans had:[12]

- Enough food to eat: 99%
- Reasonable access to medical care: 98.2%
- No chance of a single night of homelessness: 99.5%
- True poverty (destitution): 0.5 – 1.0%
- False poverty (statistically-imagined): 14.3%
- Exaggeration of poverty: 14.3 – 28.6x
- Middle-class using welfare for perks: 20%

Even though poverty in America was grossly exaggerated by those who profit from the belief in it, we can still show how prosperous the nation was in the last century. Then we will have an honest understanding of why Americans of all classes enjoy greatly improved standards of living.

The prosperity of a nation is indicated by a large government, a service economy, high wages and profits, steady savings and investments, growth in private fixed assets, an explosion of invention, growing cultural infrastructure, housing growth with increased quality, and increased spending on discretionary goods.

---

[12] § 1.2 Prosperity, Poverty, and Destitution

Poor societies cannot even conceive of disposing resources on those things.

A Large Government

A prosperous nation can afford a large government. The state tends to enlarge itself on the backs of its citizens, as they are better able to burden its expansion. The United States is now consuming almost $50,000 of taxation per working person every single year. Only half of that tax is what we carefully account for on our annual tax filing. The rest is taken from our businesses and value (*ad valorem* taxes include property, sales, and even tariffs baked into the cost of things we buy).[13] [14] [15] [16] With taxation that nearly equals the median annual wages, we can say that we are paying the government as much as wage-earning people. Like a ghostly octopus with its phantom tentacles weaving through every thread of our clothing to find our last penny, the government sneaks half of our tax away from us surreptitiously, in the form of hidden taxes, lost wages, lost jobs, price inflation for the things we buy, and lost profits that we rely upon for our retirement investments.

How has taxation changed over the years? Even during the World Wars and Great Depression, Americans paid less than half of what we are paying now. Considering that history, the argument cannot be made that we *need* this high level of taxation. Desires should be distinguished from needs. Since the 1980s, America has settled on consuming around one-third of its annual productivity in direct taxation. If we add the cost of regulations[17] and nonprofit revenues[18] [19] to obtain the total cost of American civics, we are spending ten trillion dollars per year – over sixty percent of what the entire nation produces each year! Meanwhile, state and federal tax

---

[13] *Figure 5: Total Tax per Working Person*
[14] *Figure 6: Federal Tax per Working Person*
[15] *Figure 7: State Tax per Working Person*
[16] *Figure 8: Local Tax per Working Person*
[17] (Crews Jr., Ten Thousand Commandments - An Annual Snapshot of the Federal Regulatory State, 2014)
[18] (National Center for Charitable Statistics, 2014)
[19] (Corporation for National and Community Service, 2012)

exploded in the second half of the 20th century, while local tax has increased less dramatically.[20] [21] [22] [23]

There were five spikes in federal taxation throughout the past century, coinciding with The Great War (1918), World War 2 (1944), the beginning of the Cold War (1952), the terrorist attacks of September 11th and the dot-com bust (2002), and finally, the Housing Bust (2008).[24] Overall, federal social insurance and income tax have exploded in the second half of the 20th century, but since the 1970s, federal tax has settled at about one-and-a-half times that of state and local. Prior to 1941, except for a few years, the American state and local governments were larger than the federal government.[25] This is hard evidence of vastly increased centralized power in American civics.

Before World War 2, America spent most of its money on direct market interventions. Since that time, economic intervention does not show up so readily in government spending data, because they have used heavy regulation and monetary manipulation with the Federal Reserve as new tools for market intervention. With *Financial Repression*, government reduces its own debt at the expense of others, using direct lending to itself, interest rate limitation, close government-bank collusion, and restrictions on capital movement between countries. The citizen pays for those interventions in the cost of the things they buy, lost interest, inflated prices, inflated real estate and rent, inflated property taxation, and manipulated markets that do not reflect the production that their liberty would naturally drive.

Also, prior to World War 2, America spent a lot of its tax on transportation but very little on earned retirement. Besides a moderate drop during World War 2, we have spent the same proportion of our taxes on education for over a century, making a farce out of financial paradigms for declining education performance. The largest share of tax is now spent on compulsory retirement and

---

[20] *Figure 9: Total Tax, % of GDP*
[21] *Figure 10: Federal Tax, % of GDP*
[22] *Figure 11: State Tax, % of GDP*
[23] *Figure 12: Local Tax, % of GDP*
[24] *Figure 13: Ratio of Federal to State & Local Revenues (Spikes)*
[25] *Figure 14: Ratio of Federal to State & Local Revenues (Trends)*

healthcare, which includes the largest share of welfare and redistribution in the nation's entire history. After the 1990s, *national defense share* has been lower than any time in the last century since before World War 2.[26] Our Defense Department has shed nearly half of its fixed assets since a peak in the 1970s.[27] [28] Advocates of reduced military spending will have a hard time confronting these facts.

Counting how many people are working does not mean much, because each worker does not work the same number of hours. We have to normalize employed Americans to *full-time-equivalent workers* (FTE) in order to make a sensible labor comparison. The American government is now taxing and spending over 500% more per FTE than it was before World War 2.[29] Comparing this spending to the FTE total compensation (including wages, known benefits, and transfers), we discover that the government gradually increased its spending share since World War 2, with the largest recent spike starting in 2008, peaking at seventy-one percent of the compensation of a typical worker.[30] This was driven by the largest welfare redistribution in American history, more than doubling the normal trend from the 1970s to 2008.[31]

A Service Economy

A prosperous nation can afford a service economy. That is a workforce that *mainly* services Maslow three-to-five psychological motivations: social (3), esteem (4), and self-actualizing (5). Such a nation has sufficiently satisfied Maslow one-and-two physical motivations: physiological (1) and security (2). Even the poorest amongst us consume the services of engineers, doctors, police, transportation, military, teachers, mechanics, insurance agents, lawyers, entertainers, restaurant staff, social workers, and hairdressers. Services are intangible – they cannot be touched, tasted, smelled, handled, or seen. Because of intangibility, services

---

[26] *Figure 15: Government Spending*
[27] *Figure 41: Defense-to-Non-Defense Fixed Asset Ratio*
[28] *Figure 42: Growth of Government Fixed Assets by Defense Function*
[29] *Figure 16: Government Spending per FTE*
[30] *Figure 17: Government Spending per FTE Compensation*
[31] *Figure 18: Government Redistribution per FTE Compensation*

Thomas E. Kurek

only require indirect inventories of items used in the service, such as medical equipment, computers, or tools.

The currently high level of service consumption in the poorest sectors of American society is unheard of in any other time in history and across the globe. While fixating upon income and wealth disparity, the raw consumption of services is entirely ignored. In truth, much of the ingratitude for our prosperity comes from failure to appreciate this kingly living that nearly all Americans enjoy. Since World War 2, Americans have multiplied their annual service consumption tenfold, to $25,000 per person! This voracious service consumption has exponentially risen to almost 70% of our entire GDP![32] [33]

Such enormous demand for hired help results in mountains of service jobs. Over 75% of the workforce is selling their services instead of producing tangible goods. Heaven help America if international oil and imported goods are ever disrupted significantly! Our military is aware of this Achilles' heel, and so are our enemies. Due to regulatory burden, taxation, and wage controls, American businesses are compelled to manufacture in foreign nations. Improved manufacturing efficiencies and robotics also require fewer workers for manual labor.

Another way of looking at it is that the division of labor extends to machines and foreign workers. If American lawmakers and unions inflate wages to uncompetitive levels, poor Americans do not have to suffer from inflated prices in all of the things they buy. The businesses just go overseas where labor is priced competitively, and then sell at lower prices to help Americans afford what they need.[34] This international redistribution of jobs is exactly what the destroyers of national sovereignty – *global citizens* and internationalists – have in mind. People who are looking for reasons that American labor is uncompetitive in the global market should focus on the domestic policies that inflate benefits and compensation for services.

---

[32] *Figure 47: Consumption*
[33] *Figure 48: Share of Personal Consumption*
[34] *Figure 19: Workforce Composition*

Higher Wages and Profit

A prosperous nation can afford to pay higher wages and earns more profit. The profits do not just end up in the hands of the rich. They pay for the retirement of Americans, and they finance the expansion of enterprise which creates new jobs. The jobs that pay the most are government, finance, real estate, insurance, oil, mining, and gas.[35] [36] It is not a mistake that the highest paying industries are the ones that are sustained by economic and military intervention. There is a lot of *something-for-nothing* flowing into the pockets of workers in these industries, where competition is gamed.

On the other hand, the industry that an American is in means much less to their compensation than it used to. The inequality of compensation based on industry has plummeted since 1929.[37] The ratio of profit to compensation has remained highly consistent for the past century, except for mining and real estate, in which fluctuating capital goods and land value understandably introduce factors that more dramatically impact productivity.[38] Mining, oil, gas, and manufacturing double the average profit, but the rest of the industries are very close to the average profit.[39] Except for mining and manufacturing, profits per worker range from a few thousand dollars to $17,000 a year.[40] It seems as though the "greedy" corporations, do not have much extra cash for their workers after taxation, even if they wanted to rob the retirements of their shareholders by surrendering profits.

More Savings and Investments

A prosperous nation can afford to save and invest more. Since the 1970s, American citizens and businesses have been responsibly saving, and in the past few years they have reached historically high savings rates! Adversely, the United States government has been saving nothing and accumulating large debts since the 1970s, reaching record high borrowing in the past few years.[41] The same trends hold for American surplus – which is the total savings and

---

[35] *Figure 20: Average Industrial Compensation Ratio*
[36] *Figure 21: Compensation per Worker*
[37] *Figure 22: Industrial Compensation Inequality*
[38] *Figure 23: Ratio of Profit to Compensation*
[39] *Figure 24: Ratio of Industrial Profit to Average Profit*
[40] *Figure 25: Profits per Worker*
[41] *Figure 26: Savings per Capita*

Thomas E. Kurek

investments after capital consumption. When combined, government borrowing in the last few years has wiped out the prudent diligence of businesses and citizens.[42] [43] This provides even more hard evidence of destructionism (the ubiquitous consumption of capital).[44] Few indicators could better demonstrate the greed of a society that votes to force their children to pay for their luxuries of today.

Growth of Private Fixed Assets
A prosperous nation can afford to build fixed assets. Housing values, business structures, intellectual property, and equipment have exploded in the past century, by 500 – 3,000%.[45] Housing proliferated and equipment plummeted in the years leading up to World War 2 and the subprime mortgage crisis of 2007. Intellectual property has become a large contributor to American prosperity, as business structures have declined.[46] We would expect such a dynamic in the Information Age. An alarming trend is the voracious acquisition of infrastructure by government and nonprofits. With so much government debt, it seems clear that civics infrastructure is being built very greedily in an unsustainable manner. Contrarily, business and citizens have maintained steady, sustainable growth, except during the recent subprime mortgage bubble.[47] [48]

Explosion of Inventions
A prosperous nation can afford to create new ideas. In the last century, entertainment and literature value has barely grown, but software, medical, and pharmaceutical inventions have risen by 150,000 – 400,000%! Non-medical chemical inventions plateaued in the 1970s, computing and other research has grown over 5,000%, while automobiles and aerospace are the only areas that declined in the last few years.[49] Currently software, miscellaneous research, entertainment, literature, pharmaceutical, and medical inventions

---

[42] *Figure 27: Surplus per Capita*
[43] *Figure 28: Combined Surplus per Capita*
[44] (von Mises, Socialism: An Economic and Sociological Analysis, Part V, Destructionism, Chapter 33, 2015)
[45] *Figure 30: Growth of Private Fixed Asset Value*
[46] *Figure 29: Share of Private Fixed Asset Value*
[47] *Figure 39: Share of Fixed Assets by Ownership*
[48] *Figure 40: Growth of Fixed Asset Value by Ownership*
[49] *Figure 32: Growth of Intellectual Property Value*

hold the most value. Entertainment used to dominate the share of intellectual property, but America's inventions have proliferated so rapidly that other areas now surpass society's ability to consume more entertainment. It should not be surprising that American entertainment is such a competitive industry.[50] The market has been saturated for a long time.

Dominating entertainment copyrights, video has undergone a meteoric rise in the past century, increasing by 3,200%. Music and video took a dive in the 1970s, but quickly resumed growth. Except for a plummet in music value since 2002, all areas of entertainment value have been rising. The music industry remains in crisis due to internet theft of recorded music, and oligopolies that have constrained the quality of the products in an unresponsive market that has dictated to its customers what it thinks they want. The music business is caught in a destructive feedback loop fed with popularity bias. Video takes 74% of the entertainment copyright value, with books, music, and miscellaneous items making up the difference.[51] [52]

Growing Cultural Infrastructure
A prosperous nation can afford to build cultural infrastructure. Leisure travel buildings have grown slightly in the last century, but recreation, religious, and education buildings went exponential! Education facilities dwarf the rest, with almost 3,000% growth. People who are looking for areas to reduce college costs should consider the absurdly grandiose real estate and facilities built by modern educators. Meanwhile, religious and recreation buildings have dropped off sharply since 2005.[53] [54]

Housing Growth and Quality
A prosperous nation can afford better housing. The value of housing has increased greatly for citizens, business, government and nonprofits alike, but government and nonprofits have left the rest behind in terms of growth. Civic housing ownership has increased so much that private housing cannot keep up. The share of citizen-

---

[50] *Figure 31: Share of Intellectual Property Value*
[51] *Figure 33: Share of Entertainment Copyrights Value*
[52] *Figure 34: Growth of Entertainment Copyrights Value*
[53] *Figure 35: Share of Cultural Buildings Value*
[54] *Figure 36: Growth of Cultural Buildings Value*

Thomas E. Kurek

owned housing value dropped from 87% to 85% in the last century, while civic housing increased from 1.8% to 5.5%. Business housing value declined by a few points.[55] [56]

Increased Spending on Discretionary Goods
A prosperous nation can afford to buy more discretionary durable goods. In 1925, Americans could only afford $3,500 in discretionary goods per person. Today, Americans have almost $17,000 per person in discretionary durable goods. Furniture plateaued in the 1970s, while recreational goods and motor vehicles have skyrocketed since the 1980s. Families had so much extra money that they began buying many cars per household. Coinciding with massive government subsidies of college education and student loans, educators inflated their prices to whatever money government and banks made available. This dynamic is observed in the exponential rise of educational book value.[57] Overall, motor vehicles have taken up the share of goods that the household furnishings category has lost, while recreational goods took a dive during The Great Depression, World War 2, and the beginning of the Cold War, and the other goods have maintained their share fairly consistently.[58]

A very interesting trend is that consumer durable goods have flat-lined since the housing bust. Consumers have always been growing their wealth with this discretionary spending since 1925. The only other period of stagnation occurred during the lead up to World War 2, in the 1930s. When the war began, consumers invested majorly in furnishings and household items while sacrificing other things, as they hunkered down with their families. In recent years, the luxury-obsessed Americans have taken a tiny share of their wealth and purchased jewelry and watches during this recent stagnation.[59]

Summary
These mounds of evidence show that America is more prosperous than ever, and only an attitude of ingratitude could possibly leave any American buried in envy. Short of a total system breakdown, it is unlikely that America will see the poverty it suffered during

---

[55] *Figure 37: Share of Housing by Ownership*
[56] *Figure 38: Growth of Housing by Ownership*
[57] *Figure 44: Growth of Consumer Durable Goods Value*
[58] *Figure 43: Share of Consumer Durable Goods Value*
[59] *Figure 45: Consumer Durable Goods Value per Capita*

dustbowl and the Great Depression. Those who distort what American progress really looks like, have neglected the hard work of analyzing all the facts, to discern the trends of the past century. They have no historical context, and they advance their propaganda for modern agendas upon short-term thinking and ignorance. They must learn the truth from this analysis to correctly understand our economic reality.

In short, America has built a level of prosperity unknown to human beings anywhere on the planet, during any time of history. The numbers do not lie. We must acknowledge American success as evidenced by the meteoric rise of the service economy, wages and profit, savings and investments, private fixed assets, inventions, cultural infrastructure, housing, discretionary goods, and a parasitically large government that can even attempt to feed off of all this prosperity. Instead of destroying western success with the failed policies of dirigisme, other nations should be learning from accurately curated American history, to lift their own people out of suffering with liberty, capitalism, profits, innovation, competition, small government, and voluntary cooperation.

§ 1.4 America vis-à-vis the World

"The winds and waves are always on the side of the ablest navigators." –Edward Gibbon, The History of the Decline and Fall of the Roman Empire, 1789

There is no shortage of pontificators who talk about "the world" compared to some other country. Perhaps they traveled a bit, or saw some narratives on the news. Perhaps they trusted the heartrending speech of a politician, professor, or nonprofit. Perhaps a depressing advertisement touched their guilt, or an activist entertainer beguiled their groupthink.

It is easy to go with our gut and intuition. The trouble is, we cannot possibly understand "the world" in terms of our individual experiences. We can spend years in a city, without even grasping a fraction of what life is truly like for millions of people living within a few miles from us. If we wish to understand large, complex systems, then we must look at systemic evidence. Individual experiences and stories can paint either an emblematic or atypical picture. They are not reliable.

So we must turn to the data and research. Using the impressive and authoritative World Bank indicators,[60] we can objectively estimate how the United States compares to the rest of "the world," without involving our biases. This will give us a picture of how the American experience differs from an aggregate abstraction of experience for other people across the globe.

Is America exceptional? By every reasonable measure, yes! No other nation on the planet can claim to have created such prosperity, innovation, and quality of living, in such a short time. That is why millions of immigrants have poured across America's borders for generations to access our prosperity. Latin America, from which most modern American immigrants hail, is burgeoning with a massive wealth of natural resources, but they have failed to efficiently exploit their gifts and control the corruption that arose from their culture and politics. The decaying features of America

---

[60] (World Bank, 2014)

are also cultural and political. Dysfunctional culture eventually tears down strong economies, but the process takes generations.

For our comparison, we will begin with American labor. Currently, many Americans are not working. Meanwhile, poverty hustlers myopically focus on the unemployment rate. The rising joblessness is actually found in working-age people who have stopped seeking jobs, which does not show up in the unemployment rate. Some even claim that the labor market has improved, when comprehensive analysis shows that it has not. New jobs are lower quality, lower-wage, and part-time.[61] Employers are increasingly risk-averse and picky with new hires. Aggregate employment, by accurate measure, is down significantly.[62] Foreshadowing retirement doom, adults are not having children like they used to, as youths continue to decline in their share of the population.[63]

Accordingly, American social insurance taxation is immediately consumed as interest payments continue to mushroom. In such a compulsory retirement scheme, it is hard for workers to save more than they are already taxed, so it prevents many individuals from saving privately for the future. What will happen when there is an explosion of retirees and too few working-aged people to support them? Social insurance is not a personal savings account – the taxes are handed to the present-day elderly the moment they are collected. Any additional revenue is parked in a trust fund that does not even cover a fraction of what the government has promised to taxpayers.

In the last twenty years, about nine percent of American workers are not working anymore from peak employment.[64] Compared to the rest of the world, American workers are still providing almost twice the services, such as education, law, technology, management, entertainment, financing, and food services. At the same time, Americans are not making as many things as foreigners; we have thirty percent fewer industrial workers compared to foreign workforces since 2003, and we have been running a trade deficit

---

[61] (Obata, 2015)
[62] *Figure 50: U.S. Labor Aggregate*
[63] *Figure 49: U.S. Labor by Aged Work Status*
[64] *Figure 50: U.S. Labor Aggregate*

Thomas E. Kurek

since 1976.[65] We also have nearly twenty-times fewer agricultural workers.[66]

How productive is America compared to the rest of the world? Our Gross Domestic Product (GDP) growth rate is very close to the global average, but our GDP per American is five times the global average.[67] [68] Our GDP per employed American has plummeted since 2002, indicating that productivity gains are coming from financial tricks and investments instead of labor, and underscoring the decline of American labor.

The United States has not been using its production to add lasting value to the future. In only four years since 1968 did America beat the rest of the world in Gross Capital Formation (GCF), the measure of how much added value is being invested in real growth, rather than consumed.[69] This calls into question the state of our infrastructure.

Money can be a moving target, when central banks print it or expand its supply. Honest people who want to spend money wisely and invest responsibly are forced to compete with crooks who shower irresponsible players with loans. This infects the entire economy with *dumb-money*, and the result is *dumb economic activity*, which is divorced from the actual needs and desires of most people. America is not alone in the proliferation of dumb-money. Since the 1960s, the rest of the world has been inflating their monetary supply and prices twice as much as America.[70] [71] These monetary interventions influence trade. The weaker a nation's currency, the more incentive foreigners have to buy their exports. In the early 1990s, the globe started to export a little bit more than they imported, but America has been running a trade deficit of one to five percent of GDP since the 1980s.[72] [73] Americans are buying up these

---

[65] *Figure 62: Trade Surplus/Deficit*
[66] *Figure 53: US-to-World Labor Output Ratios*
[67] *Figure 54: Gross Domestic Product Growth*
[68] *Figure 55: Gross Domestic Product per Capita*
[69] *Figure 58: Gross Capital Formation*
[70] *Figure 59: M2 Growth*
[71] *Figure 60: Consumer Price Inflation*
[72] *Figure 61: Imports and Exports*
[73] *Figure 62: Trade Surplus/Deficit*

imports, largely with credit. It is much easier to get loans in America than the rest of the world.[74]

Since the 1990s, America has not used energy for production as much as the globe, but today, that difference is vanishing.[75] Increased American exports and more efficient consumer energy usage contribute to that trend. Over the course of fifty years, America's energy usage has been halved compared to the rest of the world, but we still use three times as much energy per person.[76]

Where does the energy come from? The rest of the world imported much more energy than America until the prelude to the petrodollar system in the early 1970s, in which Middle Eastern countries agreed to price all of their oil in US dollars in exchange for weapons and American commitment to their defense. Since then, United States energy imports have blown the rest of the world out of the water.[77]

Fossil fuel energy comes from oil, coal, and natural gas. Alternative energy comes from nuclear and "green" technology (hydroelectric, geothermal, solar, wind). During the prelude to the petrodollar system in the early 1970s, global fossil fuel usage plummeted, while the United States scaled back gradually.[78] By the late 1980s, America surged past the rest of the world in alternative energy use.[79]

Almost a quarter of our energy is used for transporting people and goods on our roads, nearly doubling the rest of the world.[80] America's road sector energy usage exploded during the prelude to the petrodollar. Combined with much cheaper gasoline, over double the road networks, and many more vehicles, the transportation infrastructure has allowed Americans to consume more things, faster. This consumption is greased with superiorly affordable and

---

[74] *Figure 63: Financial-Sector-Provided Domestic Credit*
[75] *Figure 57: Gross Domestic Product per Energy Use*
[76] *Figure 72: Energy Use*
[77] *Figure 73: Net Energy Imports*
[78] *Figure 75: Fossil Fuel Energy*
[79] *Figure 74: Alternative & Nuclear Energy*
[80] *Figure 76: Road Sector Energy Use*

Thomas E. Kurek

available travel and shipping.[81] [82] [83] [84] [85] Transportation is instrumental to American prosperity, so it is an attractive target for enemies.

Rapid innovation accompanies our prosperity. America dwarfs the rest of the world in intellectual property revenues.[86] Strong legal protections for inventors and creators has fueled our ingenuity. The rest of the world also benefits from America's intellectual property infrastructure, as foreigners apply for United States non-resident trademarks and patents at six times the rate of other countries.[87] America towers over the rest of the world in scientific and technical publications, high-technology exports, research, and innovation spending, but the globe has been catching up rapidly.[88] [89] [90] [91]

Despite our impressive economic, social, legal, and martial achievements, our region is miniscule. North America is the smallest region in the world, with a declining population. The Middle East and North African region surpassed North America in 2002 and continues to grow. Latin America and the Caribbean follow, with almost double the population of North America. With the largest population decline since the 1960s, Europe and Central Asia was just surpassed by Sub-Saharan Africa. Asia and the Pacific dominate the world in population, but South Asia has grown at nearly the same rate that East Asia and the Pacific have declined.[92]

The United States' has not largely contributed to the burgeoning masses of the human race since the 1960s, with only half the rate of

---

[81] *Figure 77: Gasoline Price*
[82] *Figure 78: Diesel Price*
[83] *Figure 79: Motor Vehicles*
[84] *Figure 80: Passenger Cars*
[85] *Figure 81: Road Density*
[86] *Figure 64: Intellectual Property Revenue*
[87] *Figure 65: Non-Resident Patent and Trademark Applications*
[88] *Figure 68: High-Tech Export Value*
[89] *Figure 69: Research and Development Researchers*
[90] *Figure 70: Research & Development Expenditure*
[91] *Figure 71: Scientific and Technical Journal Articles*
[92] *Figure 82: Population, % of the World*

population growth as the rest of the world.[93] Not surprisingly, the world is filling up its available land with people at an explosive rate when compared to America, even if America is much more urbanized.[94] [95] The population of America has many more elderly people, about the same number of working-age people, and significantly fewer youths.[96] [97] There are many more females in the United States than the world in general.[98]

The rest of the world must be much less attractive and welcoming to immigrants. The United States quintuples the globe's immigrant population![99] Yet private Americans tend to transfer less money to private foreigners than people from other countries.[100] Farming and forestland is bountiful in the United States, nearly doubling what foreigners have access to, even though America ranks third behind the Russian Federation and Canada in land and water area.[101] [102] [103]

Racial demographics in the United States have greatly fluctuated in the past few years. Blacks reached an apex of 21% of the population in 1770, and gradually declined to 9%. Over the past three generations, they have risen to about 13%. During the same period, whites have plummeted to a very thin majority, with five whites for every four non-whites. The most recent apex for whites was in 1930, when there were eight whites for every one non-white.[104] Many other nations are so inferior at reporting racial statistics that an objective comparison is problematic. The most sensible inference we can make is that the United States has racial diversity that eclipses the world, due to the fact that its sustained immigration demographics also eclipse the rest of the world.[105]

---

[93] *Figure 83: Population Growth, Annual %*
[94] *Figure 84: Population Density*
[95] *Figure 90: Urbanization*
[96] *Figure 85: Age Demographics, % of Total Population*
[97] *Figure 86: Age Demographics, US-to-World Ratio*
[98] *Figure 87: Females, % of Population*
[99] *Figure 88: Immigrants*
[100] *Figure 89: Personal Transfers (Cash & Kind between Foreign Nations)*
[101] *Figure 91: Forest Land per Capita*
[102] *Figure 92: Agricultural Land per Capita*
[103] *Figure 93: Surface Area (Land & Water), km²*
[104] *Figure 94: Racial Demographics, 1690 – 2010*
[105] *Figure 88: Immigrants*

Thomas E. Kurek

By nearly every economic indicator, America has been exceptional, and still leads the world according to many indicators. However, due to profligacy in society and the government, we have stumbled into a managed decline. Our policies of destructionism lead to the consumption of capital, malinvestment, and consuming more than what we produce. As America stagnates from its foolish economic policies and retrogressed culture, the rest of the world has been catching up.

§ 1.5 Summary and Implications

"Economic progress is the work of the savers, who accumulate capital, and of the entrepreneurs, who turn capital to new uses. The other members of society, of course, enjoy the advantages of progress, but they not only do not contribute anything to it; they even place obstacles in its way." –Ludwig von Mises, Epistemological Problems of Economics (1933)

Government regulations, progressive taxation, welfare, subsidies, charities, black markets, grey markets, crime, litigiousness, cronyism, meaningless credentials, and the selective discrimination of *cultural Marxism* and *political correctness* have combined with a ten-trillion-dollar civic empire to turn America into a society where merit, honor, accuracy, and justice mean little. The redistribution of blood, sweat, merit, and honor is ubiquitous. Unemployed welfare recipients, construction workers, criminals, prostitutes, accountants, engineers, doctors, and lawyers, eat at the same restaurants, frequent the same stores, and go to the same schools and hospitals. This is the equality-of-outcome utopia that socialists have imagined from the beginning of their envy- and indignation-laden nightmare, and it is crushing the spirit and economic progress of entire nations. It is economically and socially destructive to impose even this level of unnatural equality.

Something-for-nothing is the standard, and earning is an afterthought. There is always a rationalization, because nobody wants to admit that they do not deserve their prosperity or reputation. Ask the criminal if they deserve to live as comfortably as an executive, and they will say, "Yes." They are risking jail, injury, and reputation! Ask the athletes if they deserve to live like kings, just because they are part of a cartel that robs taxpayers of billions per year from their tenuous nonprofit status and shady business deals with local politicians, and then passes on those tax robberies to contracted athletic talent – they will say, "Yes." They are competitively entertaining the masses! It is not their fault that citizens are too mollified by their own leisure to realize that their government allows this corruption.

Thomas E. Kurek

The examples of *something-for-nothing* are endless amongst the poor and the rich alike, and they all trace back to hypocritical, failed, or deliberate interventionist government policy combined with powerful institutions and unscrupulous opportunists who will take advantage of any chance to acquire more for themselves at the expense of others, without even questioning where their prosperity came from, or how it is possible. Meanwhile, hardworking middle-class workers who have lived within their means and perform critical services to keep the system running are paying the price for all of these freeloaders. The freeloaders could even be amongst the middle-class too, depending upon the size of their ill-gotten treasures.

As this injustice persists, the bureaucrats and institutionalists who created the mess turn the middle-class against itself with ignorant visions of *radical egalitarianism* – unnatural equality that destroys meaningful distinctions which assist a healthy society. *Freedom of opportunity* is slaughtered in their quest of maintaining *equality of outcome*. As the tax, regulatory, monetary, and banking policies put wealth in the hands of the undeserving rich and poor, cynical redistributionist groups create anger towards the upper-middle class, ensuring that the last semblance of the American dream will be destroyed with tax increases on successful Americans during their few good years of earning.

The cacophony of classism is pervasive, and it lends more power to the same people who created the socialist, interventionist, institutionalist, and progressive economic dystopias that we observe across the world. The more *dumb-money* they put into the pockets of those who will move the money in tune with their agenda, the less *smart-money* is accessible by hardworking citizens who are trying to earn a fair living and provide mission-oriented business output. The inter-subjectivity of pricing in economics is massively perverted by these interventionists and their armies of *something-for-nothing* recipients.

Meanwhile, much of the citizenry is too painfully misinformed and distracted to realize that the wealth of the "rich" that they envy is all fictitious, magic paper wealth, in the form of bonds and stocks that can evaporate in an instant. The fake value of this paper was created by government actions and failures to begin with. If the citizenry had been wise enough to demand that the government stop its trillion-dollar interferences, so that prices and value could correct themselves, then much of the fake paper wealth would have disappeared and taken the distorted statistics along with it.

Instead, Americans were duped by bureaucrats who knew that collapsing real estate prices not only meant affordable housing, but also massive reduction in tax revenues that would have shed thousands of government jobs. By allowing the government and banking thieves to salvage the phony value, citizens beckoned their own middle-class demise – slamming their future doors shut by increasing taxes on the upper-middle class. They continue to chant "hope and change" for charismatic politicians , when those same politicians have exacerbated all that was bad before they gained power.

These financial predators utilize an array of *poverty activists* in the entertainment, journalism, religious, civic, and education industries. They flood conversations with *the buzzwords of poverty hustling* like *income inequality* and *the one-percent*, inducing false beliefs in *prosperity incidence*. If we accept the correct definition of *prosperity* as material success, Americans of all socioeconomic classes are more prosperous than ever. The poverty activists manipulatively refer to *social deficiencies* as poverty. They use terms like *moral poverty, spiritual poverty, social support poverty, educational poverty*, or *first-world problems*. Qualifying poverty in poetic terms is effective at creating ignorant visions of people with less prosperity, but it ignores time-proven truths that show money cannot buy intrinsic goods. Money cannot buy love, correct morals, or replace bad parents with good ones. Poverty hustlers spread envy and wrath in the hearts of their targets by preaching fantasy visions of utopia and proposing redistributed money as a solution to the social deficiencies that are often the cause of poverty to begin with, and will not be ameliorated with greater wealth. The ancients scream wisdom at the poverty activists from their graves:

> *"Semper inops quicumque cupit" (whoever desires is always poor). –Claudius Claudianus circa 400 A.D.*

Because of the outrageous distortion of poverty in discourse and statistics, it is advisable to drop the term altogether. The opposite of prosperity is not poverty – it is *destitution*, a state of inadequate

Thomas E. Kurek

shelter, food, and clothing. Only 0.5 – 1% of Americans live in actual destitution,[106] which is an historical achievement beyond the imagination of the most ideologically faithful socialists of the 20th century, who were choking on the dirt of Russian dekulakization and Chinese struggle sessions. As the Chinese socialists killed off millions of their own people from democidal famine, the imagery of choking on dirt takes a realistic dimension, since those who were dying actually did try to eat dirt in order to stay alive. At the same time, the capitalism they hated was making the best of bad situations in the West, and improving destitution in ways that humanity has never before seen.

In the words of scholar James Q. Wilson, "The poorest Americans today live a better life than all but the richest persons a hundred years ago." The amenities and access available to the poorest Americans is stunning.[107] One-in-five middle-class Americans received redistribution from the government when they did not need it. The welfare slush-fund not only takes resources away from those few destitute Americans, but it also distorts price signals for productive economic activity, contributing to circulation of *dumb-money*, which is spent on luxuries like alcohol, gambling, drugs, and entertainment. America also hides its redistribution levels in subsidies that are not counted as income, as the average recipient of assistance spends 2.6 times the amount of the income they claim.

In light of these facts, most would consider current American society to be highly socialistic. Jon Stewart supported this sentiment during a debate with Bill O'Reilly in 2012, when he said:

> *"We're all socialists. This argument is about what shade of red we are, that's it." –Jon Stewart* [108]

Free-market economists would agree, but bemoan the *interventionist* policies that have corrupted our economy and society. From a technical standpoint, the massive levels of redistribution are intelligible from carefully demystified *prosperity incidence* statistics – considering income, subsidies, amenities, non-cash benefits,

---

[106] § 1.2 Prosperity, Poverty, and Destitution

[107] § 1.2 Prosperity, Poverty, and Destitution

[108] (Stewart & O'Reilly, 2012)

spending, and access to resources. Evaluating prosperity throughout history and geography should be enough to dispel illusions of American poverty. Besides its excellent performance on poverty, is American economic progress a great example to follow?

Comparing America to itself over time shows us the true story of national economic progress.[109] Data from the Bureau of Economic Analysis (BEA), Bureau of Labor Statistics (BLS), Census Bureau, and a few devoted researchers constitutes the hard evidence for that analysis.[110] The unprecedented prosperity of America is indicated by a large government, a service economy, high wages and profits, steady savings and investments, growth in private fixed assets, an explosion of invention, growing cultural infrastructure, housing growth with increased quality, and increased spending on discretionary goods.

The United States government has grown to be an enormous ghostly octopus, with phantom tentacles that seep through the threads of our clothes to find our last penny. We are currently paying the government nearly the same as all wage earning-people, after federal, state, and local taxes are combined. Half of tax is not only collected overtly – it is taken through hidden methods, price inflation, lost wages, lost jobs, and lost profits that we rely upon for retirement funds.

Detectives *follow the money* when tracking criminals. Listening to the speeches of mendacious politicians, while *following the money* of the American government will quickly turn a normal citizen into a cynic. The *institutionalist* lamentations about underfunded education, research, military, welfare, savings, and "greedy" corporate profits are a theatrical performance of Shakespearean proficiency. Either these areas have stayed the same, or they have grown monstrously. The government is even taking twice the amount of tax as they were during struggles for national survival such as the world wars and great depression. When the two-trillion-dollar cost of regulations, and two-trillion-dollars of nonprofit spending are combined, American civics is a behemoth of control and

---

[109] § 1.3 American Prosperity by the Numbers

[110] Appendix 1: Taxation, Income, Assets, Goods

Thomas E. Kurek

paternalism that would make Soviet Mother Russia greener with envy than the entire green environmental movement. The greenbacks are coming out of American pockets, but we are not enjoying greener pastures in turn.

Surrounded by this civic behemoth, economic dilettantes like Jon Stewart call for more "socialism" in the West, yet they are not imagining the Soviet, Chinese, or Cuban patterns of direct, bureaucratic government ownership of industry. They are actually invoking some hybrid of French *dirigisme* and *zwangswirtschaft* (command economy) introduced by Germans a few generations before Hitler, and adopted by fascists around the world. The government does not have to directly own industry in the zwangswirtschaft socialism pattern.[111] It uses regulation, subsidies, intimidation, regulatory capture, monetary policy, and other manipulations to force companies to do as the government pleases.

In a nation where math proficiency is not a prerequisite for fortune and fame, it is possible for rich celebrities like Jon Stewart to live under the weight of a ten-trillion-dollar civic empire and still demand more redistribution, while pretending as if seizing money from others to spend on imagined problems is an act of benevolence. The irony of leftwing Jewish Americans advocating Nazi economic features is not lost on economically literate Americans. Perhaps they drive Volkswagen cars too, and are content to forget the past in all aspects.

Nevertheless, the advocates of dirigisme and zwangswirtschaft might consider educating themselves on ownership to begin to awake from their stupor. Ownership is the power of disposal.[112] Using economic interventionism, that power is whittled away to any arbitrary point of relevance, depending upon the current agenda of the mosquito government. All the while, advocates of this "socialistic" policy can claim that this is not like Soviet communism. While that is correct, they should be offered congratulations for choosing the fascist economic pattern instead. Ownership-in-name-

---

[111] (von Mises, Socialism: An Economic and Sociological Analysis, Part V, Destructionism, Chapter 33, 2015)
[112] (von Mises, Socialism: An Economic and Sociological Analysis, Part V, Destructionism, Chapter 33, 2015)

only is still not private ownership and is still a contagion that rots the body of liberty espoused in the U.S. Constitution.

French *dirigisme* and *indicative planning* is closely related to this model of "socialism." In later chapters, these relationships will be elaborated more explicitly. Whether or not the size of American civics leaves the boundaries of dirigisme and leans into zwangswirtschaft should be argued elsewhere. The American *Code of Federal Regulations* is not the only tome of directives with price controls and quantified mandates, but it is a good place to start for the ambitious inquirer. It is sufficient for now to accept that American "socialism" looks more like dirigisme and zwangswirtschaft. Although one could ask why a foreigner like Thomas Piketty spends so much time on the United States economy to begin with, it is somewhat amusing to see a Frenchman pushing heavier *indicative planning* on a foreign nation that is already swimming in *dirigisme.*

American prosperity does not only enable a gargantuan civic empire, but it also turns our society away from maintaining their material needs towards gorging itself on psychological pursuits. The *service economy* mostly supports those kinds of transactions. Since World War 2, Americans have multiplied their annual service consumption tenfold, to $25,000 per person and service consumption is now almost 70% of America's total production. The poor and rich alike consume these services, which is an uncommon experience in history. Economic interventionism by local and foreign governments chases many jobs overseas, or else results in the importation of labor through legal or illegal channels, to affect an international redistribution of jobs. Laborers in a home nation should be more efficient than those of a foreign nation, but because of monetary policies, regulations, subsidies, and redistribution policies, laborers in home nations are priced out of their jobs. Those jobs go to machines and foreigners.

Wages and profits have increased for all Americans, and the profits pay for our retirements. The ratio of wages to profits has remained consistent throughout the past century, obliterating the fantasy of *greedy* corporations profiteering. In fact, the industries that pay the most are the ones that benefit the most from economic and military impositions by the government – including government work, real estate, finance, oil and mining. Meanwhile, government debt since the 1970s has increased gradually. The government has increased its interference so much in the past few years that it has wiped out the prudent savings and surplus of American business and citizens. This greedy action by the government is an indicator of *destructionism* (the consumption of capital), and immorality that imposes shackles upon its children to pay for the luxuries of today. The civic empire has also acquired buildings and other fixed assets at an alarming rate. Business and citizens have grown their ownership of fixed assets, but reduced their share compared to government and nonprofits. American inventions, cultural infrastructure, housing, and discretionary spending have all exploded in the past century, further demonstrating unprecedented American prosperity.

But how does America compare to the rest of the world? Is it truly exceptional? It is a childish adult, frolicking upon its laurels, while generations of economic interventions have just begun to erode an unprecedented prosperity. Production per employed American has plummeted since 2002, showing that growth is coming from financial tricks and investments. By accurate measure, employment is down, and jobs are of lower quality with less hours. Americans are not making physical goods like the rest of the world but we provide twice the amount of services. The infrastructure is degenerating as capital is consumed. While America has manipulated its currency, the rest of the world has done the same thing at twice the rate – adding even more to the export-crushing forces of heavy regulation, radical environmentalism, and aggressive taxation.

Americans take for granted their incredible road system, cars, superior alternative energy portfolio, and gargantuan energy wealth. Transportation and cheap energy make up the cornerstone of American prosperity, so it is critical to defend; the enemies of America know this. This is a major motivator for opponents to target transportation and undercut American oil and energy arrangements. Corrupt American culture that has appropriated features of ancient Greece and Weimar Germany has led to depopulation, while incentives are created for people who cannot pay for their own children to have more of them. Other nations with corrupt cultures are depopulating as well, so America is not alone.

The immigrant population of America is greased to make up the depletion of the workforce from depopulation. America has five times as many immigrants as the rest of the world, and whites are barely a majority anymore. America is the most culturally and racially diverse country in the world, but many journalists, entertainers, and educators are acting to disintegrate traditional cultural distinction.

By economic standards, America is exceptional in almost every way. But the signs of social retrogression, profligacy, and destructionism are also apparent from economic indicators. The consumption of capital, malinvestment, and voracious consumption exceeding production are allowing the rest of the world to catch up. America is in an undeniable managed decline, but this does not change what we have achieved, and how we did it. The facts of our history show a stunning victory of capitalism for the poor and destitute, with prosperity that socialists have only grasped at with miserable or deadly outcomes.

Only ignorance, short-term thinking, and ingratitude could generate the envy and wrath that *poverty hustlers* encourage to advance their agendas. By every measure, modern prosperity is unprecedented for all Americans. Nations that follow the formula for American success will help all of their citizens, and those that buy into the dirigiste fantasies will bring misery to their people. In the public discourse, we must at least agree upon the numbers, facts, and analytics so that we are operating in the realm of reality instead of our imaginations. The true tale of the American economy is sophisticated and nuanced, requiring depth and great detail to elaborate honestly. The emotionalized false tale of the American economy produces stunning class warfare stereotypes for movie scripts, but it fills our heads with inaccuracy and misdirected hostility. There is a very old cultural and political tradition that has been weaving these false tales for centuries.

Chapter 2: The Institutionalist Creed

§ 2.1 Institutionalists versus Valorists

"The faculty which produces illusory effects during waking moments is identical with that which produces them during sleep." –Aristotle, De Insomniis Part 1, 323 B.C.

How shall we refer to this cartel of ideology in a simple term? We shall call them *institutionalists*. Their smorgasbord of *dirigiste* ideology traces its roots to the vicious Jacobin Club of the French Revolution. The most popular thinker of the Jacobins, Jean-Jacques Rousseau, was "the first to teach that the imperfections of government were the only perennial source of the vices of mankind."[113] In 1762, he provided all institutionalist descendants with their tagline:

"MAN is born free; and everywhere he is in chains." –Jean-Jacques Rousseau, The Social Contract

Institutionalists despise "organized religion" that is opposed to their agenda. Throughout socialist, fascist, and Jacobin history they have destroyed the institution of the church, even murdering priests. Today, institutionalists just ridicule organized religion out of favor using their total domination of the cultural industries, or they coopt churches that will advance their agenda. Ideally, they would like the religions to promote visions that help their agendas, but they will settle for crushing organized religion, and leaving behind disorganized, balkanized, and ineffective religion that cannot gain mass power to significantly oppose them. The antithesis of *organized* religion is not some noble and purer form of worship – it is just *disorganized* religion.

If a person believes that institutional power is the solution to mankind's ailments, then their vital objective is to eradicate or coopt all institutional power that they believe stands in the way of their own "solutions," and ridicule anyone who does not affirm their agenda of the day. They illustrate their opponents as either

---

[113] (Godwin, 1793)

ignorant, mean, or bad-willed people. In socialist, fascist, and French revolutionary history, they brutally slaughtered, displaced, starved, or enslaved their opponents. Today, *institutionalists* harass, intimidate, discriminate, shame, ridicule, blacklist, and destroy the businesses of their opponents. To the institutionalist, all institutions – business, government, nonprofit, educational, journalistic, entertainment, religious – are remedies so long as their opponents are not the ones controlling them.

All men have visions, which are pre-analytic cognitive acts,[114] our intuitive sense of how the world works, and the silent shapers of our thoughts.[115] A person's visions are not often articulated to others, let alone to themselves. Visions can be social, moral, cultural, political, economic, or religious. Most importantly, everyone has a vision of the nature of mankind.

The institutionalists have an *unconstrained vision*[116] of mankind, in which mankind itself is incrementally improvable by replacing *disfavored* institutional power with their *idealized* institutional power. According to their original masterminds, such as William Godwin, Rousseau, John Stuart Mill, Marquis de Condorcet, and Baron D'Holbach, they do not think that men are naturally at odds with each other, and they believe that bad education and destructive social arrangements are the roots of human suffering. Perhaps they have never read *Lord of the Flies*, raised children, or witnessed the spontaneously emerging child soldiers in lawless regions throughout history. Thus, institutionalists are apt to disagree with the notion that,

> *"Each new generation born is in effect an invasion of civilization by little barbarians, who must be civilized before it is too late."* –*Thomas Sowell*

Conscience and virtue must be taught, earned, and honed. The idea that humans are inherently good from birth is not only falsified by history, but also by the institutionalists' incessant fixation upon peoples' intentions and character. If people were born in goodness, they would not direly need institutionalists to keep them on a

---

[114] (Schumpeter, 1954)
[115] (Sowell, A Conflict of Visions, 1987)
[116] (Sowell, A Conflict of Visions, 1987)

Thomas E. Kurek

politically correct path of righteousness with contrived central plans, cults of personality, redistribution, socially-framed educational content, and entertainment influence. The institutionalists' rejection of human sinfulness in the nature of mankind is one of their most paradoxical beliefs.

Their *unconstrained vision* of mankind sees knowledge as concentrated in the minds of the educated and experts, so they believe that power should only be wielded by those credentialed people.[117] This is a popular aspect of imperial, fascist, communist, socialist, and social democratic societies, and it leads to a status-based society that is obsessed with awards, recognition, credentials, degrees, and certifications. Intentions, credentials, conformity, and status supersede results, tests, and direct competition in the institutionalist society.

This credential obsession also brings forth pervasive *scientism* in which the scientific method is corruptly applied to subjective inquiries, allowing "experts" to give mass media a false sense of objective authority as they push institutional agendas upon the hapless audiences of television, internet, and radio. The extent of misinformation in the minds of the public, implanted by the nexus of mass media and educators, is monumental.

For instance, one-third of psychological research is not reproducible,[118] and over one-million psychologists, social workers, counselors, marriage therapists, life coaches, and substance abuse counselors consume billions of dollars helping people to deal with everyday problems. This *caring industry* has multiplied its size by one-hundred times since the 1940s,[119] and yet it feeds from this falsifiable research. Moreover, only half of their patients qualify for psychiatric diagnoses. Traditional societies had already learned how to mitigate social dysfunctions with standards like the *seven heavenly virtues* and the *seven deadly sins*. These standards have been uprooted by the institutionalists, and replaced with hedonistic eudaimonia (happiness is virtue, suffering is sin). They decide what is harmful or beneficial to people and uproot the standards of morals that were developed by the experiences of millions of people,

---

[117] (Sowell, A Conflict of Visions, 1987)
[118] (Nosek, 2015)
[119] (Dworkin, 2010)

captured in tradition. The *caring industry* workers supplant the interpersonal persuasion of priests with eudaimonia and their own set of behavioral imperatives. The *caring industry* is paid to plug the leaking holes of their relativistic, chaotic value system.

Psychology is not alone; a large share of published research is false,[120] within this institutionalist atmosphere of scientism, where the money never stops flowing to education, training, research, and certification. Bookworms without a cause leech off of each other, steal ideas, coopt and distort time-tested wisdom, or else present outrageous new interpretations of standardized knowledge that was settled a long time ago. Meanwhile, honest researchers fight the tide of agenda-driven revisionism, as they tirelessly curate, defend, and preserve the tomes of knowledge and wisdom that are persistently under attack by the neophilic institutionalists.

Peer review is a sacred phrase in academia, but it is a process which does not convey any proven level of authority or veracity.[121] With just a fraction of the annual billions spent on peer review, digital collaboration systems could be built to cheaply and effectively detect fraud and errors, improve publications, and grade the value of research. Peer review is certainly not resilient against fraud. Over half of open-access journals solicited in a recent sting operation accepted a blatantly false study.[122]

What are the consequences incurred by experts and institutionalists for participating in this widespread academic fraud, abuse of credentials, incompetence, and unethical promotion of falsehoods? The farcical outcomes include large salaries, professional honors, ennoblement from the general public, respect from society, and virtually no punishment or liability even when caught red-handed.[123] The institutionalists select from a wide array of fake knowledge and fraudulent experts to justify their agendas.

This is the swamp of imagined knowledge that they operate upon to form their ballyhooed *consensus*. The sacred consensus of experts is a groupthink fabrication that they use in their *appeal-to-authority*

---

[120] (Ioannidis, 2005)
[121] (Smith, 2010)
[122] (Bohannon, 2013)
[123] (Marcus & Oransky, 2014)

Thomas E. Kurek

propaganda. They even invoke medieval witch-hunt language when referring to those who challenge their consensus. They call their opposition *"deniers,"* and refer to their speech as *"dangerous."* This is the same language used by those who burned witches at the stake for questioning religious authority.

So far, these pseudo-priests of institutionalist education have not requested for the "deniers" to be burnt at the stake, but they have requested for them to be treated like gangsters under RICO laws (Racketeer Influenced and Corrupt Organizations Act).[124] [125] In this 21st century institutionalist society, *caveat emptor* (buyer beware) is the most practical advice to any citizen, as they consume information in classrooms or living rooms. Only traditional historical analysis, critical thinking, and evidence can counteract the pervasive falsehoods of scientism, and collectivist intimidation.

Another destructive effect of *institutionalist scientism* is the corruption of the minds of young adults, who pay for higher education with their future earnings, or other people's money. They sit in classrooms absorbing these distortions as if they are the unadulterated truths of the universe. The United States forefathers warned us of such dysfunctional intellectual atmospheres:

> *"He who knows nothing is nearer to truth than he whose mind is filled with falsehoods and errors." – Thomas Jefferson, letter to John Norvell, Jun. 11th, 1807*

In short, the *unconstrained vision* sees mankind on a continual path of *progress*, prioritizes the *intentions* of a man over his *results*, concentrates knowledge and power in *experts* and *institutions*, looks for special causes of *suffering* (such as war, poverty, and crime), attempts to create social results *directly* with concentrated power, and pursues *solutions* to problems instead of optimizations. It sees people as *far from* what they *could possibly be*, and blames external factors for their problems, so it is not concerned with prudence as much as *excuses for the deficiencies* of people. It views the institution as both the problem and the solution, so it is apt to blame

---

[124] (von Spakovsky, 2015)
[125] (Competitive Enterprise Institute, 2016)

the failures of individuals on scapegoats, demonize opposition, and jockey for total control of institutional power and influence.

It is an *idealist* vision, which makes economic and social intervention essential, through economic planning, surrogate decision-making, politically correct shaming, kangaroo courts, arbitrary legal interpretations that use twisted semantics to advance agendas, and aggressive judicial activism. It tends to collect self-pitying, self-abdicating people along the way with a mentality of insecurity, victimhood, and grievance-mongering – along with their narcissistic champions who swear they will help these downtrodden souls by defeating the scapegoats. It garners divisive *identity politics* while proclaiming *equality* at the same time. Its impetus to control, prescribe, and exhort is attractive to the ideologically irreligious or insecure religious people who use their worldviews to provide psychological escape from *fearful histories* into a *hopeful future*. These *idealists* primarily want to feel *security*.

Opposing the institutionalists are the *valorists*. They are called valorists because they prefer valor to the institution – courage of the individual in the face of the uncertainty that is always present. They do not wish to destroy institutions, but they do not see them as solutions to problems, or vehicles for the deliverance of mankind. To the valorist, the institution is an association of people and traditions that can be as destructive as constructive, and only as good as its processes, design, and the imperfect people who belong to it. Valorists expect bad actors to corrupt institutions from within, so they require checks-and-balances, collateral, and skepticism of leadership. They have a *constrained vision*[126] which sees the nature of mankind as *tragically fixed* by moral and egocentric limitations; therefore, changing human nature is vain and pointless, and society should only find ways to accurately understand human nature, and optimize the situation.

A tagline for the valorists is that *"the perfect is the enemy of the good."* They prioritize *results* over intentions, and pursue *tradeoffs* and *optimizations* instead of solutions.[127] They look for special causes of *triumph* (such as peace, wealth, or law-abidance), assuming that mankind only needs to erode gainful processes in

---

[126] (Sowell, A Conflict of Visions, 1987)
[127] (Sowell, A Conflict of Visions, 1987)

Thomas E. Kurek

order to return to its natural state of war, poverty, and crime. They see *consequential knowledge*[128] as *dispersed* throughout society and experienced people, so they are skeptical of experts and concentrated power, as they prefer to disperse power to competing forces like free market contenders, small business owners, and people who have proven themselves with results. They feel that social results cannot be directly created and maintained, so they aim to *indirectly influence social results* through social processes like liberty, rule of law, representative power, tradition, and freedom of opportunity.

Tradition is a social process that the valorists defer to over their own imaginations, as tradition aggregates generations of experience from millions of people, so that abiding people living today will not have to suffer the same errors. They believe that wise traditions can be lost and must be restored, and that bad traditions should be reformed with caution. Incremental reforms to tradition must be carefully tested, and justified by evidence and reason. Their *constrained vision* prefers not to presume how far people can go, or the reasons for their failures, instead it encourages *prudence* of the individual to *make the most* of their conditions.

They have a *realist* vision that sees economic and social intervention as usually more damaging than rectifying, preferring to establish systems of cooperation that are determined by the directly affected parties instead of third-parties, activist judges, politically correct social activists, and surrogate decision-makers. In the words of Friedrich Hayek,

> *Either both the choice and the risk rest with the*
> *individual or he is relieved of both.*
> *–F. A. Hayek* [129]

The valorists are typically confident people of faith who are apt to let go of controlling things beyond their reach – trusting the *invisible hand of the free market*, the wisdom of traditions, and the deterring effect of retribution and punishment for wrongdoing. Their impetus to compete, let go, live and let die, and defer is attractive to survival-of-the-fittest irreligious people and conscientious religious people who use their worldviews to explain a tragic world, an *unguaranteed*

---

[128] (Sowell, Intellectuals and Society, 2009)
[129] (Hayek, 1944)

future, and *triumphant histories.* Adherents to this vision have a mentality of rugged individualism, independence, self-reliance, and personal responsibility. These realists primarily want to feel *liberated.*

Qualitative practices like history and economics require analytical thinking, but visions fill the analysts with presumptions. Schools of economic thought, such as Marxist, Keynesian, and Institutionalist operate upon the *unconstrained vision,* whereas Classical and Austrian schools operate upon the *constrained vision.* Distributism is an interesting case, advocated by Catholic socialists like Dorothy Day. It cannot be called a school of economics because it simply proposes ideals, without offering quantitative methods that can be tested. Distributism is filled with the *idealist* basis of the unconstrained vision, but assuming human sinfulness, it attempts to use distributed institutional action to confront the dark side of mankind. It is likely that adherents of Distributism and the Marxist, Keynesian, and Institutionalist schools of economics, are *institutionalists.* The proponents of the Classical and Austrian schools of economics are *valorists.*

Visions of mankind significantly influence economic analysis. Perhaps only more rigorous and accurate analysis could catch failures of visions infecting economic analytical output. These failures are certainly consequential for business and government action. Political theory also becomes subject to vision-bias. In fact, societies at inflection points have constructed entirely new governments upon the basis of visions. The political atmosphere impacts economic outcomes in profound ways. For instance, communists slaughtered millions with democidal famine throughout the 20th century, while capitalists fed their people and foreign nations with charity and surplus.

§ 2.2 Visions and Nations: Continental Europe vs. America

> *"The accumulation of all powers, legislative,*
> *executive, and judiciary, in the same hands,*
> *whether of one, a few, or many, and whether*
> *hereditary, self-appointed, or elective, may justly be*
> *pronounced the very definition of tyranny." –James*
> *Madison, The Federalist Papers No. 47* [130]

The designs of entire nations embody these opposing visions. The constrained vision of *valorists* is written into The Constitution of the United States of America, with its sophisticated checks and balances. Many of the American forefathers explicitly advocated the constrained vision. This is well-elaborated in *The Federalist Papers*:

> *Ambition must be made to counteract ambition. The*
> *interest of the man must be connected with the*
> *constitutional rights of the place. It may be a*
> *reflection on human nature, that such devices*
> *should be necessary to control the abuses of*
> *government. But what is government itself, but the*
> *greatest of all reflections on human nature? If men*
> *were angels, no government would be necessary. If*
> *angels were to govern men, neither external nor*
> *internal controls on government would be necessary.*
> *In framing a government which is to be*
> *administered by men over men, the great difficulty*
> *lies in this: you must first enable the government to*
> *control the governed; and in the next place oblige it*
> *to control itself.* [131]

Contrarily, nations that deploy large government, high taxes, and strong centralized power, are based upon the *unconstrained vision*. Examples include the French revolutionary government, Rousseauean "General Will," and the socialist nations that built upon French revolutionary thought and German idealism. Condorcet rejected the notion of *checks and balances*, centuries

---

[130] (Hamilton, Madison, & Jay, 1788)
[131] (Hamilton, Madison, & Jay, 1788)

before modern activists complained about a "do-nothing congress," or "partisanship" holding back the imagined "progress" of society.

America looks increasingly like the French and socialist regimes throughout history, and less like what the American forefathers designed and this was entirely predictable. The continental European ideology was mostly imported by progressives and socialists beginning in the 19th century, and has presently consumed the majority of America's Democrats, and some Republicans. Obama expressed animosity towards checks-and-balances and belief in *economic command-and-control* when he said,

> *"Whenever Congress refuses to act, Joe and I, we're going to act. In the months to come, wherever we have an opportunity, we're going to take steps on our own to keep this economy moving."* –Barack Obama, *Tuesday, February 21st, 2012, Eisenhower Executive Office Building, with Vice President Joe Biden*

The economic ignorance of this statement is phenomenal. The economy does not move or stop based upon the words that a politician puts on paper. The only economic results a bureaucrat can affect is to exacerbate shortages, minimize the damage of taxes, optimize the civility of market exchange, and reward some by punishing others. The economy moves on its own within these optimal or destructive conditions created by the government. Even in anarchy, there is an economy, and the economy moves without the interference of bureaucrats.

This ignorance is repeated by those who claim that Bill Clinton single-handedly created American prosperity in the 1990s with his reluctant acquiescence to Republican congressional balanced-budget plans. The sea of prosperity sprung from the technological fruition of American satellites, cell phones, cell towers, personal computers, software, internet, and robotics, along with retraction of Russosphere competition in the global markets from the collapse of the Soviet Union.

Bill Clinton's policies had infinitesimal contribution to that prosperity – in fact, he tried to implement socialized medicine through HillaryCare in 1993, and his modifications to the Community Reinvestment Act, failure to defeat Al Qaeda, and transfer of missile technology to the Chinese were all disasters that have led to deep problems in America today. The outrageous boondoggles of government bureaucrats are easily whitewashed when America's hard workers unleash economic revolutions, as they did in the 1990s. The bureaucrats hide their mistakes under the success of citizens while blaming crises on their political opposition. An explanation must be provided as to how policies specifically exacerbated or alleviated conditions. Bill Clinton's failures required his successor to confront very serious issues.

Obama's economic promises are equally as counterproductive to long-term American prosperity. Belief in *centralized power* and disdain for checks-and-balances go hand-in-hand. His threat of unilateral action was a targeted circumvention of congress, called the *We Can't Wait* initiative, which imposed serious economic interventions that rewarded his political party's voters at the expense of other Americans. Democrats claimed that this $447-billion economic intervention was the *solution* to the economic issues of the day. Republicans claimed that this enormous debt and public sequestering of private capital was not a wise *tradeoff*, and would damage more than it repaired in the long run.[132]

To date, Obama has bypassed congress on environmental policy, Palestinian foreign aid, illegal immigration, tax, and education financing. With these actions, he effectively told the American people that he and his experts know better than their elected representatives. Even worse, he has covered up his circumvention of congress with clever deception. In a 2014 speech, he claimed that,

> *"The truth is, even with all the actions I've taken this year, I'm issuing executive orders at the lowest rate in more than 100 years. So it's not clear how it is that Republicans didn't seem to mind when President Bush took more executive actions than I did."* [133]

It would be clear to him if he was being honest. Not only did his administration do the calculated research to generate that deceptive statistic, but they also obfuscated the fact that executive orders are

---

[132] (Epstein, 2011)
[133] (Obama, Remarks by the President on the Economy, 2014)

not the only tool that he uses to exercise executive action. As of December 17th, 2014, Obama had issued more executive actions than any President since Jimmy Carter, when his executive orders are combined with memoranda.[134] He had also issued twenty-eight presidential policy directives, which is another one of his executive action tools. By the time he finishes his presidency, it is conceivable that he will surpass every president since Truman in executive action. As a lawyer who studied the Constitution, these facts are not lost on him, as he inks his signature on all of these executive actions.

It would be difficult for Obama to claim ignorance, as his knowledge of the mechanics of government is well-demonstrated. For example, he joined other constitutional scholars in a 2001 Chicago Public Radio interview, in which he bemoaned the court-focused litigation strategy of the civil rights era,

> *"But the Supreme Court never ventured into the issues of redistribution of wealth and sort of more basic issues of political and economic justice in this society. And to that extent as radical as people tried to characterize the Warren court, it wasn't that radical. It didn't break free from the essential constraints that were placed by the founding fathers in the Constitution, at least as it's been interpreted, and the Warren court interpreted it in the same way that generally the Constitution is a charter of negative liberties. It says what the states can't do to you, it says what the federal government can't do to you, but it doesn't say what the federal government or the state government must do on your behalf. And that hasn't shifted. One of the I think tragedies of the civil rights movement was because the civil rights movement became so court-focused, I think that there was a tendency to lose track of the political and community organizing and activities on the ground that are able to put together the actual coalitions of power through which you bring*

---

[134] (Korte, 2014)

*about redistributive change and in some ways we
still suffer from that."* [135]

Some explanation is necessary to whittle away this ideological
jargon to its bare substance. Although Obama does a decent job at a
basic explanation of "negative liberties," the notion itself is empty
rhetoric. There is no such thing as a "positive" or "negative" liberty.
This fake concept has been advanced by communists, Marxists, and
the socialists of the Frankfurt School, like Erich Fromm. It uses
multiple fallacies to seem plausible, including:

- Framing: selective influence over the perceptions of
  meaning
- Unstated assumptions
- Ideographs: virtue-words like *liberty* and *positive*
- False equivalence: asserting equality between two
  unequal things
- Argument from analogy: drawing irrelevant justification
  from analogies

Examples are helpful to understand the concepts. The First
Amendment of the U.S. Constitution is what they would call a
negative liberty. In reality, it should be unqualified, and correctly
referred to as simply, *liberty*. The government works for us. It is
obliged to defend our *liberties*:

> *Congress shall make no law respecting an
> establishment of religion, or prohibiting the free
> exercise thereof; or abridging the freedom of speech,
> or of the press; or the right of the people peaceably to
> assemble, and to petition the Government for a
> redress of grievances.*

Chapter ten of the Soviet Union's communist constitution is filled
with what they would call *positive liberties*. To accept this fantasy
concept, a person must believe that government-coerced healthcare,
education, entertainment, and jobs do not constrain their liberty.
They also must be foolish enough to believe that these guarantees
are actually *free* and not paid for by their own *forced labor* or

---

[135] (Obama, Interview of Illinois Senator Barack Obama on Chicago Public
Radio WBEZ Chicago 91.5 FM, 2001)

surrender of private property. They also must believe that the "universal" government-coerced services are not quality- and quantity-constrained by economic realities. Implicit in these beliefs is that the government does a better job at deploying all of these massive services than liberated, competing citizens who have personal stakes in the outcome of service delivery. Examples of *positive liberties* in the Soviet Union's communist constitution include:

> *Article 118. Citizens of the U.S.S.R. have the right to work, that is, are guaranteed the right to employment and payment for their work in accordance with its quantity and quality... abolition of unemployment.*

> *Article 119. Citizens of the U.S.S.R. have the right to rest and leisure. The right to rest and leisure is ensured by the reduction of the working day to seven hours for the overwhelming majority of the workers, the institution of annual vacations with full pay for workers and employees and the provision of a wide network of sanatoria, rest homes and clubs for the accommodation of the working people.*

> *Article 120. Citizens of the U.S.S.R. have the right to maintenance in old age and also in case of sickness or loss of capacity to work. This right is ensured by the extensive development of social insurance of workers and employees at state expense, free medical service for the working people and the provision of a wide network of health resorts for the use of the working people.*

> *Article 121. Citizens of the U.S.S.R. have the right to education. This right is ensured by universal, compulsory elementary education; by education, including higher education, being free of charge; by the system of state stipends for the overwhelming majority of students in the universities and colleges; by instruction in schools being conducted in the native language, and by the organization in the*

*factories, state farms, machine and tractor stations
and collective farms of free vocational, technical
and agronomic training for the working people.*

*Article 131. It is the duty of every citizen of the
U.S.S.R. to safeguard and strengthen public,
socialist property as the sacred and inviolable
foundation of the Soviet system, as the source of the
wealth and might of the country, as the source of the
prosperous and cultured life of all the working
people. Persons committing offenses against public,
socialist property are enemies of the people.*

*Article 132. Universal military service is law.
Military service in the Workers' and Peasants' Red
Army is an honorable duty of the citizens of the
U.S.S.R.*

These are the *positive liberties* that Obama correctly implies are absent from the American system of government. In reality, they are not liberties at all. They mandate the surrendering of liberty to the government, under the assumption that an army of bureaucrats can better decide for us what quality, type, and character of essential services that we should have. These positive liberties from the government require *forced labor* through taxation or regulatory constraint, which is then redistributed in some form, to recipients in whatever way the current bureaucrats deem righteous. They compel the citizens to *compulsory government service*, under the presumption that they cannot reach their full potential without such arrangements.

The socialists claim that a person without the tools to reach their full potential does not have full liberty. How would they know? Any individual's potential is determined by their biology, environment, morals, character, and earned intrinsic goods that are impossible to accurately measure. If positive liberties were applied honestly by these socialists, then an entrepreneur who can move mountains with their genius deserves millions of tax dollars, and a dimwitted citizen does not deserve a high school education. If they spend the tax money on the dimwit, and fail to provide mountains of capital for the entrepreneur, they are robbing citizens of their positive liberties.

Opponents of socialism rightly believe that free markets, private charity, and voluntary cooperation can better grade and align capital to merits and needs, and that disruption of these processes by central planners harms many more people than it helps.

The positive liberties that institutionalists seek to impose are nothing more than *compulsory government service* industries at the expense of *forced labor*. There is no liberty in such an arrangement. A citizen is compelled to pay for it, and compelled to be subjected to its interference within their free markets. The government-financed services are never free, universal, efficient, nor sufficient. Socialist nations throughout history have proven that these compulsory government services bring waste, misery, and failure to nations.

When Obama referred to *negative liberties* and implicitly advocated *positive liberties* through redistribution of wealth, along with "political and economic justice," his aims were intelligible to the initiated. In translation, he wishes to use the institutions to tear down the political and economic possessions of some Americans, while giving handouts to groups of people he thinks need more political and economic advantage. He admitted that the Constitution limited the civil rights movement from his positive liberty schemes of forced labor, favoritism, discrimination, and seized assets, and believes that the civil rights leaders should have focused on whipping up voters to achieve these goals through legislation and executive power. Fourteen years after he made this comment, it seems that he has succeeded in his *solution* which is just another boondoggle in the history of institutionalists and the unconstrained vision. Although it is an oxymoron, it would be much more accurate to rename "positive liberty" to "compulsory liberty."

Most notably, Obama did not start this alien ideological invasion of America. Franklin Delano Roosevelt demanded many of the same *compulsory liberties* that the communists had in their constitutions – including entertainment, healthcare, education, jobs, housing, retirement, price controls, and food. He called it the *Second Bill of Rights*, and presented it in his 1944 state of the union address.[136] While presenting this plan to Americans, FDR implied that people who opposed this plan were like Hitler and the fascists. Apparently,

---

[136] (The Heritage Foundation, 2016)

presidential bombastic dishonesty was alive and well in FDR, as much as our modern presidents. FDR knew that the fascists, communists, and democratic socialists were proponents of these *compulsory liberties*, which would actually make FDR and Obama like the fascists, using FDR's logic. Fascist economies are dirigiste economies.

While FDR's compulsory liberties were never adopted as constitutional amendments, they have been imposed upon Americans incrementally through legislation, including the New Deal, Lyndon Johnson's Great Society, and ObamaCare. Just like the collapsing socialist and fascist states, America's compulsory liberties have faced unserviceable liabilities, debts, and insufficient quality of services for which they took responsibility. FDR ascribed subjective terms to the mandated liberties, like "good," "adequate," and "decent," as all institutionalists have done. They hide behind their vagueness, so that they can make excuses for expansion or failure. The answer to the failure of compulsory liberty is always more forced labor, more promises, and more power for the government. With the mandates of compulsory liberties, life becomes more collectivized in all areas, and we lose control of our own conscience, intellect, and property.

When modern commentators bemoan the "polarization" of American politics, they should check the history of ideology instead of assuming it has something to do with changing times or "extremists" who refuse to conform to the demands of the institutionalists. There is nothing new about the changes that institutionalists have brought to America. Weimar Germany did very similar things which led to the rise of Adolph Hitler. Also, there is nothing unpredictable about this polarization. Institutionalists have incrementally imported foreign ideology that is based upon the unconstrained vision, in complete contravention to the design of America, and along with it, a collectivist environment of scientism and ill-gotten consensus.

In a coup de grâce, they have also imported beliefs in compulsory liberty which is normal in socialist constitutions, but completely anathema to the American tradition. *Valorists* who affirm the *constrained vision* have just woken up to this hostile takeover of the nation. Conflict and polarization is guaranteed whenever radicals destroy and replace entire traditions and value systems. Obama and his wife admitted to this in plain words during his first presidential campaign:

> *"We are five days away from fundamentally transforming the United States of America."* – Barack Obama, October 30, 2008

> *"We are going to have to change our conversation; we're going to have to change our traditions, our history; we're going to have to move into a different place as a nation."* –Michelle Obama, May 14, 2008

It seems as though only American conservatives were taking them at their word, and have been proven to be prescient in their loathing of the Obama administration from the beginning. Now those most wise and benevolent Americans are branded as "extremists" for speaking the truth and defending the American nation from this hostile takeover, or *"fundamental transformation."*

In reality, modern institutionalist assaults on the American nation are not new at all. There is nothing "progressive" about the agenda of Obama, Bernie Sanders, Hillary Clinton, nor any modern institutionalist. It only requires knowledge of history and ideology to realize how timeworn their platform truly is. It would behoove all Americans to become familiar with the *unconstrained* and *constrained visions* of mankind,[137] and their corresponding political experiments throughout history. From the unconstrained vision of mankind emerges an institutionalist blueprint for civics, and from that blueprint emerges delusional economic interpretations.

---

[137] (Sowell, A Conflict of Visions, 1987)

§ 2.3 The Institutionalist Fantasy Economy

"If you happen to read fairy tales, you will observe that one idea runs from one end of them to the other--the idea that peace and happiness can only exist on some condition. This idea, which is the core of ethics, is the core of the nursery-tales." –G.K. Chesterton[138]

Under the veil of this fairy-tale economy, we have reached a point of subversive tyranny in which civic institutional power exceeds the combined earning power of all Americans! The United States economy currently produces sixteen trillion dollars in value per year. The federal, state, and local government combined is seizing six trillion dollars per year, and another two trillion in regulatory impositions. Wealthy *institutionalists* are mainly responsible for another two trillion in tax-free civic activity by charitable and uncharitable nonprofits.

This powerful ten-trillion-dollar civic empire is not enough for the institutionalists. Even though all Americans combined only earn nine to eleven trillion dollars per year, they want to increase taxes on successful Americans during their couple of years of high earnings, and choke off the last remnants of the American dream. The handful of elites who control the government and institutions do not fear the poor, and they do not fear the rich. They can buy off or collude with either of those groups. It has always been the task of institutionalists to neutralize the upper-middle class (bourgeoisie), because when the bourgeoisie combines its decentralized economic and social power it can affect real change in the government and institutions on behalf of its workers and interested parties.

Most Americans are familiar with the institutionalist fairy tale that is used to manufacture consent of the hapless poor and egocentric do-gooders. They speak of education, environment, energy, health care, housing, jobs, immigration, urbanization, and identity segregation. All of these policies impact our economy.

---

[138] (Chesterton, 1915)

Education

According to the fairy tale, there was some kind of golden age of American education in the 1960s and 1970s, that was ushered in by higher taxes and legislation. This is false. Inflation-adjusted education spending per student has increased by 300% since the 1960s, while they outrageously request even more money for education. A rational person would demand that they slash education spending by two-thirds and stop wasting money, to recreate the education finance of the 1960s.

They bemoan the hordes of college graduates who cannot find work and live with their parents, but it is their own centralized education financing and segregation of education, industry, and apprenticeship that has created the mismatch between knowledge and productive work. They lament the cost of college but it is their billions in subsidies, easy loans, and handouts that have allowed universities to skyrocket the prices they charge. They complain about the quality of education, but they are the ones who chose to use a large share of education for social engineering instead of perennial, empirical, and rational knowledge.

Now they ask for "college loan forgiveness" so that all Americans will be made to pay for those few who "followed their heart," and refuse to take responsibility for their own choices. This tyrannical injustice harms all parties involved, including the future students who will have increased incentive to pursue wasteful, inefficient education. If any third-parties should take responsibility for overpriced, ungainful education, it is the educators and university administrators who sold the services to students and consumed the capital from those students. When the colleges cough up the money they took from the students, then the responsible parties will be aligned. In no instance should any American agree to forgive education loans, and force innocent taxpayers to foot the bill for the free choices between greedy colleges and naïve young adults.

Energy & Environment

In the eyes of the institutionalists, oil companies and manufacturers are greedy destroyers of the earth instead of the engines of historically unprecedented prosperity and peace that we have enjoyed in the past century. The institutionalists claim that free people cannot form cooperatives and build new energy infrastructure

Thomas E. Kurek

themselves. Instead, government regulation, taxation, and price inflation must be imposed upon the American people to expand our energy industry. In 2009 they tried to pass the American Clean Energy and Security Act, which was narrowly defeated in the senate by Republicans.

It would have established a *cap and trade* program which would force Americans to pay for green energy research by coercing energy companies to spend money on research and development. To understand this swindle, it is best to think of it on a personal level. It would be as if the government banned cheap cars, by forcing you to buy cars that cost at least $40,000. In effect, you are coerced into paying for cutting edge research, indirectly. With *cap and trade*, you do not even get to enjoy a better product – your "green energy" does the same thing for you. The Democrats' intervention would have cost a family of four $829 per year on their household energy bill, and $743 per driver on gasoline.[139] Besides robbing a family of $2,315 per year for gas, welfare, and household bills, the indirect costs rippling through the economy would have been immeasurable, as all products, food, and real estate would have taken on additional energy costs and passed those costs on to all consumers in the form of higher prices, from the Cost of Goods Sold (COGS).

Republicans warned of the direct costs, indirect costs, job losses, and national security risks. Democrats remained tone-deaf, despite irrefutable evidence from calculations and foreign green energy programs. In Spain, the taxpayer was forced to pay $762,200 for every new green energy job, as it killed 2.2 regular jobs in turn. Simultaneously, there are national security byproducts of this economic suppression, leading Republicans to demand that China and India accept these standards along with the United States – another compromise Democrats were unwilling to make. Jobs and industry flee from countries with green energy programs, which leads to growth of countries like China that frequently vote against United States security interests in the United Nations. China confronts environmental problems only as they relate to its greater interest for growth. Chinese actions and words on green energy are not closely matched.[140]

---

[139] (Beach, Campbell Ph.D., Kreutzer Ph.D., Lieberman, & Loris, 2009)
[140] (Ma, 2010)

As other nations gain the fleeing business, the green energy programs rob their host nations of productivity (the Democrats' plan would have lost $9.4 trillion between 2012 and 2035).[141] For example, Spain faces the devastation of nearly a decade of depression-level unemployment (17-27%), brought about from a combination of *institutionalist* policies, including their green energy program. In Germany, green programs have crushed the poor,[142] and oppressed the middle class.[143] American Democrats are not worried about this prosperity-destroying imposition, because they will whip up class warfare to steal from Americans who live within their means. Their overt green energy program of 2009 had provisions to redistribute revenues to low-income households.

These *cap and trade* and *green energy* programs are some of the most insidious liberty-crushing deceptions conceived by modern institutionalists. They capitalize on the fear, shame, and guilt of those who believe in them, then use the force of government to seize between 5-10% of hard-working American families' net income. That money is handed to the energy companies, and armies of lawyers, bureaucrats, salespersons, managers, nonprofits, and paper-pushers. The American taxpayer that is forced to pay for this gets nothing but reduced prosperity. The collusion between *business* and *government* is solidified in this web of tyranny, with all of the institutionalists benefitting at the expense of everyone else.

Alternative energy is an exciting prospect to engineers and scientists. However, energy companies should be made to approach consumers, and ask them for investments to pay for this infrastructure. All of the citizens who pay for green energy infrastructure should receive corresponding ownership in the energy company in corporate stocks, with a normal investment vehicle. Getting robbed by a hidden web of government-imposed taxes and price inflation is not a liberty-oriented policy. Nor is it fair free market activity, as other businesses still must earn their capital honestly and persuasively.

The bad news is that the United States already has a *cap and trade* program. It simply has less teeth than the failed legislation

---

[141] (Beach, Campbell Ph.D., Kreutzer Ph.D., Lieberman, & Loris, 2009)
[142] (Zubrin, 2015)
[143] (Spiegel Staff, 2013)

Thomas E. Kurek

Democrats tried to pass in 2009. Thirty-three states and Washington D.C. have now adopted a *Renewable Portfolio Standard* that punishes and incentivizes energy companies to spend their money on worthless pieces of paper called *Renewable Energy Certificates.* These papers certify that the energy company has met green energy production standards dictated by the state's portfolio standard. Of course, the costs of these fabricated commodities are passed on to American customers who get nothing in return for their higher bills. They might blame corporations when the price of their groceries go up, or when their employer cannot give them bigger raises because their lease and energy bills are more expensive. But behind the scenes it is the greedy ghostly octopus of institutionalist imposition that is forcing the price inflation with its sticky and beguiling arms.

The institutionalists criticize subsidies to oil companies, which is a rare event, since they advocate subsidies to almost anything else a person could imagine. In fact, the subsidies given to oil companies are miniscule – 0.8% of the industrial value in 2013. Most of the subsidies are given for the environmental, research, and conservation motives of the government,[144] and if they are removed then the companies would either pass on the costs to the customers or stop the activity requested by the government, so the question of oil subsidies rests upon whether or not these goals are valuable to taxpayers. If the government forced the oil companies to do the same thing without tax subsidies, the cost would just find its way into regulatory burden and become buried in the cost of oil to all consumers, in a decreased transparency that is not preferable to subsidy. So it is duplicitous for environmentally-focused institutionalists to demonize oil subsidies when they know the environmental basis of them.

Even worse, they characterize *tax breaks* for oil companies as subsidies, even though other businesses receive similar tax breaks. They also frequently levy accusations of profiteering by pointing to the large gross profit, but because the oil industry is so enormous, large gross profit means nothing in relation to the question of industrial profiteering. Large industries have a large volume of sales, many customers and shareholders. These failed profit-police

---

[144] (Loris & Dubay, 2011)

should be looking at *industrial profit margins* for a meaningful comparison. Although the oil industry pays its workers well, mining is much more profitable. Major oil and gas was ranked 114 out of 215 industries for profit margin in 2011.[145] So much for the institutionalist demonization of the oil companies.

Their views on land management and conservation are equally problematic. They believe that private owners will not preserve the value of land, so they force all Americans to pay for the mismanagement of endless wilderness. As of 1999, the government owned one-third of all the land in the United States! The mismanagement of that land by federal agencies has left a trail of deleterious economic and environmental impacts.[146]

Perhaps the most egregious consequence of institutionalist environmental action is the slaughter and suppression of innocent human life in the name of biodiversity and anthropomorphism (ascribing human features to animals and insects). The biodiversity and land management policies rob the poor and middle class by inflating rent and real estate costs through supply constraint and bureaucratic expenses. A particularly tyrannical case resulted in the death of a child.

For two decades, the residents of Chesapeake Ranch Estates in Maryland sought community action to save their homes and lives from a pest called the Puritan Tiger Beetle. This insect burrowed into the ground beneath their properties, eroding the soil, collapsing the earth or dropping it into the ocean below. Roads in the community were closed due to this erosion. By enforcing the Endangered Species Act, the biodiversity lawyers prevented residents from saving their properties with simple methods. They even prevented alternative action that could harm a local crab habitat, even though that species is not endangered.

Twenty years after the crisis began, the punctual bureaucrats finally allowed the homeowners to apply for an *incidental take permit* which will finance a habitat and relocation for the pest, but the government is only willing to allow them to save one-in-six properties. The bureaucrats also have no problem involving other

---

[145] (Perry, Oil Industry Profit Margin Ranks #114 out 215, 2011)
[146] (Annett, 1999)

Thomas E. Kurek

taxpayers in the situation. The U.S. Fish and Wildlife Service issued a $2.4 million grant to gain control of 225 acres of their shorefront property for their own interests.[147] Not only did they take the money from unrelated taxpayers, but they also paid no price for the death of 12-year-old Wendy Miller, who was crushed in 1996 from the collapsing soil. She would likely still be alive today if the residents were free to save their land as they pleased. It is a tragedy that the environmentalists will never take responsibility for, even though they are covered in blood.

Although pollution, ecology, and natural resources are concerns that need public attention, the action to handle those concerns must be rooted in hard evidence, prioritization of citizens directly affected, and evaluation of realistic alternatives. Instead, the institutionalists prioritize imagined impacts, indirectly impacted citizens, and single-minded ideological perceptions. They take the situation beyond the realm of reason and into apocalyptic visions of epic proportion.

Their secular apocalypse is best illustrated in a documentary called *Earth 2100*.[148] It follows the life of a woman named Lucy, born in 2009. As the fictitious story goes, in 2015, global warming negotiations break down between the West and the overpopulated East (India & China). The East expects the West to bail them out with free technology and resources. The "greedy" capitalistic West refuses. Gas shortages compel Lucy's family to move to Miami and then a global-warming induced hurricane destroys the city. She meets her husband during an environmental activist protest against high water prices, in the wake of water shortages.

As America descends into poverty, suffering, and crime from energy and environmental degradation, Lucy escapes to the progressive oasis of New York City in 2050. The city now has green energy, clean public transportation, and pervasive hydroponic and community gardens. Its engineers, including Lucy's husband, are busy erecting flood barriers to prevent rising sea levels from swallowing New York. By 2075, New York is flooded, and most of the global population is dying from starvation and disease. International trade stops and all essential services break down.

---

[147] (Hyman, 2011)
[148] (Bednar, 2009)

American civilization and democracy is destroyed completely. Lucy lives out the rest of her life with some friends and family, in a newly dystopian world.

Careful observers would notice that the cartoon style was eerily reminiscent of communist propaganda throughout history. Is it a coincidence that a company called *Guerrilla FX* and some activist artists brought the tale to life, as its animations were interspersed between interviews and narration? Many of those involved in the tall tale have been feeding from socialist dogma since they first stepped onto their university campuses. Some usual suspects collaborated on the film – Obama's associates like John Podesta, John P. Holdren, Tom Daschle, Van Jones, and Al Gore's associates like Alex Steffen. Organizations affiliated with participants include the Center for American Progress, the Council on Foreign Relations, the Pacific Institute, Green for All, the Environmental Defense Fund, the Earth Institute, Google, and Yale, Harvard, and Columbia Universities.

The radical environmental policies of the institutionalists turn valid challenges into exaggeration, subjugation of nations, price inflation, extortion, much economic destruction, and even death. Wendy Miller is not alone in her outrageous demise. Destitute people around the world are forced into dependency or desperation from the declining economic conditions caused by irrational environmental policy.

Cultural Marxism & Identity Segregation

Many institutionalists are also cultural Marxists, who socially divide people by filling their heads with fear, guilt, identity crises, and victimization, so that they can inspire the kind of division and self-abdication that begs for institutional power. A full understanding of cultural Marxism requires knowledge of *transculturation, dialectal materialism*, communist Antonio Gramsci's principles of *cultural hegemony*, and The Frankfurt School's *critical theory*, which are beyond the scope of this book. *Political correctness* is a byproduct of cultural Marxism, most concisely defined as social self-censorship. Many will see these principles through the lens of political correctness.

Cultural Marxists seek to exploit and exaggerate the grievances of groups of people. Taking advantage of vulnerable minds and circumstances is a hallmark of institutionalists. As Obama's Chief of Staff, Rahm Emanuel, and Hillary Clinton said:

> *"You never want a serious crisis to go to waste, and what I mean by that is it's an opportunity to do things that you think you could not do before...if the problems are big enough that they lend themselves to ideas from both parties for the solution." –Rahm Emanuel, Wall Street Journal CEO Council, Washington D.C., November 19th, 2008*

> *"I'm actually excited by this opportunity...never waste a good crisis...don't waste it when it can have a very positive impact on climate change and energy security, and that's what we're trying to do." – Hillary Clinton, European Parliament, Brussels, March 6th, 2009*

Their fellow institutionalists in the media see the general public as stupid and desperate for enlightened surrogate decision makers:

> *"You know – that's the problem with this country. They say that there's not enough bipartisanship. There's too much...We have Democrats for one reason – to drag the ignorant hillbilly, half of this country, into the next century, which in their case is the 19th. I'll tell you this about Americans – about the American electorate, the voter... They're too stupid. They're like a dog. They can understand inflection. They can understand fear. They can understand dominance. They don't understand issues." –Bill Maher, TBS's Lopez Tonight, October 26th, 2010*

This patronizing and detached attitude could not better demonstrate how institutionalists are prone to rote opportunism and arrogant application of centralized power. By instilling fear of racial and gender identity, they are inducing their followers to become scared of the imagined liability of their own face. Typical American targets of *identity politics* are women, immigrants, religious minorities, non-white races, and homosexual people. The scapegoats for cultural Marxists are drawn down the lines of ideology, race, religion, economics, gender, and family unit organization. Respectively, current scapegoats for the aggrieved groups of citizens are conservatives, whites, Christians, executives and entrepreneurs, men and traditional women, and traditional suburban families.

The term *non-white races* is appropriate since whites cannot be called a majority race anymore in many locations. To refer to a "white majority" in most of America would be entirely fallacious. In powerful areas of the country, there are more "minorities" than whites, such as Washington D.C. where non-hispanic whites made up 35.8% of the population in 2013 and blacks made up 49.5%. White males only constitute about twenty-seven percent of America, making the combined aggrieved *identity targets* for cultural Marxists a sizeable plurality, in grand irony. If a white male wanted to exercise discrimination, he would be self-limiting his capacity for optimal cooperation in exclusion of seventy-three percent of America. That kind of irrational discrimination against a massive majority (minorities and women) would have painful business consequences.

On the other hand, cultural Marxists can get away with discrimination against minority populations such as white males, traditional women, or devoted conservatives. For instance, women only make up around 28% of the computer and software workforce, but Yahoo's *diversity* imposition and layoffs left the company with 80% female management.[149] [150] *Diversity* is a code word for favoritism towards non-white races and women. The discriminatory preference for diversity is an economic wrecking ball that has just begun to destroy productivity in companies. *Inclusion* and *diversity* policies are economic tar that impedes business results as much as the discrimination that it claims to confront. Cultural Marxists are free to discriminate with diversity preferences, but their companies will suffer in turn as they fall behind the competition that is only concerned with the results of their workers.

Identity segregation is the process that cultural Marxists use to instigate social groups to fight each other, and blame each other for their perceived collective problems. They employ mass psychology

---

[149] (Masunaga & Lien, 2016)
[150] (Nash, 2016)

Thomas E. Kurek

and propaganda through movies, songs, political speeches, journalism, religious sermons, and school indoctrination. Their common technique is to point to stories in history or the news, and take them out of context of the time and place.

So a modern cop killing a suspect, whether justified or not, becomes an extension of racial civil rights from three generations ago. Then they turn the story into a melodrama, and wrap it in a personified narrative to manipulate the emotions of the targets. So the killed suspect is not just a criminal who was doing awful things to his community; he becomes an extension of the egos of all people who share his skin color – even those who were being tormented by criminals like him. The story is exaggerated without hard evidence, and the cultural Marxists claim that the story is generalized for all of society. Consequently, the audience comes to believe that a crisis exists. The target population now feels indignation, pride, and fear against another group of people, opposed to their own personal *identity*. They then demand institutional power to confront the imagined crisis.

The duplicitousness of cultural Marxists is easily revealed by taking note of how they treat women and non-whites who oppose their agenda. For generations, they have expended substantial resources marginalizing, ridiculing, and assassinating the character of conservative racial minorities and women like Margaret Thatcher, Sarah Palin, Michele Bachmann, Star Parker, Thomas Sowell, Herman Cain, and Ben Carson. They fear these people more than any, because their minority persona and conservative ideology is a simple and powerful weapon that can reveal the manipulation. With total domination of entertainment, education, and journalism, it is easy for cultural Marxists to inculcate false indignation based on identity.

Details on the topic could fill a book, but onslaughts of feminist misandry, homosexual false equivalence, and anti-conservative prejudice are common. Even though women as a whole make less money than men, it is for the same reason that whites make less than asians – free choices. The gender pay gap myth has been debunked since the 1970s, and received elaborate treatment in 1981 on PBS.[151] Despite these facts, for nearly two generations, cultural Marxists have turned "equal pay for equal work" into *big lie propaganda* – if they repeat it enough then the masses will believe it.

In recent years, President Obama and his appointees have demonstrated their cultural Marxism many times, particularly with targeted racial groups. A dysfunctional outcome of this abuse of authority is the *Black Lives Matter* movement. The dynamics of crime will be discussed in later books, but for now, it is enough to mention that crime is cultural. Racial hate crimes only make up five-in-ten-thousand violent victimizations and two-incidents-per-one-hundred-thousand minorities. Despite this fact, cultural Marxists have used mass media, education, and civic power to persuade the masses against reality. Racial hate crime exists, but the facts show that it is miniscule, and certainly not a crisis. It has even plunged by two-thirds since 1995.[152]

There is also not an epidemic of police brutality. There are over thirteen million arrests every year, but only 1,100 suspects shot by the police. Of those, only 600 are killed, and half are mentally ill, and thus likely to behave erratically during an arrest. When police shoot suspects in only 0.008% of arrests, it is not an epidemic of police brutality – it is a minor and terrible reality of apprehending destructive human beings, with a handful of bad cops thrown in the mix.

Against the facts, the cultural Marxists continue to dramatize stories of every ambiguous event they can get their hands on. They use cultural power to turn these uncommon events into mass panic, and deceive people with personified narratives. Analysts know that in order to make a generalized claim, there must be generalized evidence. Stories and case studies are not generalized evidence that can justify claims of crises and systemic problems that need great attention.

Equally misleading, bad researchers argue false causation from statistical correlations. A good example is the claim that Hollywood is bigoted against women. They point to the dearth of female

---

[151] (Sowell, Firing Line: The Economic Lot of Minorities, 1981)
[152] (U.S. Federal Bureau of Investigation - FBI, 2014)

producers in Hollywood compared to the number of total women in society instead of the number of certified and qualified female producers available to the labor market. This sleight of hand is enough to reveal sophisticated deception. The researchers who do these calculations know the truth – they are professional analysts. Unfortunately, their audience does not pick up on the analytical errors.

Emotionally swayed by these personified narratives and distorted statistics, the affected targets ultimately see insignificant experiences through the lens of prejudicial self-victimization, and it is from that delusion of injustice in their own mind that they themselves become the new destroyers of cooperation and harmony. They begin to perceive bigotry within harmless comments and actions, devoid of ill-intent. Meanwhile normal people with functional minds see these "offensive" events as either isolated (if truly bigoted) or innocuous. They say to themselves, "Well, of course there is some bigotry, but this experience does not mean that it is inescapable or prevalent. And what exactly has it taken from me? I can walk away from the offender. Also, other people face the same kind of disapproval and ostracism more often from reasons other than physical identity. A committed conservative is treated like the devil in many cliques."

The Economic Impact of Cultural Marxism
There are devastating economic consequences for atomizing society into aggrieved *identity groups*, because productive industry depends upon peaceful and mission-oriented cooperation. This social infestation of all business activity cannot be fully appreciated without understanding the *utility of labor*. Goods, resources, and time-usage face limits, so they all must be economized. Even unemployed people – independently wealthy people, babies, retirees, and dependents – must choose how to spend their limited time. Agitation of the mind and body is a human feature; we seek activity of some sort every waking moment. Babies scurry and kick around to satisfy their impulse for activity that has yet to be set to purposeful action. They show us that even being freed of work can lead to restlessness and boredom. So pleasure in activity is subjective, but people do not obtain *direct* pleasure from work. Labor is conducted because of *indirectly pleasurable results* that counterbalance the overriding sense of tedium or pain.

Purposeful labor is a foundation of this indirect pleasure, but it leads to satisfaction only up to a certain point. When the actual product of labor is less satisfying than the pain and tedium caused by working, work only continues because of the three *indirect pleasures of labor*. When those are exhausted, then labor has more disutility than utility, and a person will seek to end the work.[153] There are three different categories of these *indirect pleasures of labor*.

The first is self-serving accompanying circumstance *(ulterior motives)*. A government official may not have much true passion for governance and political theory, but they enjoy the power, influence, and status that accompanies the office. A teacher might not genuinely be thrilled by knowledge and scholarship, but they enjoy the power and nurturing feeling they obtain from their influence over other people's children.

In the case of the politician, she will outwardly perform the duties of her office, while abusing it to create her cult of personality and service her power impulses. In the case of the teacher, she will outwardly teach the students by the plan, but seize opportunities to indoctrinate them and reward obedience over brilliance. Jobs that offer more of these self-serving circumstances typically pay less, because more people are willing to accept them for ulterior motives, sacrificing some pay for the perversion of the work that they obtain. Examples of *ulterior motives* include job security, less competition, more creative freedom, fewer physical risks, less pain, lower effort, heavy fringe benefits, status, power, attention, socializing, luxurious working environments, less challenging thinking, less physical strain, and easier tasks.

These *ulterior motives* may not even be fully articulated to the worker in their own minds, as they may have surrounded their self-image with powerful rationalizations. Actions always speak louder than words. If a politician is enthused by research on political theory and lectures on history, then they will spend their time on those things. If a teacher loves knowledge and discovery, then they will spend their time on epistemology and research, and their

---

[153] *Figure 95: Disutility of Labor*

passion will come out in their delivery of the knowledge itself. They will focus on teaching *how to think* instead of *what to think*.

A second indirect pleasure of labor is the satisfaction a person obtains from completing tasks. This is not pleasure from the work – it is joy of being *freed* from the work. It is a common feeling after being rid of something tedious, painful, difficult, or unpleasant. *Achievement pride* can be a powerful motivator, but it does not keep a roof over head or food on the table. And it is certainly not a direct pleasure from the work itself.

The third and final indirect pleasure of labor is *positive incentive*. Examples include economic thriving, earning a living, self-actualization, and acknowledgment from society that the goods or services are valuable enough to others that they wish to exchange their wealth. These positive incentives raise the self-respect of the individual in a free market. This is the most crucial motivator of work.[154]

In the institutionalist society, the indirect pleasures of labor are skewed. The *ulterior motives* become more prevalent and they crush *achievement pride* and *positive incentives*. People realize that their work is not fairly rewarded or acknowledged. Bad economic signals from currency manipulation, government intervention, or cartels and criminal organizations distort what goods and services are really worth to people. The workers feel overburdened, and that their tasks are too unpleasant. A hatred of work emerges and stifles the drive to produce good results. In a free market society, this bad dynamic is held back by consequences of violating a fair market. *Ulterior motives* in labor exist in the capitalist system, but they are restricted by systemic corrective forces.

Labor chosen through voluntary cooperation aligns the *positive incentives* most accurately to individuals, making the most of each person's situation. Coercion and restriction in that process interferes with the incentives. Cultural Marxists isolate people into groups that share a preoccupation with therapeutically commiserating comrades. This preoccupation puts many *ulterior motives* into their minds. Skepticism, loathing, and mistrust of

---

[154] (von Mises, Chapter IV The Socialist Community under Stationary Conditions, 1922)

outsiders such as white males and native-born Americans, are just the most obvious byproducts. Sharing a psychological kinship based on grievance and fears isolates the cultural Marxists from broader exposure to outgroup people who are cooperating in mission-oriented activity that is free of prejudice.

So they bring these activist *ulterior motives* into their education and workplace. A woman who pursued a tax-funded *women-in-engineering* program in part for feminist pride, will be loath to discover later in life that her social grievance does not bring joy when solving technology problems. She will transform her social grievance into antisocial workplace attitudes, like trying to prove herself against male coworkers, interpreting innocuous experiences with male coworkers as sexist, or scapegoating her own setbacks on imagined chauvinism – eliminating her capacity for self-criticism and growth. This is how cultural Marxists set up their victim groups for self-sabotage in careers. A person without this *ulterior motive* whose love of technology was pure, will have maximized their *positive incentives*.

The cultural Marxists will also act in biased ways that run counter to the business mission. They will select "minority- and women-owned" vendors, instead of the most competitive vendor irrespective of what its owners look like. When the best product or talent is not selected, the market receives irrational, quality-destroying signals. The "minority- and women-owned" business is not incentivized to become more competitive, so the proliferation of productivity is impeded.

These barriers can work in the opposite way as well. With fear of some inescapable, ubiquitous discrimination, many cultural Marxists may pursue jobs that are socially gratifying to them instead of intellectually and physically gratifying. They may opt to "stick with their own kind" instead of pursuing the work that truly interests them the most. These self-limiting fears then prevent the individual from following their most willful path. They will infect their business mission-orientation with social concerns, and approach their work expecting to be socially gratified in their quest for *social justice*.

One of the most destructive manifestations of this *identity segregation* is workplace *diversity* policies and actions. Amongst qualified colleagues, work products do not usually benefit from skin color, gender, or sexual preference. Taking action based upon *diversity* results in stupid business activity because it prioritizes something that does not impact the end product. Workers should be looking past superficial characteristics of each other, and focusing on the goals and objectives that bind them in work activity.

In short, identity-based commiseration leads to skepticism of outgroup-people, reduced mission-orientation, antisocial attitudes, wrathful ulterior motives, scapegoats for setbacks, prejudiced business deals, constrained options, and prioritization of factors irrelevant to business. All of these things are devastating to voluntary cooperation and objective work. The *diversity* culture reveals a profound irony. They claim to fight discrimination, but they impose *the same negative effects* that exist when there is proven discrimination!

Hatred towards minorities or women would lead discriminators to make poor business decisions, for instance. In that case, *diversity* action would attempt to socially preempt such discrimination. The notion itself is absurd – an adult is not going to change their heart. They will respond to law suits or incentives, but preaching at adults about values like they are children is not an effective method for social influence. The irony is that cultural Marxism and *identity segregation* have systematized these negative effects in the workforce, and wrapped them in false righteousness.

So the cultural Marxists are guilty of that which they accuse ubiquitous discriminators, and their impact is to place landmines in the fields of productive business and voluntary cooperation. This interferes with fundamental labor processes in economic activity. The *ulterior motives* introduced by cultural Marxism eat away at *achievement pride* and *positive incentives*, increasing the *disutility of labor*. In effect, it transforms dysfunctional social paranoia into negative economic impact within labor markets. Such tar in the gears of labor could be observed qualitatively but it would be difficult to quantify. *Identity segregation* is an insidious social virus with economic symptoms, like a painful disease that evades diagnostic tests.

Prosperity Support Industries

Healthcare, immigration, housing, military, criminal justice, scientific research, guilds, and culture are industries that *support* constructive economic output. The topics are covered extensively in the next Alvarism book. The related *institutionalist* claims will be presented briefly here with minimal counterarguments. They say that *healthcare* is poorly delivered in America and much better in socialist nations, with markets that are centrally coerced by the government. They imply that *immigrants* have all been the same throughout history, so no special distinction needs to be made today for variance in different immigrant populations. They believe that a person who is motivated to immigrate through any method is better served in the nation that they choose, and that the nation is better served with more immigrants of any kind, so they destroy deterrents for illegal immigration and refuse to enforce the law, while creating incentives for illegal immigration.

In regards to *jobs*, the institutionalists claim that unemployment is down because of government intervention, and that more government intervention would increase positive impact. They support price controls on labor like maximum and minimum wages, while they blame dissatisfaction with wages and opportunities on "greedy" corporate executives or discrimination. They claim that the Great Recession of 2007 was due to "Wall Street greed," instead of three decades of government intervention like redlining, the Community Reinvestment Act, and the Federal Housing Administration policies. The rally cry for decades was "affordable housing for all," and housing has only become less affordable in government-coerced markets, as they propped up the fictitious values of housing with bailouts that shackle our children with punishing debt.

Their philosophy of security claims that crime and war can be eradicated with social pressure and controls. As usual, institutionalists blame failures of institutions and ideological opponents for the suffering. They treat violence with a therapeutic, rehabilitative attitude, denying its root in the nature of mankind. Pacifism and disarmament ideals are popular amongst them, with notable advocates such as Bertrand Russell, Einstein, Jeremy Bentham, John Stuart Mill, Norman Angell, and Neville Chamberlain.

Thomas E. Kurek

Institutionalists vehemently oppose vigilantism, honor culture, and trusting security decisions to individual citizens. They believe that the police and military must be responsible in full for controlled violence to confront crime and war. The institutionalists believe that the citizens will make mistakes, and experts will make fewer. The discomfort institutionalists have with a person being able to defend themselves vividly reveals the extent of life and treasure they are willing to sacrifice on their altar of imagined progress. There is always an institutional scapegoat for criminals and belligerent nations. They think that the drug dealer had no choice because of his poor education and poverty, even though the majority of his peers chose law abidance. They think that the rogue nation developing nuclear weapons and financing terrorists had no choice, even though its neighbors thrived with less resources and chose peace.

As with every other issue at hand, the institutionalists blame externalities and disregard prudence and self-agency. The institutionalist fantasy economy is falsified by meticulous analysis of each industry for which they propose policies. They make their claims based upon insufficient details, and because their intentions sound benevolent, there are masses of people who believe them. Much patience and diligence is required to elaborate the true state of business and industrial intelligence. This maturity is eradicated by the emotionalized environment of propaganda and groupthink that the institutionalists nurture.

§ 2.4 Institutionalists and Old Ideas Posing as Progressive

*"Their sense thus weak, lost with their fears, thus
strong,
Made senseless things begin to do them wrong;
For briers and thorns at their apparel snatch;
Some sleeves, some hats: from yielders all things
catch.
I led them on in this distracted fear,
And left sweet Pyramus translated there:
When in that moment,--so it came to pass,
-- Titania wak'd, and straightway lov'd an ass."
–William Shakespeare, A Midsummer Night's
Dream*

Perhaps Shakespeare's fanciful tale was more of a prophecy than a play, warning us that those who are distracted by fabricated fears, irrationality, and intoxicating potions become harmed by senseless things, and may even fall in love with a political party represented by a donkey. Regrettably, the weavers of "progressive" stories lack the merits of Shakespeare. Their ideas are very old, but they promote them as trendy and new. Intoxicated Americans sit huddled in the dark, like tiny tykes who just heard a scary story from a mean elder sister. Playing on her siblings' deepest fears and ignorance of the adult world, the nightmare-weaving elder sister paralyzes the tykes in their manipulated imaginations.

Other times, the children sit in wide-eyed wonder, as the elder sister preaches fairy-tale visions of utopia, equality, rainbows, and world peace. Playing on her siblings' deepest hopes and dreams, she gives them delusions of grandeur in some imagined utopian future. It is too hard to keep up with all of the names that these fearmongers and utopia-weavers call themselves in our society. Sometimes they choose the name progressives, socialists, democratic socialists, liberals, anti-clericalists, populists, syndicalists, Labour, Jacobins, communists, Peronists, or Democrats. Even conservatives are not immune to this ideology. In the United States, there are some progressive Republicans that share these visions.

Springing from Leo Strauss' formative thinking and disillusioned 1960s Democrats, neoconservatism tends to see the world in "binary

Thomas E. Kurek

good/evil terms," has a "disdain for multilateral organizations," and wishes to enact alternatives to *social democratic* institutions instead of significant reformation.[155] [156] William F. Buckley Jr. characterized the neoconservatives as *idealistic*:

> *"I think those I know, which is most of them, are bright, informed and idealistic, but that they simply overrate the reach of U.S. power and influence." –* *William F. Buckley[157]*

Whether popularly conceived as rightwing or leftist, they all share a vision of the world that looks essentially the same, no matter how they spin it, dress it up, or color it. Understanding their vision helps to explain how they can come to perceive the economic reality so incorrectly, bordering on delusional fantasy. It is also important to understand what their fictitious tale looks like, so that we can identify it in movies, songs, news reports, political speeches, religious exhortations, and classrooms. Economic, historical, and political analyses are subject to the bias of visions, so understanding these visions is critical. A person who masters knowledge of these visions will fortify their own thinking and readily find errors in the thinking his fellows. Positive business and economic decisions will follow.

---

[155] (Clarke, 2009)
[156] (Kristol, 1995)
[157] (Buckley, Jr., 2004)

§ 2.5 Summary and Implications

"It is impossible to calculate the moral mischief, if I may so express it, that mental lying has produced in society. When a man has so far corrupted and prostituted the chastity of his mind as to subscribe his professional belief to things he does not believe he has prepared himself for the commission of every other crime." – *Thomas Paine*[158]

Socialists, progressives, democrats, neoconservatives, fascists, communists, Peronists, and Jacobins fall under the ideological umbrella of *institutionalists*. Their policies vary, but they have similar visions. In societies where their ideology dominates, large institutions emerge within the five cultural industries – civics (government, business culture, and nonprofits), religion, education, entertainment, and journalism. Institutionalists believe that the ills of the world are made by institutions, so it is paramount that they obtain total control of them. In the past they have murdered, enslaved, displaced, or starved their opponents. Today, they use financial and cultural means to intimidate, ridicule, shame, and destroy the careers and businesses of their opponents.

The *unconstrained vision of mankind* leads them to believe in solutions to problems instead of optimizations, tradeoffs, or checks and balances. They seek to replace *disfavored* institutional power with their *idealized* institutional power, feeling that in the process, they will advance the progress of mankind and improve mankind itself. According to them, knowledge itself is concentrated in experts, so they believe that power should be given to them – surrogate decision makers must call the shots for the simple-minded masses. This leads to an obsession with institutional status, awards, certifications, and degrees, instead of demonstrated capability by virtue of work products. Conformity, intentions, and credentials surpass results, tests, and direct competition. A brilliant businessman with little education will never be respected as much as an Ivy League lawyer who runs a nonprofit with mixed results.

---

[158] (Paine, 1794)

Thomas E. Kurek

The notion of a self-educated man like Abraham Lincoln is anathema to them.

The obsession with appearances in the institutionalist society leads to pervasive *scientism*, in which experts apply phony scientific methods to qualitative inquiries that are not well-suited to deductive methods. In turn, a disturbingly large share of published research is falsifiable, and the lauded *peer review* does not sufficiently detect fraud and errors, improve publications, nor accurately grade the value of research. When experts are caught in fraud or incompetence, they face farcical consequences, because it is more important for institutionalists to maintain the illusion of integrity for their institutions, agendas, and processes, than to maintain individual integrity and justice. Journalists, politicians, and the public feed from this swamp of fake knowledge as if it is Biblical scripture and institutionalists deride skeptics as heretics, deniers, and they even seek to bring federal gangster charges against them (with RICO laws). The *idealist* characteristic of the *unconstrained vision* makes social and economic intervention essential.

Opposing the institutionalists are the *valorists*. They have a *realist* vision of mankind that sees human nature as tragically fixed, and the quest to change it as arrogant, futile, and causing more harm than good. They look for optimizations and tradeoffs instead of solutions. They trust decentralized power, competition, free markets, tradition, lessons from history, and they are confident to let go of grandiose things with a spirit of faith. The institutionalist *idealists* of the unconstrained vision primarily want a feeling of *security*, whereas the valorist *realists* of the constrained vision want a feeling of *liberty*. The institutionalists typically align with leftwing political movements and the valorists typically align with rightwing movements – but this tendency is not a guarantee.

Conversely, conservatives are not immune to this kind of idealism. Institutionalist thought underlies ostensibly "rightwing" movements, such as fascism or neoconservatism. Even worse, many see conservative institutionalists as moderate voices of reason; however, to identify a center position requires definition of polar opposites. Those political opposites are incorrectly identified in America as "left" and "right."

Casual observers misperceive centrism because the opposites they imagine are the nearly-anarchical caricature of rightwing policy versus a communist leftwing policy. Neither of these are seriously in play within the United States. The serious political contenders in the United States have been a European-styled social democracy that emulates Weimar Germany and borrows "positive liberty" notions from the Soviet Constitution, versus a small-government, free market Republic that honors the intent of the original U.S. Constitution.

Currently, the leftwing choice is exemplified by The Progressive Alliance (former members of Socialist International), and finds sympathy with some Republicans. They are all institutionalists. The rightwing choice is exemplified by Constitutional Conservative caucuses within the Republican Party, with thought leaders in Stanford's Hoover Institution, The Heritage Foundation, Cato Institute, and Ludwig von Mises Institute. They are valorists. The political party and caucus names are apt to change, but the ideological dichotomy of institutionalists and valorists will not. This knowledge is useful to any international observer, as they can apply the concepts to their own political parties.

The United States forefathers believed in the *realist*, constrained vision of mankind, and wrote it into the formative laws of the nation. For the past century, the *idealist* ideological invaders have moved American governance towards French Jacobin thought and German socialism. Modern institutionalists like Obama advance policies like the *We Can't Wait* initiative, massive social and economic interventions, and attempt to write Soviet *positive liberties* into legislation through cultural and congressional action, since they cannot achieve the same goals with the courts due to the U.S. Constitution. Franklin Delano Roosevelt tried to advance these *positive liberties* with his Second Bill of Rights in 1944. Even in 1944, their agenda was not "progressive" or new, as it has been experimented with in pieces across Europe, Latin America, and Asia for well over a century. The *fundamental transformation* of America that Obama spoke of is significant. If the path America has been treading for a century is not changed, it truly will become a nation against its design within a generation.

Just like any other monopolist reacting to a threat against their absolute power, the institutionalists of today make every attempt to destroy their challengers. They usually deride voices of liberty as "extremists." On the contrary, if we affirm the fundamental design of the United States, all institutionalists are extremists. Those who cannot perceive their alien characteristics are measuring the wrong things, because their knowledge of ideology and history is lacking. If we define *moderate* and *extreme* simply by popular opinion instead of rational universal standards, then we should say that Etruscan human sacrifice was *moderate* in its day. Instead, we should define our inquiry based on reason and evidence, ignoring popular opinion. In that case, the institutionalist extremists have a sizeable majority in America.

Consequently, it is not hard to hear their economic fairy tale. They are in full control of the current establishments. They dominate education, entertainment, journalism, civics, and they even control half of religious institutions. Episodes of their narrative are injected into the brains of the masses nearly every time they turn on the television, take a class in school, watch the news, hear a political speech, or pick up a magazine. When a significant counter-enclave like Stanford Hoover Institution, Fox News Channel, or Hillsdale College collects even a fraction of the market share, the establishment acts as if this dissent is worse than foreign enemies of America.

In a way, their paranoia and hatred is justified. It only takes one voice of reason to dispel their entire fairy tale. So they must maintain totalitarian domination of knowledge, opinion, values, visions, and culture at all costs. They participate with opponents, only when they believe they can make an example of them while creating an illusion of objectivity. Masterminds like William F. Buckley Jr., Milton Friedman, and Thomas Sowell utterly destroyed the institutionalist narrative in open confrontation throughout the 1970s and 1980s, so now they either character assassinate or stonewall the most brilliant *valorists*.

The institutionalist fairy tale contains exhortations on education, energy, environment, identity politics, healthcare, immigration, justice, and war. On *education* they say we need to spend more money, even though we are already spending 300% more than we did in the sixties – a time that they claim was superior to today. They blame unemployed college graduates on markets instead of unaccountable education services that are divorced from apprenticeship and industrial aims. They blame low quality education on society and financial concerns instead of modern education philosophy and teachers colleges.

Institutionalist plans for *energy* entail hidden theft. Using state legislation for Renewable Portfolio Standards and Renewable Energy Certificates, they impose the cost of infrastructure expansion onto customers, without exchanging stocks and ownership of the energy companies. In this way, they finance their production goods with coerced price increases upon all essential needs of citizens. If the middle-class citizen can be duped into believing that they are saving the earth with green energy, then they will go along with the theft quietly, and let all of the lawyers, managers, salesmen, and bureaucrats get rich off of the price hikes, while the citizen is left with reduced prosperity.

Democrats tried to nationalize this tyranny in 2009 with the American Clean Energy and Security Act. Institutionalists impose these programs despite the harm they have done to working families in Europe. Forcing others to sacrifice for their grand schemes without compensation is standard operating procedure. It is bad enough to play Santa Claus with other peoples' money, but it is outrageous to play with peoples' lives. Biodiversity, conservation, and land management bureaucrats have affected deadly results and destroyed entire communities with their policies. Very powerful nonprofits, educators, and other institutions collaborate on green energy propaganda that takes on the tone of apocalyptic religious visions.

Corrupting two major components of prosperity – energy and private property usage – is not enough for the centrally planned schemes of institutionalists. They also corrupt labor markets with legal advantages for unions, and cultural Marxism. Labor markets allow citizens to sell their services, and those services are *the* nearly exclusive means by which any American can survive and thrive. Most citizens do not own production goods, resources, or commercial land. This makes the manipulation of labor markets incredibly cruel.

Thomas E. Kurek

Understanding the corruption of labor requires knowledge of the motivations for labor. *Direct* pleasure is never obtained from work, and people sometimes confuse *indirect* pleasures for *direct* ones. The three indirect pleasures of labor are *ulterior motives*, *achievement pride*, and *positive incentives*. Interventionist and socialist societies increase *ulterior motives* and destroy the other two pleasures of labor in the process, which ushers labor into a race towards mediocrity and misery. Even millennia before economic theory was well-developed, Aristotle implied:

> *"Pleasure in the job puts perfection in the work."* – Aristotle, Nicomachean Ethics, Book X(5)

Cultural Marxism divorces this kind of honest pleasure from the worker by rewarding their politically correct *ulterior motives*. Preemptive prejudicial oppression such as *diversity* and *identity politics* systematize discrimination, resulting in economic destruction. The actual work can never satisfy gender and racial paranoia. The cultural Marxists suffer from antisocial, prejudiced, self-abdicating, self-loathing, and tyrannical attitudes. The workplace culture takes on a wasteful therapeutic atmosphere to confront this social dysfunction.

By targeting groups of citizens with overstated victimhood, they segregate citizen identity into categories that have nothing to do with productive business. They then use this cultural segregation for legal, institutional, and business standards that destroy merit and justice, while doling out honor, advantage, and power to people who did not earn it through objective achievement and competition. It is not enough for cultural Marxists that the law punishes proven discrimination. They exaggerate injustice done to aggrieved identity groups, and then impose productivity-destroying policies as they nurture paranoia.

This pattern leads to economically destructive national results as well. The disproven *gender wage gap* is attributable to free choices of women since the 1970s. *Racially-motivated violence* against minorities is not a crisis. The number of racial hate crimes per minority has plummeted to less than two-in-one-hundred-thousand since the early 1990s. Subversive elements in our government and nonprofits instigate racial riots. Using false equivalence, big lie propaganda, generalization of personified narratives, and other manipulative methods, cultural Marxists spread paranoia in their target groups. It is a perfect formula for increasing the power and public mandate of *institutionalists*.

Unfortunately, while it benefits powerful leaders, it does not benefit the economy. It increases the *disutility of labor* in a manner that is difficult to measure, like a stealth virus. The aggrieved groups build up commiseration and *ulterior motives* which lead to skepticism of outgroup-people, reduced mission-orientation, antisocial behavior, prejudiced business deals, and prioritization of factors irrelevant to business. It systematically enacts the prejudice and discrimination that they claim to oppose.

In relation to prosperity support industries like healthcare, institutionalists also distort the issues through their idealist visions. Their prioritization of *intentions* over *results* allows for continuous failures to be whitewashed by flamboyant altruism. Their leaders incessantly repeat phrases such as, "it's the right thing to do," like a religious mantra spoken from a church pulpit. Critical thinking is a victim on their altar of good *intentions*.

Although there are some exceptions, the vast majority of entertainers, journalists, lawyers, bureaucrats, social justice religious leaders, and educators are not well-versed in mathematics and analytical thinking. Their college programs required basic calculus, at most, and perhaps one course in rudimentary statistics. These are not people who are good at, or particularly enjoy isolated, quantitative, methodical, and tenacious thought. Their knowledge of economics and unadulterated history is equally lacking. So they rely upon their trusted chart-makers and historical revisionists to find justifications for what they already believe. They are steeped in *confirmation bias*.

They even overtly pay experts to provide *confirmation bias* and propaganda tactics. President Obama asked a group of historians to help him find a way to communicate his ideas about *income inequality* without being accused of *class warfare*.[159] A person with intellectual integrity would never ask academics to help them propagandize their predispositions. An analytical thinker only asks for truth, higher precision, and accuracy. In effect, institutionalists

---

[159] (Dovere, 2012)

Thomas E. Kurek

simply trust the wrong experts and care more about their own visions than what is actually true. They spend more time perfecting their rhetoric than they do evaluating evidence.

Simultaneously, their trusted *experts* are aware of their own fraudulence. They simply lack integrity, and know that they can get paraded around international media, and make incredible money off of their deceptions by giving the institutionalists the arguments for what they want to believe. There are many tricks they use in their fabrications, but mainly they construct the problem definition in an irrelevant way, leave out data, assumptions, and context, and draw irrelevant conclusions from their poorly constructed problem definitions (*ignoratio elenchi*). In the words of Thomas Paine, they are prepared for the commission of every other crime. They are laughing all the way to the bank while they destroy our society from the halls of influence and power.

The fairy tale economy is advanced by many modern, wealthy, and influential institutionalists. Whether these leaders are using civics, education, journalism, entertainment, or religion, their nursery rhymes are omnipresent in the institutionalist society. In one way or another, their agenda has the economic effect of increasing *something-for-nothing* across the board. Power, money, jobs, honor, awards, and a multitude of privileges are doled out to elite institutionalist leaders and their favored classes of citizens, at the expense of others. They compress the middle-class to one homogenous group, and set up systems that only allow distinction based upon obedience to the agenda. In every institutionalist society, they have destroyed the upper-middle class (bourgeoisie), by fomenting enmity towards the rich. The rich amplify their power, and the upper-middle-class gets destroyed, slamming the door shut for middle-class prosperity.

Today, Western institutionalists are not using gulags, death camps, or democide, but they are using culture war, financial manipulations, and duplicitous laws to compress the entire middle-class, and erect an oligarchy of well-connected, wealthy elites who are ideologically pure in their support of institutionalist agendas, while the destroyed bourgeoisie is relegated to subordinate status.

Just like Shakespeare's Titania was intoxicated by a mischievous fairy, fell in love with a donkey-faced simpleton, and believed that harmless things were crises, those who feed from the institutionalists are placing imagined utopia and fear of oppression above reality, and consequently support policies that are unjustified and harmful to society. Any policy is foolish when it is based upon falsehoods. Even worse, many institutionalists believe their own fiction.

Their ultimate effect of *compressing the middle-class* ushers in the destruction of the American dream. According to the dream, a liberated and industrious person has a high chance of accessing prosperity commensurate with their talent and effort. Free markets, good culture, and a small government used to enable that American dream. Now, a pervasive parasitic system doles out *something-for-nothing* under the weight of a ten-trillion-dollar civic empire, and turns the journey to prosperity into a stroll over quicksand. Institutionalist visions and policies are to blame, and valorists are a dying breed spending their last breath to blow out the engulfing flames which are turning the U.S. Constitution to ash.

Part 2: Personal Considerations and Charting the Course for Prosperity

Photo 5: COL(R) Buzz Aldrin sets foot on the moon, photo taken by Apollo 11 Commander Neil Armstrong, July 21st, 1969

Chapter 3: Inequality, Wrath, and Envy by Diktat

§ 3.1 Concepts and Limitations of Prosperity Analysis

"When there is mutual fear, men think twice before
they make aggression upon one another."
–Hermocrates of Syracuse, circa 413 B.C.

Knowing the accurate portrayal of the American economy,[160] and
the warring ideological forces that rip it apart in the halls of
institutions,[161] is not enough to obtain the *economic sovereignty* that
optimizes prosperity for all. We must discover the concepts and
limitations of prosperity estimates on a personal level – whether we
are addressing wealth or income. The men who obtain *something-
for-nothing* do not fear the men from which their mosquito tongues
draw blood. They either hide behind economic fallacies or moral
superiority with false claims of compassion, kindness, and charity.
Their aggression ultimately translates to either *seized property* or
forced labor. Understanding common economic fallacies in
prosperity analysis is a crucial ingredient for effective insect
repellent.

Wealth is not Income

It is a misconception that income is the same thing as wealth. In a
population that spends almost all of the money they earn
immediately, it is easy to see how this fallacy came to bear. Wealth
is actually surplus. Income is only a pathway to surplus, which also
requires wise spending decisions. A person who has a decent income
but spends a large share of it on annual leisure travel is not going to
become wealthy. The typical annual cost for pets are $700 to $1,000,
tobacco and marijuana cost $1,000 to $2,000, and alcohol costs
$1,500. A person who owns three pets, smokes, and drinks alcohol
spends at least $5,500 a year on those choices and then wonders why
their neighbor can afford annual leisure travel. A third neighbor

---

[160] Chapter 1: American Socioeconomic Indications & Warnings

[161] Chapter 2: The Institutionalist Creed

Thomas E. Kurek

with the same income who chooses none of these things is gaining wealth.

Wealth is not just about income and savings. Access to unearned resources is not always monetized. If a person inherits a house from their family, takes advantage of tax-subsidized housing, or lives with their parents or friends, they only have to maintain a fraction of the income as a person who must pay for their own housing in full. A person living on unearned real estate may show up in statistics as poor compared to a person who must earn all of their own living expenses with twice the income. If a person is receiving government housing subsidies, food stamps, or other kinds of welfare, they can earn less than their peers who do not receive welfare. If a person is promised future benefits paid for by future workers, they do not need to earn as much income as a person without those government benefits. If a young adult is given a college subsidy or vehicle from their parents, they've consumed wealth, and can earn less income for a number of years than their peers who paid for these things with their own earnings.

There is a lot of talk about *income inequality*, but less about wealth. An honest person would never claim that "all of the money or assets" in America are owned by a percentage of the population. Money changes hands frequently and when it is held in a bank it is being used for lending and investment. *Net worth per capita* captures liabilities and assets. The household statistics cited by *poverty hustlers* deceive the public, since households have different numbers of people, and different numbers of earners. The most reliable wealth data available comes from the IRS SOI, since wealthy estates are subject to the inheritance tax.

Other measures exaggerate wealth. When capital gains from investments are reported, the person may have held that investment for ten years, and lost more money to inflation than they gained from their return on investment. Yet the government still reports that investor as wealthier, and taxes them for those gains, even though they lost money in real terms. *Personal wealth* measures that account for estates instead of just financial assets are therefore the most accurate available for discerning the real wealth of Americans. Using the IRS SOI Personal Wealth data, we discover that wealth disparity between the top 1-2% of the population and the average citizen has declined by 30% since the 1970s. *Average net worth* has steadily risen.[162]

This completely falsifies the *institutionalist* mantra that "the rich are getting richer while everyone else is getting poorer." There are certainly some wealthy bandits in every society, and they almost invariably maintain their heists with government collusion or complicity. In recent American years, the tools of the bandits have included taxpayer bailouts, stimulus, subsidies, price fixing, cartel activity, and government regulation to crush their competition and provide them with unearned advantage. The policies of institutionalists create these injustices while purporting to help the middle-class. If the public really wanted to make "the wealthy" pay for the government at higher rates, then going after the income tax of the upper-middle class is the worst way to do it. They would only shut the door to middle class mobility, during their own few good years of high earnings in their lives.

Zero-Sum Imagination

Considering that destitution in America is so low, and by every reasonable measure prosperity has exploded within the last century, despite depressions, wars, and disasters, it should be curious to honest people how it is possible to believe in widespread American destitution. As we previously elaborated,[163] part of the problem is a statistically and conceptually creative definition of poverty itself. Another problem is the imaginative vision that wealth is distributed like cutting pieces of a pie. This is the *zero-sum fallacy*.

In this fallacious and economically ignorant idea, the economic pie is fixed, and anyone who has a larger portion is necessarily taking from everyone else. One man's gain must be another man's loss. The real economy does not work like that. Goods and services can be created, destroyed, rightfully owned, or misallocated. The real economy "pie" grows or shrinks in the aggregate. Thomas Sowell described the misconception very well:

> *"If there really were some pre-existing body of income or wealth, produced **somehow**—manna*

---

[162] *Figure 46: Net Worth of the Wealthy vs. Average Net Worth*
[163] § 1.2 Prosperity, Poverty, and Destitution

Thomas E. Kurek

*from heaven, as it were—then there would of course be a moral question as to how large a share each member of society should receive. But wealth is **produced**. It does not just exist **somehow**. Where millions of individuals are paid according to how much and what they produce is valued subjectively by millions of other individuals, it is not at all clear on what basis third parties could say that some goods or services are over-valued or under-valued"[164]*

Third parties could only blame mispriced goods and services on the institutionalist banditry that brings coercion to the exchange process. In reality, new wealth is being created all the time, and it builds upon wealth that already existed. The process by which wealth is exchanged and priced is another issue altogether. As we have already shown,[165] the *wealth pie* has been expanding bountifully in America throughout the past century. People cooperate, and make new wealth for each other, through the process of exchange and production. That is why by every honest measure, even the poorest of Americans live better than all but the richest people a century ago.[166] In very simple terms, if one person builds a hut to sleep in, it does not hurt another person sleeping in a hammock. The only thing that can impede the person sleeping in the hammock is if the hut-builder uses the force of government or cartels to interfere with his labor, or prevents him from building his own hut. Otherwise, the same process of cooperation and bargaining can be chosen by anyone.

Thieves, manipulators, and zero-sum-game believers are after *something-for-nothing*. Their *modus operandi* is an improper transfer of ownership, ironically, making them the only ones guilty of creating the problem they claim to be solving. They use processes that actually do make one man's loss another man's gain, including government redistribution, market manipulation, crime, monetary inflation, financial repression, and economic intervention.

---

[164] (Sowell, Intellectuals and Society, 2009)
[165] § 1.3 American Prosperity by the Numbers
[166] § 1.2 Prosperity, Poverty, and Destitution

Even with these illicit actors in our midst, there is still no such thing as a *zero-sum game* in economics. Instead, the unscrupulous actors clog up free trade with their *something-for-nothing* schemes, and put poisonous additives into pieces of an ever-growing or shrinking pie. The pie will endlessly morph in unfathomable ways, despite bad actors that make pieces of it taste terrible.

Level Playing Fields

Poverty hustlers use the phrase "level playing field." To think of such an absurdity in economics, is reminiscent of the old moonwalk carnival ride, also known as the inflatable playpen. While the rest of the toddlers try to go about their business enjoying themselves, the *poverty hustlers* bounce around telling the more vulnerable children they are not getting their *fair share* of airtime. Soon this mob of bratty toddlers begins stomping on the ground next to the neighbors they envy. The peaceful toddlers who were content to play nice eventually all get knocked over by the mob of brats and their fake crusade for equal airtime.

By trying to create a *level playing field*, the poverty hustlers only create chaos. They destroy *freedom of opportunity* in the process. The economic playing field is in flux and it always will be. It is better that it is in flux because of the peaceful activity of everyone sharing it, than because of a mob of brats who cannot tolerate some kids bouncing higher than others. The *level playing field* will only exist when everyone has been knocked down and nobody is moving.

Only if the world was made of identical twins, and all children were raised in laboratories, would there be equal opportunity. Human beings would have to also choose to spend every moment of their lives in the same way, so that all skills and knowledge gained would be the same. Logically, the notion of equal opportunity then becomes a paradoxical performative contradiction, since without diversification of skill and knowledge, competition would be constrained to varying willpower, and the division of labor that increases productivity and enables economic growth would become impossible. In the real world, *freedom of opportunity* is possible, but trying to obtain *equal opportunity* interferes with progress and

productivity. George Reisman, Ph.D. and Dr. Thomas Sowell
address these concepts in depth.[167] Sowell notes:

> *"The fact that one person's productivity may be a
> thousand times as valuable as another's does not
> mean that one person's merit is a thousand times as
> great as another's. Productivity and merit are very
> different things. An individual's productivity is
> affected by innumerable factors besides the efforts of
> that individual—being born with a great voice being
> an obvious example. Being raised in a particular
> home with a particular set of values and behavior
> patterns, living in a particular geographic or social
> environment, merely being born with a normal
> brain, rather than a brain damaged during the
> birth process, can make enormous differences in
> what a given person is capable of producing.*
>
> *Moreover, third parties are in no position to second-
> guess the felt value of someone's productivity to
> someone else, and it is hard even to conceive how
> someone's merit could be judged accurately by
> another human being who 'never walked in his
> shoes.'"* [168]

Because all interventions require time, labor, and resources,
attempts to create *equal opportunity* against what arises from
happenchance and the deliberate actions of millions of people, will
necessarily reduce *freedom of opportunity*. The resources would
otherwise be directed towards enhancing pluralistic opportunities
that are determined by the free choices of millions of people. What
is ideal and what is possible are often in conflict. There are very
productive jobs for blue and white collar wage earners. High levels
of income are accessible to many varieties of citizens, from every
corner of the nation, because of *freedom of opportunity*.

---

[167] (Reisman, 2015)
[168] (Sowell, Intellectuals and Society, 2009)

Unaccounted Resources

A *previously-earned resource* contributes greatly to the prosperity of people. For example, does an elderly person who has paid off their house and raised their children need as much income as a young parent? A *state-redistributed resource* such as *welfare* provides *something-for-nothing* to nearly half of Americans, and much of this redistribution is not counted. These people spend 2.6x more than the income that is reported for them.[169] For instance, does a welfare recipient, whose neighbors are subsidizing their food, healthcare, and housing need as much income as a taxpaying, independent worker who earns all they consume? Businesses are also recipients of *state-redistributed resources* through regulations, subsidies, or competitive advantages. Their competitors must be more productive to compete with this *corporate welfare*.

An *inherited resource* is the tradition of families and friends. A person who has inherited a house, college tuition, vehicles, trust funds, stocks, businesses, petty cash, and car insurance can make half as much income as a person who has been paying their own expenses for their entire lives. These resources represent a massive stock of unaccounted wealth. *Charitable resources* provide recipients with unaccounted wealth. This could be a college scholarship, subsidized medical care, assistance with living expenses, and many other redistributed items.

Finally, there are *fringe benefits* which deliver "free" things to people and remain unaccounted in their personal accounts. For example, government workers, soldiers, and public school teachers receive fringe benefits worth fifty- to one-hundred-percent of their base salary. Private worker benefits are typically only seventeen- to twenty-five-percent of their base salary. Consultants and corporate managers write-off expensive meals and other activities as "expenses" and then do not pay taxes on them. The personal boons for those who consumed the write-offs are unaccounted.

Government workers receive a generous *per diem* payment when they travel, and many find ways to travel cheaply – living with friends, finding cheap deals, taking meals from their clients – and then they pocket the remaining money. The *per diem* payments

---

[169] (Rector & Sheffield, The War on Poverty After 50 Years, 2014)

Thomas E. Kurek

throughout locales in New York State range from $140 to $380 for lodging and meals.[170] A five-day government assignment in New York City is a $1,900 tax-free bonus for a bureaucrat who has a friend to stay with. This daily expense schedule for government workers is tacit admission that the cost of living variation alone accounts for a significant portion of income inequality. It is amusing that the same elected officials who keep their money so exactly doled out for themselves when they travel, then turn around and whitewash the cost of living implications that negate much statistical income inequality.

Most Americans have access to some kind of *unaccounted resources*, but there are those who have much more, and they are typically either considered poor or wealthy. The middle-class kings of unaccounted resources are soldiers, public school teachers, and government workers. Thorough analysis of all their fringe benefits reveal that their total compensation packages nearly double the median income – most of which is not included in income distribution statistics. Their complaints about compensation should be met with offers to exchange their benefits for cash, so they can start paying the same tax that everyone else pays.

Many people with significant unaccounted resources pursue lower incomes and will show up in wealth distribution reports as impoverished, while Americans who must pay their own way for everything show up as richer. In reality, these people have similar prosperity, even though income statistics indicate otherwise. In fact, the wage-heavy American may be less prosperous, because they must earn all that they spend to live in a similar way to lower-income Americans consuming unaccounted resources. They also pay taxes on all their wages and salary.

It is important to note that this dynamic is difficult to quantify. It is such a large consideration though, that it should be kept in mind for all prosperity comparisons. Tracking net worth in conjunction with income for individuals over the course of many years may help to fill in this analytical gap, but many non-cash resources would still be unaccounted for.

---

[170] (U.S. General Services Administration, 2016)

Moments in Time versus Lifetimes

One of the biggest *poverty hustling* deceptions is to refer to people who happen to have a high income in a particular year of their life as "wealthy." Income statistics do not represent poor and rich people. They capture a snapshot of what people earned in one year. Does a person earn more money at the beginning or end of their career? For decades, Americans have earned almost triple the amount of money at the end of their careers compared to the beginning, despite peers in older age classes dragging down aggregate income by retiring and working fewer hours.[171] Correcting for depopulation, *income inequality* from job experience (age) ranges from 0.19 to 0.27 – almost half of what poverty hustlers peddle around in their statistics.[172]

Is life a snapshot in time, or the sum of everything that has happened since a person was born? If a person makes a fortune in one year, then they are painted as rich "fat cats" by poverty hustlers. That same person may have been earning very little money for the past ten years, while risking a lot for a big payoff. In those low-income years, the class warriors would paint the same person as a poverty-stricken victim. Confusing annual snapshots of income statistics with flesh-and-blood people leads to great misconceptions of income inequality. Poverty hustlers paint visions of lifelong destitution or affluence in their targets' minds, but they point to snapshots in time that only catch people in typical parts of their careers.

The Cato Institute performed an analysis of this concept with a cross-tabulation of annual and lifetime income. They showed that 34.3% of households in the top annual income quintile were also in the lowest three lifetime quintiles, and 28.8% of households in the lowest annual income quintile were in the top three lifetime quintiles. This means that about a third of people who have low levels of lifetime income, make the top level of income during a good year. At any given time, there is a large portion of people who are being taxed at top rates, and considered "rich" based on a snapshot in time, who are in fact, the farthest thing from "rich." The same is true for wealthy people sometimes having bad years and showing up

---

[171] *Figure 99: Head of Household Median Income by Age*
[172] *Figure 100: Head of Household Total Income by Age*

as "poor" in the statistics. There are also diverse and well-distributed scenarios between those extremes.[173] These studies indicate exceptional income mobility in America, even if it is blunted by the byzantine web of taxation.

Prosperity and Intangibles

Happiness and prosperity are sometimes confused. Happiness is intangible. Measuring happiness on a universal scale would require that we could measure the happiness of a murderous psychopath, alongside the happiness of two parents who just gave birth to their first child. If we asked either of them whether they felt truly happy in the moment of their deeds, they would confirm. A child in poverty, with loving parents, and a sweet lollipop in their hand is the happiest being on the planet in his own mind. That child's parent, unsatisfied with their religion, love life, family, or job can be perfectly safe and secure, with a sweet lollipop in their hand, and think that they are one of the unhappiest people on the planet.

A field called *happiness economics* ignores this extreme subjectivity and acts as ammo for political agendas. It is yet another example of *scientism* in the *institutionalist* society. In truth, happiness economics can only measure the relative placation of the population at a current moment in time. One man's happiness is not the same as another's, and the values which produce psychological results will vary over time, so conflating prosperity and happiness is a false endeavor. When people treat the concept of prosperity poetically, we run into the same problems that face happiness economics. It is blatant scientism.

Economics is not just evaluation of systems of goods and services. It is the study of *scarce resources* with alternative uses – whether that is labor, time, raw materials, or goods of varied orders. Whether the economy is under the boot of socialism, dirigisme, or the chaos of anarchy, *rationing* and *competition* will be features of all economies. The only question is which set of processes optimize the use of scarce resources. No politician will ever eliminate scarcity, competition, or rationing, but they certainly can lie about it, and guide the public into the worst outcomes.

---

[173] (Metcalf, 1997)

Consequently, economic calculation is subjective enough without highly abstract intangibles riding on top. Where do values and pricing meet? Any man who makes a choice between satisfying one of two desires must make value judgments. People make these choices on a momentary basis, as they judge how to spend their time, money, resources, and prioritize their activities. Those decisions are only as rational as the individual. Judgments of value cannot precisely measure, but they can align, arrange, classify, and grade. That subjectivity of an individual's value judgments cannot be directly compared to that of others, but if free people are left to free markets, where the inter-subjectivity of their value judgments creates a scale for individuals to align their own value judgments with that of the market, then exchange value is the unit of calculation.

Money is just a proxy for this economic exchange value. Comparing diverse cultures across the globe and history reveals the pitfalls of quantitative measurement of intangibles – there are wild differences in what satisfies different people. The term *quantitative intangible* itself is an oxymoron. *Institutionalist* politicians and groupthink-economists across the globe have recently adopted the *scientism* of *quantitative intangibles*, including *happiness economics*. They are the same ones who interfere with the inter-subjectivity of pricing in economics through currency manipulation.

When governments interfere with the currency, they rejigger the society-wide economic settings of value judgments from the population. People who value truth and self-determination would be outraged at such tyranny. The first U.S. Mint in Philadelphia was established on April 2nd, 1792, and it enacted a death penalty for devaluation of money. Around the late 17th century, the currency counterfeiting and debasement problem was so great in England that many counterfeiters were executed. Sir Isaac Newton not only became the father of physics, and a prolific Christian theologian – he was the tireless Warden of the Royal Mint. He would even disguise himself in bars to collect information on criminals. His diligence, brilliance, and morality brought much monetary corruption in England under heel. Are there any Americans with the character of Sir Isaac Newton? Do our modern universities and churches even try to produce such people?

Our egregious monetary policies would offend Newton enough, but the *institutionalist* desires to treat intangibles in a deductive manner are cut from the same cloth of mysticism that he opposed in his own day. Intangibles can be empirically treated, but we must ask the right questions and use the right measures. A high degree of inductive reasoning is required. The trouble is not that certain economists are trying to measure such things; the problem is the speculation they are drawing from qualitative observations. Happiness will never be a relevant measure of prosperity until a person can convincingly argue that a true-believer in Mayan human sacrifice, enslaved and marching to his own butchery with a smile on his face, was as prosperous as the hypnotized masses who prayed in joy over his corpse.

By now it should be clear that measuring income alone is not a good measure for prosperity, and that intangibles are not either. Another approach to assess prosperity is to measure access to material comforts. As described earlier,[174] The Heritage Foundation showed that the kind of punishing deprivation that people imagine when they hear the term "poverty," is not common at all in America. In fact, just 1.5% of poor households claimed that they often did not have enough food. That is only 0.14% of American households. Air conditioning, video games, numerous televisions, computers, cell phones, washers and dryers were common features of households considered to be statistically poor.[175] Luxuries of this nature were unimaginable to all but the richest people just four generations ago.

Summary

The general public is grossly misled by poverty hustlers focused on income inequality. Their charts are false to begin with, but even if they were correctly constructed, they rely upon ignorance of basic economic truths to produce manufactured consent for their agendas. In short – wealth is not income, wealth is surplus, income is only a pathway to wealth, the economy is not a zero-sum game that divides like a pie, one man's prosperity is not necessarily another man's loss, unaccounted resources massively contribute to prosperity, lifetime

---

[174] § 1.2 Prosperity, Poverty, and Destitution

[175] (Rector & Sheffield, Air Conditioning, Cable TV, and an Xbox: What is Poverty in the United States Today?, 2011)

prosperity cannot be discerned from taking a snapshot of income distribution during a moment in time, and intangibles such as happiness should never be confused with prosperity.

§ 3.2 Manufactured Income Equality

*"Statistics show that of those who contract the habit
of eating, very few survive." –George Bernard Shaw*

Correcting common economic fallacies is not enough to show how
badly *prosperity incidence* is misrepresented. One of the primary
statistics that poverty hustlers use is fallacious *income inequality*
presentations. Their statistics are distorted with numerous
omissions that surprise nearly everyone who discovers their
methods. In the *institutionalist* society, people simply assume that
these poverty hustlers are inherently compassionate human beings.
Realistically, we cannot tell whether they are liars or dupes, but
they are one or the other. If they are not opportunistic liars, they
could be truly wonderful and tragically misinformed people.

Statistical Tricks of Income Inequality Proponents

First of all, most statistics that are based on households must be
normalized to a per-person basis. Unless we know how many people
are living in the house, we cannot make any presumption as to how
much wealth or income-per-person is distributed. Houses are
inanimate objects and they do not earn income. The people living in
them use wealth and earn income. Year-after-year, the top-quintile-
income households contain over double the residents as the lowest
quintile. Larger groups of people need more money, so there is
nothing alarming about the highest quintile even having double the
amount of income as the lowest quintile.

Even worse, not all people living in a home earn income. We call
people who bring money into a household, *earners*. A house can
have anywhere from zero to a dozen *earners*. Asserting household
income without correcting for the number of *earners* confuses a
wealthy person without a job (statistically "poor") with a rented
house of a dozen struggling young adults (statistically "rich"). So the
alarming hockey-stick curve of *income inequality* does not correct for
how many mouths the income feeds, nor how many people are
actually earning it. Consequently, the relation of *household income*
to how well individuals are paid is entirely meaningless. Some
poverty hustlers go further to distort the narrative by calling
household income, *family income*. They have no evidence that the
thing they are calling a *family* is made of parents and children or a

few roommates. It is just empty propagandistic rhetoric that targets naïve heart strings.

Another common error is the failure to correct for *part-time labor*. A person is not necessarily getting a raw deal if they only work fifteen hours a week and still get paid enough to survive. Many people with high incomes have worked fifty-or-more hours per week for their entire lives. Many of them have worked hard in academia, research, or investments, getting paid very little during many years of their lives. The annual income statistics do not capture the fact that they are trying to catch up from behind, even if they currently have very high incomes. In order to best approximate equal work hours to income, we must convert part time labor to *full-time equivalent* (FTE) workers.

It may be shocking to learn that many income inequality statistics do not adjust for most of taxation, such as all income and ad valorem taxes and fees charged by state, local, and federal governments combined. If we look at a person's income before the government has taken what it demands from them, we are deceiving ourselves massively. The person does not have access to the money that the government takes, so they do not have access to that prosperity. Whatever income is seized by the government through any tax vehicle is effectively *forced labor* of the corvée serfdom variety. Excluding *tax dynamics* from income distribution calculations is one of the most duplicitous distortions. If all tax dynamics are not corrected for, then income statistics are meaningless in terms of personal prosperity, because it includes what the government takes from the person as if that person can actually use that money for themselves.

Common income inequality statistics also exclude some or all kinds of government transfers – welfare, social security, Medicare, Medicaid, veterans' benefits, and other sources of prosperity. There are people drawing from a combination of all these transfers. It is difficult to separate the benefits based on whether they were *earned* from contributions (like veteran's benefits and Medicare) or *unearned* and redistributed (Medicaid, welfare). A prudent government would do a better job at tracking these categories to manage its own budget.

Finally, income inequality statistics are rarely adjusted for the variance of monetary value across *time and space*. Because of inflation, we must adjust all monetary values by inflation when comparing year-to-year changes in any economic phenomena. This adjusts for variance across *time*. Also, the same things cost more or less in different cities and countries. A person can earn less money in a smaller city and have the same purchasing power as a person with a much higher salary in a metropolis. This is called Purchase Power Parity (PPP), and even the government acknowledges it by factoring it into their own employees' travel expenses and relocations with *cost of living adjustments* (COLA). It feeds cynicism when the government is more careful about paying its own people than with accurately reporting poverty analysis to the American people. The fluctuation of PPP in America is about thirty percent. We must use it to adjust for prosperity variance across *space*.

The Real Income Distribution Indicator

By correcting for these factors, we arrive at the *Real Income Distribution* indicator (RID), which is what should be used for assessments of *prosperity distribution* between individuals in terms of income. *Real income* is almost entirely flat, with very little inequality, compared to *anarchical income* (before-tax income), and after-tax income without welfare and other transfers. The commonly reported *household income distribution* that is not corrected for any of these factors is absolutely preposterous.[176] It does not even look like the other three series at all, for the reasons we have just elaborated. The politicians and activists who cite this fabricated income inequality are either dupes or liars.

A mathematical construct called the Gini Ratio measures inequality between series. A Gini Ratio of *zero* represents perfect equality, while a value of *one* represents perfect inequality. When we calculate Gini Ratio on *real income*, we find that poverty hustlers have been exaggerating *income inequality* by around 250 to 300% for decades![177] The government debt contracted from 2008 to 2011 completely blunted the income inequality created by the housing bust. The poverty hustlers' value of income inequality falsely

---

[176] *Figure 1: Income Distribution by Quintile, 2011*

[177] *Figure 4: Income Inequality Index*

includes all of those factors we have corrected, and is stated to run between 0.45 and 0.54. The *real income* Gini Ratio has barely fluctuated since 1984, hovering around 0.19.

Even correcting for the distorting factors of *taxation, cost of living, inflation, welfare, redistribution, part time labor*, and the *household-versus-earner* fallacy, we are left with income disparity from *age* and *industry*. Income is greatly affected by worker *age* which conveys job experience, and also the productivity of the *industry* in which a person works. Mining and oil is more productive than entertainment. Age is a serious income factor as well, since a person is paid more as they gain experience. Industrial income inequality has plummeted since 1929 from 0.16 to 0.07.[178] This could only be imposed upon us with dirigisme. Industries in reality should have widely varying productivity and revenues to match. The Federal Reserve and government interference has distorted that accurate grading of value increasingly for almost a century. Job experience (age) income inequality has ranged from 0.19 to 0.27 since 1967, and averages 0.23.[179]

It is safe to say that when the effect of *age* and *industry* are considered in conjunction with *real income*, we completely wipe out all income inequality, showing a regressive, socialistic income distribution that robs remuneration for productivity in whole. We would like to think that our income prosperity is purely affected by the size of our employer, experience, education, skill, supply, demand, and value of the job itself. Unfortunately, due to regressive socialistic redistribution, government interference, progressive taxation, unaccounted resources, part time labor, and cost of living, our prosperity opportunities are completely gamed.

At the current time, America's income distribution is about as close to extreme socialism for labor as a society could get. Many of those ultra-rich few have only become wealthy by using this game to their advantage, but their poverty-hustling politicians continue to deceive the public into punishing the upper-middle-class. They do not even whisper the notion that if there is justice to obtain and vengeance to enact, it would be a raid of the stocks, bonds, and real

---

[178] *Figure 22: Industrial Compensation Inequality*
[179] *Figure 100: Head of Household Total Income by Age*

Thomas E. Kurek

estate that were obtained through government collusion. In general, punishing the future for the sins of the past seems to be an easy deception to promote when society is filled with indignation.

Despite the common misinformation circulating within most classrooms, newsrooms, and legislatures – there is not enough income inequality to adequately justify fair compensation for the real productivity of workers. The dirigiste policies of the *institutionalists* have caused compensation arrangements that are completely unfair. Yet, based upon their false claims of income inequality, the poverty hustlers demand legislation and regulations that create even more of this unfairness. Real income inequality should have a Gini Ratio of 0.35 on average to reflect the disparity of productivity and incentivize people towards work that fulfills the more valued needs of society.

The myth of *income inequality* is not the only misinformation driving bad economic policies. The poverty hustlers also promote false beliefs in disparity of economic progress. In fact, the *real income* for all Americans increased generously during the technology boom of the 1990s, and also during the George W. Bush years from 2000 to 2007. Since the housing bust of 2007, real income has been completely flat with the exception of two changes. The lowest 20th percentile of income earners actually *lost* income while the highest quintile sharply *gained* income after the stimulus and bailout spending.[180] In fact, the lowest income earners only significantly gained real income during Reagan and George W. Bush's years in office.

While all other income classes stagnated, and the poorest lost income, the government interventions sharply increased the income of the highest earners. Those who claim that government spending has helped the poor, have deceived everyone. It has only helped the wealthy by using tax debt to legitimize overpriced stocks, bonds, derivatives, real estate, and other holdings, while suppressing productivity and labor markets.[181] Financial repression imposed by the Federal Reserve sucked capital out of the private sector and into the government. Now, those same institutionalists bemoan income inequality, when it is proven that their government intervention is the only thing that has contributed to artificial income inequality in the past few years. It is alarming that poverty hustlers in society support and enact laws based on statistical misrepresentation, and then they actually harm disadvantaged people in the process of their meddling.

Government Spending is not Investment

Another group of losers since 2008 are adults between the ages of 30 and 50. The amount of government debt forced upon them is truly outrageous. The stimulus and bailout laws were formally called The American Recovery and Reinvestment Act (ARRA), Public Law 110-343 and the Troubled Asset Relief Program (TARP). Some claimed that the federal government was borrowing from the future to save our nation today; but, the future is an abstraction and nobody can borrow from it. The people who will pay this debt are productive Americans between the ages of 30 and 50.

In an Orwellian, institutionalist trick of the tongue, the proponents of this debt actually called the spending *investments*. Such people cannot be taken seriously. If the debt contracted by the United States Government was truly an *investment*, then it should have predicted a *return on investment* that would pay down the debt that already existed. It should have also taken collateral from those who directly benefitted from it, which happen to be the only ones whose income has increased. *Private gains* with *public losses* is not an investment – it is redistribution from the middle class, poor, and younger taxpayers to the destroyers of the economy today.

The Sources of Real Income Gains

What is the source of the excellent increases in *real income* for all Americans? Many people assume that increases in income must be from wages, but that is not the case. An impressive analysis by BEA economist Arnold J. Katz revealed fascinating implications. Since 1969, there are fewer workers per household, and they are choosing to live as unrelated individuals. In addition, the elderly had large income increases. Self-reported income from Census measures showed slower rate of growth than the national accounts (Bureau of Economic Analysis), because of sharp increases of transfers-in-kind and employment benefits. The income per capita increases were concentrated in two components – pension payments and property income. In the past decade, there have been large increases in income from S-corporations and partnerships,[182] the common business legal structures chosen by small business owners.

These observations indicate that income growth may be somewhat illusory. Instead, there has been shuffled wealth, increased benefits, pensions, and gains from manipulated real estate markets. On the other hand, advisors to the U.S. Congress Joint Committee on Taxation have shown that middle-class and poor Americans have made substantial gains in the past three business cycles, since 1979. This fact conflicts greatly with the class warfare animus of poverty hustlers, but it confirms The Heritage Foundation's amenities and food security analysis. The truth is a synthesis – middle-class and poor Americans have gained income from manipulated sources instead of their productivity.

When we consider the steady increase of net worth in America, the amenities data from the Department of Energy, and the income gains from manipulated sources we arrive at a disturbing trend in American prosperity dynamics: it seems that productivity is not being compensated fairly. The accurate income observations presented here lend more evidence to destructionism and suppression of the upper-middle class with financial, cultural, and tax methods. Because the middle class path to wealth is compressed to near-equality, the American dream is an illusion.

---

[182] (Katz, 2012)

Taxation and Income

Indirect consequences of taxation are fairly intuitive. Business owners have to treat taxation as an expense, so increased business tax leads to lost jobs, lost profits, lost benefits, lower wages, or increased prices. Business owners will try to do the best to optimize their operations when forced to pay more taxes. This is also true for the hidden tax imposed by government regulations, which mushroomed to $1.863 trillion in 2013,[183] a cost that was greater than American food or energy expenditure. When the government issues an edict with threat of illegal operational status, business owners pass the cost on to the customers through their prices, or they scale back the quality and size of their business. In some cases, taxes and regulations can cause a business to shut down or cancel products and services due to shortages or infeasibility.

Technically, the minimum wage is not a tax, but it is a regulation that produces similar effects. The cliché, "nothing in life is free," applies here. The lack of transparency and complexity of multi-level tax transactions makes it nearly impossible for the normal citizen to judge whether or not specific regulations and taxes are wise tradeoffs. Only with detailed analysis can we even begin to intelligently discern these tradeoffs.

Ad Valorem Taxes

Ad valorem means "according to value" and it is a frequently-ignored form of taxation. It includes property, sales, inheritance, expatriation, value-added, and tariffs. Who pays *ad valorem taxes*, and to what extent? Certain ad valorem taxes can affect people with very little wealth. Renters end up paying high property taxes, which are hidden in the cost of their rent. Why do we ignore these taxes in common discussions of wealth distribution? What good is measuring "income disparity" when we do not measure the total money that people are free to use for their own purposes?

Income-Related Taxes

It is a fallacy that the poor do not pay *income-related taxes*. In fact, the combination of taxes levied upon any person just to do their job is a dizzying array. We can identify at least eighteen income-related

---

[183] (Crews Jr., An Annual Snapshot of the Federal Regulatory State, 2014)

taxes that are mostly taken through hidden channels that a wage-earner rarely sees. They are prefixed with a running count, and capitalized in the following paragraphs.

The money that the government takes from our paychecks directly is obvious. Employers print these deductions on the paycheck. They are typically: (1) Federal Income Tax, (2) Social Security Tax, (3) Medicare & Medicaid Tax, (4) State Income Tax, and (5) Local Income Tax.

People who do not live at their place of business must drive to work or take public transportation. That transportation is taxed in numerous ways through (6) Property Tax, (7) State Gasoline Tax, (8) Federal Gasoline Tax, and (9) Road Usage Tax & Tolls. For a typical middle-class commute in 2013, gas taxes and property tax combined ranged from $500 to $2,000. If we use public transportation, these costs are hidden in our fare, redistributed tolls, and non-vehicle property taxes, which are used to subsidize the public transportation business. We are still paying the taxes, indirectly. The less robotic among us will need a place to sleep, so they can rest for the next day of work. We are charged (10) Real Estate Tax, hidden in our rent, or directly levied on our households. To be fair, we would only count 25-35% of that tax as work-related, since we spend that much of our life working, and sleep is also needed to function during the time that we are not working.

There are a host of taxes that are hidden from us, paid by our employer behind the scenes, based upon every dollar they pay to us. Those hidden taxes are – (11) Social Security Employer Tax, (12) Medicare & Medicaid Employer Tax, (13) Federal Unemployment Tax (FUTA), (14) Worker's Compensation, (15) State Unemployment Tax (SUTA), and (16) Real Estate Tax on facilities workers need to do their jobs.

Most employers need to be able to call us. Sometimes, we even have to use our personal phones to do business. So we buy phone services, and immediately face (17) Phone & Communications Taxes. From the money we have left over, we must pay (18) Sales Tax on basic things we need to keep living and working.

With all of these taxes in mind, the notion that "the poor pay no tax" is a myth. They pay significant *income-related taxes*, in ways that are mostly hidden to them. The wage income of any worker is heavily taxed, in at least eighteen ways, just so that the individual can have the privilege to continue to work. Let us call the comprehensive tax rate that combines these eighteen taxes, the *income-related taxes* (IR taxes).

Reviewing 2012 snapshots of income-related taxation gives an impression of how deceptive poverty hustlers have been with their demands for even more punishing tax scams.[184] [185] The highest quintile of household income has five times as many earners as the lowest quintile. If those "rich" people were not making at least five times as much money as the "poor" people, then the "poor" people would have higher incomes. Interestingly, there are about as many non-earners in each quintile – around thirty-two million people per quintile.

Even though low-income Americans pay significant hidden taxes, if their tax is spent on the welfare they consume first, it is entirely used up before there is any net positive contribution to the tax pool. In other words, whatever tax low-income people make is not enough to pay for all the redistribution that their neighbors are consuming. So the notion that low-income Americans contribute to military spending, infrastructure, roads, school, or anything else is false. On a categorical basis, the taxes of the "poor" do not even cover the amount of redistribution that they consume. Only 40% of Americans contribute tax to something more than welfare for themselves and their neighbors.[186] When only four-out-of-ten taxpayers are financing the government, we have a very perverted and parasitic tax structure.

National Production and Income-Related Tax

There are two major sources for income and production data. One set of household income data comes from the U.S. Census Bureau's Current Population Survey (CPS). It reports regular pre-tax cash income and excludes capital gains and lump-sum payments. A drawback is that it is taken from only two in ten-thousand houses, and of those, half of the income reported is by people who are not

---

[184] *Table 1: Taxation & Income Quintiles, 2012*
[185] *Table 3: Income Quintiles, 2012*
[186] *Figure 2: Tax Burden for Income Quintiles, 2011*

earning it. The CPS surveys give us a microeconomic view of income, from a 0.02% sample set of the population, half of which is collected from second-hand testimony. This measure is also known as *money income*.

A macroeconomic view of income uses the national economic accounts analyzed by the Bureau of Economic Analysis (BEA). This measure counts much more than just regular income. It includes all participation in production (labor and owned capital), government and business transfers, dividends and interest, income from nonprofits, private welfare funds, and private trust funds. The measure is also known as *personal income*. Personal income is more comprehensive than money income because it employs administrative data that is not available on the household level. It inflates the notion of income a bit by considering "quasi-individuals" on par with flesh-and-blood human beings. These "quasi-individuals" act on behalf of other people, such as non-profit institutions serving households, private trust funds, and noninsured welfare funds.[187]

Comparing the two measures yields astonishing congruence, after correcting for the additional data that *personal income* tracks and *money income* ignores. If we apply our *income-related tax* model to money income, we arrive at $3.13T in total income-related taxes. The BEA reports $3.3T in taxation of personal income from national accounts. The rest of tax for the year from various fees, charges, and ad valorem channels totals $2.8T. Our estimation of income-related taxes, of course, includes a portion of the ad valorem taxes. Subtracting the ad-valorem portion and reconciling with the BEA data yields congruence within a small margin of error. With these methods, we have sufficiently explained the gap between the government tax accounts, and the common reports of tax rates applied to our earnings.[188]

In 2013, we had $6.1T in total taxation, and another $1.9T was taxed to us indirectly through regulatory costs hidden in the things we buy. The implications of this are astounding. According to *personal income*, our government is only allowing us to keep $5.2T of our total income per year after the $6.1T they take through state,

---

[187] (Ruser, Pilot, & Nelson, 2004)
[188] *Table 2: Summary Wage Tax Table, 2012*

local and federal taxes combined. After tax and regulatory cost, Americans are only left with $3.3T per year in income at their liberty to spend as they please. That is only $24,397 per working American, while we are forced to pay $58,765 per working American as our price of the government we have chosen.

Of course, we spend and consume more than $24,397 per working person, in the form of personal debt, paying for taxes and regulations hidden in the cost of our transactions, utilizing properties we already own, or transferring them through in-kind transactions. A person could spend $50,000 in one year, not realizing that an enormous proportion of what they spent found its way into government hands, above and beyond the direct income taxation they saw on their paycheck.

We simply have a very cloudy concept of where the money is going when we buy things, where the money came from, and the relationship of our consumption to the larger economic forces. This veil over monetary transactions makes it very easy for third parties to inject themselves and leech our earnings without our informed consent. Gross Domestic Product (GDP) is the measure of what America ultimately produces. In 2013, it was $17T, while civics was consuming $10T (with nonprofits added to regulations and taxes), and *personal income* was $11.3T.

When the dust settles, what is left for America to build for the future and leave behind? Recalling that surplus is wealth, when our governance costs over half of what we produce, and more than individual people gain every year, can we call America a liberated nation? It may be for the time being, based upon previous generations who left behind more than they took. But this system cannot last long without destroying our wealth. In fact, surplus per capita has plummeted since 2006. The responsible parties for the bleeding are not individual households and private businesses. The responsible party is government.[189] [190] [191]

In only four years since 1968 did America beat the rest of the world in Gross Capital Formation, the measure of how much added

---

[189] *Figure 26: Savings per Capita*
[190] *Figure 27: Surplus per Capita*
[191] *Figure 28: Combined Surplus per Capita*

value is being invested in real growth, rather than consumed.[192] If we are so wealthy, why can we not even beat the world average in capital formation? The real economy will not tolerate financial tricks and illusions as does the *imagined institutionalist economy*.[193] Comparing total taxation and income-related tax to national production lends more evidence to American destructionism.

People who feel bad about their financial situation today must think twice about believing the poverty hustlers. Not only are their policies destroying *real income* and American productivity, but what is the point of working hard when the moment success is gained, the institutionalists will steal most of those gains for their programs? This wasteful and enormous system of spending and control is choking job growth and productivity, and sucking the prosperity right out of America.

More Income Inequality is Needed

The false belief in income inequality is a major driver of the envy and hatred that keeps this parasitic system growing. In fact, almost all income inequality in America can be reduced to statistical tricks, and what inequality remains is due to normal career progression and age. We need more income inequality so that the most productive careers have maximum incentive. There should be no shortage of doctors or engineers in an advanced economy. We continue to see shortages in critical professions because institutionalists have interfered with the labor markets in such ways that constrain the most productive labor. With their typical habit of treating symptoms instead of the disease, the institutionalists now travel the world with trade agreements, looking for immigrants to fill the unjust labor situations they have created with their own policies.

---

[192] *Figure 58: Gross Capital Formation*
[193] § 2.3 The Institutionalist Fantasy Economy

§ 3.3 Illusory Career Paths and Wealth Erosion

"For there's one thing, my lords, it's safe to say;
Lovers must each be ready to obey
The other, if they would long keep company.
Love will not be constrained by mastery;
When mastery comes the god of love anon
Stretches his wings and farewell! he is gone."
–Geoffrey Chaucer, The Canterbury Tales (The
Franklin's Tale)

Chaucer describes the hazards of coercing the closest relationships in our lives. When a person must live under the psychological or physical dominion of their peers, they soon seek to break free so that their willpower and interests can be satisfied in liberty and cooperation. The same is true in labor relationships. The hardest-working and rarest talents in society are being set to the greatest *forced labor* by the government and cartels, while more common jobs avoid taxes and are compensated unfairly. Coerced workers underperform and adopt passive aggressive behaviors that decrease productivity. As with dominated lovers, dominated workers develop resentment and apathy.

Unfortunately, much resentment and apathy is created by the fictitious stories of *institutionalists*. In the very beginning of this book, the story of Cato demonstrated the experience of many observant Americans – we all have access to nearly the same prosperity outcomes, brought about by what popular culture would call *socialism*, but what is actually *dirigisme*.[194] We shop at the same stores, eat at the same restaurants, and see the same doctors, with minor distinctions that are related more to our family support, government subsidies, progressive tax brackets, and lifetime spending choices than how much money our employers give us.

When a poor person is rushed into the hospital after a car accident, taxpayers will spend one million dollars saving their life, while people wasting away from chronic diseases go bankrupt fighting to get tests and procedures approved between their doctors and insurers. The doctors and insurers hesitate in fear of the

---

[194] § 1.1 Redistribution of Blood, Sweat, and Merit

medical boards and lawyers, but spend everyone else's money prodigiously when an easy diagnosis and tax funds are available. These inversions of justice and insults to our society persist ubiquitously, while *poverty hustlers* pour acidic falsehoods into the minds of the most impressionable.

Throughout this book, we have unveiled the real American economy,[195] [196] and we have shown how this incredibly unjust system has been inflicted upon us.[197] [198] We have disproven the common myth of *income inequality* and demonstrated how America needs *more* income inequality to drive activity towards productive endeavors.[199] Now it is possible to look at compensation for typical careers in America.

The fabled American "middle class" has not existed for at least a generation. Lifetime income analysis reveals five income classes for career paths in America. To discover the new American socioeconomic classes, we use the average, minimum, and maximum salaries for professions and apply the typical compensation for career progression. Then we consider the typical educational requirement, and its total price. We assume that everyone had to borrow the money to pay for college, and apply the standard interest rate to the loans. A living wage is assumed to be the minimal cost of living for everyone, and their childhood living costs are subtracted. Some day they will pay those costs for one child in the average two-child family.

The *income-related tax* is taken from each year of their earnings, and they all retire at age seventy. Irregular benefit compensation, such as that which is given to union workers, government employees, and public school teachers is added, and it is not taxed. The average profession is assumed to have a standard 21% benefit package. A running total of *income* and *benefits* less *living costs*, *taxes*, and *school loans* gives us the *lifetime accrued disposable*

---

[195] § 1.3 American Prosperity by the Numbers

[196] § 1.4 America vis-à-vis the World

[197] Chapter 2: The Institutionalist Creed

[198] § 3.1 Concepts and Limitations of Prosperity Analysis

[199] § 3.2 Manufactured Income Equality

income for each profession.[200] All other comparisons of income for professions are deceptive, as they almost invariably presume that progressive taxation, education, fringe benefits, and opportunity costs do not exist.

From this accurate analysis, new socioeconomic classes emerge: the *destitute*, the *persistent*, the *robbed*, the *gaming*, and the *wealthy*. The *destitute* are the truly poor Americans representing only 0.5 – 1.0% of the population.[201] The *persistent class* includes people who spend their lives in associate positions or technician services, agriculture workers, non-union blue-collar workers, religious ministers, and also unemployed people on welfare. They usually have high school or liberal arts college degrees.

The *robbed class* includes professions that have historically received top compensation because of the rarity of intellect, and mental rigor required for the work. In the *institutionalist* society, their productivity is collectivized and their wages are suppressed by cartels, regulations, and government intervention. Because the end product of *the robbed* is often immaterial, the institutionalists easily collude with government to use immigration law and offshoring to access cheaper labor. Foreigners also take advantage of United States intellectual property and education infrastructure. Taxpayer-funded grants are used for research which is conducted by foreign labor. The taxpayers pick up a large share of the cost for this underhanded activity. The *robbed* professions feature scientists, high technologists, engineers, mathematicians (STEM), economists, finance workers, and many lawyers.

Because the labor market is gamed, the market rates for jobs do not adequately reflect rare skills, high intelligence, and hard work; but, devious government is not the only culprit. *Private cartels* are formed by businesses colluding with *each other* to reduce competition and fix prices or supply. Most nations in the world punish private cartels under antitrust laws. A class action lawsuit against tech giants Apple, Adobe, Google, Intel, Intuit, Pixar, and Lucas has uncovered a wage-fixing cartel in the tech industry that

---

[200] *Figure 96: Lifetime Accrued Disposable Income*
[201] § 1.3 American Prosperity by the Numbers

has robbed countless tech workers of hundreds of millions in wages.[202]

Dozens of other tech companies were implicated in the evidence, beyond the seven that were named in the lawsuit. Their price fixing drove unearned money to third parties in the stock market – a process that inflates pensions and real estate values in-part. That money should have been competing for rare labor resources instead of inflating financial assets. Rather, these major tech companies became yet another contributor to the *something-for-nothing* corruption of America. The *robbed* class has millions of workers who were indirectly affected by this recent tech cartel, since the wage-fixing of so many large companies has a rippling effect through the nation on technology wages in other companies.

The fourth income class in America is highly counterintuitive. The *gaming class* includes those modern professions that typically (but not always) use some form of coercion to inflate their compensation. For instance, union blue collar workers, government employees, and public school teachers offload so much of their compensation to benefits, that they not only underreport their compensation, but they also avoid significant taxation. A typical public school teacher will gain almost five-hundred thousand dollars in tax avoidance over the course of their career from their benefits. Other *gaming* professions eliminate their competition through government collusion to inflate their wages. For instance, news anchors benefit from Federal Communications Commission (FCC) licensing and broadcast regulations along with the media oligopolies that emerged from them.

Monopolistic licensing from medical boards and medical school accreditation constrains the supply of medical labor as well. Nobel laureate Milton Friedman has warned about the American Medical Association (AMA) inflating medical costs since 1962.[203] Two generations later, salaries of doctors are inflated by 200% compared

---

[202] (Ames, 2014)
[203] (Friedman, Medical Licensure, 1962)

to other developed nations,[204] accounting for $58 billion in unnecessary medical costs in 2008.[205]

Constraining the supply of doctors does more than inflate their salaries. The costs of medical school are also inflated by these constraints induced by healthcare "guilds." There are 22% fewer medical schools than a century ago, and they must serve a population that has exploded by 300%. Contrarily, the number of law schools increased by 50% during the same time period, and legal compensation is now in tune with other professionals.

If the medical cartel broke its hold on constraining the supply of labor, and suppressing cheap services for basic medical care, the cost of medical school would decrease in turn. Not only should there be competing ratings and licensure agencies that are broadly acceptable, but with information technology, malpractice and performance records, and consumer reviews of doctors can act as a greater quality assurance system than professional "guilds."

Essentially, those in the *gaming* class are using licensure, professional societies, government benefits, tax avoidance, and unions to defeat competition and inflate their compensation. These are old tactics of *guild socialism*, which led to both *syndicalism* and the *zwangswirtschaft* (command economy) pattern of the fascists. Meanwhile, the professionals in the *robbed* class are having their competition artificially enlarged by third parties, government interventions, and cartels. If these injustices were corrected, we could expect the *robbed* and *gaming* classes to converge in both taxation and income.[206] [207] As it stands, *income-related taxes* are entirely regressive. The least gainful professions are taxed the most, while benefit-heavy professions enjoy massive tax avoidance.[208]

Finally, we arrive at the much-fabled "rich" boogeymen spoken of in the horror stories preached by poverty hustlers. The actual *wealthy* are few and far between. They include the *top* artists,

---

[204] (Perry, The Medical Cartel: Why are MD Salaries So High?, 2009)
[205] (Farrell, et al., 2008)
[206] *Figure 96: Lifetime Accrued Disp*
[207] *Figure 97: Lifetime Accrued Income-Related Tax*

[208] *Figure 98: Accrued Tax-to-Income Ratio, End-of-Life Outcomes*

Thomas E. Kurek

actors, athletes, CEOs, investors, lawyers, surgeons, and aristocrats. The key word is *top*. Very few people in those professions earn the kind of wealth that society is led to believe by sensational journalism and political opportunists. The outrageously exorbitant "CEO pay" that institutionalists decry is only calculated for the top public companies (typically transnational corporations), or 0.002% of US companies.[209] The median CEO earns less *lifetime disposable income* than the median doctor.[210] The average tenure for a CEO is only eight years of their career and they are paid widely different packages based on their return on talent.[211]

The danger of confusing the *wealthy* with other classes of Americans is that an angry, envious, and ignorant electorate will support policies that actually destroy their own paths to prosperity. Increasing tax on individuals who make over $125,000 a year, not only further punishes some of the most burdened tax donkeys in the *robbed* class, but it also ensures that when hard working Americans have a few good years of income, they cannot keep it to get ahead.

These unjust policies will slam the door shut on the American dream, by manipulating perceptions about what it means to be wealthy. While very few Americans would take issue with increasing taxes on the truly *wealthy* class, the risk of increasing tax on them is capital flight. They are in a good position to use every legal and physical trick imaginable to avoid paying those taxes. The *wealthy* are not geographically constrained. Essentially, they live in elite communities with multiple properties and the freedom to move at will. The *gaming* live in very nice communities, while the *robbed*, the *persistent*, and the *destitute* live everywhere. Moving is a significant burden for any class but the *wealthy*.

Careers and income aside, wealth disparity is also decreasing, as we have already shown.[212] The net worth (wealth) of a person is their assets less liabilities. Assets include tangible items (real estate, equipment, durable goods) and financial items (deposits, mutual funds, pensions, stocks, bonds). Liabilities include any form of debt and property taxes. In a society where financial assets and

---

[209] (Bamberger, 2012)
[210] *Figure 96: Lifetime Accrued Disposable Income*
[211] (Burnison, 2013)
[212] *Figure 46: Net Worth of the Wealthy vs. Average Net Worth*

real estate had been artificially gamed for decades, the housing bust of 2008 was the natural consequence that rectified much of the *something-for-nothing*.

If the government had let the failed parties take responsibility for their own losses, our society would already be recovered, and wealth would be distributed more correctly according to market value. Nobel economist Joseph Stiglitz suggested that the banks should fail in 2009,[213] when governments were forcing their societies to reduce their standards of living for an entire generation to reward the people who failed. Poverty hustlers not only distort wealth disparity with bogus statistics and propaganda, but they decry inequality made by their own politicians' economic interventions. It is a truly delusional and contradictory advocacy position. To wit, the actions of the Obama administration and his appointed Federal Reserve chairpersons have exploded net worth by nearly $27 trillion,[214] with their banking and spending policies.

The cost of this unjust redistribution of wealth is not just the face value. The tool used to do it is called *financial repression*, in which government debt is financed at favorable terms, sucking capital out of the private sector. In this case, the Federal Reserve set the *real* interest rate below zero, by ensuring that the inflation rate was greater than the rate paid. In this way, the government induces malinvestments for all who benefit from the interference, which suppresses job growth, income, output, and wealth in the private sector.

The economy is then hobbled while the government prioritizes financing itself instead of the productive sector. Institutionalists are guilty of making the rich richer with their spending policies, and they are also responsible for suppressing economic productivity by distorting value across the board. As with income analysis, the numbers become less meaningful because they are not counting the right things and they have effectively rewritten the markers on the measuring stick. The effect of *wealth erosion* and *financial repression* is thus measurable indirectly, as demonstrated in this

---

[213] (Evans-Pritchard, 2009)
[214] (ZeroHedge, 2014)

Thomas E. Kurek

book. Americans and Europeans have just experienced one of the greatest swindles in history.

To add insult to injury, the educators that our culture has sanctified have been scamming us for a generation. In 2013, the United States spent $1.5 trillion on education and training! Outstanding college debt topped $1.3 trillion in 2015,[215] and college no longer has a high chance of leading to gainful employment. A full 49% of recent college graduates are underemployed, only 52% of them have full-time employment, while 41% of them are making less than $25,000 per year and only 17% of them are making more than $50,000 per year.[216]

In a mind-numbing revelation that anyone who read this book could have predicted, Brookings Institution has shown that Bachelors of Arts degrees for graduates from low-income families do not lead to significantly higher lifetime compensation than those with high school diplomas.[217] Bachelors of Arts degrees for graduates from households with median or above income have led to higher income. Brookings is investigating explanations that include family resources, child neighborhood, and the types of colleges. It is incomprehensible that they are not considering what kind of college degree was obtained.

For many college degrees, there are too many colleges offering uncompetitive programs, which are not respected by the labor market. For instance, the career prospects vary greatly for a first-tier and third-tier law school. The same could be said for Bachelors of Art degrees in humanities programs. The most obvious explanation as to why graduates from middle- and upper-income families make more money is that their culture encourages them to pursue competitive (and often *boring* degrees). The cultural influence on choice is powerful. Why is Brookings Institution not investigating the most obvious paradigm?

Manipulated markets, inflated stocks, gamed pensions,[218] government spending, unfair tax schemes, real estate swindles,

---

[215] (Kane, 2016)

[216] (Lavelle, Silverstone, & Smith, 2015)

[217] (Hershbein, 2016)

[218] (Dubay, 2005)

banking schemes, financial repression, labor cartels, unions, professional societies, licensors, and education scams have been robbing the most productive and responsible Americans. The amount of corruption we sustain leaves citizens without *economic sovereignty* and the youth of today are confused by *institutionalist* activists. We have evidence of destructionism in labor markets, and the illusory career paths have already responded to this extreme corruption by directing labor away from the most productive endeavors.

If Chaucer could instruct modern institutionalist labor activists as well as he instructed medieval Europeans about love, he might say, "*Jobs will not be constrained by mastery; When mastery comes, the workers anon stretch their wings and farewell! They are gone!*" Instead of picking up the dire needs of the economy, new workers fled to delusions in their heads about how they imagined the world to be. Meanwhile those who choose the *boring* jobs continue to toil diligently while being robbed by this corrupt system.

§ 3.4 Lifetime Prosperity

"If ye love wealth better than liberty, the tranquility
of servitude than the animating contest of freedom –
go from us in peace. We ask not your counsels or
arms. Crouch down and lick the hands which feed
you. May your chains sit lightly upon you, and may
posterity forget that ye were our countrymen!"
–Samuel Adams, speech at the Philadelphia State
House, August 1ˢᵗ, 1776

In their hearts, Americans long for liberty and the animating contests that Samuel Adams described. Unfortunately, we do not have a prayer unless we can dispel the economic myths of the *institutionalists*. A general model for prosperity analysis is the tool that Americans need to correctly perceive the economic reality of their own personal life, and the lives of others. The model is a formula called *Lifetime Prosperity*. It measures the amount of resources a person has consumed and accrued up to the current point in their life.

First, we borrow from Haig-Simons-Hicks (HSH) income, to define income in a given year as *consumption* plus the *change in net worth*. Consumption accounts for all items used by the person – unearned resources, welfare, government resources, business resources substituted for individual needs (such as business meals), fringe benefits, subsidies, paychecks, royalties, advantages from regulatory boons, and even illicitly acquired resources. This means that if a person got a paycheck, lived in a rent-controlled or subsidized house, or ate a steak that was bought by their boyfriend, it is all counted as *income*. The change in net worth can be negative or positive:

Equation 1: Lifetime Prosperity Income (LP Income)

$$LP\ Income = Consumption + \Delta(Net\ Worth)$$

But using this income model is not enough to estimate *prosperity distribution*. The *prosperity* that an individual enjoys in a given year is actually their *LP Income* plus the *wealth* they had access to in that year. Recalling that wealth is surplus, the major categories of wealth are *financial accounts*, *property holdings*, and *shared access. Financial accounts* include stocks, retirement income accounts, retirement healthcare accounts, trust funds, inheritance, pensions, savings, education accounts, debts and negative financial accounts. *Property holdings* include real estate, cars and other vehicles, amenities, furniture, jewelry, durable goods, and any other material thing in the possession of the individual. *Shared access* includes living with a friend, parent, or other person who pays the bills, or a government or institutional program not yet elected but available based on the special status of the individual. Essentially it is personal access to a share of earned or unearned communal or state property. If a person is living for free in a friend's mansion, they are incredibly wealthy during that time, and that wealth would be classified as *shared access*:

Equation 2: Prosperity

$$Prosperity = LP\ Income + Wealth$$
$$= Consumption + Wealth + \Delta(Net\ Worth)$$

With *prosperity* defined, we can consider how *progressive taxation* affects it. Progressive taxation punishes people who earn a high income during a few years of their lives. It does not "tax the wealthy," but it does crush the pathway to wealth. Many highly productive careers have a low income for at least a third of their entire career. Their few years of high income can represent the pathway to wealth they have earned, from sacrificing so many years before they succeeded. If they are taxed punitively during those few years of bounty, it just means that people who are already wealthy will not be joined by hard-working nouveau riche. It also punishes those who earn conventional income through a paycheck. Those who consume government or business expense accounts, welfare, or fringe benefits avoid taxation for that income. If taxing the wealthy was the sincere goal, then taxes on *financial accounts, property*, and *shared access* would be increased.

Income tax hobbles low income earners as well, because it also means that people who prefer to live frugally cannot amass wealth as easily. Consider the previous equation for prosperity.[219] Most poor people have low or negative wealth (debt). Their only pathways to wealth are to reduce their consumption, remain dependent upon

[219] *Equation 2: Prosperity*

others, or to keep as much of their income as they can. Wage and salary taxes obtrude into that pathway. *Ad valorem taxes* siphon off their wealth, and *income taxes* siphon off their consumption and increased net worth. If people could keep what they earn, and tax was shifted off of income, then people who choose to live humbly could amass wealth simply by spending as little as possible.

As we calculated *income-related tax* before, we must now consider other tax burdens to obtain the total taxation imposed on a person. There are *ad valorem taxes* on consumption including, but not limited to sales tax (AT_C). This is taken from the consumption of personal resources including recently earned income and existing wealth (C_P). Then there are ad valorem taxes on standing wealth of all sorts (W), such as property tax (AT_W). Tax is levied upon gains made from investments, which is essentially income generated from wealth itself. That is called capital gains tax (IT_G), charged on financial account income (I_{FA}). Finally, we have the income-related taxes on our wages, salaries, and all earning-related activities, including *ad valorem taxes* (such as gas tax) levied upon that which is required for our jobs (I_E). This is the income-related tax (IT_{IR}). The total tax burden on an individual is then:

Equation 3: Tax Burden

$$Tax\ Burden = Consumption_{Tax} + Wealth_{Tax} + Capital\ Gains_{Tax} \\ + Income\ Related_{Tax}$$

$$= AT_C * C_P + AT_W * W + IT_G * I_{FA} + IT_{IR} * I_E$$

Tax avoidance is the tax that would be charged on what a person has consumed through untaxed channels, such as divorce alimony, child support, fringe benefits, gifts, expenses incurred by third parties (government, businesses, friends), and deferred income that is taxed at lower rates later (C_E). There is also tax-exempt standing wealth, such as resources maintained by other people (shared access wealth), or tax-exempt properties (W_E). This boon is defined as:

Equation 4: Tax Avoidance

$$Tax\ Avoidance = Consumption_{Tax\ Exempt} + Wealth_{Tax\ Exempt}$$

$$= AT_C * C_E + AT_W * W_E$$

This gives us a person's total tax balance. If it is negative, then they contributed to the government. If it is positive, then they got an advantage that others would have had to pay tax on if the laws disallowed their methods of tax avoidance:

Equation 5: Tax Balance

$$Tax\ Balance = Tax\ Avoidance - Tax\ Burden$$

$$= AT_C(C_E - C_P) + AT_W(W_E - W) - IT_G * I_{FA} - IT_{IR} * I_E$$

At last we can derive the equation that poverty hustlers imply with their rhetoric, but never justify with their numbers. It considers our previous annualized equations, but aggregates them over the lifetime of an individual. Ideally, we should weight the wealth of the individual during the time period that they possessed it, not necessarily lining up with annual snapshots of their life. Such a calculation may be infeasible without precise data from banking information systems. Assuming that all previous changes in net worth have been reconciled with their accounts in previous years, and that wealth during each year of the individual's life is weighted by their age, where i is the age in years, beginning at birth and ending at the current age of the person, and n is the current age of the person:

Equation 6: Lifetime Prosperity

$$Lifetime\ Prosperity$$
$$= \sum_{i=0}^{n} Consumption_i + \sum_{i=0}^{n} \frac{Wealth_i}{n} + \sum_{i=0}^{n} Tax\ Balance_i$$
$$+ \Delta(Net\ Worth)_n$$

The calculations in this book have approximated this model as closely as possible where claims about *prosperity distribution* were offered. If the institutionalists and poverty hustlers want to get honest about increasing prosperity for the poor, then they must adhere to this model. To deviate from it leads to false claims about *wealth disparity* and *income inequality*.

Prosperity incidence occurs throughout our lives, and prosperity itself requires long-term planning and incentives. Nearly every concern today induces citizens to focus on short-term consumption choices. There are so many hidden taxes that even the most diligent cannot keep track of their tax balance. Insidious institutionalists propose value-added taxes (VAT) that will make transparency even worse. The secret to prosperity is long-term planning and careful accounting of consumption, wealth, income, taxes, and unearned resources. *Economic sovereignty* requires us to insist that our government adopts policies that acknowledge these truths, and that we use the knowledge to guide our own habits.

§ 3.5 Summary and Implications

"On the other hand, I realized that no ideals existed outside the two worlds of socialism and nationalism. They were the only two concepts for which people were ready to die if necessary. At the time, I therefore undertook to form one common world out of these torn nationalist and socialist worlds – founded on a new definition of the two concepts...They realize that this state has arrived at a lasting synthesis of nationalism and socialism and that, in the long run, this state will develop a powerful attraction, similar to that of the ideas of the French Revolution at the time."
–Adolph Hitler [220]

Adolph Hitler is one of the most infamous institutionalists of all time. He wove a centrist illusion over fanatical plans, and then sold it to a desperate population that willingly offered their wild imaginations for exploitation. Hitler's statements on National Socialism employed *argument-to-moderation* fallacy, just as today, institutionalists encourage citizens to believe that "the truth is somewhere between" and to shun the "extremists." Also, in conjunction with our classification of institutionalists,[221] Hitler associated his fascism with the emergence of Jacobin Club atmospheres. Russian communists did the same thing.

Modern Western society, taking on aspects of the society that gave rise to Hitler, is helplessly vulnerable to sophisticated manipulation. If we are to recover from the coming calamity, then we must learn *economic sovereignty*. There are three prerequisites for economic sovereignty: accurate portrayal of the economy,[222] knowledge of the warring ideologies that violate economic sovereignty,[223] and concepts of prosperity analysis.[224] Modern

---

[220] (Hitler, 1940)

[221] Chapter 2: The Institutionalist Creed

[222] Chapter 1: American Socioeconomic Indications & Warnings

[223] Chapter 2: The Institutionalist Creed

[224] Chapter 3: Inequality, Wrath, and Envy by Diktat

Thomas E. Kurek

societies across the globe have none of these three prerequisites in abundant supply, so economic sovereignty is sparse. Violations of economic sovereignty ultimately manifest in the form of *seized property* or *forced labor*, affected by both legal and illicit methods.

The good news is that concepts of prosperity analysis are not complicated. *Wealth* is not *income* – it is surplus. Few can become wealthy by having a couple years of impressive income. Many wealthy and "poor" people are consuming unearned or un-monetized resources that completely evade statistical measurement. The *zero-sum fallacy* that leads people to think that one man's gain is another man's loss is one of the most absurd misnomers. Wealth is *produced* and does not exist *somehow*. Goods and services are created or destroyed, rightfully owned or usurped (in part or whole), and well-purposed or misallocated.

Because *zero-sum* believers are after an improper transfer of ownership, they are guilty of that which they accuse – inspiring crime and rationalizing government redistribution, market manipulation, and financial repression. Their policies introduce coercion into the exchange and production processes, so they *are* responsible for making one man's gain another man's loss. That interference also corrupts economic inputs that would otherwise direct capital towards more efficient and desired purposes.

The "playing field" is not level, thanks to institutionalists. Tax policies, bailouts, stimulus spending, redistribution, welfare, regulation, and failure to prosecute private business cartels that impose their own wage- and price-fixing schemes have turned the "playing field" into a volcano that immolates everyone who tries to reach the top, while the institutionalists float above the entire thing on their clouds of fake compassion. This attempt to *level the playing field* by imposing more congruent outcomes creates chaos, malinvestment, and wasted human activity and resources. Equality of outcome is unjust to maintain and impossible to even approximate. America cannot even attain *equal opportunity* because of biological differences, environmental exposure, accident of birth, and the combined choices every person has made with every second of their lives. On the other hand, *freedom of opportunity* is attainable, but it will necessarily be eroded by attempts to create *equal opportunity* and *equal outcomes*. Such interventions rob the many to artificially advantage the few.

Studies of amenity access, wealth, destitution, and corrected income statistics prove that American prosperity is incredibly equal and well distributed. There are numerous types of *unaccounted resources* that contribute trillions to prosperity, and completely evade the statistics of the poverty hustlers. There are *previously-earned resources* such as paid-off houses that others must actually earn, which contributes greatly to prosperity in a society that has manipulated its real estate prices for decades. Fifty years ago, a blue-collar factory worker could afford a single family home on a single income. Today, their college-educated children cannot even afford to live alone in a rental. People sitting on significant resources from the past can easily take a low income and live a better life than a privately employed serf with twice their income.

State-redistributed resources come in *personal* and *corporate welfare* flavors. The *personal welfare* that "poor" people spend raises their income to 2.6x more than the income that they report. *Corporate welfare* uses government subsidies, regulations, or other competitive advantages induced by law. These unaccounted business resources benefit workers in that company or industry at the expense of those businesses without the legal advantages. *Inherited resources* include any kind of gift from acquaintances, spouses, or family members – houses, college tuition, vehicles, stocks, gas money, food money, bar tabs, restaurant tabs, entertainment tabs, etc. People consuming these boons use unaccounted wealth that their peers must earn for themselves – and it does not show up on their personal income reports.

Charitable resources include the same things as *personal welfare* and *inherited resources*, but they are doled out by private nonprofits. With nonprofits taking in $2 trillion in revenues per year, this is a significant resource – almost 25% of the value of *money income* for all Americans combined. Meanwhile, *fringe benefits* give employees per-diem travel payments, health, vision, and dental care, company meals, retirement and pension financing, life insurance, paid time off, education and training, fitness, hazard pay, and more. This compensation is rarely taxed, or even counted carefully by the recipient. Lastly, the consumers of all the types of *unaccounted resources* enjoy tax avoidance that is impossible for people who buy the same things in cash.

One of the greatest tricks of the institutionalists is to convince the public that their poverty reports represent helpless people who are eternally stuck in a life of misery, or greedy rich people oppressing everyone else. In fact, their statistics only capture *moments in time* and not *lifetimes*. A huge portion of income inequality is created by normal things like job experience (age), irregular income (investment payouts, house sales, sales commissions), and industrial production trends. Confusing annual snapshots of wealth and income with flesh-and-blood people is one of the biggest misconceptions in this discourse. The institutionalists have people believing that a lottery winner or a person obtaining a generous payout at the end of their career is a greedy tycoon while some young adult with an entry-level job and all of their living expenses bankrolled by their parents is a pitiable mendicant. Flesh-and-blood human beings move between income categories so much that a third of people with the lowest lifetime income make the top quintile of income during their good years.

Confusing *intangibles* with prosperity leads to very corrupt notions. There is an entire field of absurd *scientism* called *happiness economics*. Happiness is impossible to measure on a universal scale due to its extreme subjectivity and fluctuation of definition even within the minds of specific individuals over time. The only thing that can be measured is the relative placation of the population at a current moment in time. Such indicators would only be useful to institutionalists who already use power to placate the population.

At most we can say that physiological and security deficiencies universally degrade happiness (Maslow 1 & 2 needs, respectively). In an advanced economy, where those needs are nearly universally satisfied, associating happiness to prosperity is meaningless. At best it will measure a person's psychological weakness to be unsatisfied with a honey-laden bowl of creamed wheat instead of a Belgian waffle, or a jog on the trails instead of a game of golf. The "happiness economics" survey respondent can be a criminal and elated about their latest heist, or miserable about their latest arrest. Immorality in society that is not captured by the justice system would also result in amorphous happiness measurements, considering psychological phenomena such as "duper's delight," in which liars are elated when they realize that their lies succeeded.

While prosperity should not be conflated with *intangibles*, intangibles indirectly influence prosperity. Intoxicated and immoral societies will destroy themselves economically from the inside out, as Opium-War China and Ancient Athens discovered. Economics investigates the measurement of scarce resources with alternative uses. That includes labor, time, raw materials, capital, and goods of varied orders. Consequently, *rationing* and *competition* are features of every economy, no matter which control processes prevail (socialism, capitalism, dirigisme, or anarchy). The question is which processes optimize the use of those resources, and bring the best outcomes to the most people.

The inter-subjectivity of pricing also introduces a high degree of subjectivity into the economy. Pricing is like grading a school essay – it is not an exact science. Using millions of people to independently determine prices in free markets helps to eliminate the bias that misprices resources and labor. When economic planning is imposed by a handful of people operating with intangibles in their minds, societies experience very destructive outcomes including the collapse of socialist economies, slow-drip robbery, consumption of capital (destructionism), and the stagnant injustice of dirigiste economies.

Even worse, megalomaniacal bankers interfere with the currency itself, using inflation, quantitative easing, and financial repression. In doing this, they *change the grading scale* for pricing, rejiggering the subjective valuation of millions of people, as they modify the value of capital to favor the things for which the government and its surrogates have chosen. The greatest heists in history are perpetrated by bankers, and they have swindled modern America on an unprecedented scale. Thomas Jefferson and John Taylor would agree:

> *"Banking establishments are more dangerous than standing armies...the principle of spending money to be paid by posterity, under the name of funding, is but swindling futurity on a large scale." –Thomas Jefferson to John Taylor, May 28, 1816*

Even with common economic fallacies dispelled, inequality claims can still prevail. Fortunately, the counterfeiting methods of inequality are simple. The most common trick is counting *household income* instead of individual income. Other deceivers compare tax returns without separating the statistics into single or joint filers. The worst violators even call it *family income* when their data cannot possible tell them whether or not it represents a family in a home. The wood and concrete of a household does not make income – a working person makes income with their labor. Houses have different numbers of people and earners. The highest quintile of household income has twice as many mouths to feed and five times as many income earners. There would be a problem if the top income quintile did not have at least five-times as much income as the lowest quintile.

Another inequality counterfeit method is counting *part-time labor* as equal to *full time labor*. A person who is working twenty hours a week with enough to live is not getting a raw deal. In order to compare income accurately, the millions of part-time workers must be converted into Full-Time Equivalents (FTEs). Poverty hustlers also tend to ignore the totality of taxation associated with labor. *Taxation dynamics* blunt inequality because people are charged higher rates as they attain more prosperity. Typical statistics do not count all of the forms of redistribution and welfare that half of the nation consumes. Hundreds of billions in resources consumed by the "poor" go unaccounted.

Even *monetary time-and-space variation* is unaccounted within inequality reports. The value of money itself changes with geography (space). The same thing in one location has wildly different prices in another location. Measures such as Purchase Power Parity (PPP) approximate this phenomenon. The government acknowledges this as they line their own workers' pockets with variable per diem travel payments. Government cost of living adjustments can fluctuate by 300% across localities in a single state! It is highly dubious that the poverty hustlers in government jobs who create inequality reports suffer from amnesia on this point. If they pay themselves such varied rates when they travel, why do they not adjust their income statistics to reflect cost-of-living adjustment? Less frequently, inequality statistics fail to correct for inflation (monetary variation over *time*), which would exaggerate present-day inequality.

Correcting for all of the distorting factors of *household income, part-time labor, taxation dynamics, redistribution and welfare,* and *monetary time-and-space variation,* we arrive at the Real Income Distribution indicator (RID). The Gini Ratio is used to measure inequality of a series, and RID Gini Ratio shows that since 1984, there is very little income inequality in real terms. It also shows that poverty hustlers have exaggerated income inequality by 250-300% during the same time. There are other normal contributors to inequality reports. Income is affected by industrial productivity – it matters what industry a person chooses for their career. But inequality based on industry has plummeted since the 1920s, due to the exodus of manufacturing and rise of the service industry, along with harmful government market interference. Even income inequality from job experience (age) is larger than RID inequality.

Although real income is affected by job experience and industry, we cannot easily incorporate those into RID inequality. It is safe to say that when the effects of age and industry are considered, most of income inequality based on real productivity is completely wiped out. What is left is a regressive, socialistic income distribution that robs remuneration for productivity in the whole.

The claims of poverty hustlers are the exact opposite of the truth – there is not enough *income inequality* to reflect the real value of jobs. Free trade will need to increase income inequality by nearly two-thirds to restore justice to labor markets. An advanced economy should never have a shortage of doctors and engineers, but critical professions are constrained due to institutionalist interference with the labor markets. Restoring innate income inequality will incentivize the most productive work activities once again.

The problems of redistributive robbery go deeper than the suppression of industries and professions. Considering prosperity distribution on a broader level, alarming trends emerge. While all Americans have enjoyed increased *real income,* the elderly have had the largest increases due to sharp increases in welfare, pensions, transfers, real estate inflation, small business profits, and employment benefits. In the aggregate, Americans have not gained income from fair payment for their services. The lower income brackets have gained income from government redistribution, and the higher income brackets have gained prosperity from pensions, benefits, and manipulated real estate markets. Which Americans are gaining prosperity based upon competitive achievement instead of institutional coercion?

Comparing American income to national productivity is an even more dismal affair. In 2013, the Gross Domestic Product (GDP) was $17 trillion, the cost of civics was $10 trillion, and the *personal income* of all Americans was $11.3 trillion. After the total cost of taxes and regulations, the government only allows Americans to keep $3.3T of their earned money – that's $24,397 for the worker and $58,765 for the government. That is equivalent to consigning Americans to *forced labor* from January to September of every year. Revolutions have started for much less. The only thing that protects the heads of American bureaucrats is the ignorance of the nation, the unprecedented prosperity placating everyone, and the cunning immaterial shackles of modern servitude.

This monstrous burden on the American people has been affecting the nation in ways that are not obvious. The indirect consequences of tax and regulatory cost are numerous. Businesses have to treat tax and regulation as an expense, which leads to lost jobs, lost profits, lost benefits, lower wages, increased prices, or halted expansion plans. Even worse, the regulations are a hidden tax. The business must pay for the cost of compliance, and then they have to pass the higher costs on to everyone else. Regulations currently cost Americans two-trillion dollars every year. This level of government burden even causes businesses to shut down, or cancel products and services due to shortages or infeasibility.

A particularly insidious propaganda tact is for institutionalists to refer to government spending as "investment." In fact, nobody can "borrow from the future," they only force a tyrannical amount of debt onto workers between the ages of 30 and 50. Thomas Jefferson understood this so why have our modern bureaucrats lost his wisdom? The fools who swindle futurity will be crawling into their graves around the time that their dirty deed sinks its fangs into their children. They will not even be able to hear their children curse their name and damn their legacy with tortured fury.

Also, the government projects that they imposed will never be "investments." They have no reasonably calculated *return on investment* to pay down existing debt, and the *collateral* is not taken from those whom the programs directly benefit. This reaps *private gains* from *public losses*; private businessmen are put in jail for the same schemes. Moreover, sixty-percent of the nation does not even contribute to these public projects, and the *robbed class* shoulders the greatest burden by far. This is not equality under the law. It is the process of supplanting the indentured servants, chattel slaves, and sweatshop workers of the past with new corvée serfdom from the most diligent and distractedly analytical citizens.

Another trick the institutionalists use is to pretend like *ad valorem* taxes do not exist. These are taxes levied "according to value," such as property, sales, inheritance, expatriation, value-added, and tariffs. Many are paid without consent of the governed, hidden in the cost of the purchase. For instance, renters pay property tax in the price of their rent. Benefit-heavy jobs and people living off of others avoid many *ad valorem* taxes. These taxes are almost entirely ignored in prosperity distribution analysis.

Whitewashing outrageous tax burden is not just a pastime for institutionalist swindlers. American workers have little understanding of the total tax that is levied on every hour they work – also known as *income-related taxes* (IR Taxes). There are the *payroll taxes* that everyone sees on their paycheck – Federal Income Tax, Social Security, Medicare, Medicaid, State Income Tax, and Local Income Tax. There are the *employee taxes* that the government hides by charging to our employer for every dollar they pay us – Social Security Employer Tax, Medicare and Medicaid Employer Tax, Federal Unemployment Tax (FUTA), Worker's Compensation Tax, State Unemployment Tax (SUTA), and Real Estate Tax on worker facilities. Finally, there are *transportation and communication taxes* that workers must pay to travel to work and communicate with their employers and clients – State Gasoline Tax, Federal Gasoline Tax, Road Usage Tax and Tolls, and the Property Tax used to fund public transportation and roads during work-related travel. The *communications taxes* are levied upon the portions of internet and phone usage related to work activity. From whatever money is left, we must pay *sales tax* on many of our purchases.

Those are the eighteen *income-related taxes* that are mostly unseen, unavoidable, and completely regressive – taking much more from the middle class than common reports indicate. The taxation reports almost exclusively present *payroll taxes* alone – a fraction of the tax levied upon our labor. This is how institutionalists mislead people into believing that "poor" people pay no tax. Even though low-to-middle-income Americans pay an enormous amount of *income-related taxes*, only the top forty-percent of American earners contribute to taxes beyond welfare payments to their neighbors. The labor taxation shell game is enough to give the brightest economist vertigo and the obscurity of *income-related taxes* leaves most workers with no prayer to understand exactly how much corvée serfdom they are set to by the government.

Assuming that an American can get their head around the nationwide economic reality, the ideologies that lay out a smokescreen over that reality, economic fallacies, and the byzantine web of taxation – the question remains, what can they do about it? Perhaps they can choose a particular career over another? Analyzing typical career paths in the United States for lifetime compensation, exceptional fringe benefits, living costs, progressive taxation, and career-specific education and training costs reveals five socioeconomic classes in America: the *destitute*, the *persistent*, the *robbed*, the *gaming*, and the *wealthy*.

The *destitute class* is truly poor, with insufficient food, shelter, and clothing, but they are only 0.5 – 1.0% of America. The *persistent class* is the largest portion of America. They have high school or liberal arts college degrees, and they are either unemployed on welfare, or they work as associates, technicians, agricultural workers, religious ministers, or non-union blue-collar jobs. Over the course of their lives, they will make between $750,000 to $1.25 million dollars of income and benefits after taxes, education cost, and living cost. We refer to this value as their lifetime disposable income.

The *robbed class* is where the rarest and most talented minds meet the most disciplined worth ethic. It includes engineers, high technologists, computer programmers, mathematicians, scientists, economists, finance workers, and most lawyers. In the past they were the best-compensated people because of a natural labor shortage from the difficulty of the work and rarity of talent to perform it. Today they have been completely *robbed* through regulations, government interventions, taxation, private cartels, and offshoring. The *private cartels* that robbed technology workers have been sued for hundreds of billions to punish their wage price-fixing. By the end of their careers, people in the *robbed class* will have made between $1.25 and $2.25 million in disposable income.

Above the *robbed class* are the most gainful professions in this society. They do not even deserve the money that they earn, because they take advantage of some government-enabled scam that inflates their compensation, reduces labor competition or allows them to avoid taxes and offload compensation to benefits. The *gaming class* currently includes unionized blue-collar workers, government employees, public school teachers, news anchors, and doctors. The workers in these industries are not necessarily malicious in their usurpation. Many cannot even count the monetary value of their tax avoidance, fringe benefits, industry-coerced labor shortages, oligopolistic broadcasting or professional licensure, and school accreditation. Although Nobel laureates like Milton Friedman have warned about the consequences of these arrangements for decades, and the lifetime disposable income analysis here turns him from analyst to prophet, the facts are nearly absent from public discourse.

Above the *destitute*, the *persistent*, the *robbed*, and the *gaming* classes, resides the top income-based socioeconomic class: *the wealthy class*. They are few and far between with only a few thousand people in their ranks at any given time. They are not the stereotypical corporate "fat cat," that poverty hustlers dream up in their creative imaginations. They are the *top* actors, artists, athletes, CEOs, investors, lawyers, surgeons, and aristocratic gentry. The keyword is *top*. Very few people in those professions earn more than the *robbed* or the *gaming* classes.

Along with the fantasy of corporate "fat cats," comes the CEO pay myth, which is just a hateful propaganda campaign to manufacture consent for oppressive tax schemes. These CEO pay statistics are only calculated on CEOs from the top 0.002% of companies in the United States, which are typically enormous transnational corporations. The lifetime disposable income of the average CEO is less than the average doctor, and nearly equal to a public school teacher. The envious imagery of distorted CEO pay conveniently distracts the public from the *wealthy* entertainers, lawyers, gentry, investors, and surgeons.

Even worse, the tax increases are not proposed for those few thousand people in the *wealthy class*. Instead, they will punish the tax donkeys in the *robbed class* during the few good years of their careers in which they make between $125,000 and $300,000. Those Americans already surrender nearly half of that money to the government through combined tax channels, and with the oppressive tax designs of the institutionalists we can be sure that the imprisoned American dream will finally be executed by firing squad.

What if their new income taxation schemes were only aimed at the few thousand people in the *wealthy class*? The risk then becomes capital flight. People in other income classes are fairly restricted in where they can obtain work and raise their families. People in the *wealthy class* have so much money that they can use legal and physical tricks to avoid paying taxes. They are not geographically constrained like everyone else.

These realities leave few options for those whose hearts are filled with the burning desire to use government to steal from others so they can pretend to be heroes of the downtrodden. In reality, government size and redistribution is beyond maxed-out, and there is no amount of new usurpation that will improve the lives of Americans. Inactive people must become productive, prices must plummet, and government spending must decrease to shepherd capital towards efficient processes.

Beyond the deluded interpretations of income classes and income taxation, institutionalists rarely speak of actual wealth, which is measured by *net worth* – the assets a person has left after their liabilities. Assets are *tangible* items such as real estate, equipment, and durable goods or *financial* items such as deposits, mutual funds, pensions, stocks, and bonds. Liabilities are any form of debt and property taxes. Financial assets and real estate have been gamed for decades, providing unearned, undeserved wealth to many. The bailouts and stimulus of 2009 deepened this injustice as they exploded *net worth* by $27 trillion – a massive amount of *something-*

for-nothing paid in fabricated financial assets derived from Federal Reserve activity.

Nobel economist Joseph Stiglitz suggested that the banks should fail. Instead, the government imposed a policy of *financial repression* to finance government debt in favorable terms, which sucked capital out of the private sector and destroyed jobs. The Federal Reserve set the *real* interest rate below zero by insuring that inflation was greater than their offered rate, which chased capital into the government sector. The artificial inflation of *net worth*, *financial repression*, and *gamed income arrangements* combined constitute one of the greatest swindles in history. If the "economic justice" or "social justice" that institutionalists proclaim is to be attained, they would have to go after standing *net worth* in financial assets and real estate, or the income of the *gaming class* – not the future income of the baby boomers' children who have already been robbed by their parents' irresponsible government debt.

And how can Americans even get a chance to be robbed blind by the government? Education does not guarantee success. Modern education scams have robbed the youth, delayed family creation, and exploded spending on education and training to over $1.5 trillion. As of 2015 there is also $1.3 trillion in outstanding college debt while 49% of recent college graduates are underemployed, 41% make less than $25,000, and only 17% of them make over $50,000. The prospect of education leading to "the American dream" is dismal at best.

If we reject all of the economic fallacies, and employ the relevant concepts of income and prosperity analysis, we arrive at a measure called *lifetime prosperity (LP)*, which is a comprehensive model for individual prosperity over the course of a person's life. *LP Income* includes all annual consumption plus the person's change in net worth. *Consumption* includes all the items consumed by the person – unearned resources, welfare, government resources, business resources substituted for individual needs (like business meals), fringe benefits, subsidies, paychecks, royalties, advantages from regulatory boons, gifts, food bought by spouses and parents, and illicitly acquired resources.

The prosperity that an individual enjoys in a given year is their *LP Income* plus the *wealth* they had access to in that year. *Wealth* includes *financial accounts*, *property holdings*, and *shared access*. *Financial accounts* are stocks, retirement income accounts, retirement healthcare accounts, trust funds, inheritance, pensions, savings, education accounts, debts and negative financial accounts. *Property holdings* include real estate, cars and other vehicles, amenities, furniture, jewelry, durable goods, and any other material thing in the possession of the individual. *Shared access* is personal access to a share of earned or unearned communal or state property such as living with a friend, parent, or other person who pays the bills, or a government or institutional program not yet elected but available based on the special status of the individual.

LP Income and *wealth* alone are not sufficient to determine a person's prosperity. We must calculate their *tax balance*, which is their *tax avoidance* minus their *tax burden*. If the tax balance is negative, then they contributed to government and if it is positive, then they got an advantage that others must pay tax on if the laws did not privilege one form of consumption over another. *Tax avoidance* is the tax that would be charged on what a person has consumed through untaxed channels such as fringe benefits and divorce alimony. It also includes tax exemptions on standing wealth such as shared access resources that are maintained by other people. A person's *tax burden* is the combined tax on their consumption, wealth, financial account income (capital gains), and all income-related tax.

With these factors combined, we finally have a measure that poverty hustlers, socialists, and many institutionalists imply with their visions and rhetoric, but never justify with their numbers. *Lifetime Prosperity* takes a person's accrued *LP Income*, combined with their age-weighted *wealth* during each year of their life, and their aggregated *tax balance* for each year of their life. It shows us a person's total individual prosperity from birth through their current age. Accurate claims about *prosperity distribution* cannot be made without using this model.

Economic sovereignty is a glimmering hope that all Americans desire, but few can articulate. Without an accurate portrayal of the economy,[225] knowledge of the warring ideologies that violate *economic sovereignty*,[226] and concepts of prosperity analysis,[227] the glimmering hope will never become reality. A large government, institutions, private cartels, or even a mob-like activist electorate can combine to violate individuals, as they have done to create the modern economic quagmire. *Argument-to-moderation* was once employed by Adolph Hitler very successfully. Today, the wise path for our economy is not served by any centrist position. The truth has been obscured by all common discourse. Replacing this common discourse with the concepts of prosperity analysis is a giant leap towards the path of wisdom that can lead us away from the darkness of parasitism in which we have lived for decades.

---

[225] Chapter 1: American Socioeconomic Indications & Warnings

[226] Chapter 2: The Institutionalist Creed

[227] Chapter 3: Inequality, Wrath, and Envy by Diktat

Chapter 4: Onwards to Economic Sovereignty

§ 4.1 Schematics of the Robotic Nurse

"To take from one, because it is thought his own industry and that of his fathers has acquired too much, in order to spare to others, who, or whose fathers, have not exercised equal industry and skill, is to violate arbitrarily the first principle of association, the <u>guarantee</u> to everyone the free exercise of his industry and the fruits acquired by it." –*Thomas Jefferson*[228]

The metropolis of institutionalists is a *robotic nurse* that tranquilizes citizens into codependency and serfdom. Its *compulsory liberty*[229] violates the first principle of association, as described by Thomas Jefferson. Consequently, those who pursue the intent of FDR's Second Bill of Rights and the communist Soviet Constitution cannot call themselves Americans. They are the original inventors of the *robotic nurse* that divorces human beings from their self-agency, nature, and liberty. But when people are relieved of the things that make them human, they become deranged, and they need to escape from the frustrations of being inhuman.

The *robotic nurse* mechanically dispenses whatever pain reliever the patient prefers – narcotics, alcohol, entertainment-obsession, over-socialization, religious fanaticism, wanderlust, promiscuity, or anthropomorphism (ascribing human features to animals). The founders of the United States gave America a system that optimized liberty and productivity. The *robotic nurse* uses its financial parasitism to maximize instant gratification, luxury, and vice. The more that citizens suckle from its lifeless, cold-steel teats, the more deranged they become. Eventually, nothing seems to satisfy them, and by the time their hallucinations end, the *robotic nurse* has stolen most of their lives.

---

[228] (Jefferson, 1816)

[229] § 2.2 Visions and Nations: Continental Europe vs. America

This corrupt social dynamic is inseparable from the economic atmosphere. Economic freedom preserves personal freedom. The pervasive attitude of entitlement, arrogance, envy, and wrath necessarily eroded *economic sovereignty*. The robotic nurse was the *raison d'être* and crowning "achievement" of the institutionalists. With total control of the culture, their mechanical creature was nearly uncontested. But its greatest enemy is within the chest of every human being – the valor, virtue, and willful self-reliance that the angels on our shoulders persistently whisper into our ears. This is an opponent that the robotic nurse will never defeat, and it is the sleeping giant that will crush the institutionalists in time.

In all cases, we can say that the institutionalist arrangements violate *economic sovereignty* and are thusly un-American. Most American institutionalists are strictly misled. Deep inside, they desire economic sovereignty like the *valorists*, but they do not have a prayer to access it for numerous reasons. Their consciences are manipulated by the poverty hustlers,[230] even if their intuition tells them that they are living in a highly egalitarian, "socialist" society.[231] They are completely misled on the economic history of America,[232] and how the nation compares to the world.[233] The ideological visions that form their assumptions about the world are divided between a fake left (Democrat) and right (Republican) dichotomy, when the real ideology is somewhere along a continuum between *institutionalists* and *valorists*.[234]

If it seems as if America is polarized and unrecognizable from its past, it is because institutionalist ideology is anathema to the design of America, but has been the increasingly prevailing ideology for decades.[235] Whether by accident or by deception, institutionalists have created economic fairy tales that have become prevalent public

---

[230] § 1.2 Prosperity, Poverty, and Destitution
[231] § 1.1 Redistribution of Blood, Sweat, and Merit
[232] § 1.3 American Prosperity by the Numbers
[233] § 1.4 America vis-à-vis the World
[234] § 2.1 Institutionalists versus Valorists
[235] § 2.2 Visions and Nations: Continental Europe vs. America

Thomas E. Kurek

opinions, and those opinions hamper productivity.[236] [237] Understanding the concepts of *prosperity analysis* will help citizens to protect themselves from the manipulations of the politicians and activists who give the robotic nurse its oil changes.[238] The prosperity concepts immediately falsify beliefs in income inequality and wealth disparity.[239] They also reveal counterintuitive compensation for major career paths.[240]

In the beginning of this book, the story of Cato demonstrated that the *rich* and *poor* alike are obtaining unprecedented levels of *something-for-nothing*, in many different forms.[241] The system of *ubiquitous redistribution* consumes *forced labor* of workers through obscure taxes, regulatory costs, social, and institutional processes. That system encourages wasteful activity, and inspires a therapeutic social order to cover up the misery that comes with parasitic living. Citizens disown responsibility and seek scapegoats, and it is hard to discern the self-reliant from the mollycoddled or the meritorious from the privileged. The privileged are not necessarily wealthy people, but anyone who is living off of the productivity of other people instead of their own toils.

The institutionalist society obscures accurate measurement of value, divorces productivity from remuneration, and collectivizes the output of labor. *Freedom of opportunity* is sacrificed on the altar of *equal outcome*. The intellectual poison is so hallucinogenic that the institutionalists cannot correctly perceive the terrible level of equality that already exists. They clamor for even more power and redistribution to "solve" the problems that they created.

Accurate definitions help us to discern truth, but institutionalists peddle over thirty propagandistic phrases for *class warfare* – known as the *buzzwords of poverty hustling*. Poverty activism induces the audience to form beliefs about *prosperity incidence*, but their claims are distorted by various omissions. Americans who are "under the

---

[236] § 2.3 The Institutionalist Fantasy Economy

[237] § 2.4 Institutionalists and Old Ideas Posing as Progressive

[238] § 3.1 Concepts and Limitations of Prosperity Analysis

[239] § 3.2 Manufactured Income Equality

[240] § 3.3 Illusory Career Paths and Wealth Erosion

[241] § 1.1 Redistribution of Blood, Sweat, and Merit

poverty line," spend 2.6x the income that they report – so a person reporting only $15,000 actually spent $39,000 after all of their subsidies are counted.

Prosperity is defined as success in material terms alone, but *poverty hustlers* love to brainwash people with poetic specializations of poverty to confuse the economic discourse. They will speak of things like the "poverty" of spirit, family, morality, or love. In truth, those are social dysfunctions that redistribution and money cannot ameliorate, and that many rich people also suffer. Ancient wisdom says, "whoever desires is always poor," and that is enough to halt poetic poverty distortion in its tracks.

Destitution is the antithesis of prosperity. A destitute person lacks adequate shelter, food, or clothing. Very few Americans are destitute, despite the outrageous exaggerations of the poverty hustlers. The *destitute* in America only suffer because of the wasteful redistribution to the *imaginary poor* class. Even worse, the poverty hustlers fill the heads of the most vulnerable people with desires that go beyond satisfactory human needs, thereby inculcating envy and wrath. Poverty is the natural state of mankind and does not need to be explained. All that needs to be done for everyone's poverty to increase is for consumption to exceed production. When people are not using their life to produce, they are regressing themselves and their neighbors to the natural state of mankind. Superfluous redistribution exacerbates real poverty, as the extra money is spent on vices and enablers of poverty.

American abundance could not be clearer when around 99% of Americans have enough food to eat, reasonable access to medical care, no chance of a single night of homelessness, and 20% of middle class people are using welfare just for perks. Destitution is between 0.5 and 1.0%, while statistically-imagined poverty is 14.3% (an exaggeration of 14.3 – 28.6x). Not only is destitution rare in America, but our economic history shows undeniable prosperity at the national level. Large governments, service economies, high wages and profits, steady savings and investments, growth in private fixed assets, explosion of invention, growing cultural infrastructure, housing growth and quality, and increased spending on discretionary goods are all impossible without broad national prosperity.

America has demonstrated all of these indications over the past century. Our success at lifting people out of poverty is unprecedented in human history. Short of a total system breakdown, it is unlikely that America will see the kind of poverty observed during Dustbowl or the Great Depression. Unfortunately, modern institutionalist policies have thwarted the liberty, capitalism, profits, innovation, competition, small government, and voluntary cooperation that gave rise to our prosperity.[242]

Comparing America to itself over time is very helpful, but we also must compare America to the world, in our quest to present American economic progress accurately. Frequently, people use their own unreliable experiences from travel or foreign residency to compare foreign nations. Even a person living in a city for their entire life will have a limited conception of what life is like for their millions of neighbors. Our personal experiences can paint an atypical or emblematic picture in our own minds. So we must compare American data to the world's data in order to have an accurate assessment of America versus "the world."

The first revelation is that America has created more prosperity, innovation, and quality of living in the shortest time compared to the world. America is truly exceptional by the numbers. Foreign societies have failed to use their abundant resources and labor as productively because of environmental disadvantages, political and cultural inadequacy. On the other hand, in the last decades, America has increasingly pursued the same institutionalist policies that have hampered the rest of the world. Currently, America still leads "the world" in nearly every meaningful indicator, but its policies of destructionism, consumption of capital, malinvestment, retrogressed culture, increasing redistribution, and crushing civic expenditure has allowed the rest of the world to begin catching up.[243]

Overall, the American socioeconomic indicators and warnings do not bode well. Merit, honor, justice, and accurate valuation mean little in the institutionalist economy, overwhelmed by a $10 trillion civic empire filled with regulations, progressive taxation, welfare, subsidies, combined charities that exceed the entire food and energy

---

[242] § 1.3 American Prosperity by the Numbers

[243] § 1.4 America vis-à-vis the World

markets, black & grey markets, crime, litigiousness (from over one-million lawyers), cronyism, meaningless credentials, hypocritical discrimination of diversity policies, cultural Marxism, and political correctness. The equality-of-outcome utopia imagined by socialists is as close as it could ever be, as workers of all types essentially have access to the same lifestyles, and this equality imposed by the civic empire is economically and socially destructive. The inter-subjectivity of pricing goods and services is fully corrupted by the radical egalitarianism and interventionist policies.

Meanwhile, poverty activists in the entertainment, journalism, religious, civic, and education industries flood conversations with the *buzzwords of poverty hustling*, inducing false beliefs in prosperity incidence. The modern notion of poverty is so distorted as to be meaningless. Massive welfare payments have given American "poor" people more prosperity than many college graduates. These massive levels of redistribution are intelligible from carefully demystified prosperity incidence statistics that respect income, subsidies, amenities, non-cash benefits, spending, and access to resources. Evaluating destitution and prosperity throughout history and geography should be enough to dispel illusions of American poverty.

Poverty hustlers bemoan government spending on things they do not like, but their lamentation of underfunded education, research, military, welfare, savings, and "greedy" corporate profits is a theatrical performance of Shakespearean proficiency. Either these areas have stayed the same, or they have grown monstrously. The government is even taking twice the amount of tax as they were during struggles for national survival such as the world wars and great depression. The modern American civic empire does not follow the communist model of socialism – direct state ownership. It is actually invoking some hybrid of French dirigisme, indicative planning, and zwangswirtschaft (command economy) introduced by Germans a few generations before Hitler, and adopted by fascists around the world. The government does not have to directly own industry in the zwangswirtschaft socialism pattern. It uses regulation, subsidies, intimidation, regulatory capture, monetary policy, and other manipulations to force companies to do as the government pleases.

Thomas E. Kurek

By most economic standards, America is exceptional in almost every way, but the signs of social retrogression, profligacy, and destructionism are also apparent from economic indicators. The world is catching up to America as we are mired in malinvestment and voracious consumption which exceeds production. America is in an undeniable managed decline, but this does not change what we have achieved, and how we did it. The facts of our history show a stunning victory of capitalism for the poor and destitute, with prosperity that socialists have only grasped at with miserable or deadly outcomes.

In light of the economic reality, how can the majority of politicians, professors, and journalists present such distorted economic claims? Their biases come from their visions of humanity and the world – which are not drawn along clean leftwing and rightwing politics. *Visions* comprise our intuitive sense of how the world works – they are the silent shapers of our thoughts (social, moral, cultural, political, economic, or religious). The significantly competing ideologies are *institutionalism* and *valorism*. Although these visions are not often articulated even to ourselves, all people operate somewhere between the two.

An *institutionalist* has an *unconstrained vision* of mankind. Their tagline is, "Man is born free; and everywhere he is in chains." He believes that mankind is malleable and must be changed with collective power. Consequently, men are not naturally at odds with each other and the roots of human suffering are bad education and social arrangements. They see institutions as both the problems and solutions – blaming failures of individuals on scapegoats, demonizing their institutional opposition, and seeking total control of institutional power and influence. They will use the institutions to impose *solutions* and achieve *general, grandiose goals* such as eliminating poverty. This makes them prone to believe that newer things are inherently better (*neophilia*), and that the "progress" of humanity is undeniable, priming their slogans with terms like "forward," "progress," and "the future."

Institutionalists prioritize peoples' *intention, credentials*, and *conformity* while they pursue their *solutions* instead of *tradeoffs*. They seek special causes of *suffering*, in things like war, poverty, and crime. To them, economic and social intervention is *essential*.

They aim to *directly* influence outcomes with surrogate decision making, economic planning, politically correct shaming, kangaroo courts, arbitrary and contradictory legal interpretations, and aggressive judicial activism. Their quest to concentrate power amongst experts and institutions comes from their belief that knowledge is centralized in experts and institutions. The self-educated man is anathema and they seek persuasion and consensus in their activities. The institutionalist builds a status-based society that is impressed by awards, recognition, credentials, degrees, and certifications.

To the institutionalist, the problems of people are due to external factors, so they are concerned with excuses for deficiencies instead of prudence. They will seek *special knowledge* that is institutionally-affirmed by experts and consensus, but when they are uncertain, they will defer to their *imagination*. Their impetus to *control*, *prescribe*, and *exhort* attracts *ideologically irreligious* and *insecure religious* people whose worldviews provide psychological escape into a *hopeful future* from *fearful histories*. They are *idealists* who want to feel *security*. Political ideologies that have emerged from institutionalist visions include socialism, progressivism, neoconservatism, fascism, communism, Peronism, corporatism (all but kinship and communitarian), French dirigisme and indicative planning, German idealism, German SPD, democratic socialism, the Jacobin Club (French revolutionary thought), Islamists, and most Democrats.

The notion that Islamists are regressive and backwards-looking in all aspects is absurd. They envision a necessarily better future unified by Islamic collusion with the power of state. Likewise, fascism is derived from guild socialism, and confused professors associate its historical symbolism for genuine adherence to tradition even has Hitler pointed to the Übermensch and a new dawn of mankind with materialist and socialist principles. The invocation of reactionary history in propaganda and by extreme elements is betrayed by the actual policies and governmental agendas of fascists and Islamists. They have shopping malls, credit cards, internet, long-range missiles, and increasing participation of women in their workforces. This is one of many cases where rightwing and leftwing categories fail to unify ideology. The institutionalist and valorist ontology succeeds.

Thomas E. Kurek

Opposing the institutionalists throughout history are the *valorists* who have a *constrained vision* of mankind – asserting that the nature of mankind is fixed, flawed, and always operates within those constraints. Their tagline is "the perfect is the enemy of the good," which is reflected in Aristotle's golden mean, the writings of Confucius, Shakespeare's King Lear, and the Pareto principle. Men are naturally at odds with each other because of egocentricity and sin, so the roots of human suffering are innate within every individual. Consequently, it is vain and pointless to even try to change human nature. Instead, we should seek to better understand our nature and optimize the situation. *Valorists* only wish to use institutions with checks and balances to achieve *specific, limited goals* such as assisting distressed people.

Seeing all human experience as rooted in history and nature, *valorists* encourage patience, endurance, and prudence – they are prone to *stoicism*. They care little for intentions and credentials. They prioritize peoples' *results*, *tests*, and *direct competition*. They pursue *tradeoffs* and optimizations instead of solutions, and seek special causes of *triumph*, such as peace, wealth, and law-abidance. A valorist sees economic and social intervention as questionable, instead, aiming to *indirectly influence social and economic results* through social processes like liberty, rule of law, representative power, tradition, freedom of opportunity, free markets, and corporate business governance. They advocate decentralized power, viewing knowledge as dispersed amongst experienced individuals who specialize. To the valorist, a self-educated man is ideal, while precision and accuracy trump persuasion and consensus.

Valorists are not impressed by credentials and status, aiming for a *discretion-based society*, where individuals are judged by unique demonstration, rugged individualism, independence, self-reliance, and personal responsibility. They do not presume how far people can go, or the reasons for their failures. Contrarily, they encourage the individual to make the most of their conditions at all times. Their ideal knowledge is *mundane* – that which has demonstrative consequence in the real world, and justified by reason, evidence, and results. When they are uncertain, they defer to *tradition* instead of their imagination. The valorist's impetus to compete, let go, live and let die, and defer attracts *survival-of-the-fittest irreligious* people and *conscientious religious* people who affirm an *unguaranteed future*, and *triumphant histories*. They are *realists* who want to feel *liberated*. Political ideologies that have emerged from the valorist vision include federal republic, commercial republic, fiscal conservatism, classical liberalism, federalists, corporatists (kinship and communitarian only), cold warriors, social conservatism, Tory, constitutionalists, Whig, some Republicans, and some libertarians.

An artifact of the institutionalist vision is *scientism* – in which the scientific method is corruptly applied to subjective inquiries. Mass media and cultural leaders use *scientism* to manufacture consent for their agendas, and only traditional historical analysis, critical thinking, and evidence can counteract it. Because of the domination of institutionalist visions for the past century, the world is swimming in scientism. We are also swimming in their schools of economics – Marxist, Keynesian, and Institutionalist. The *valorists* support the Classical and Austrian schools of economics. Although distributism is not a valid school of economics, since it refuses to formulate, it is based upon the unconstrained vision while claiming to moderate negative effects with distributed institutional action. As such, it necessarily leads to institutionalist economic approaches. Catholic and social justice advocates of distributism should abandon this fallacious economic disposition and instead, prioritize grace and truth described in John 1:14 as the imperative, which begs for realism.

Ideological visions are not constrained to segments of society. Entire nations have been built upon visions. The U.S. forefathers wrote valorist principles into the Constitution and Federalist Papers. They rejected centralized power and gave us checks and balances so that the government could avoid totalitarianism. By contrast, French revolutionary thought and German idealism created large governments, aggressive taxation, and strong centralized power from the institutionalist visions. Progressives and socialists sometimes give lip service to balance of powers and competition, but they do everything they can to circumvent it. Modern institutionalist Presidents have used copious executive actions to circumvent congress – including executive orders, executive memoranda, and presidential policy directives.

Socialist intellectuals of the Frankfurt School introduced the Orwellian terminology of *positive liberty*. In truth, it should be called *compulsory liberty*, oxymoronically, since it is actually *compulsory government service* at the expense of *forced labor* and *seized assets*. There is no liberty in that arrangement. Compulsory liberty creates an array of entitlements. Consequently, institutionalists claim that actual liberty, freedom, and rights are *negative liberties*. Actual liberty makes a person free to do something, and compels the government to defend that freedom; that is, the *defense of permitted actions*. A compulsory liberty entitles people to something, and the government must provide it — an *imposition of mandated actions*. These two concepts could not be more foreign to each other, for any human being with a shred of integrity.

Essentially, *valorists* reject the notion of *compulsory liberty* and only accept actual *liberty* as a valid role of government. Institutionalists promote compulsory liberty and frequently restrict actual liberty. Examples of actual liberty include free speech, religion, petition, press, assembly, privacy, keeping and bearing weapons, self-incrimination, due process, compensation for public seizure of property, trial by jury, fair punishment, state and local authority, voting (suffrage), equal protection under the law, and *voluntary* servitude. Examples of compulsory liberty include compulsory healthcare, entertainment, education and training, jobs, housing, retirement, guaranteed market prices, minimum wage, maximum wage, food, compulsory military or government service, housing subsidies, cell phone subsidies, energy subsidies, childcare, refugee support, family intervention, and coerced community service.

Institutionalists always deceive people by calling their *compulsory liberties* "free," as in "free healthcare," or "free college." *Valorists* assert that these entitlements are never "free." Wherever the money comes from, it translates to *forced labor* or *seized assets* of citizens. The institutionalists claim that compulsory liberty saves money on marketing and that centralization improves quality, price, innovation, and expansion better than competition and profit. Valorists insist that every entitlement still must obey the laws of economics — scarcity, rationing, and competition. Consequently, competition optimizes quality and price, while profit optimizes innovation and expansion. Imposition of compulsory liberty erodes those superior processes.

Compulsory liberties come from institutionalist visions of mankind and the world. Chapter ten of the Soviet Constitution is filled with compulsory liberties, but communists are not alone in the quest. In 1944, FDR proposed a Second Bill of Rights which contained many of the same compulsory liberties mandated by the communists. Since then, they have been imposed through incremental legislation. FDR, Lyndon Johnson, and Obama advanced those policies more than other Presidents. American institutionalists will continue to use civic power across the board to advance compulsory liberty through legislation. The valorist opposition is very simple – they will insist that it is unjust, it is less effective than actual *liberty*, it will explode prices, it will kill innovation and quality, and it will always hurt more people than it helps in the long term. They will also argue that it is un-American, based on our Constitution and statements such as the Thomas Jefferson quote at the beginning of this section.

Why should we study ideological visions so comprehensively in an economics pursuit? The answer is simple – in complete contravention to the economic history evidenced by the numbers, institutionalist visions and political theories have led to their completely delusional economic opinions. Their most glaring insanity is shrugging off the $10 trillion cost of American civics (federal, state, local tax, regulatory costs, and nonprofit activity), while they demand more tax and civic power. During the same year, total U.S. productivity (GDP) was only $16 trillion, and all American income from labor and investments was only $9 to $11 trillion! A civic power that controls as much income as all American earners combined is an insufferable tyranny.

Institutionalist views on education would bring Noah Webster back from the dead to perform the lead role in a ghostly horror film of vengeance. They bemoan education quality and access but blame it on budgets that are too small. They hail the 1960s as the golden age of education, and blame corporations for unemployed college graduates, demanding college loan bailouts and tax-funded college education. In reality, there is more money than ever in education and training with a 300% increase since the 1960s. Overpriced college is a result of the easy loans and government subsidies pushed by institutionalists in the first place.

Thomas E. Kurek

The quality of education is depressed by their social engineering schemes, curriculum changes, patronization of ineffectual students, and indoctrination agendas. Corporations and consumers are not responsible for the mismatch between knowledge and productive work. Overfunded education that incentivizes impractical courses of study created the unemployed graduates. In a pure fit of tyranny, they suggest raiding the taxpayer's pockets to bail out their poorly chosen college loans, instead of going to the people who took their money. The universities and professors should refund their defrauded customers if the services are deemed unsatisfactory.

Institutionalist education corruption is on par with the distortion of the energy and environmental industries. A citizen might wonder if there are any scientists and businessmen left who have been operating without conflicts of interest. The institutionalists have apocalyptic visions of climate change, pollution, and animal extinction. They think oil companies profiteer and use government subsidies and they are passionate about conservation, land management, biodiversity, and anthropomorphism. Institutionalist environmentalists advocate increased taxes and regulations to improve energy and environment. In reality, everyone wants cheaper energy and clean environments, but the approach for valorists always entails tradeoffs and optimization instead of idealistic gambits.

In 2009, the Clean Energy and Security Act proposed by Democrats would have taken 5-10% of Americans' net income, paid to lawyers, bureaucrats, managers, nonprofits, and energy companies. Republicans blocked that monstrosity, but the United States already has similar swindles at the local level. Thirty-three states and Washington D.C. adopted a Renewable Portfolio Standard (RPS) that punishes fossil fuel and incentivizes companies to spend their money on Renewable Energy Certificates (RECs). The cost of that useless piece of paper is passed on to energy customers. In fact, these schemes rob people every time they buy something. Manufacturing, warehousing, retail, and commercial real estate are forced to pass on the higher energy costs to consumers through higher prices or reduced quality.

In further insult to the middle class, green energy plans rob them twice, by subsidizing low-income energy bills, exacerbating the burden on people with a net positive tax burden. To wit, German and Spanish green energy have been economic disasters. As usual, institutionalists do not learn lessons of failure from each other because their imaginations and egos prevail.

In truth, there is nothing inherently wrong with green energy if it was developed with fair market procedures. Energy companies should approach consumers and ask for normal investments to pay for their infrastructure, and the citizen should receive corresponding ownership in corporate stocks and bonds from the energy company. The technologies are conceptually attractive, but must be constrained by respect for reality. For instance, expansion of public transportation with subways and buses is economically and environmentally inferior to software-optimized decentralized ride sharing.

But institutionalist education, energy, and environmental delusions pale in comparison to their disruption of personnel. A prevalent and poorly-understood sociological trend has wreaked havoc on labor markets. *Cultural Marxists* divide the population into groups that can be exploited to increase institutional power. Modern targets are women, immigrants, religious minorities, non-white races, and homosexuals. Current scapegoats for cultural Marxists are conservatives (ideology), whites (race), Christians (religion), entrepreneurs, executives, business owners (economics), men and traditional women (gender), and traditional suburban families (family unit organization).

Cultural Marxists use the process of *identity segregation*, with the mass psychology of fear, guilt, shame, and identity crises to induce their targets to separate themselves from other groups based upon egoistic identification. This instigates social groups to fight each other and blame each other for their perceived collective problems. *Political correctness* (PC) is the social self-censorship that locks in the hypocritical standards of the cultural Marxists. A full understanding of *cultural Marxists* (also known as Social Justice Warriors) is beyond the scope of this book. It requires a basis in *transculturation, dialectal materialism*, Antonio Gramsci's communist principles of *cultural hegemony*, and The Frankfurt School's *critical theory*.

Thomas E. Kurek

The economic impact of cultural Marxism is what concerns us here. Essentially, it poisons the sociological basis for peaceful and mission-oriented cooperation that business thrives upon by atomizing society into aggrieved *identity groups*. This increases the disutility of labor – our will to avoid work activities. The *utility of labor* is motivated by three *indirect pleasures* – ulterior motives, achievement pride, and positive incentives. The ultimate goal is to maximize positive incentives for labor, and people without ulterior motives tend to do that.

The cultural Marxists' preoccupation with commiserating comrades in their identity groups fills their heads with ulterior motives. This process also eliminates the capacity for self-criticism and growth and leads to skepticism of outgroup-people, reduced mission-orientation, antisocial attitudes, wrathful ulterior motives, scapegoats for setbacks, prejudiced business deals, constrained options, and prioritization of factors irrelevant to business. So cultural Marxists set up their aggrieved identity groups for self-sabotage in their careers and this is devastating to everyone's voluntary cooperation and objective work. Identity segregation transforms dysfunctional social paranoia into negative economic impact within labor markets. *Diversity* programs claim to fight discrimination, but they impose the same negative effects that exist when there is proven discrimination.

The institutionalist creed gives rise to many economic fallacies and social dysfunctions. In America, this creed currently dominates education, entertainment, journalism, civics, and half of the religious institutions. These five cultural industries gain ideological conformity and lack serious competition in the institutionalist society. They rely upon false beliefs in centrism and argument-to-moderation fallacy, such as "the truth is always somewhere in the middle," in order to distort the definitions of *moderate* and *extreme*. If popular consensus dictates what is moderate, then Etruscan human sacrifice and Iroquois Indian cannibalism were *moderate* norms in their time and place. Instead, if we set our standard as the U.S. Constitution, reason, evidence, virtues, and classical history, then the institutionalists are always the extremists, and they will always be, no matter how popular their influence becomes.

With the accurate depiction of the United States economy elucidated, and with the fictitious institutionalist story dispelled, we can understand how *prosperity analysis* itself has been distorted in modern institutionalist societies. The *concepts of prosperity* analysis are straightforward. *Wealth is not income*; it is surplus. Profligate spending choices prevent people from acquiring wealth. The people who consume unearned or un-monetized resources can earn much less than people who must pay for the same things in cash. Average American net worth (wealth) has increased, while the net worth disparity for the top 1-2% of the population has declined 30% since the 1970s. Household statistics deceive the public on wealth disparity. "Rich" houses have twice as many people and five times as many earners as "poor" houses. Another distortion of wealth comes from the fact that capital gains from investments held for long periods of time actually lose money to inflation, but they are taxed and reported as if they did not.

Zero-sum imagination corrupts institutionalist prosperity analysis. In reality, wealth is not distributed like cutting a piece of pie (the zero-sum fallacy). One person with more wealth is not necessarily taking from everyone else – one man's gain is not necessarily another man's loss. Goods and services are actually created or destroyed, rightfully owned or usurped (in part or whole), and well-purposed or misallocated. Wealth is *produced*; it does not just exist *somehow*. Goods and services are only under-valued or over-valued when there was coercion involved in the exchange or production. Zero-sum believers aim for an improper transfer of ownership – they are guilty of that which they accuse, using government redistribution, market manipulation, crime, monetary inflation, financial repression, and economic intervention.

Advocating *level playing fields* is another great deception in prosperity analysis. If the field was curated with liberty, contractual agreement, and fair marketplace exchange process, it is already optimized. The attempt to "level the playing field" by imposing more congruent outcomes creates chaos, malinvestment, and wasted human activity and resources. Equal outcome is unjust to maintain and even impossible to approximate. Equal opportunity is better, but freedom of opportunity is the best. Because of biological differences, environmental exposure, accident of birth, and the combined choices people have made their entire lives, nobody

Thomas E. Kurek

will ever be the same. That diversity is an asset when peaceful and voluntary cooperation is allowed. Attempts to create *equal opportunity* will necessarily reduce *freedom of opportunity* because it robs the many to artificially advantage the few.

The exclusion of *unaccounted resources* from prosperity analysis is perhaps one of the greatest sources of false conclusions. People with significant unaccounted resources pursue lower income, because they can afford to. They show up in income statistics as much poorer than they actually are. Wage-heavy compensation cannot avoid tax, and it is fully counted in the statistics. Meanwhile, unaccounted resources are very large considerations, but difficult to quantify. There are six types of unaccounted resources. *Previously-earned resources* are time-varying items that give advantage to one class of consumer in the past or present. For instance, an elderly person who paid off their house appears poor in the income statistics, but they could be better-off than a young person making twice their income. It was infinitely easier for them to cover their biggest expenses, compared to their children, due to increasing corruption of the real estate markets over time.

There are two kinds of *state-redistributed resources*. *Welfare* is what people assume – handouts from the government of almost anything that can be imagined. Much of welfare and state subsidies are not accounted for as personal income or wealth for the people who consume them. Welfare recipients spend 2.6x more than their reported income, so they appear much poorer in the statistics than they actually are in real life. *Corporate welfare* is the other kind of state-redistributed resource. It is any government regulation, subsidy, or competitive advantage induced by law, resulting in unaccounted business resources for those who benefit – employees, investors, shareholders, and participating consumers.

Inherited resources are largely unaccounted. They include houses, college tuition, vehicles, trust funds, stocks, businesses, petty cash, car insurance, gas money, food money, etc. People consuming these boons from others in their lives have unaccounted wealth that their peers must earn for themselves. The providers of these *inherited resources* can be spouses, boyfriends, parents, family members, or friends. The beneficiary shows up as "poorer" in the income statistics than they actually are. This increases the appearance of inequality in the statistics. *Charitable resources* are the fifth type of unaccounted resources and they essentially include the same things as *welfare* and *inherited resources*, but they come from a private nonprofit.

Finally, *fringe benefits* round out the unaccounted resources that inflate claims of *inequality*. In addition to not being counted very well, they mostly provide the recipient with the additional value of tax avoidance. That tax avoidance should be counted as income, since others consuming the same things must not only pay for the boons with their counted income, but they also must pay tax on that income. *Fringe benefits* include per diem travel payments, health care, vision care, dental care, company meals, retirement and pension financing, life insurance, end of life care, paid time off, sick leave, maternal leave, paternal leave, education and training reimbursement, overtime pay, unemployment benefits, workers compensation, fitness, and hazard pay.

What would phony economic visions be without total confusion of real people and categories of people? Confusing annual snapshots of categorical income with flesh-and-blood people is a great misconception. A third of the people with low lifetime income make the top level of income during a good year. An enormous portion of income inequality is created by normal things in life: job experience (age) and irregular income (investment payouts, house sales, inheritance, and sales commissions). Job experience comes with age, and older people with greater experience are paid more, because they have higher productivity. The *job-experience (age) income inequality* Gini Ratio has ranged from 0.19 to 0.27 from 1967 to 2014. This is almost half the value that *poverty hustlers* peddle in their bogus statistics.

Injecting intangibles into economic policies is not only a task of propagandistic poverty hustlers. There is a formalized field called *happiness economics* that makes a fake science of it. The practice is a farce because measuring happiness on a universal scale is impossible due to extreme subjectivity, even within the same human being from year-to-year. It is another example of *scientism* amongst institutionalists. Their collection of happiness data only measures the relative placation of the population at a current moment in time, which would only be useful to institutionalists who are trying to use power to placate the population to begin with.

A valorist would assert that prosperity and happiness should never be conflated. At most we can say that Maslow 1 (physiological) and Maslow 2 (security) deficiencies universally degrade happiness. But in a prosperous society where Maslow 1 & 2 needs are nearly universally satisfied, happiness indicators are tenuous at best. Economics measures *scarce resources* with *alternative uses* – labor, time, raw materials, and goods of varied orders. *Rationing* and *competition* are features of every economy, despite the control processes (socialism, capitalism, dirigisme, anarchy). The question is which system optimizes the use of the resources. Those who inject intangibles into these analyses are out for political manipulation – not discovering truth.

Despite these facts, intangibles are certainly peripheral to economics. The inter-subjectivity of pricing in economics, makes it a subjective system. When people exchange – setting prices and agreeing to pay prices – they are making these choices based upon their own intangible values. Pricing and buying is like grading school essays – it is not like calculating a formula. *Currency interference*, including inflation, quantitative easing, and financial repression, rejiggers this subjective valuation of millions by changing the value of capital to favor government choices. And government experts are horrible at making those choices for other people. The economic planning by a handful of elites, operating with overriding intangibles in their minds, is a very dangerous and destructive arrangement, which has caused the collapse of socialist economies, and stagnant injustice in Western dirigiste economies for centuries. America is suffering these failures right now.

With the concepts of prosperity analysis in mind, it becomes easy to evaluate American income distribution. The statistics of *income inequality* are counterfeit and those who create and promote them are either liars or dupes. Their counterfeit methods include using *household income*, not correcting for *part-time labor*, and ignoring *taxation dynamics*, *welfare*, and *cost of living*. Their *household income* statistics are meaningless because houses do not make income – people do. Houses have different numbers of people and earners in them – the highest income quintile has twice as many people to feed and five times as many people earning money for the household, compared to the lowest quintile. Egregiously, they count the millions of part-time labor income recipients as equal to full-time labor. This part-time labor deception skews income statistics. A person who only works 20 hours a week and can still survive is not getting a raw deal. Jobs must be converted to Full-Time-Equivalents (FTE) for equal comparisons of earners.

The *taxation dynamics* of income inequality advocates are also skewed. Many income inequality statistics do not correct for all of the taxation that the government takes through all channels. Counting money that is given to the government and inaccessible to the earner is the height of deception for prosperity analysis. They also ignore significant portions of *redistribution and welfare.* Common income inequality statistics do not include all sources of government transfers. A "poor" household typically spends 2.6x its reported income, and this prosperity is excluded from the statistics. Perhaps the least discussed deception of income inequality advocates is the *cost of living adjustments* (COLA, related to Purchase Power Parity, PPP). Monetary value changes across time and space. In one location, money can buy the same things for less. The government acknowledges this with their per-diem payment schedules, which can vary in a single state like New York by nearly 300% for food and shelter. Income inequality statistics do not correct for this variation. Also, at one point in time, the same value of money is not worth as much because of inflation. Some income inequality statistics do not adjust for real inflation year-to-year.

If we correct for these counterfeit methods, we arrive at the Real Income Distribution (RID). It shows that the hockey-stick curve of income inequality is a gross falsehood – income distribution since 1984 is nearly flat, barely fluctuating, with a Gini Ratio hovering around 0.19. Poverty hustlers have inflated their claims of income inequality by 250-300%. The income inequality that results from working in more or less productive industries has plummeted since 1929 to an average of 0.07. A healthy society would have a much larger industrial income inequality because the real value of industries varies greatly. This is another indicator of the misallocation of capital in labor markets.

Job experience (age) income inequality has ranged from 0.19 to 0.27 since 1967 and averages at 0.23. Real income is affected by job experience and industry, but we cannot easily incorporate those into the Real Income Distribution. It is safe to say that when the effect of age and industry are considered for real income, we completely wipe out all income inequality, showing a regressive, socialistic income distribution that robs remuneration for productivity in whole. We are left with tyrannical equality, where income does not reflect the real value of jobs. Real Income Distribution should have a Gini Ratio that hovers around 0.35.

The sources of income gains are not encouraging for the economy. The government bailouts and stimulus response to the housing bust decreased real income for the lowest income quintile and increased income for the highest quintile. Everyone else's real income has stagnated since the housing bust. There are fewer workers per household since 1969, and they more often choose to live as unrelated individuals. The elderly had large income increases due to overly generous pension payments and corrupt real estate income. Small business income (S-corporations and partnerships) have shown large increases in income in the past decades. Income gains in the lower income quintiles have come from government redistribution instead of wages, while higher income earners have gained prosperity from pensions, benefits, and manipulated real estate markets.

One of the most absurd institutionalist claims is that government spending is just an "investment." Government projects will never be "investments." They have no reasonably calculated *return on investment* to pay down existing debt, and the *collateral* is not taken from those whom the programs directly benefit. This imposes *private gains* with *public losses*. Private parties are put in jail for the same schemes. Moreover, nobody can "borrow from the future," they can only force 30-to-50 year olds to pay for the profligacy of today. The amount of government debt forced upon Americans under the age of 50 is tyrannical.

Institutionalists are not even honest about the impact that their government action has upon citizens. There are many indirect consequences of taxes and regulations. Businesses have to treat tax and regulations as an expense, which translates to lost jobs, lost profits, lost benefits, lower wages, increased prices, lower quality of goods and services, and halted expansion plans. Regulations are hidden taxes, costing Americans $2 trillion per year through the price of the things they buy. Taxes and regulations can even cause businesses to shut down, or cancel products and services due to shortages or infeasibility. *Ad valorem taxes* greatly decrease the purchasing power of the poor and middle class, but they are ignored in prosperity distribution analysis. These are taxes "according to value" – property, sales, inheritance, expatriation, value-added, and tariffs. Renters pay property tax in the cost of their rent. Government spending, benefit-heavy jobs, and people living off of others get away with evading *ad valorem taxes.*

Counting payroll taxes is insufficient to account for all of the capital withheld from workers by government mandate. This outrageous manipulation greatly underestimates the amount of taxes taken from all Americans. To fix this problem we calculate the *income-related taxes.* They are all of the taxes that are levied upon every hour we work, directly and indirectly. Most Americans are familiar with the *payroll taxes* – they are the printed deductions on our paychecks. They include Federal Income Tax, Social Security Tax, Medicare, Medicaid, State Income Tax and Local Income Tax. *Employee taxes* are those which the government hides by charging them to our employers for every dollar they pay us. They include Social Security Employer Tax, Medicare & Medicaid Employer Tax, Federal Unemployment Tax (FUTA), Worker's Compensation Tax, State Unemployment Tax (SUTA), and Real Estate Tax on worker facilities.

Very few Americans take the time to calculate the tax on their transportation to-and-from work. These *transportation taxes* include State Gasoline Tax, Federal Gasoline Tax, Road Usage Tax & Tolls, and the portion of Property Tax used to fund public transportation and roads. We also use our phone and internet for work most of the time. There are significant *communication taxes* paid in the cost of those bills. With whatever money we have left, we must then pay *sales tax* when we buy many things. Low-income Americans pay huge amounts of *income-related tax*, but not enough to cover the welfare they use. Only 40% of Americans contribute to taxes beyond welfare payments to themselves or their neighbors.

Income distribution statistics and income-related tax analysis show that the American government has been a redistributive institutionalist hellhole for decades. The most dismal revelation comes from comparing this income scenario to national production. Using the income-related tax model on the data stated in *money income* and *personal income*, we explain the government's understatement of our taxation. According to personal income, the government only allows us to keep $3.3T of our income after the total cost of government and regulation. That leaves $24,397 for the working American, and $58,765 as the government burden on the earner.

This is effectively *forced labor* from January to September of every year. Revolutions have started for less. People simply do not perceive the financial tricks since they are comfortable for now. In 2013, Gross Domestic Product was $17 trillion, the cost of civics was $10 trillion, and the personal income of all Americans was $11.3 trillion. The tolerance of a government that spends more of our money than we do is destroying national wealth. Surplus per capita has plummeted, and our gross capital formation has lagged behind the world average for almost fifty years. We need more income inequality to incentivize the most productive work activity, and we need to obliterate the size of government to restore healthy economic processes.

Because of the interventions of the institutionalists, Americans have access to very similar prosperity outcomes. They eat at the same places, see the same doctors, and enjoy similar leisure. Variations in wealth occur less from productivity and talent than from family connections, government policies, tax, and life choices. The hardest-working and rarest talents in the labor market are being robbed with financial and regulatory tricks. This does not bode well for healthy labor markets. Dominated workers develop resentment and apathy.

Much talk is devoted to the "poor," "rich," and "middle class." As we have already demonstrated, income disparity in general is nonexistent in the whole. But can different career paths lead to higher prosperity? To find out, we must calculate the lifetime disposable income for different career paths including exceptional fringe benefits, equal living costs, progressive taxation, tax avoidance, and career-specific education and training costs. What emerges are the *five American socioeconomic labor classes.*

The *destitute* are less than one-percent of Americans who are truly poor, with insufficient food, shelter, and clothing. The *persistent* have high school or liberal arts college degrees. They are associates, technicians, agriculture workers, non-union blue collar workers, religious ministers, and unemployed people on welfare. The *robbed* were historically the best-compensated people from the mental rigor and rarity of intellect required for their work, but now they are completely robbed through regulations, government interventions, taxation, cartels, and offshoring. They are scientists, high technologists, engineers, mathematicians, economists, finance workers, and most lawyers.

The *gaming* have professions that use some kind of coercion to inflate their compensation, reduce labor competition, avoid taxes, and offload their compensation to benefits. They include union blue-collar workers, government employees, public school teachers, news anchors, and doctors. Their labor industry tactics are similar to the old patterns of guild socialism, syndicalism, and the zwangswirtschaft (command economy) of the fascists.

The "greedy" *wealthy* people stereotyped by professors and journalists alike are few and far between. They are rarely the corporate, suit-wearing, white men who seem to be a favorite scapegoat of hatred for the self-loathing institutionalist population at large. In reality, they are the *top* actors, artists, athletes, CEOs, investors, lawyers, surgeons, and aristocrats. The keyword is *"top."* Few people in those professions earn more than the *robbed* and the *gaming* classes. CEO pay largesse is a deception propagandized by Democrats, based on only 0.002% of the top transnational corporations in the world.

American Democrats also have a habit of confusing other classes with *the wealthy*, leading to policies that punish the hardest working tax donkeys in *the robbed* class who make between $125,000, and $300,000 in a few good years of their career. Even worse, those beasts of burden will surrender half of that income to the government through one tax channel or another. On the other hand, the risk of increasing taxes on the *truly wealthy* is capital flight. Those people have so much money that they can use legal and physical tricks to avoid paying taxes. They are not geographically constrained like everyone else.

But as we noted in the concepts of prosperity analysis – income is not wealth; it is only a pathway to wealth. Wealth is surplus, best represented financially as a person's net worth. That is calculated as an individual's assets less their liabilities. Assets include tangible items such as real estate, equipment, and durable goods, and financial items such as deposits, mutual funds, pensions, stocks, and bonds. As with income distribution, wealth disparity has been decreasing for decades. The trouble with wealth distribution in America is similar to the labor market manipulations. Real estate and financial assets have been gamed for decades, providing unearned, undeserved wealth to many. The bailouts and stimulus of 2009 made this injustice worse. Nobel economist Joseph Stiglitz suggested that the banks should fail. The Obama interventions exploded American net worth by $27 trillion – a massive amount of *something-for-nothing* captured in unjustly distributed wealth.

A key tool for gaming American wealth is the *financial repression* of central banks. In this process, government debt is financed at favorable terms which sucks capital out of the private sector. The central bank sets the *real* interest rate below zero by insuring that inflation is greater than that rate. This induces malinvestments and punishes most people to give favor to special interests. The gamed compensation for careers and gamed wealth, combined with central banking financial repression have created one of the greatest swindles in history. It is most disturbing that a supposedly-educated democratic electorate has participated in the swindle.

But government, licensing, and accreditation councils are not the only culprits. *Private cartels* have recently suppressed wages for technology workers. Price-fixing can be done by oligopolies and cartels as well as the government. Meanwhile, education scams have robbed the youth, delayed family creation, and exploded spending on education and training to $1.5 trillion in 2013, with $1.3 trillion in outstanding college debt in 2015. This has not led to higher productivity – with 49% of recent college grads underemployed, 41% of them earning less than $25k, and only 17% of them earning over $50k. Poverty hustlers try to blame everything except culture, government, and career choice for stagnation of college graduates from low-income families. In reality, culture, government, and career choice are the things that impede economic mobility.

With the economic concepts, labor, and wealth trends elaborated, it is possible to arrive at a general model for prosperity analysis. The indicator is called Lifetime Prosperity (LP) and it is the most comprehensive model for individual prosperity. It starts with *LP Income*, which includes all annual consumption plus change in net worth.[244]

Consumption includes all items consumed by the person – unearned resources, welfare, government resources, business resources substituted for individual needs (like business meals), fringe benefits, subsidies, paychecks, royalties, advantages from regulatory boons, gifts, food bought by spouses and parents, and illicitly acquired resources. Next, the *prosperity* that an individual enjoys in a given year is their *LP Income* plus the *wealth* they had access to in that year.[245]

Wealth includes *financial accounts* – stocks, retirement income accounts, retirement healthcare accounts, trust funds, inheritance, pensions, savings, education accounts, debts and negative financial accounts. It also includes *property holdings* – real estate, cars and other vehicles, amenities, furniture, jewelry, durable goods, and any other material thing in the possession of the individual. Finally, a large part of American wealth is *shared access* – personal access to a share of earned or unearned communal or state property like living with a friend, spouse, parent, or other person who pays most of the bills, or a government or institutional program not yet elected but available based on the special status of the individual. A mansion with a swimming pool only shows up on statistics as the wealth of one person or the household, but in reality, all of the owner's family members and friends enjoy access to that wealth – even when they show up as "poor" in the statistics.

What is income and wealth without taxation? Total *tax burden* is the combined tax on our consumption, wealth, financial account income (capital gains), and income-related tax (not just income

---

[244] *Equation 1: Lifetime Prosperity Income (LP Income)*
[245] *Equation 2: Prosperity*

tax).[246] *Tax avoidance* is the tax that would be charged on what a person has consumed through untaxed channels like fringe benefits and divorce alimony, and tax exemptions on standing wealth such as shared access resources they use that are maintained by other people.[247]

Finally, the *tax balance* is a person's total tax account. If it is negative, then they contributed to the government, if it is positive, then they got an advantage that others would have had to pay tax on if the laws did not privilege one activity over another.[248] To arrive at Lifetime Prosperity (LP) we must use the previously defined annualized formulas, and aggregate them over the lifetime of the individual.[249]

The approaches in this book have approximated the LP model as closely as possible with available data, since accurate claims about *prosperity distribution* require the *Lifetime Prosperity* model. It is the measurement that poverty hustlers, socialists, and many institutionalists imply with their visions and rhetoric, but never justify with their numbers. Their ideas only evade complete obliteration because this model is not demanded by the public. They capitalize on our ignorance and lack of precision.

The *robotic nurse* is a wickedly complicated design, because it did not emerge overnight. It was created with un-American ideologies and policies that infected our nation slowly over a century. If we do not accurately understand the economic history of America,[250] the way that we compare to the world,[251] the ideology of institutionalists and valorists,[252] and the economic misconceptions of institutionalists,[253] [254] we will never destroy the robotic nurse with *economic sovereignty*. We might begin to reclaim our liberty by

---

[246] *Equation 3: Tax Burden*

[247] *Equation 4: Tax Avoidance*

[248] *Equation 5: Tax Balance*

[249] *Equation 6: Lifetime Prosperity*

[250] § 1.3 American Prosperity by the Numbers

[251] § 1.4 America vis-à-vis the World

[252] Chapter 2: The Institutionalist Creed

[253] § 1.2 Prosperity, Poverty, and Destitution

[254] Chapter 3: Inequality, Wrath, and Envy by Diktat

taking Thomas Jefferson's first principle of association very seriously; that is, the guaranteed free exercise of our personal labor and the fruits acquired by it.

§ 4.2 Policies and Conclusion

"Hang (and make sure that the hanging takes place in full view of the people) no fewer than one hundred known landlords, rich men, bloodsuckers...Do it in such a fashion that for hundreds of kilometers around the people might see, tremble, know, shout: 'they are strangling, and will strangle to death, the bloodsucking kulaks.'" – Vladimir Lenin, Lenin's Hanging Order, August 11th, 1918 [255]

The Russians, Germans, and Chinese had no excuse for their economic devastation, considering that the sentiments of Thomas Jefferson were resounding from sea-to-sea throughout capitalist Western lands for generations prior to their socialist crusades. Although the Russian slaughter began with Lenin, it climaxed during Stalin's reign. In 1929, successful Russian farmers known as *kulaks* were declared enemies of the state. Stalin announced the "liquidation of the kulaks as a class" to affect forced collectivization of Russian agriculture. Kulaks were placed into three categories: those to be shot or imprisoned at the discretion of the local secret police, those to be displaced to Siberia, the Urals, or Kazakhstan, and those to be sent to labor colonies in their own districts. In all cases, their property was seized by the state for redistributive purposes. This *slavery-with-massacre* was known as *dekulakization*.

The Chinese socialists immediately began implementing their own versions of dekulakization as soon as they usurped total power in 1950. Their oppression and slaughter culminated with a program in 1958 called The Great Leap Forward, in Orwellian-insult to thinking human beings. It is a habit of institutionalists to describe their thieving and murderous programs with inspirational terms like "progress" and "forward."

The Chinese, Russians, Germans, and French slaughtered intellectuals perceived to be a threat to their ideology, while their favored wealthy denizens were welcomed to the ruling oligarchy. In just a short period of socialist history, the ensuing famine,

---

[255] (Service, 2000)

imprisonment, slavery, massacres, and refugee crises killed 14.5 million Russians from 1930 to 1937 and 30 million Chinese from 1958 to 1961. Within a much smaller geography, the French slaughtered around 217,000 people for ideological motives during the September Massacres, Reign of Terror, and Vendée Massacre. Nazi Germany killed 21 million people from 1933 to 1945.

This process of neutralizing the upper-middle class with slaughter or robbery is called *vorardennes*. The Ardennes workhorse was called "rustic, hard, and tireless" by Julius Caesar, and he recommended their use in heavy cavalry units. The Latin root *vor* means to eat something greedily, giving rise to words such as voracious, devour, and carnivore. As institutionalists coalesce power they tend towards *vorardennes* either gradually or quickly. Dekulakization, The Great Leap Forward, the Reign of Terror, and the National Socialist Twenty-Five-Point Plan are infamous examples.

In all cases of *vorardennes*, this social suicide is perpetrated by mobs of peasants led by their brainwashing elites. The upper-middle class is always their target of slaughter and robbery for a number of reasons. First of all, the upper-middle class has great power, when they associate with each other. They represent their workers' interests in very real ways. They know their workers personally. The natural socioeconomic hierarchy driven by free market productivity institutes a level of cooperation and independence that gets in the way of the institutionalists' thieving central plans. As vorardennes proceeds, the middle class is fully compressed and left powerless to affect their own destiny without the oligarchy's blessings. Meanwhile, the elites and their manufactured peasant mobs obtain absolute power over the entire nation.

In addition to the elimination of hierarchical socioeconomic classes, vorardennes also slams the door shut on middle class economic mobility. By deceiving the mobs of "poor" and middle class people into thinking that their programs will only punish the rich, they gain manufactured consent to permanently trap the middle class in stagnation. By killing economic mobility, the institutionalists do not have to worry about a reemerging upper-middle class, nouveau riche, or bourgeoisie that can challenge their power in the future. The ideologically conforming, totally compressed middle class becomes the beast of burden for the wealthy oligarchs who wield institutional power in business and government.

If this robbery of the middle class and stagnation of economic mobility sounds familiar, it is because *economic sovereignty* research has shown that modern institutionalists perpetrate vorardennes with legal and financial tricks instead of murder and violence. Considering that FDR's Second Bill of Rights espoused the same goals as the tenth chapter of the Soviet Union's constitution, it should not be surprising that Western "democracies" have attained the same results of dekulakization through gradual, subversive, and invisible financial methods. The elites and the "poor" continue to use each other in order to subordinate the upper-middle class and siphon the sweat off of the backs of productive workers.

As with other *vorardennes* societies, the new indentured servants are the hard-working, and exceptional middle class. Regrettably, most of them are completely blind to the complex web of robbery that sets them to *forced labor* with the invisible shackles of the rich and "poor." In Ancient Rome, America, Germany, France, Sweden, China, and Russia, government has used a segment of the population as beasts of burden – slaves, prisoners of war, indentured servants, and private-cartel-robbed workers. *Forced labor* in the twentieth century is imposed upon the middle class with nonviolent methods and information asymmetry.

In the institutionalist, *vorardennes* nation, the beasts of burden are any members of the middle class who are disfavored by the central plans of the day, or cursed with rare talents, ambition, prudence, and a strong work ethic. The upper-middle class is too busy with their careers, while the wealthy, well-connected oligarchy, and the "poor" have all the time in the world on their hands to cause trouble, impose their will, whip up mob-like fury, and distract themselves with intoxication, socializing, and leisure. It is the habit of all institutionalists to provide a steady stream of vice to keep people distracted long enough to never fully appreciate the truth of their situation.

Ultimately, *economic sovereignty* research has demonstrated that America drifted from its principles many years ago. Today, we cannot call this nation truly American, and we will not recover the strengths that made America great without defeating the institutionalists and reversing vorardennes. If we continue on the same path, we will become more like Germany and Russia and our forefathers will be relegated to a fanciful chapter of history. But hope is never lost in the heart of a *valorist*. There are specific actions we can take to recover American *economic sovereignty*.

Undercut Institutionalist Price Manipulation

Whether induced by government mandate or institutional action, the prices for very basic services and goods in America are bloated like a handful of party balloons, turned-obnoxious as they block our view and fetter our hands. These balloons were cheerful when the institutionalists preached their utopian visions of "free" or "affordable" *compulsory liberties* for everyone; in reality, they affected the exact opposite. Healthcare, real estate, green energy, education, and all goods and services touched by union labor must be brought under heel. The price inflation for those basic items must be deflated at the source.

In the healthcare industry, licensing, regulatory, and accreditation functions must relax and medical labor must increase to at least 200% of its incidence during the 1960s. The centralization brought about by the Democrat party's ObamaCare legislation must be reversed, and competition for out-of-pocket medical payments must be unleashed. To reduce third-party payments in medicine from government or private insurance, high-deductible catastrophic insurance will become the norm, and everything else will be paid for by tax-exempt medical savings accounts. Milton Friedman elaborated this plan in 2001.[256] When the medical savings are not used for medical service, they become taxable income. Simply reducing the amount of money paid to healthcare providers by third parties, would reduce the costs of healthcare services that actually matter. All-told, reigning in medical waste can slash costs by thirty- to forty-percent.

But healthcare is just as critical as real estate. Housing has never been more expensive since institutionalists decided to subsidize loans, impose regulations, and offer tax dollars to

---

[256] (Friedman, How to Cure Healthcare, 2001, winter)

Thomas E. Kurek

unscrupulous developers for "low income" residents. Inflation of commercial real estate even infects the prices of goods and services. They are inducing free markets to make costly real estate choices with institutional power, so that they remain blameless for outrageous rent and mortgage prices, crime surges, school redistricting, and displacement. These subsidies, quotas, and government litigations must end immediately. A complete platform for restoring integrity to real estate markets should be based upon Thomas Sowell's brilliant analysis in *The Housing Boom and Bust*.[257] Citizens should pay close attention to the rent-vs-buy ratios when choosing to buy homes or rent. If they spend more money in interest, maintenance, and property tax over the course of a loan than they would spend on rent, it does not make sense to purchase real estate.

What Americans lose on healthcare and real estate inflation is joined by green energy activities. While new energy technology is appealing for many reasons, the impositions of government with Renewable Portfolio Standards and Renewable Energy Certificates must end, and any form of cap-and-trade scheming must be forbidden by the electorate. If energy companies wish to build for their future, they must approach the citizen and ask for investments or cooperatives like any other business. The citizens who invest will reap the rewards of the new energy infrastructure. Enriching lawyers, middlemen, and bureaucrats at the expense of the middle class is an atrocious violation of *economic sovereignty* and the principles espoused by the American forefathers.

Likewise, in no case should a union worker use legal force to obtain gains that their work cannot justify with competition. Public sector unions must end, per the admonishments of FDR. Legal privileges for union strikes and collective bargaining must end as well. Workers must be free to associate and form unions, but in no case should their jobs be protected for any reason. Right-to-work laws must expand, and union price-fixing must be treated in the same way that monopolies and private cartels are treated with antitrust laws.

---

[257] (Sowell, The Housing Boom and Bust, 2009)

Finally, education subsidies must end, and public school must be paid for with vouchers so that educators are competing for their income. Prices must be eviscerated back to 1960s levels, and efficiency will be increased by a better division of labor between instructors, curriculum designers, lesson-plan creators, and administrators. Digital assets and licensing of private content will flourish in a privatized education market. The best instructors will not even require licensure. They will be wise, successful, experienced elderly citizens with a lifetime of knowledge to convey. Students will receive the tests and content from the most brilliant academics, and instructors will improve by focusing on delivery.

When all of this institutionalist price inflation ends, poor and middle-class Americans will be amazed at how little they require charities and government to subordinate them to their redistribution and paternalism. An aggregate fifty-percent price reduction for the costs of education, energy, housing, commercial real estate, union labor, and healthcare will do much more than minimum wage and "living wage" deceptions. They will bring the fundamentals of our economy into abundant reach of the vast majority of Americans. The liberated capital will then once again drive capitalist innovation and prosperity. Jobs will become more satisfying as human energy is taken from unjustified work activities and bureaucracy. Relieving distress for the most desperate Americans with entrepreneur-partnered work programs and disability communities will reduce welfare to pennies-on-the-dollar.

The Classic Way to Wealth

When exposed to the knowledge of *economic sovereignty* for the first time, a frequent question emerges: "what can the average citizen do to deal with the temptations of the *robotic nurse?*" It is a somewhat tragic inquiry, because honestly, there is so much out of the control of the average citizen. They can actively demand that the politicians they vote for adopt the reforms and principles in this book. Entertainers and journalists can spread the knowledge in their stories. Clergy and educators can spread the values throughout their congregation and student body. Activists can disarm their opponents with the facts presented herein. But when professional investors are on their knees and scattered in fear of how the global cabal of institutionalists will wreck their next business cycle, how does the citizen optimize their own lot? Business thrives on standards and predictability, and the institutionalists' massive power plays obliterate those features.

We must learn Benjamin Franklin's *Way to Wealth*, which is a summary of his advice on procuring wealth through industry and frugality – thereby securing virtue and honesty. A man who is in debt or financially codependent has a more difficult time acting honestly, as "*it is hard for an empty sack to stand upright.*" The same applies to America's awful indebtedness and welfare schemes. The institutionalists have turned our nation and a third of its population into empty sacks. It is time to fill these sacks with bounteous and hearty nourishment! So what makes the industry and frugality that Franklin speaks of?

First of all, individuals must take full responsibility for their own sustenance, their idleness, pride, and folly. He says,

"The taxes are indeed very heavy, and, if those laid on by the government were the only ones we had to pay, we might more easily discharge them; but we have many others, and much more grievous to some of us. We are taxed twice as much by *our idleness*, three times as much by *our pride*, and four times as much by *our folly*; and from these taxes the commissioners cannot ease or deliver us, by allowing an abatement. However, let us hearken to good advice, and something may be done for us; *God helps them that help themselves.*"

Secondly, individuals must not wish and hope for better times. They must become people of patience, zeal, and action. He says,

"*Industry* need not wish, and he that lives upon *hopes* will *die fasting.* There are no *gains* without *pains*...He that hath a *trade* hath an *estate*; and he that hath a *calling*, hath an *office of profit and honor*...If we are *industrious*, we shall never *starve*; for, at the working man's house hunger looks in, but dares not enter. Nor will the bailiff or the constable enter, for *industry* pays *debts*, while *despair increaseth* them...*Diligence* is the mother of good luck, and God gives all things to industry. Then plough deep while sluggards sleep, and you shall have corn to sell and to keep. Work while it is called today, for you know not how much you may be hindered to-morrow. *One*, today is worth *two* tomorrows, as Poor Richard says; and further, never leave that till tomorrow, which you can do today.

If you were a servant, would you not be, ashamed that a good master should catch you idle? Are you then your own master? Be ashamed to catch yourself idle, when there is so much to be done for yourself, your family, your country, and your king."

Thirdly, we must take responsibility for our own spending, embrace frugality, and despise wasteful culture. We must evict the government from being our financial stewards. We must take no debts for things we do not need, and pay not a dime of interest to lenders to obtain today, what we can pay in full tomorrow,

"But with our industry we must likewise be *steady*, *settled*, and *careful*, and oversee our own affairs with *our own eyes*, and *not trust too much to others*...Trusting too much to others' care is the ruin of many; for in the affairs of this world men are saved, not by faith, but by the want of it. If you would be wealthy, think of *saving* as well as of *getting*. The Indies have not made Spain rich, because her outgoes are greater than her incomes... And further, what maintains *one vice* would bring up *two children*. You may think, perhaps, that a little tea, or a little punch now and then, diet a little more costly, clothes a little finer, and a little' entertainment now and then, can be no great matter; but...beware of little expenses; A small leak will sink a great ship... But what madness must it be to run in debt for these superfluities? We are offered by the terms of this sale, six months' credit; and that, perhaps, has induced some of us to attend it, because we cannot spare the ready money, and hope now to be fine without it. But, ah! think what you do *when, you run in debt you give to another power over your liberty*... Creditors have better memories than debtors; creditors are a superstitious sect, great observers of set days and times."

Finally, although industry, frugality, and prudence are excellent pathways to wealth, *force majeure* is ever looming over our heads – such as a medical illness, a natural disaster, an offense by a criminal or terrorist, a vile and immoral betrayer who walks into our love-lives or business affairs. So we must comfort our brothers and sisters as best we can, to relieve their distress when they are truly destitute and honest with us on a personal level, and be prepared with virtue and faith, to endure the most heinous and unfair circumstance with our own spirits – not demanding government to do charity for us,

"This doctrine, my friends, is reason and wisdom; but, after all, do not depend too much upon your own *industry*, and *frugality*, and *prudence*, though excellent things; for they may all be blasted, without the blessing of Heaven; and, therefore, ask that blessing humbly, and be not uncharitable to those that at present seem to want it, but comfort and help them. Remember, Job suffered, and was afterwards prosperous."

In the development of this book and Alvarism research, this author has experienced the endurance, frugality, industry, and prudence that Benjamin Franklin suggests. He could not have survived and prospered without those choices. Benjamin Franklin's financial wisdom is one of the most timeless and crucial set of standards for the *valorist* that has ever been captured in writing.

Education

High school education should include a foundation in *economic sovereignty*. For adults, community efforts should be made to spread the knowledge through churches, civic organizations, and small group discussions. The economic indicators and data sources used in this book should be published to a public website.[258] [259] Further research should be conducted upon the principles in this book. Education is a continual quest for refinement, and considering that this knowledge is currently obscure, the challenge is proliferation first, and expanded research afterwards.

Propaganda Resistance

Confronting misinformation requires more than the knowledge of what is true. The propaganda and rhetorical tricks surrounding prosperity, poverty, and destitution should be thwarted wherever they are found.[260] Organizations, politicians, entertainers, educators, and journalists that participate in poverty hustling, economic distortions, and class warfare should be monitored and records should be made to capture their harmful activity. This could be a feature of a larger website, as these subversive elements could

---

[258] § 1.3 American Prosperity by the Numbers

[259] § 1.4 America vis-à-vis the World

[260] § 1.2 Prosperity, Poverty, and Destitution

be tracked in the same way that Southern Poverty Law Center purports to track hate groups.

Ideological Hardening & Influence Countermeasures

Valorist civic organizations should be organized in the same way that the TEA Party was organized, in order to deconstruct the false left-right paradigm of the modern Democrats, Libertarians, and Republicans. Valorists should seek to evict the institutionalist majorities in the nation through coopting, infiltration, and subversion, since there is no other way to confront such an overwhelming power. These covert elements will redirect funds, influence, and activities towards *valorist* agendas under the pretense of *institutionalist* affirmation. Simultaneously, the agenda, principles, and history of valorist ideology should be openly and loudly proclaimed by overt activists. Convergence of the covert and overt valorist activities would proceed in the same way that The Progressive Alliance and Socialist International has used the American Democrat to converge America towards *social democracy*. The *valorist* movement would undercut that subversion.

Industrial Intelligence, Labor Equality, Identity Integration

Specific economic fallacies of institutionalists on prosperity, income, wealth, education, energy, environment, career paths, and personnel should be thoroughly debunked on a public website. This industrial intelligence would become a gold-standard resource for business journalism. Civil rights laws must be reformed to prohibit the systematized discrimination of "diversity," affirmative action, disparate impact, and identity politics. Political caucuses must not dole out advantages to groups of people because of their identity. If the political agenda cannot be put in universal terms, then it should indicate that it will lead to inequality under the law, or an area of civic activity in which the law should not be operating.

Discrimination must still be punished as *identity integration* proceeds. Current financing for civil rights should be drastically reduced, and remaining funds should be directed towards investigating and punishing provable discrimination. The American Constitutional principle of *due process* and "innocent until proven guilty" must defeat the French and Russian collectivist terror from which "diversity" policies derive. The novel theory presented in this book which shows how *identity segregation* increases the disutility of labor and harms labor markets should be promulgated and demonstrated through further research.[261]

Standardize Lifetime Prosperity, Lifetime Disposable Income Analysis

To correct the pervasive misnomers about income, wealth, and socioeconomic classes, the concepts and limitations of prosperity analysis must be respected. All politicians, educators, and journalists who violate those principles must be discredited. The general model for *Lifetime Prosperity* should become the measure by which poverty and prosperity is evaluated.[262] Lifetime disposable income estimates should be published for every career before college students choose their paths.[263] That data should be associated to the greatest needs in the labor market, and a private entity should establish a website where universities and alumni associations can corroborate their employment and compensation information. Because of the IRS, the government already has lifetime income data associated to every citizen's social security number. Any notion that reports of lifetime prosperity are infeasible is a deception. Cross-referencing property tax records with income tax and census records will produce a highly accurate estimate for every citizen.

End Guild Labor Market Interference, Banking, and Real Estate Swindles

The various institutional tricks used by the *gaming class* to swindle the labor market should be confronted with the force of law. Countervailing accreditation, licensing, and professional associations should be established, and monopolies of power in those areas should be treated in the same spirit of antitrust laws. In no case should guilds or unions have the effective power of a monopoly or cartel in labor markets. Drastic tax reductions should be given to each citizen who makes impressive income during any five years of their life. This will incentivize greater innovation and risk-taking by normal Americans.

---

[261] § 2.3 The Institutionalist Fantasy Economy

[262] § 3.4 Lifetime Prosperity

[263] § 3.3 Illusory Career Paths and Wealth Erosion

In order to free capital from government and banking misappropriation, Americans could have private trust funds for buying a house in cash. The median house price of their location would be set as the limit of the account. If they spent money only on living expenses, with cost-of-living-adjustments considered, and put the rest of their earnings in the trust fund, the government could exempt them from all income taxation until they filled the account. Once they filled the account they must use the cash to purchase a house within one year. This would turn housing back into a marked-to-market industry, and destroy the thieving real-estate casino that banking institutions and government have imposed for two generations. Increasing home ownership is not achieved by incenting debt serfdom with creative loans and tax subsidies – it is achieved by incenting pure, unleveraged equity and the lowest interest payments possible. When normal Americans can quickly pay for their house in cash, those interest payments will be minimized.

If these union, guild, licensing, and real estate scams were corrected, in just one generation, the unionized blue-collar workers, government employees, and public school teachers would return to the *persistent class*, the *robbed class* would no longer be *robbed*, and doctors and news anchors would be compensated similarly to engineers, economists, and average lawyers. Labor across the board would actually be worth its fair-market price, with a vibrant diversity of remuneration driven by the free market responses to real productivity. Healthcare and education would become affordable again. Broadcast news media would lose its legacy oligopolistic advantages gained from Federal Communications Commission (FCC) licensure, and would face competition from high-integrity newcomers, improving the quality of journalism.

Taxes and government employee compensation packages would be reduced, so we would also ameliorate government debt. The *persistent class* could afford their own doctors, housing, and food without assistance. Capital would be freed up for generous private charity for the *destitute class*. We would have a normal, honest labor market, where productivity incentivizes activity.

Unfortunately, prying the ill-gotten spoils from the *gaming class* will require a nationwide explosion of truth and conviction. The institutions that protect the current usurpation will not give up their scams without a fight. The customers must demand it and affect it – using righteous civic power to destroy the scams that are maintained with corrupt civic power.

Total Tax Transparency

Reigning in the economic tyranny of our modern government is a much loftier quest. *Total tax transparency* is the first place to start. If citizens continue to be deceived about the massive amount of taxation that the government takes from hidden channels, they will not understand the extent of their servitude. State and federal legislatures must require all government agencies and their taxed surrogates to inform (via receipt or report), the end-sources of revenue precisely what tax and regulatory cost was paid on their labor or purchase price. That means that if Environmental Protection Agency regulations cost $3.00 for a full tank of gasoline, the customer must have access to that information via receipt or publicly available reports. Any tax that is infeasible for such reporting should be illegal.

Voter Responsibility

As this book has shown, America has reached a condition of ochlocracy (mob rule) – the evil form of democracy first coined by Polybius,[264] and admonished through the wise traditions of history. In Rome it was known as *mobile vulgus* – "the fickle crowd" – and characterized by demagoguery, the tyranny of the majority, and domination of emotion over reason. Republics in history had prevented such legal retrogression by requiring some form of responsibility to vote.

Until shortly before the civil war, black males could actually vote in a number of states, and over half of white males could not vote anywhere in America.[265] The standards for voter responsibility were poll taxes and property qualifications. America made a dire mistake when it began toying with suffrage laws. As it turns out, when women spend most of their lives trying to get three out of twenty babies to survive infant mortality, voting is not a very relevant

---

[264] (Polybius & Paton, 117 B.C.; Translation, 1922)
[265] (Thorpe, 1898)

activity. When maternal death and infant mortality were conquered by science, female voting became more than a fanciful notion of academics and rich women. It was a very pragmatic social adaptation.

In regards to race and suffrage, the Civil War ended racial justification for chattel slavery, and legal arguments for racial disenfranchisement in turn. Yet power hordes used tricks to hold on to their advantages at the polls and the Voting Rights Act of 1965 confronted those tricks. Unfortunately, it opened the floodgates of ochlocracy and voter fraud that we suffer from today.

The mistake certainly was not opening suffrage to women and blacks. They were wrongly denied self-agency with bureaucratic hypocrisies, much like affirmative action, identity quotas, and diversity programs impose today. In suffrage reform, the mistake was removing all civic responsibility as a qualifier to vote. Ochlocracy was easily predictable from this foolhardiness. Today, with only 40% of citizens financing American government beyond redistribution to their neighbors, the oppressed middle-class citizens who pay the cost of government are completely shackled by upper- and lower-class parasites who collude with each other for their own interests. Because taxes and property qualifications were deemed Constitutional for the first three generations of the American Republic, there will be no problem introducing new voter qualifications to end the oppressive ochlocracy brought about by "the fickle mob."

We will ratify a Constitutional amendment to weight votes by lifetime-accrued tax balance. In doing so, we will not discriminate by gender, race, or any other identity concern; we will only ensure that "he who pays the piper calls the tune," in accordance with true justice. The more a citizen pays in tax over their lifetime, the greater relevance their vote carries. In the past this was impossible, even with property and poll tax qualifications. They ensured that an educated elite prevented mob rule from an illiterate majority. Today, after a century of social insurance, welfare, income and property taxation, it is very easy to estimate a specific citizen's total tax balance. Their social security numbers are associated to all of those transactions. The first outrage is that our tyrannical government has access to such business intelligence, but the people who pay the tax do not.

This plan is the ultimate hedge against ochlocracy. Awarding civic power to those who give the most to the government provides the check-and-balance needed for suffrage. It removes corrupt civic signals by neutralizing the bias of criminals, black-market purveyors, rich tax evaders, and self-entitled citizens who persist on the generosity and forced labor of productive citizens. Modern *vorardennes* succeeds because the people who are getting robbed have no power against the short-sighted masses. Earning civic relevance throughout a lifetime of devotion will obliterate vorardennes in one generation.

It will also reduce incentive to remain on government subsidy. As a citizen consumes government subsidies, they reduce their tax balance and lose civic relevance. Naïve and disruptive signals from youth voters will also be thwarted. The greatest shift of power goes from them to the elderly. People cannot vote when their tax balance is below half of the median income (approximately $25,000 today). People with no "skin in the game" will no longer be able to extort the tax donkeys of the middle class. A side effect will be a desire to pay "fair" taxes or else render oneself meaningless in the voting booth. This will encourage a much more appropriate tax burden.

There is a concern that wealthy citizens will run away with the vote in such a weighted voting system. This is completely falsified by the numbers. The greatest shift in power will go from the youth to the elderly. The socioeconomic shift in power will not only be the height of justice, but very moderate. The current socioeconomic breakdown of voters, old suffrage weight, and new suffrage weight respectively is:

1. Destitute – 1.3M voters, 1% (old), 0% (new)
2. Persistent – 83M voters, 64% (old), 50% (new)
3. Robbed – 20M voters, 15% (old), 19% (new)
4. Gaming – 26M voters, 20% (old), 30% (new)
5. Wealthy – 95k voters, 0.1% (old), 1.7% (new)

Consequently, the *wealthy* will not run away with our civic power. In fact, their nonprofit financing is responsible for that today. They will be greatly challenged by the increased power of productive middle class voters. Still, these estimates are very inaccurate, since so many in the *gaming* class evade taxation through benefits and tricks. In truth, the *persistent* will lose much less civic mandate, the *robbed* will gain much more, and the *gaming* and *wealthy* will gain much less. The socioeconomic power shift will not be drastic at all – it will just be enough to incent citizens to loathe and respect taxation at the same time. It is a perfect balance of power where the risk and choice rests with the individual. As a consequence, rational civic engagement will increase, when "he who pays the piper calls the tune."

All Tax Collection is Paid by the Government

State and federal tax filing, reporting, and collection should be paid for by the government. Hourly fees will be collected by each citizen, business, and accountant, from the government agency responsible for the taxation. Not a single second of a citizen's time will be uncompensated for doing the work of the government's tax collection. This will deter complicated tax manipulations imposed by special interests and government tyrants. It will also obliterate the cost that government currently imposes upon private citizens and businesses to do their work of collecting and accounting, as the government gains a powerful incentive to simplify their hamster wheels of bureaucratic waste. Much human life under the green visor will be liberated for the joy of America.

Constrain Civic Power – Spending Limits and Nonprofit Antitrust

An absolute constraint on total civic power through spending limits must be achieved. In any year, regulations cannot cost more than 10% of GDP or *personal income*, and combined federal, state, and local spending cannot exceed 20% of GDP or *personal income*, whichever is lower. These enormous amounts should be generous enough, for the cost of government imposition. In struggles for national survival from war, insurrection, or natural disasters, exceptional spending may be conducted.

Nonprofits must be subject to new antitrust laws, when their industrial activity is found to interfere with markets, rendering their humanitarian mandate dubious. The two-trillion-dollars that they currently throw around is already dubious "humanitarian" activity. Reforms must be made to ensure that they are lifting

Thomas E. Kurek

people up instead of capturing them and holding them down or else acting as tax havens and crony nepotism vehicles.

Reduce Tax Exemption for Government and Nonprofits

When the government takes its dollars into a market to lease or buy property for instance, there is an unjust competition for those products and services. Paying no tax on the acquisition or the spending, the government has easy money compared to private citizens and businesses who are annihilated by taxes. Previous legal considerations have deemed government taxation of itself to be self-destructive. Modern revelations falsify that claim. If the government must pay full price and tax on everything it buys, like a private citizen or business, then it cannot inflate the prices of those things when it throws its billions of spending around. For instance, it cannot as easily infect a locality and inflate the prices of housing, food, real estate, parking, lodging, and conferences. Its dollars become equal to that of a private entity.

To prevent the government from shuffling its own tax money back to itself, even at a slower velocity, the new taxes government pays on its purchases will instead be funneled into a general fund to pay off government debt and municipal bonds. This will introduce a healthy association of debt reduction to government spending. Although nonprofits will pay taxes on all purchases for the same reasons, they will retain their corporate tax exemptions for revenues and donations to incent private charity.

Wean Adult Dependents off of Welfare

Partnerships with small business entrepreneurs will be forged in the short term to provide jobs to welfare recipients. Work requirements for all but the disabled will be introduced, for any form of government subsidy. As the citizens gain skills and self-sufficiency through gainful production, the welfare payments to the entrepreneurs will erode. Participating businesses will be required to gradually replace welfare sources of revenue with business revenues on a standard schedule. The participating businesses will be required to justify market viability and competitiveness.

End Minimum Wage Laws and Other Price Controls

There are few things worse than price controls on labor, which create unemployment, hobble the most vulnerable workers who need to gain skills, increase prices of basic items, reduce the quality of services and products, and impede innovation and business expansion. Some combination of those effects is always the result of the government forcing people to hire each other for more or less than their time is worth to the market. The people who are duped into thinking that this helps them are shocked to discover that they will pay for their wage floor in the cost of their products and services, smaller quantities, unemployment, reduced hours, and less job mobility.

Moreover, repression of youth experience is another great victim of minimum wage laws. Our young adults should have nine years of part-time work experience by the time they are twenty-five. Contrarily, many enter the workforce nearly inept and undisciplined in any meaningful aspect of working for a living. Minimum wage laws make jobs inaccessible to youths. Instead of filling our businesses with low-wage youthful workers, those youths are living like spoiled brats, corrupting and indebting themselves with all of the free time they enjoy.

Milton Friedman expressed the awful reality of minimum wage and other price controls, and two generations of research have proven him to be prophetic. In the process of *vorardennes*, such impositions compress the middle class further, so that people who do the job that a high school kid should be doing are paid almost as much as many college graduates. There is no economic sense in distorting the value of labor with legal tyranny, any more than there is "fairness" in such arrangements. Price controls on labor are just one more major contributor to the endless amount of *something-for-nothing* in our society.

Introduce Civic Malfeasance Laws for Government Officials

The process of impeachment and firing corrupt government workers is too onerous thanks to self-imposed privilege and public sector unions. Firing government employees should be as easy as firing private sector employees on employment-at-will contracts. Introducing laws for civic malfeasance would compel government officials to always serve the interests of objectivity and reason instead of propaganda and special interests.

If an official's activities, reports, research, or policies can be shown to be in provable contravention to significant industrial practice and mundane knowledge, they will be petitioned by industrial representatives. If they do not correct their misinformation and activities after a successfully adjudicated challenge, all of the employees associated with the malfeasance will face a series of sanctions – termination, jail, pension forfeiture, or demotion. Today, enormous government agencies run by unelected officials perpetrate the highest levels of failure and corruption without any consequence. Civic malfeasance laws will turn them back into public servants and end the reign of public overlords.

Transform American Research and Development

Appropriations for research and development will no longer be under the control of any government official. The money will be put into a trust fund for direct innovation, and invested like venture capital. Engineers, scientists, mathematicians, and computer programmers will direct the use of the funds with a nationwide association. Members must have worked in those jobs for at least five years, and their voting stock for the disbursement of research dollars is weighted by their tax balance. This will bring about a new era of American high technology, by eliminating the control of foreign interests, transnational corporations, universities, and bribed government officials who corrupt American innovation.

The Greatest Tax Revolt in History

Naturally, many of these actions to restore *economic sovereignty* suffer from great conflicts of interest. When medical doctors, educators, union workers, government employees, private cartels, and any business with a subsidy is leeching off of the taxpayer or from favorable legal privileges, why would they actively surrender their own stolen prosperity? Even if they affirm the logic and evidence presented here, they would require a morality and conscience that is an exceedingly rare feature for any group of human beings. The people who are gorging themselves on golden eggs laid by the *robbed* and *persistent* classes will not kill that goose willingly.

Consequently, every American with a conscience, who cares about the future of their children and the nation, and every American who is being robbed by this parasitic system must consider the necessity of the *greatest tax revolt in history*. This last resort would depose all politicians who will not implement *economic sovereignty* reforms, and replace them with the leadership that will restore economic sovereignty. It will bring the government to its knees and remind it that it does not exist on the mandate of people with negative tax balances, but that it exists by the graces of those with positive tax balances.

Even the notion of such a tax revolt will strike fear into the hearts of every tyrant in our society today. They know that they would be completely powerless against such a coordinated financial revolt. As we speak, America's prisons are full of dangerous people. Contrary to propagandistic accolades, around 88% of those people are locked up for very serious crimes – mostly violent ones. "Nonviolent" drug criminals comprise only 12% of the prison population. Due to this overwhelming burden of our justice system, the United States government would not even have the capacity to imprison a significant number of those who join the tax revolt.

The revolt would be an asymmetric financial insurgency. Trusted parties would gain access to 256-bit Advanced Encryption Standard (AES) keys, to use for communication with their cells of business owners. The central authority that coordinates the precision tax denials would remain unknown. The business owners would recruit willing employees to participate. When orders are given to execute, the cells will withhold their business and income tax payments, and use methods to fool the government into thinking that all is above board. In this way, the government agencies will lose initiative and have the shortest response time from the inception of their own bankruptcy.

Leadership similar to the hacktivist group Anonymous would issue demands and status updates on the progress of the financial insurrection. Localities with the highest levels of dirigisme and most vulnerable budgets would be targeted first. These would mainly be progressive metropolises – the worst offenders of *economic sovereignty*. The government bankruptcies would cascade into a total breakdown of social cohesion, and all of the heroic tax-balance-

Thomas E. Kurek

positive citizens upon which everyone else has been surviving, will gain their rightful place as the determinants of government policy.

The plan is ingenious, because if the *institutionalists* strike out at a plurality of the tax-balance-positive citizens who joined the revolt, then they will kill the source of their own existence. The realization that the true civic power in our nation is completely based upon those 40% of Americans with a positive tax balance will give those oppressed serfs the confidence they need to realize that they are invincible against their oppressors, if they act in unison. The incentive for those who join the tax revolt is not only gaining their rightful civic power and *economic sovereignty*, but also, the promise that the new leadership will allow them to keep all of the tax that they withheld during the insurrection.

Ayn Rand's imaginative entrepreneurial strike described in her book, *Atlas Shrugged*, was shortsighted in its consideration of who are the real serfs of dirigisme. Innovators and entrepreneurs are certainly important, but there are few of them in any economy. It is likely that any society operating with any form of dirigisme has a plurality of citizens whose liberty is held hostage with the outrageous financial tricks described in this book. Only by recruiting a large number of those business owners and employees, for a coordinated tax revolt, will it be possible to depose the economic parasites who have been controlling the system for decades. If the actions to restore *economic sovereignty* cannot be implemented through normal legal and business channels, this last resort should be explored by those with the ability to pull it off.

Conclusion

Economic freedom preserves personal freedom and *economic sovereignty* secures personal sovereignty. We are not masters of our own destiny anymore, after decades of dirigisme under a civic empire tended to by hypnotized serfs. Our personal sovereignty and freedom eroded, trailing their economic counterparts. There are arguments for social reformation, and they are certainly valid. Unfortunately, money is power, and power is the determinant. Without economic sovereignty, any social concern will dissolve in the maelstrom of corruption that institutionalist economic policy breeds.

The misinformed youths suckle the *robotic nurse*, mollified, and begging for more of the disease that created their disillusionment. Various polls for the past decade indicate that around half of them have unfavorable views of capitalism, and large pluralities have favorable views of socialism. That dismal inversion of reality makes this book, and the principles of *economic sovereignty* a last chance to save Western society from utter destruction. When the population is so ignorant that they beg for more of the things that created their problems, destroyed nations of the past, and brought modern nations to their knees, there is a severe crisis.

We might wander about our cities, proud of the pervasive equality. The "poor" cashier at the morning coffee shop has two children, who thrive as much as any other middle class child in America. Through government programs, she steals money from the man that bought coffee from her – his tax is buying the housing, the clothes, and food for her kids. Nobody is buying his living requirements. His housing and education debts cannot be settled for decades because of how much tax is robbed from him. He cannot consider having children because his finances are maxed out. The cashier does not even thank him for keeping her alive and allowing her to procreate while he cannot afford a family of his own.

He sits down at a table to catch his breath from his sixty-hour work week. The bright-eyed cashier smiles at him, with plenty of energy from her easy, thirty-six-hour work week. A disheveled professional woman sits down next to him and says hello,

"You look like you've had a rough week."

"Well, it's a typical week. I fight the traffic, barely get a free second to myself, I'm buried in debt, while these 'poor' people keep having babies that they force me to pay for, and they're living in the same neighborhoods that they also force me to pay for. I was born with unique talents, and did the right thing my whole life. These tax freeloaders don't even realize how much they're robbing from people like us. It's just not right. There's no justice in this place. There's no good reason to aspire to anything different than the norm," Cato confirmed with resignation.

"Maybe that's exactly the attitude they want us to have, the people who pull the strings of this *robotic nurse*. If we're trapped in stagnation, and there's no distinction of honor and outcome, then we're nice and docile, with nothing to compete for. I can relate. I've got the same middle class drudgery as you in my life. I spent my twenties hanging out in bars, doing dumb things with dumb men, and traveling the globe to stupid foreign places. I'm not better-cultured for it. Leisure tourism only serves vices, and it's the same in every city – only the veneer of the experience changes. All of my shallow girlfriends fed from the same poisoned well. 'Blow all your money on overpriced college, wine, travel, style, plastic surgery, socializing – whatever.' Now we're all broke, in debt, and I can't really say that anybody is satisfied or their character has improved. We've all got those few good men that we let go because of our envy, sloth, vanity, wanderlust, and total self-absorption. None of them want us anymore because they can get friendship from anyone, and we can't give them youthful romance or children anymore. We're all miserable and it's only going to get worse from here," she lamented in commiseration.

"I sympathize with your troubles. The *robotic nurse*. I get it. That's really clever. This grey concrete nightmare of socialism really is a robotic nurse, isn't it? Those are some hard lessons you've learned. It seems like almost everyone I know is facing the same kind of resentment and regrets. And all of our parents are busy destroying whatever resources are left in our families, while bankrupting our government and inflating our currency. They're too self-absorbed to even stop and think about how easy their lives were at our ages – how they could get jobs without college degrees, and buy new single-family homes and cars in their early twenties. Do you think we're even going to have a country left by the time our careers are over?" he inquired with earnest solidarity.

"We have a chance. You seem like a simpatico American. There is a movement of people like us, called the *valorists*. They have a plan to fix this nightmare. The American dream has been dead for decades. Either we continue as we are, and our situations will continue to degrade ever-so-subtly, as it happened to the Japanese and social democracies across the globe. Or a black-swan event will occur and crash this entire system that is already hanging by a thread. It's up to us to force the rich and the fake 'poor' people to become self-reliant again. They will continue to use us as their serfs until we refuse and resist," she testified with conviction.

"Right. Fake poor people? Like the ones who can pump out babies on our dime, live in the same neighborhoods on our tax dollars, eat at the same places, go to the same schools, and essentially live the same lives as people like us who slaved away our whole lives?" Cato inquired.

"The same," she confirmed.

"Who are the *valorists*, and how will we reclaim our lives from this *robotic nurse*? Is there a plan?" he questioned with intrigue.

"I'll tell you all about them. The winds of change are blowing. Either we'll have a great reformation with peaceful methods, or there will be a monstrous revolt when the system crashes. We might have had half of our lives stolen from us by this *robotic nurse*, but our achievements during the rest of our lives will forge the most critical upheavals since World War 2. If we fail, everything that is awful today will be infinitely worse. Are you prepared to take responsibility for such a challenge?" she queried, cheerfully.

"I've been destined for this my entire life. When do we begin?" Cato resounded.

"We are all destined. The victory is already written on our hearts. We begin today. With the traditional American and *valorist* principles at our disposal, we will overcome these challenges and restore *economic sovereignty* to the American people," her deep conviction mated with his own through their gaze, into the heart of their valorous souls.

Appendix 1: Taxation, Income, Assets, Goods

The following figures are derived from authoritative sources including the Bureau of Economic Analysis' (BEA) National Income and Product Accounts (NIPA) for macroeconomic perspective and the US Census Current Population Survey (CPS) for a microeconomic perspective. Professor Sahr's conversion factors were used for inflation-adjustment.[266] The Bureau of Labor Statistics (BLS) Consumer Expenditure Survey (CES) tables were used to discern characteristics of households.

The following BEA NIPA tables were used: Personal Income,[267] Wages and Salaries by Industry,[268] Compensation of Employees by Industry,[269] Corporate Profits Before Tax by Industry,[270] Corporate Profits After Tax by Industry,[271] Saving and Investment by Sector,[272] Full-Time Equivalent Employees by Industry,[273] and tables related to transfers.

The following Census tables were used: Households by Type,[274] and CPS tables related to income quintiles, market income, transfers, and tax.

The following BLS CES tables were used: Number of People in Consumer Unit, and Number of Earners.[275]

Government spending, revenue, and taxation data were accessed from Christopher Chantrill's websites.[276] State and Local tax rates were derived from methods described by Marr and Huang.[277] Because elderly transfer receipts were included for a total income

---

[266] (Sahr, 2014)

[267] (U.S. Bureau of Economic Analysis, 2014)

[268] (U.S. Bureau of Economic Analysis, 2015)

[269] (U.S. Bureau of Economic Analysis, 2015)

[270] (U.S. Bureau of Economic Analysis, 2015)

[271] (U.S. Bureau of Economic Analysis, 2015)

[272] (U.S. Bureau of Economic Analysis, 2015)

[273] (U.S. Bureau of Economic Analysis, 2015)

[274] (US Census Bureau, 2014)

[275] (Bureau of Labor Statistics, 2014)

[276] (Chantrill, 2014)

[277] (Marr & Huang, 2012)

picture in this analysis, state and local tax rates were adjusted to include the elderly paying state and local taxes.

It required all of these disparate sources of data, dozens of spreadsheets, and many syntheses to estimate welfare, taxation, income, and industrial characteristics in an accurate fashion that respects as many of the complex factors in play as available data will allow. There are many factors that must be considered for a realistic model – cost of living index, inflation, unaccounted taxation, welfare, and transfers. Possibly the worst unaccounted factor is how many people are actually in the household, and how many earners are actually drawing income in the household. Higher income households have many more people living in them and many more earners.

Real Income accounts for all earned income (wages, salaries, capital gains), all taxation (federal, state, local), inflation (where time series are concerned), all transfers (welfare, social insurance, pensions, veterans' benefits), and also geographical differences in prices and salaries to buy the same things (cost of living index and purchase power parity). Age and net worth are significant income-impacting factors, but correlating that data meaningfully is problematic, so they were not used here. "Reported" income is the false, typical, household income model.

The appendices are not formatted for consistency, but to maximize the space usage for charts, figures, and tables.

On *Figure 25, Profits per Worker*, Mining, Oil, Gas sinks to $15k, and rises to nearly $120k, off the chart.

Two-dimensional stacked chart series are depicted from bottom-to-top in the chart, corresponding to the legend items listed from left-to-right, top-to-bottom.

Surplus is savings and investment after capital consumption.

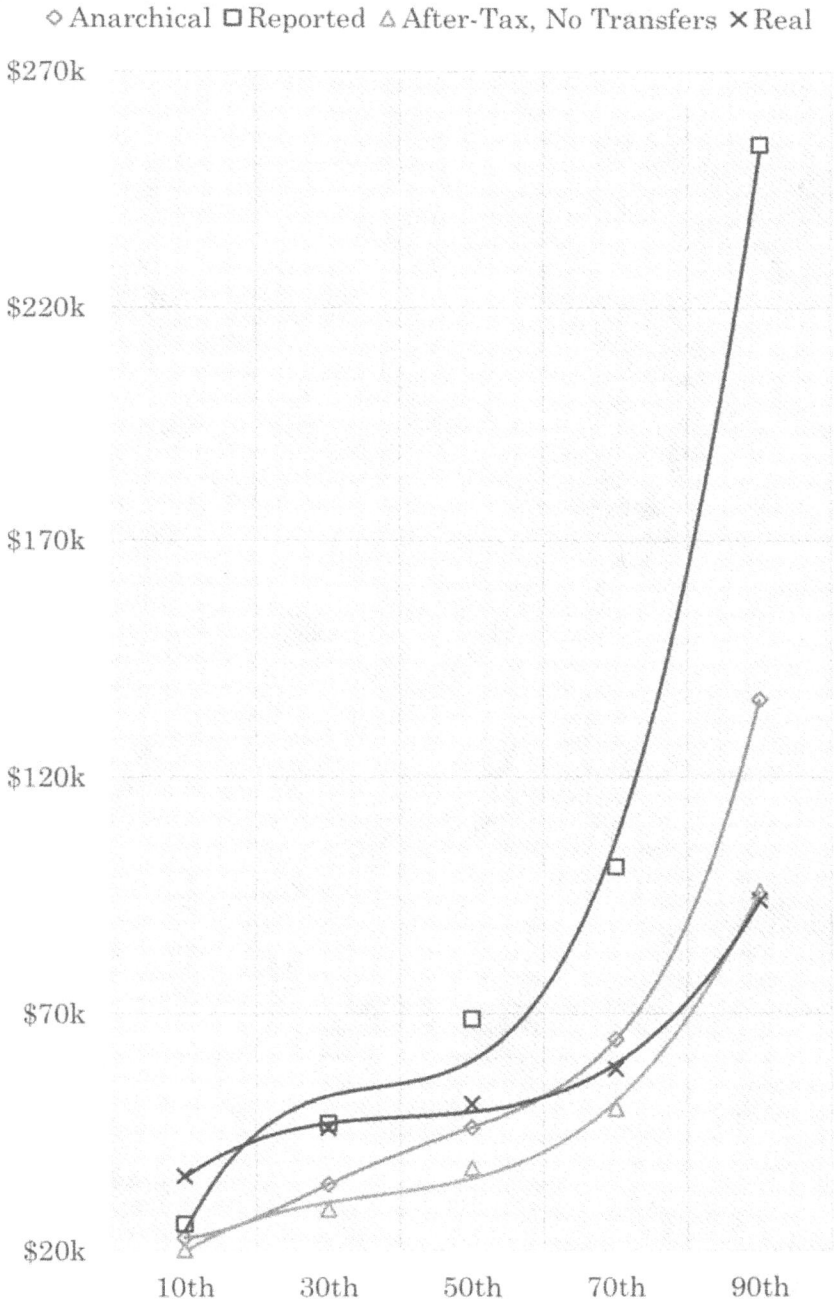

Figure 1: Income Distribution by Quintile, 2011

◇ Anarchical □ Reported △ After-Tax, No Transfers × Real

$270k

$220k

$170k

$120k

$70k

$20k

10th   30th   50th   70th   90th

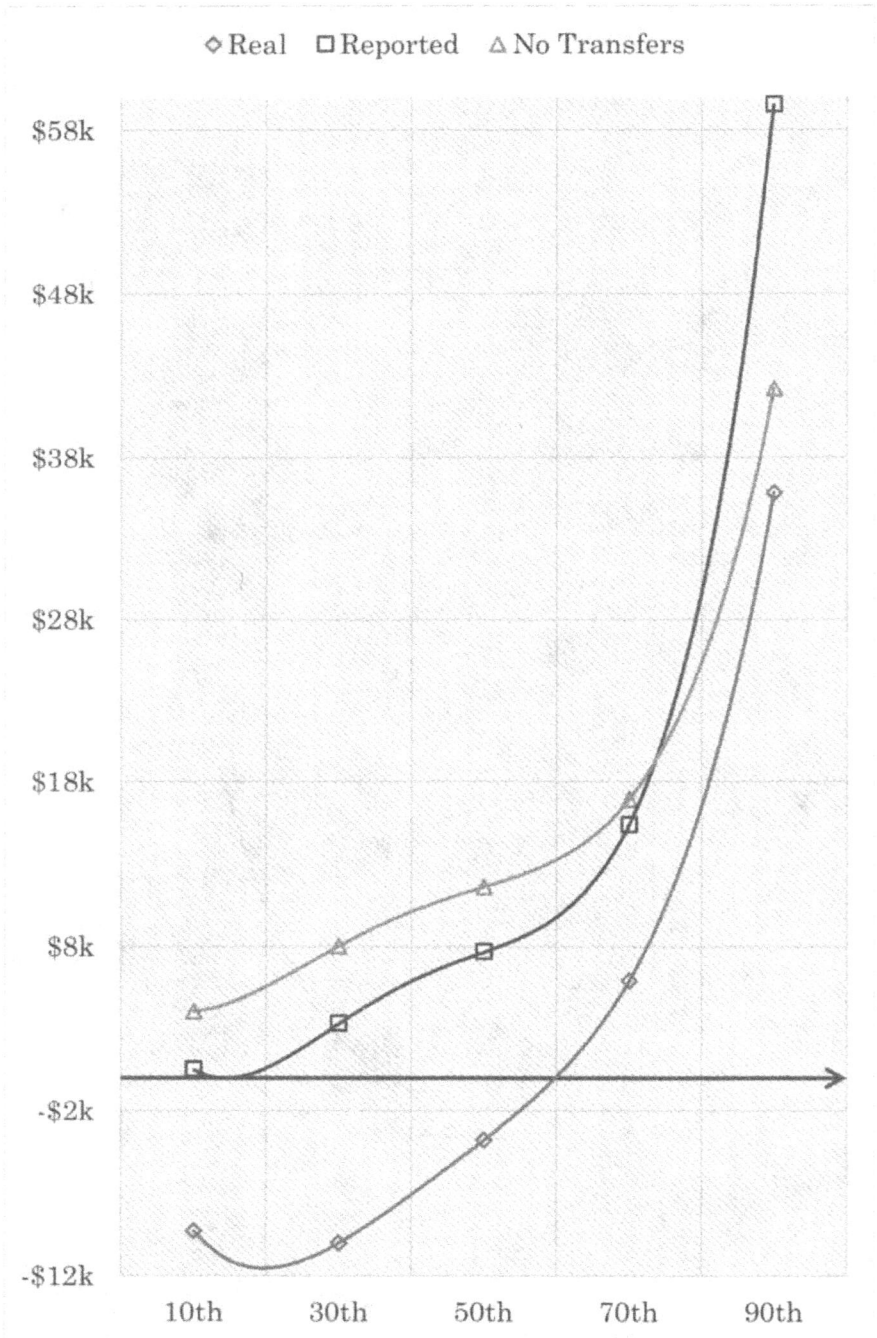

Appendix 1: Taxation, Income, Assets, Goods
Figure 2: Tax Burden for Income Quintiles, 2011

◇ Real   □ Reported   △ No Transfers

Thomas E. Kurek

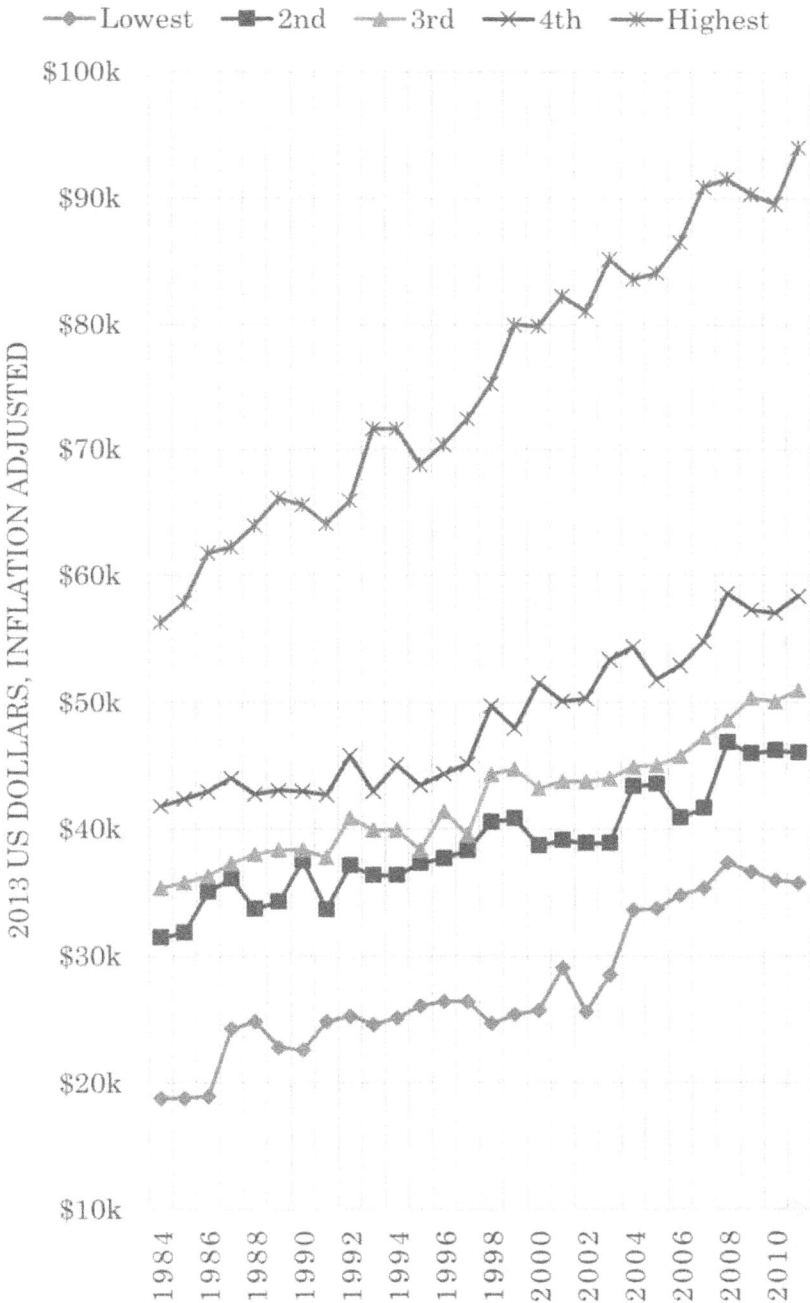

Figure 3: Real Income per Earner

Figure 4: Income Inequality Index

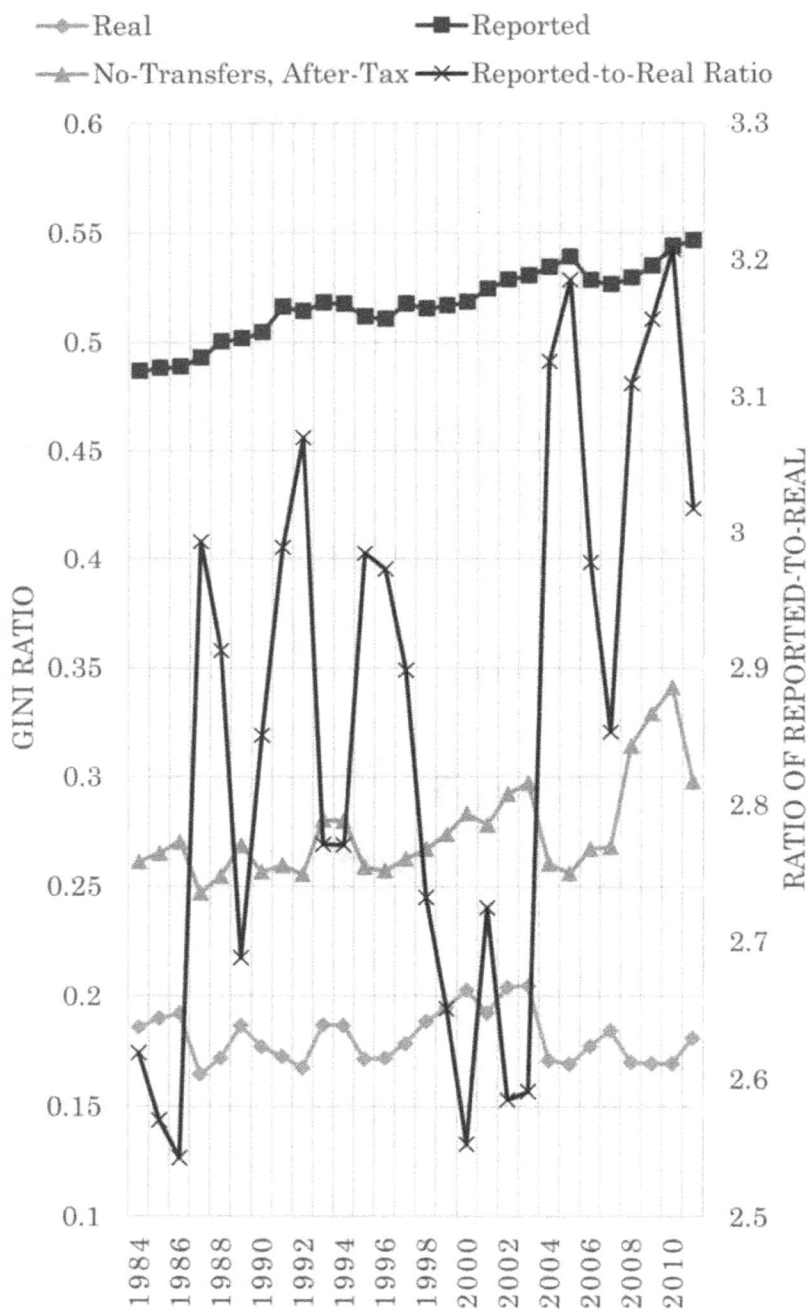

Figure 5: Total Tax per Working Person

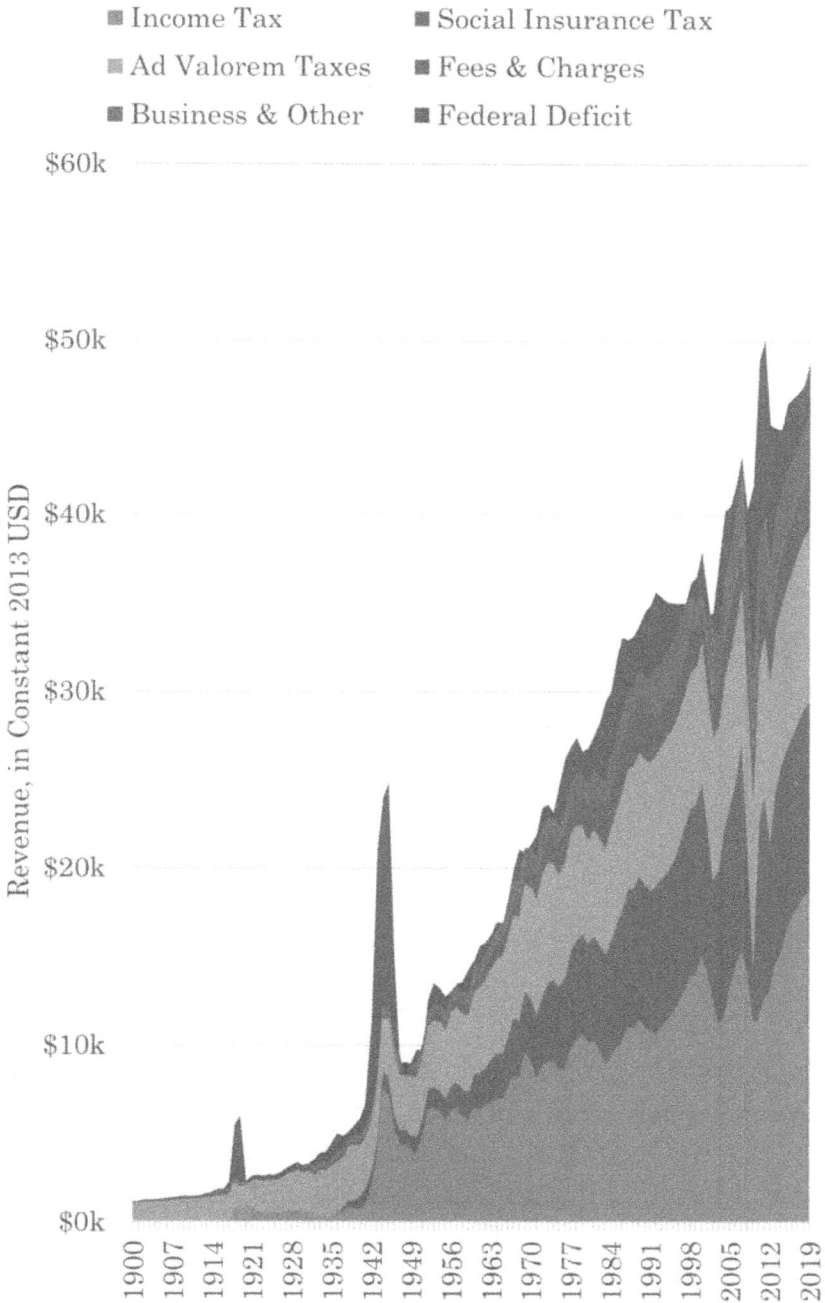

Legend:
- Income Tax
- Social Insurance Tax
- Ad Valorem Taxes
- Fees & Charges
- Business & Other
- Federal Deficit

Y-axis: Revenue, in Constant 2013 USD
$60k
$50k
$40k
$30k
$20k
$10k
$0k

X-axis: 1900 1907 1914 1921 1928 1935 1942 1949 1956 1963 1970 1977 1984 1991 1998 2005 2012 2019

Figure 6: Federal Tax per Working Person

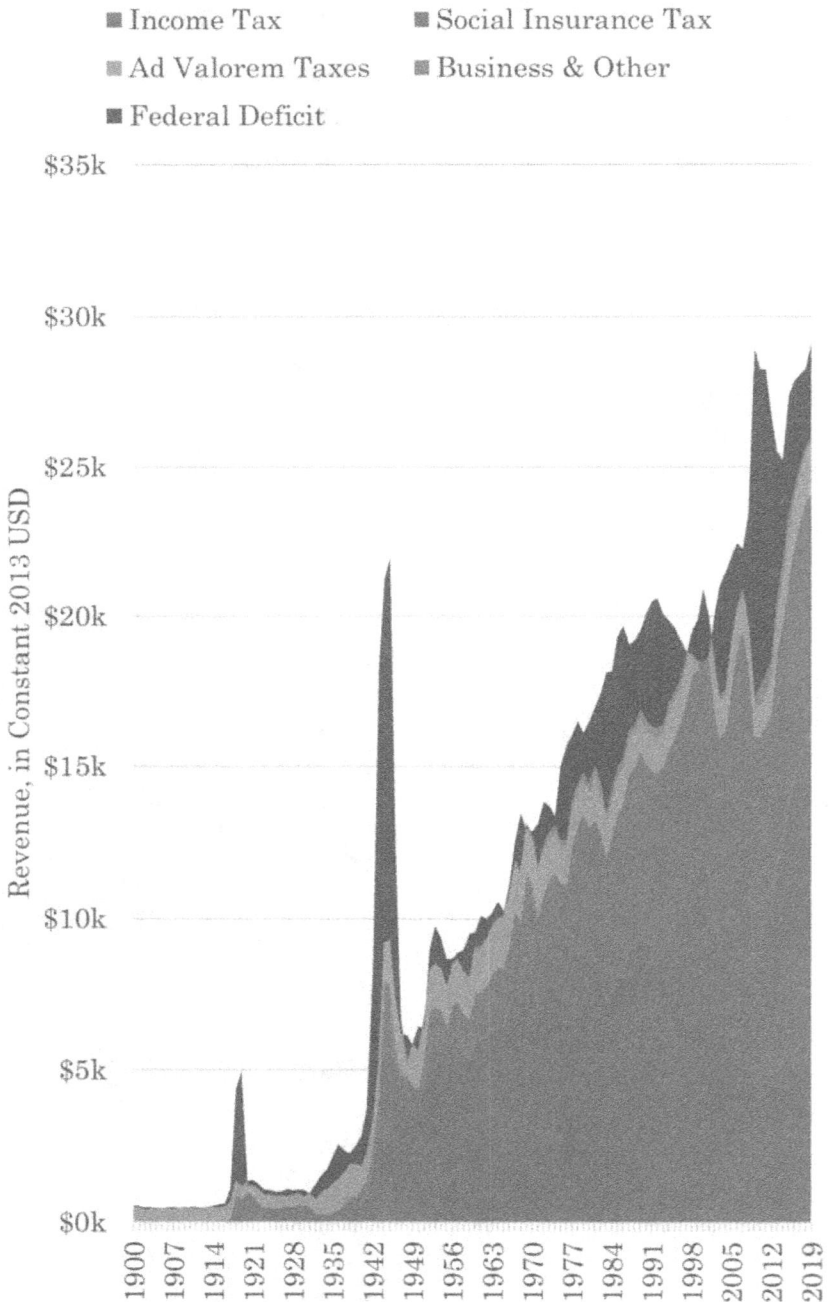

- Income Tax
- Social Insurance Tax
- Ad Valorem Taxes
- Business & Other
- Federal Deficit

Thomas E. Kurek

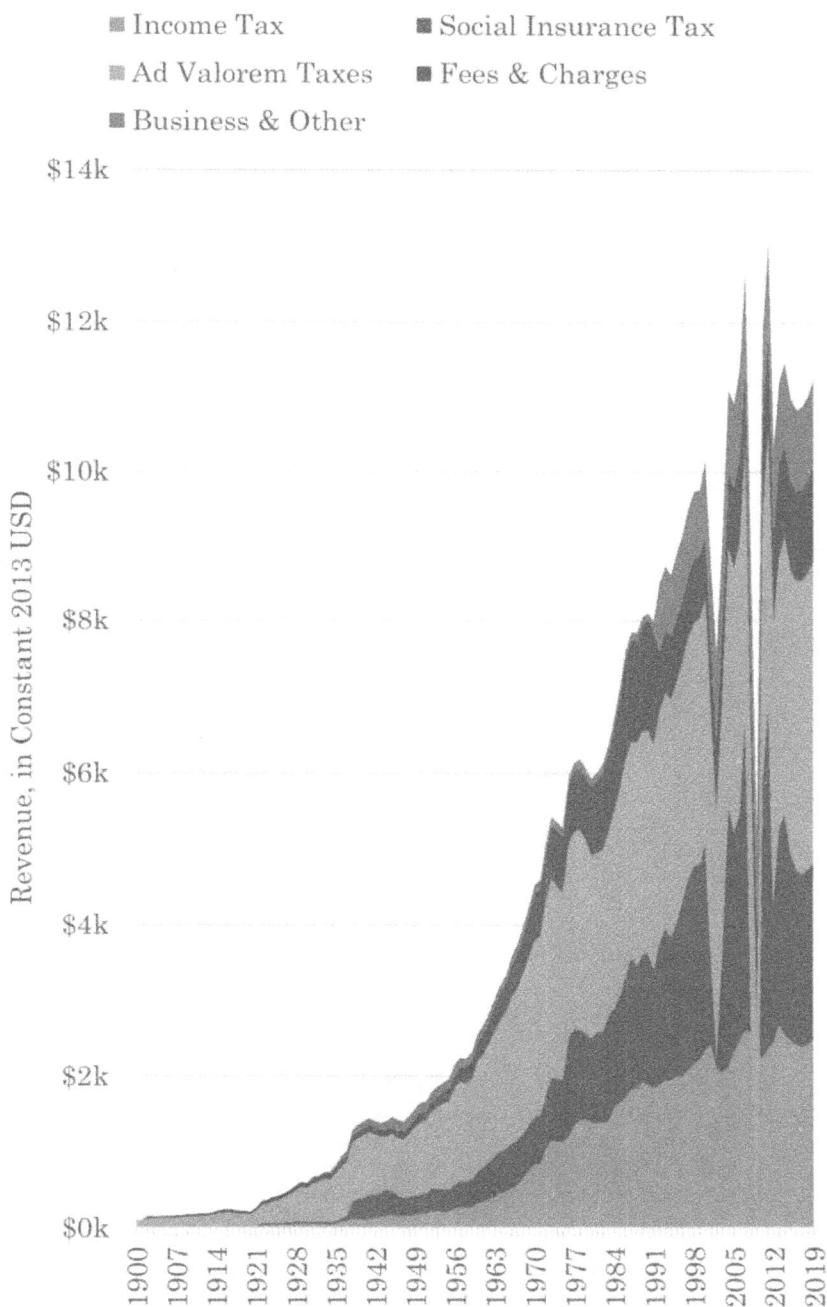

Figure 7: State Tax per Working Person

Income Tax   Social Insurance Tax
Ad Valorem Taxes   Fees & Charges
Business & Other

Appendix 1: Taxation, Income, Assets, Goods
Figure 8: Local Tax per Working Person

■ Income Tax   ■ Social Insurance Tax

■ Ad Valorem Taxes   ■ Fees & Charges

■ Business & Other

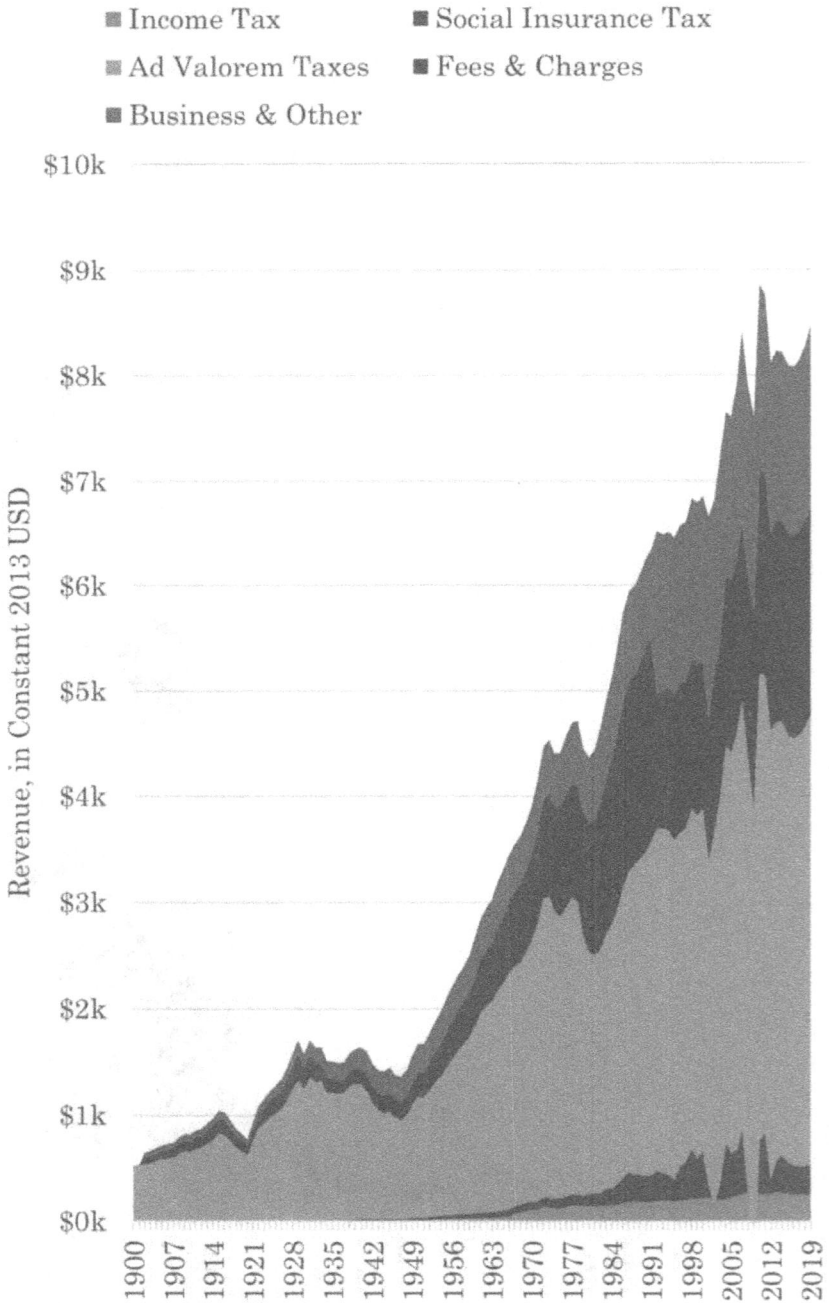

Thomas E. Kurek

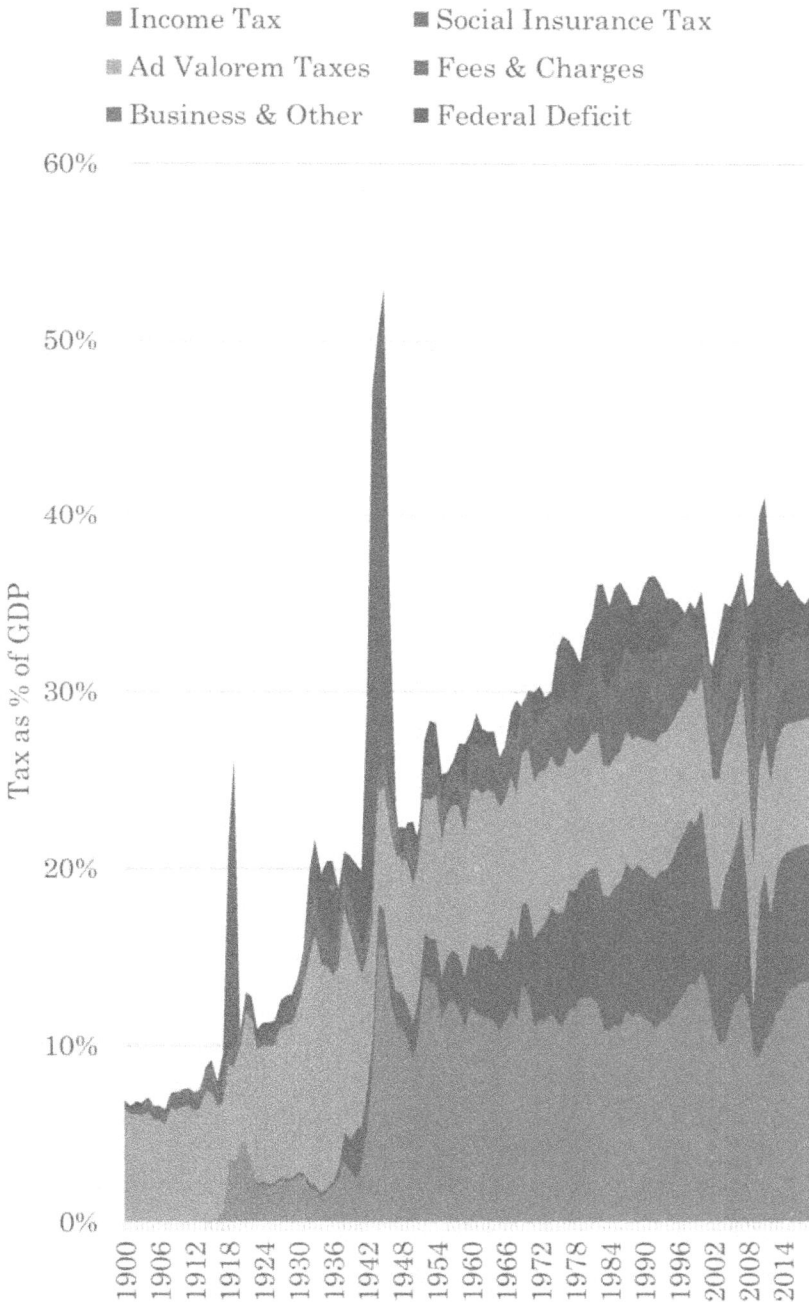

Figure 9: Total Tax, % of GDP

Legend:
- Income Tax
- Social Insurance Tax
- Ad Valorem Taxes
- Fees & Charges
- Business & Other
- Federal Deficit

Appendix 1: Taxation, Income, Assets, Goods
Figure 10: Federal Tax, % of GDP

■ Income Tax   ■ Social Insurance Tax

■ Ad Valorem Taxes   ■ Business & Other

■ Federal Deficit

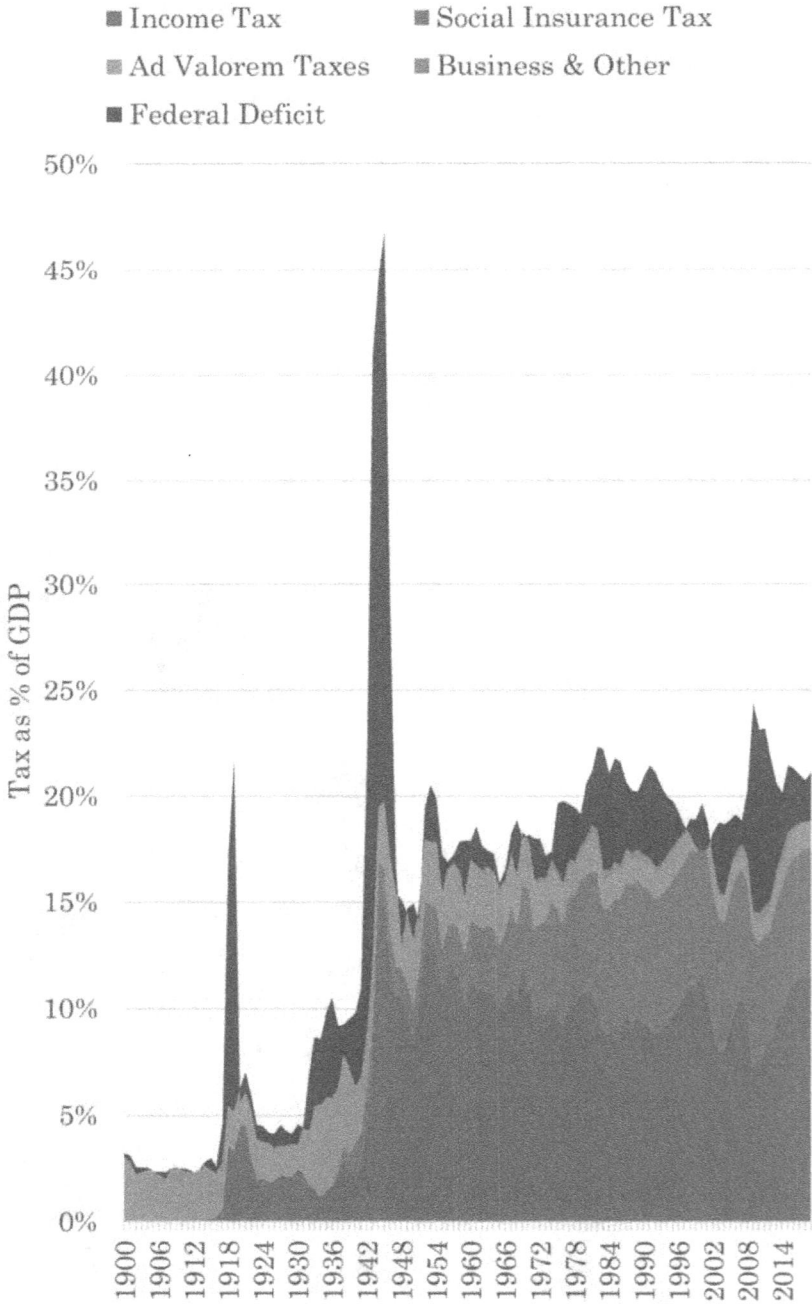

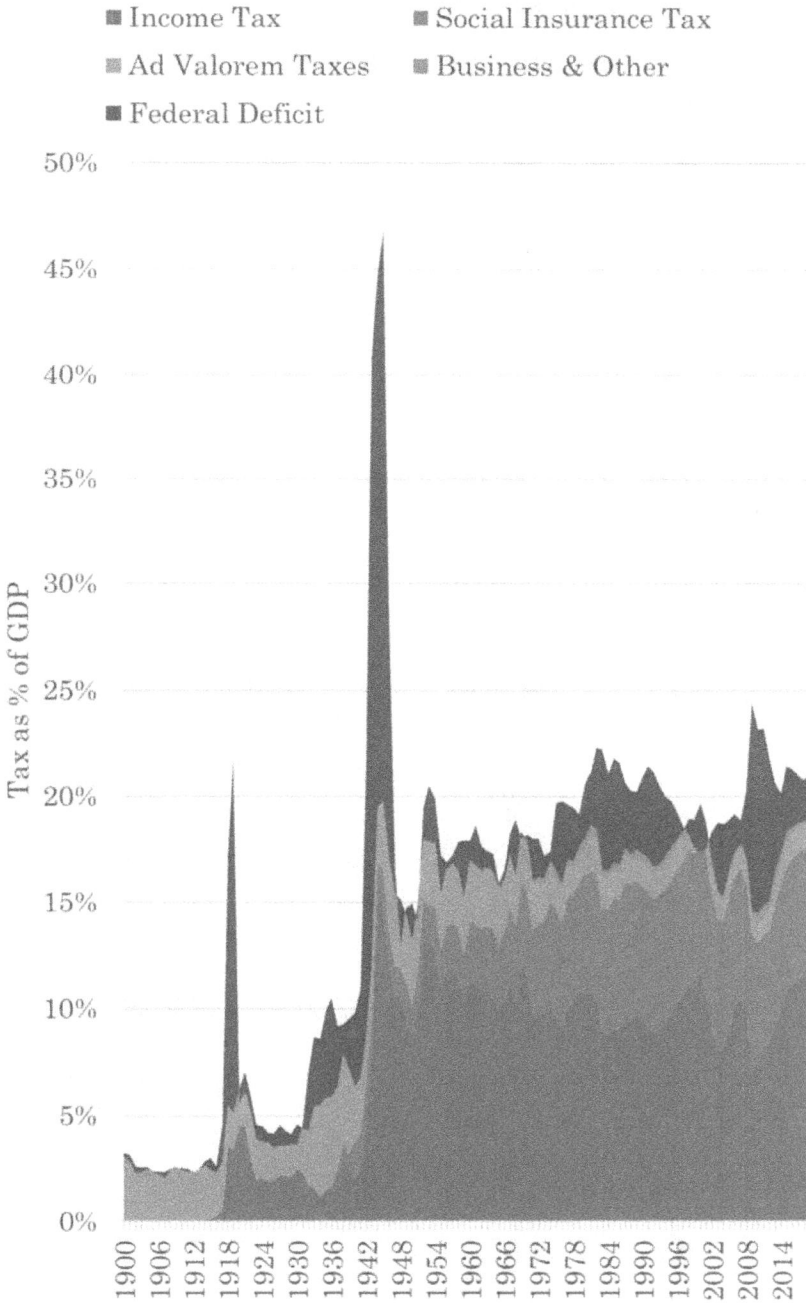

Figure 11: State Tax, % of GDP

Legend:
- Income Tax
- Social Insurance Tax
- Ad Valorem Taxes
- Business & Other
- Federal Deficit

Appendix 1: Taxation, Income, Assets, Goods
Figure 12: Local Tax, % of GDP

- Income Tax
- Social Insurance Tax
- Ad Valorem Taxes
- Fees & Charges
- Business & Other

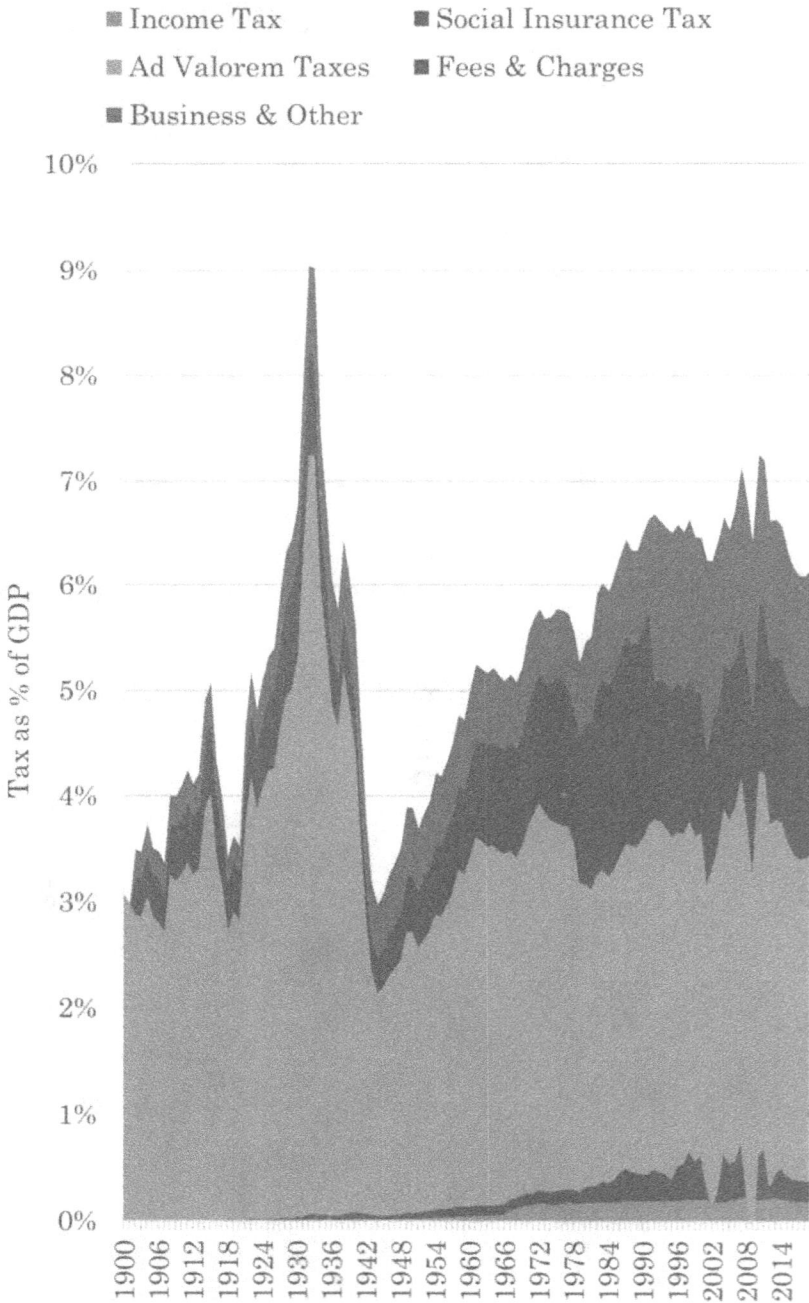

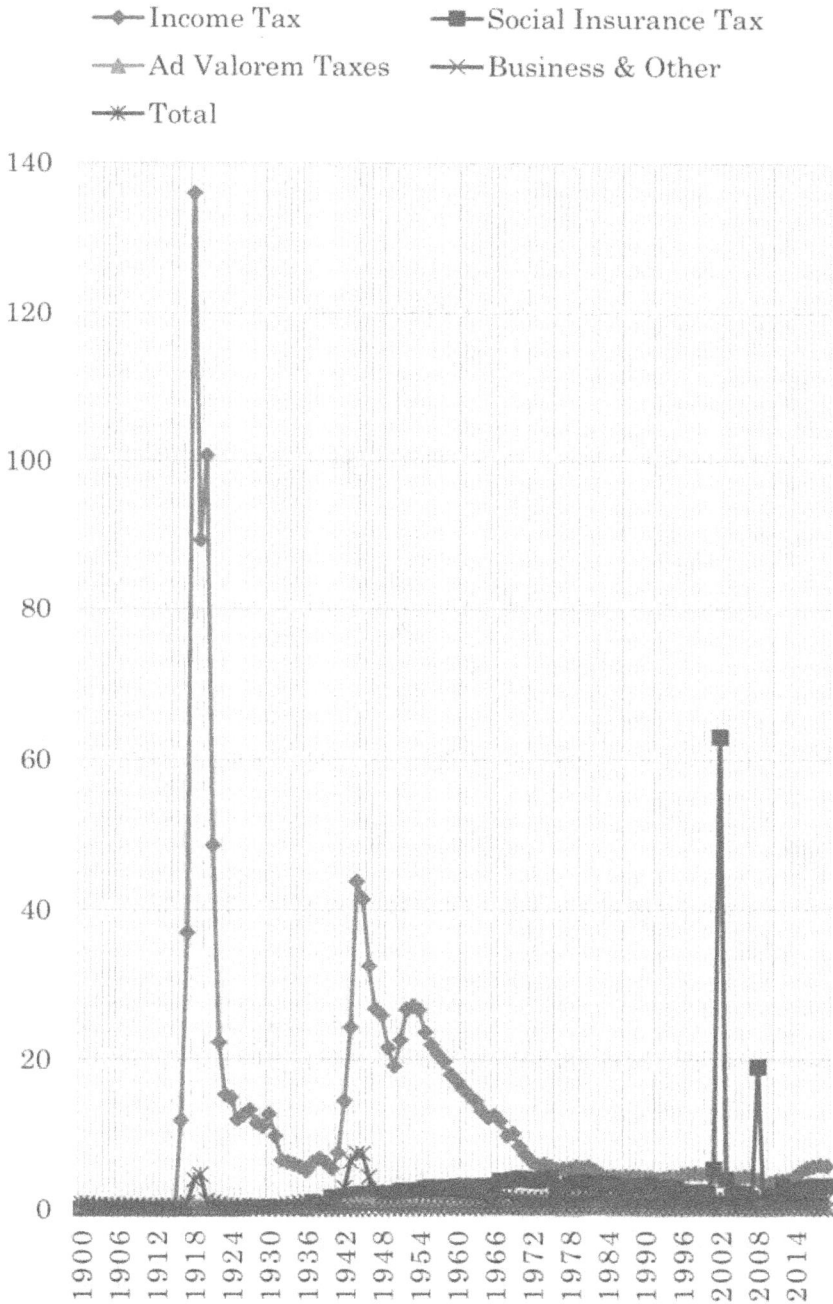

Figure 13: Ratio of Federal to State & Local Revenues (Spikes)

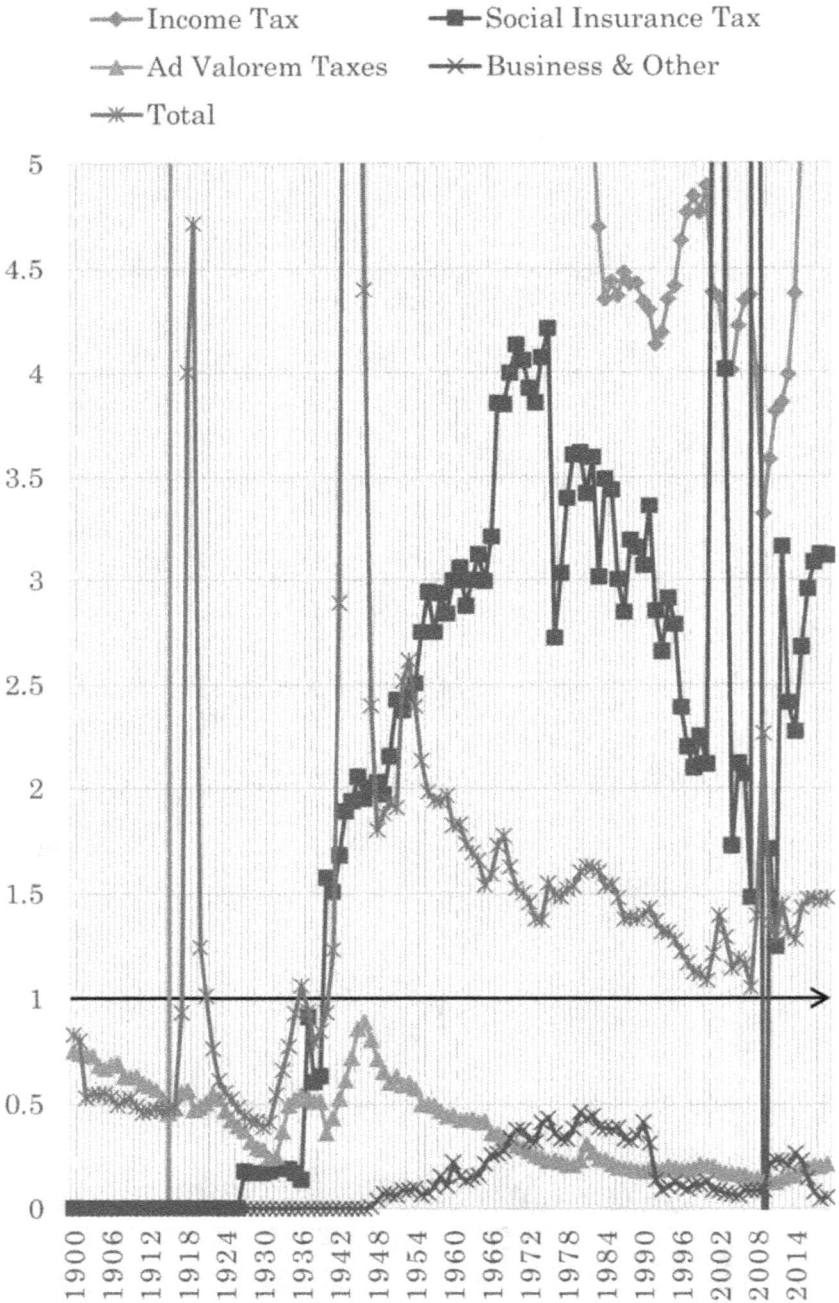

Appendix 1: Taxation, Income, Assets, Goods

Figure 14: Ratio of Federal to State & Local Revenues (Trends)

Thomas E. Kurek

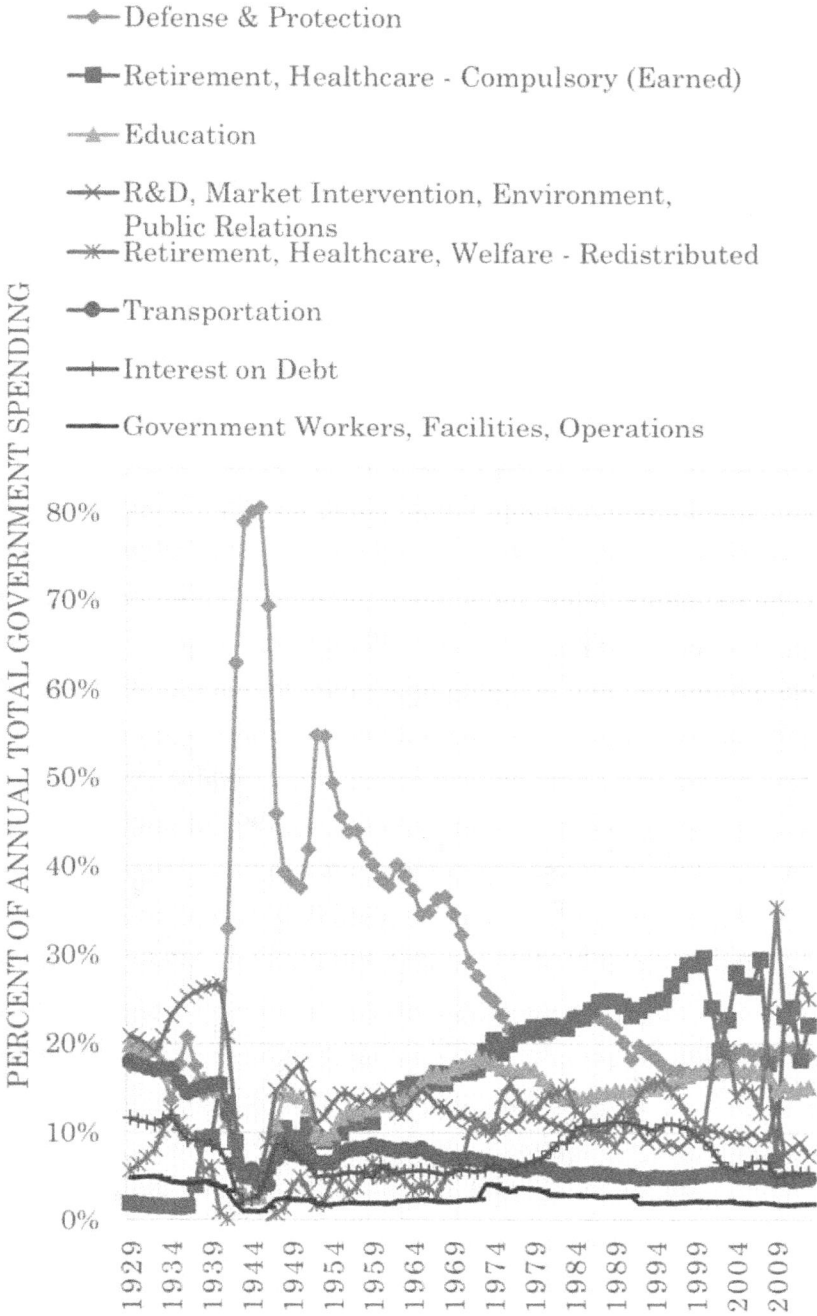

Figure 15: Government Spending Distribution

—◆—Defense & Protection

—■—Retirement, Healthcare - Compulsory (Earned)

—▲—Education

—✕—R&D, Market Intervention, Environment, Public Relations
—✳—Retirement, Healthcare, Welfare - Redistributed

—●—Transportation

—+—Interest on Debt

——Government Workers, Facilities, Operations

Figure 16: Government Spending per FTE

- Government Workers, Facilities, Operations

- Transportation

- Interest on Debt

- R&D, Market Intervention, Environment,
  Public Relations
- Retirement, Healthcare, Welfare - Redistributed

- Education

- Retirement, Healthcare - Compulsory (Earned)

- Defense & Protection

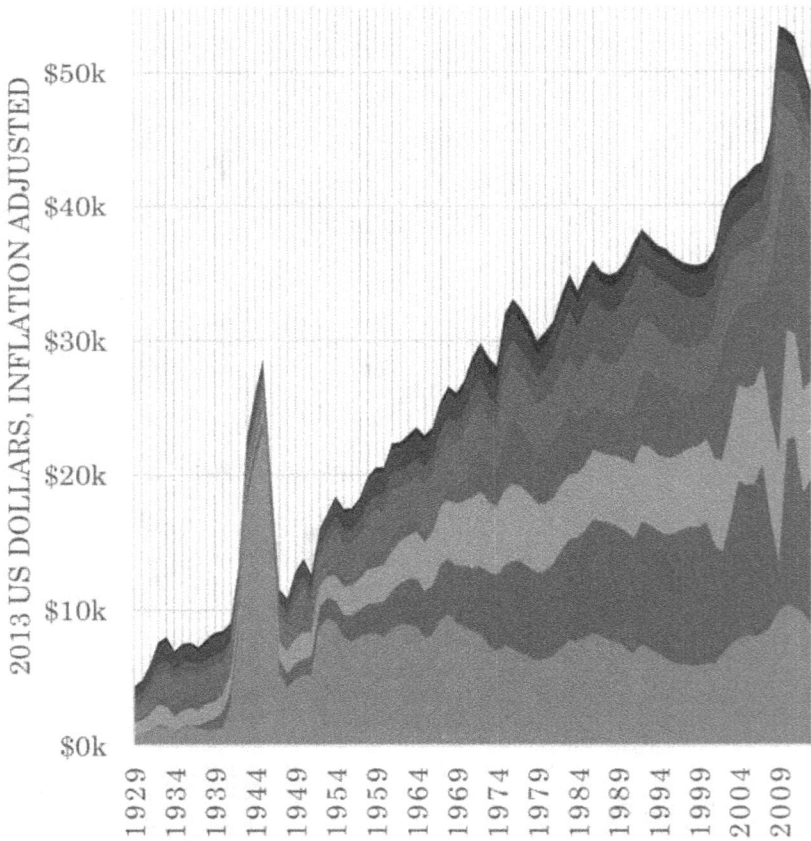

Figure 17: Government Spending per FTE Compensation

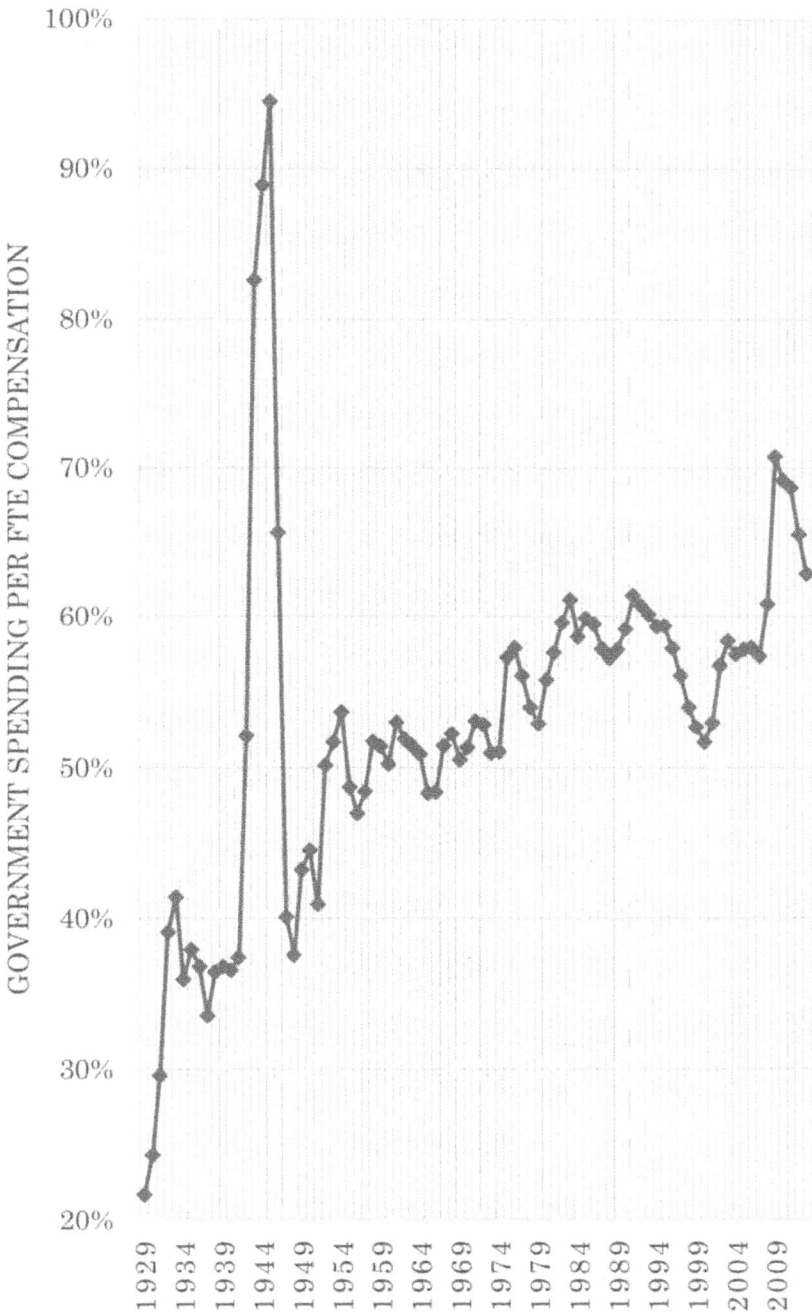

Figure 18: Government Redistribution per FTE Compensation

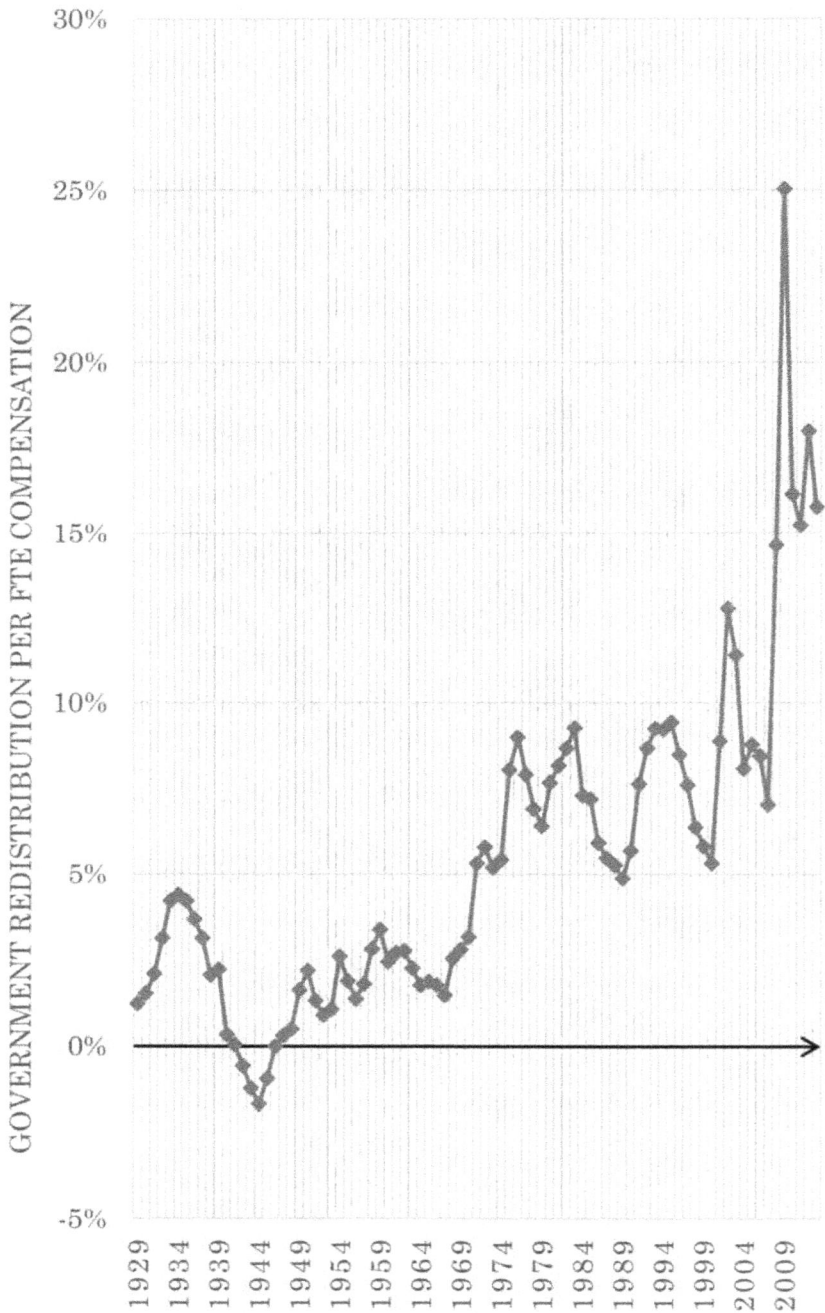

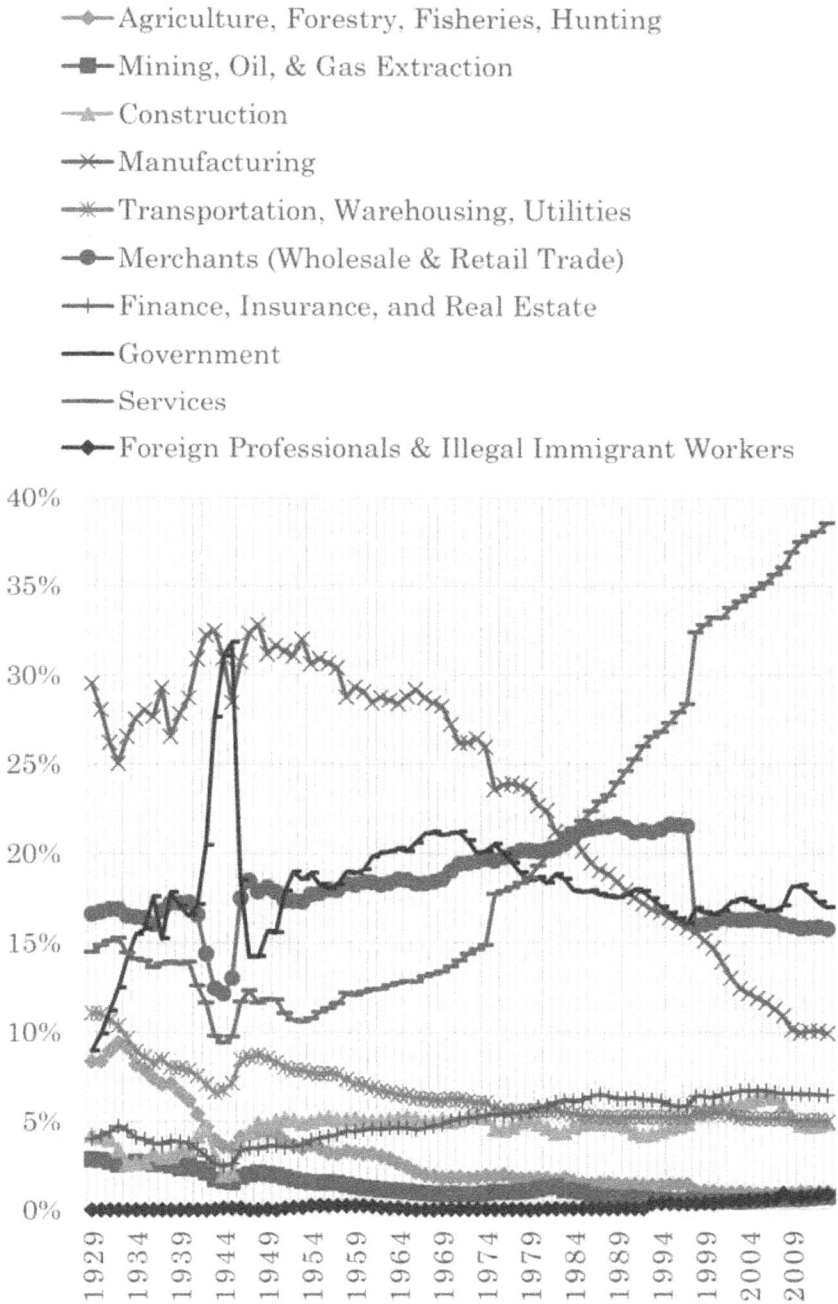

Figure 19: Workforce Composition

Legend:
- Agriculture, Forestry, Fisheries, Hunting
- Mining, Oil, & Gas Extraction
- Construction
- Manufacturing
- Transportation, Warehousing, Utilities
- Merchants (Wholesale & Retail Trade)
- Finance, Insurance, and Real Estate
- Government
- Services
- Foreign Professionals & Illegal Immigrant Workers

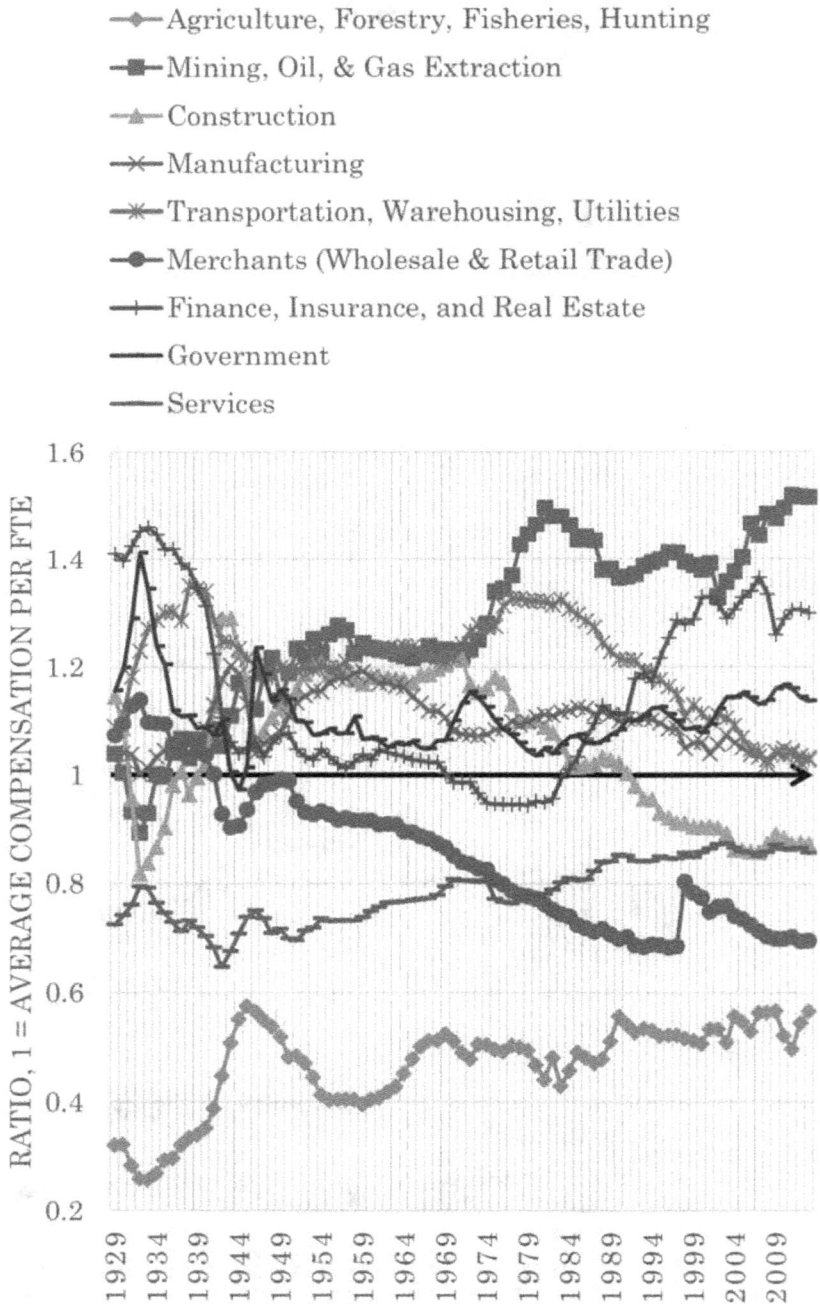

Appendix 1: Taxation, Income, Assets, Goods
Figure 20: Average Industrial Compensation Ratio

—◆—Agriculture, Forestry, Fisheries, Hunting
—■—Mining, Oil, & Gas Extraction
—▲—Construction
—✕—Manufacturing
—✳—Transportation, Warehousing, Utilities
—●—Merchants (Wholesale & Retail Trade)
—+—Finance, Insurance, and Real Estate
——Government
——Services

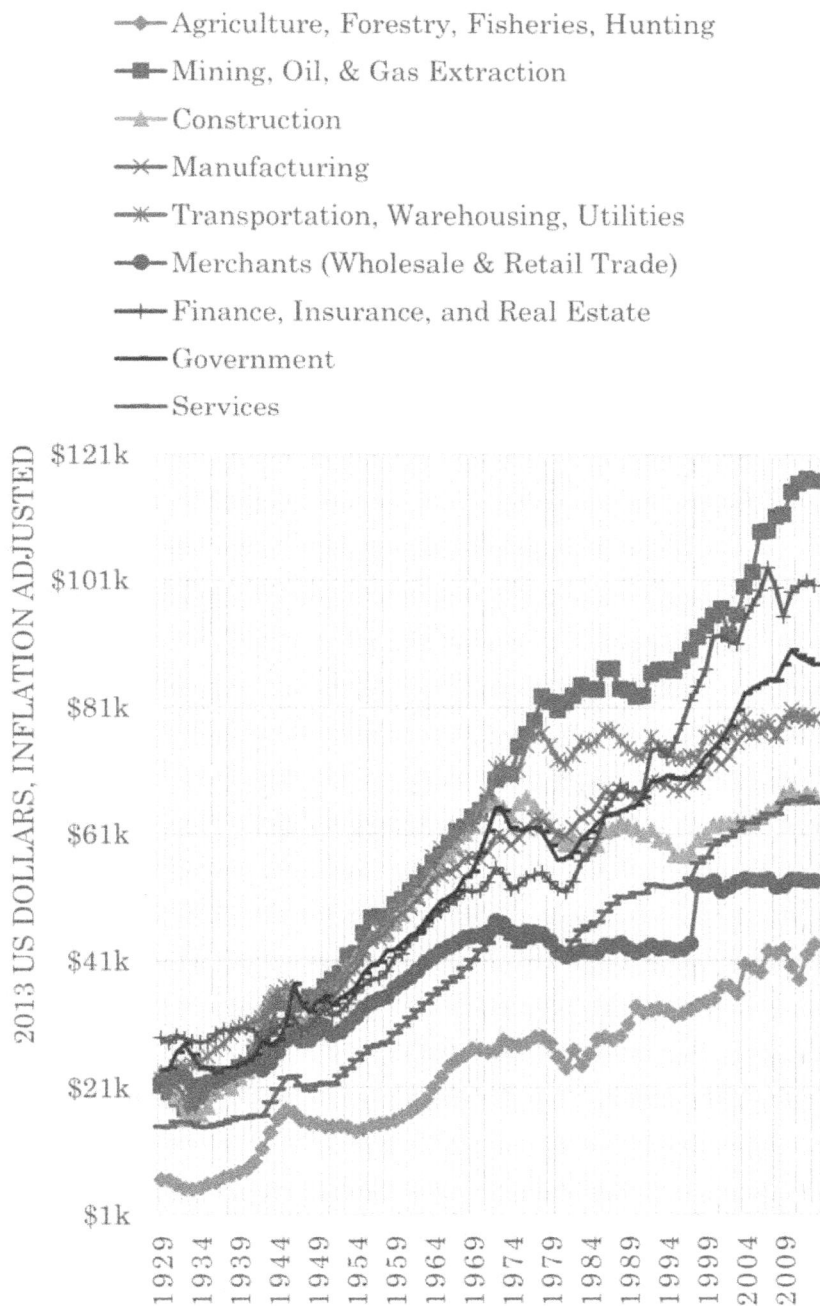

Figure 21: Compensation per Worker

—◆—Agriculture, Forestry, Fisheries, Hunting

—■—Mining, Oil, & Gas Extraction

—▲—Construction

—✕—Manufacturing

—✳—Transportation, Warehousing, Utilities

—●—Merchants (Wholesale & Retail Trade)

—+—Finance, Insurance, and Real Estate

——Government

——Services

Figure 22: Industrial Compensation Inequality

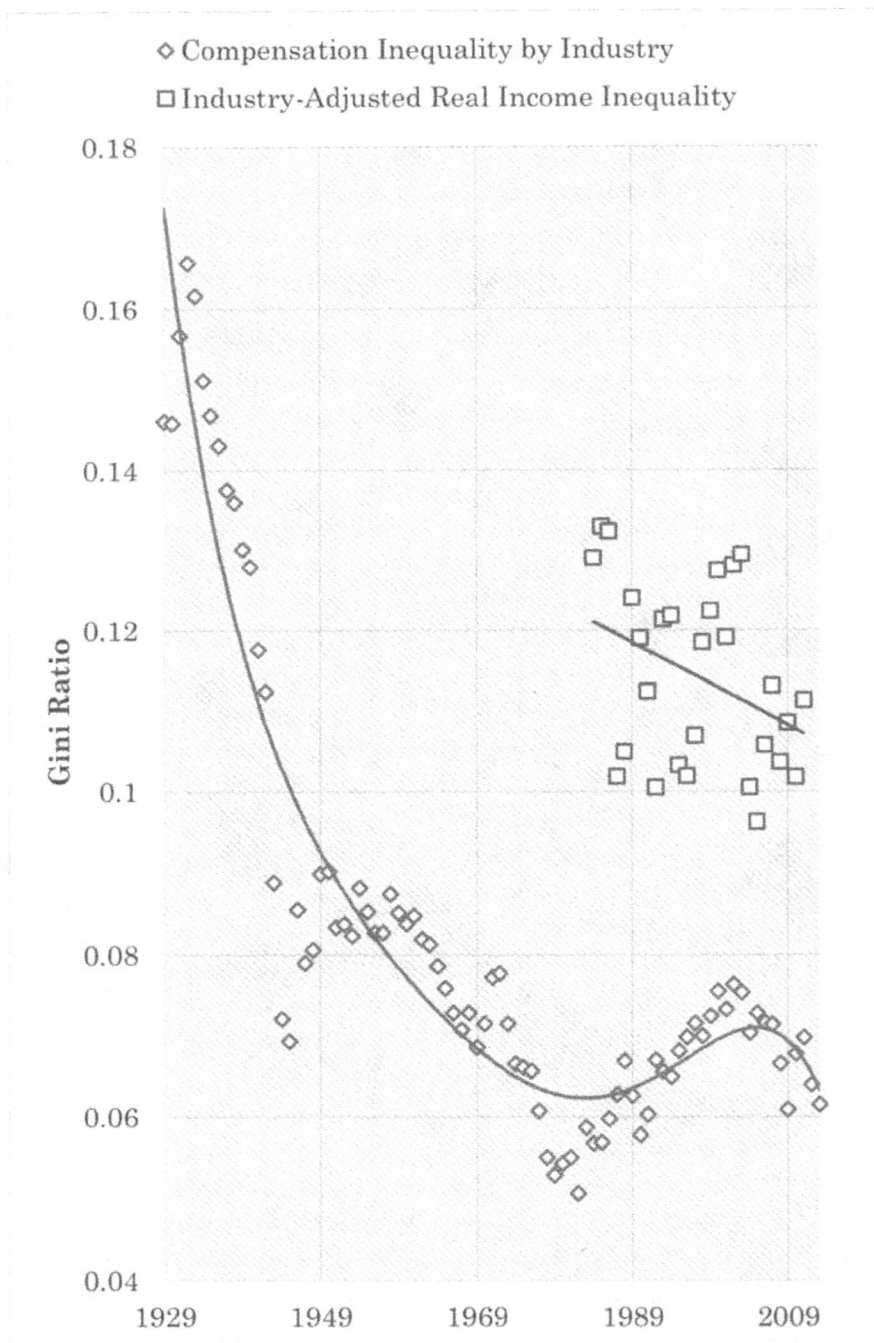

◇ Compensation Inequality by Industry

□ Industry-Adjusted Real Income Inequality

Thomas E. Kurek

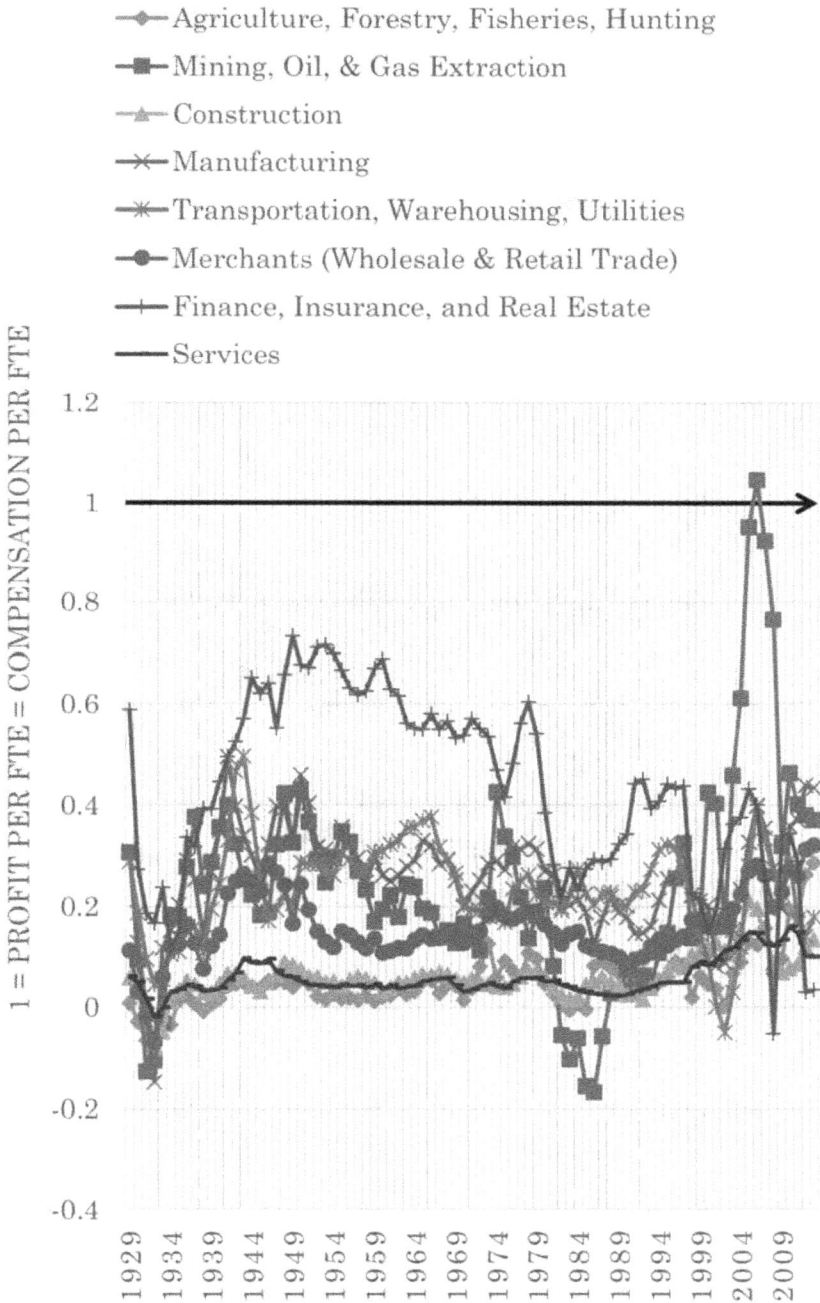

Figure 23: Ratio of Profit to Compensation

—◆—Agriculture, Forestry, Fisheries, Hunting

—■—Mining, Oil, & Gas Extraction

—▲—Construction

—✕—Manufacturing

—✳—Transportation, Warehousing, Utilities

—●—Merchants (Wholesale & Retail Trade)

—+—Finance, Insurance, and Real Estate

——Services

Figure 24: Ratio of Industrial Profit to Average Profit

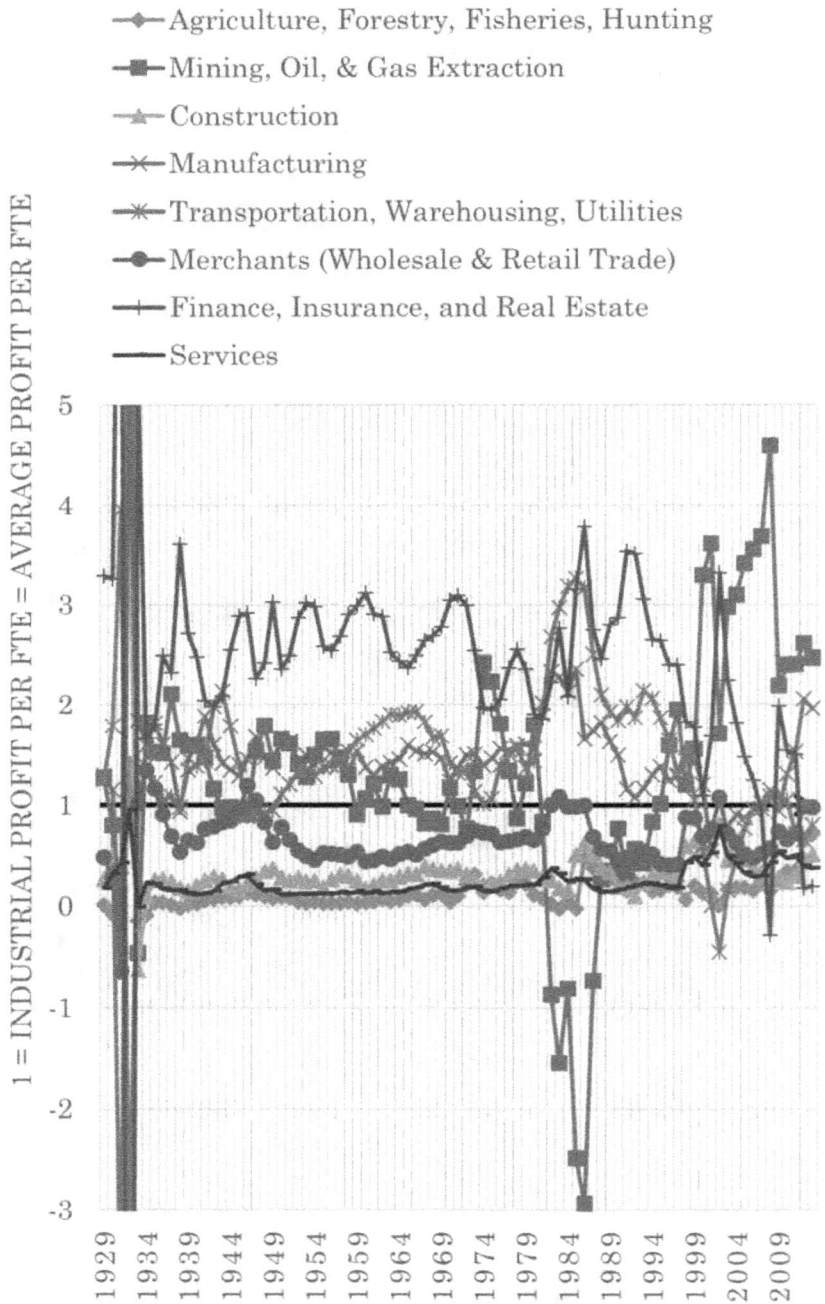

─◆─ Agriculture, Forestry, Fisheries, Hunting

─■─ Mining, Oil, & Gas Extraction

─▲─ Construction

─✕─ Manufacturing

─✳─ Transportation, Warehousing, Utilities

─●─ Merchants (Wholesale & Retail Trade)

─┼─ Finance, Insurance, and Real Estate

─── Services

Thomas E. Kurek

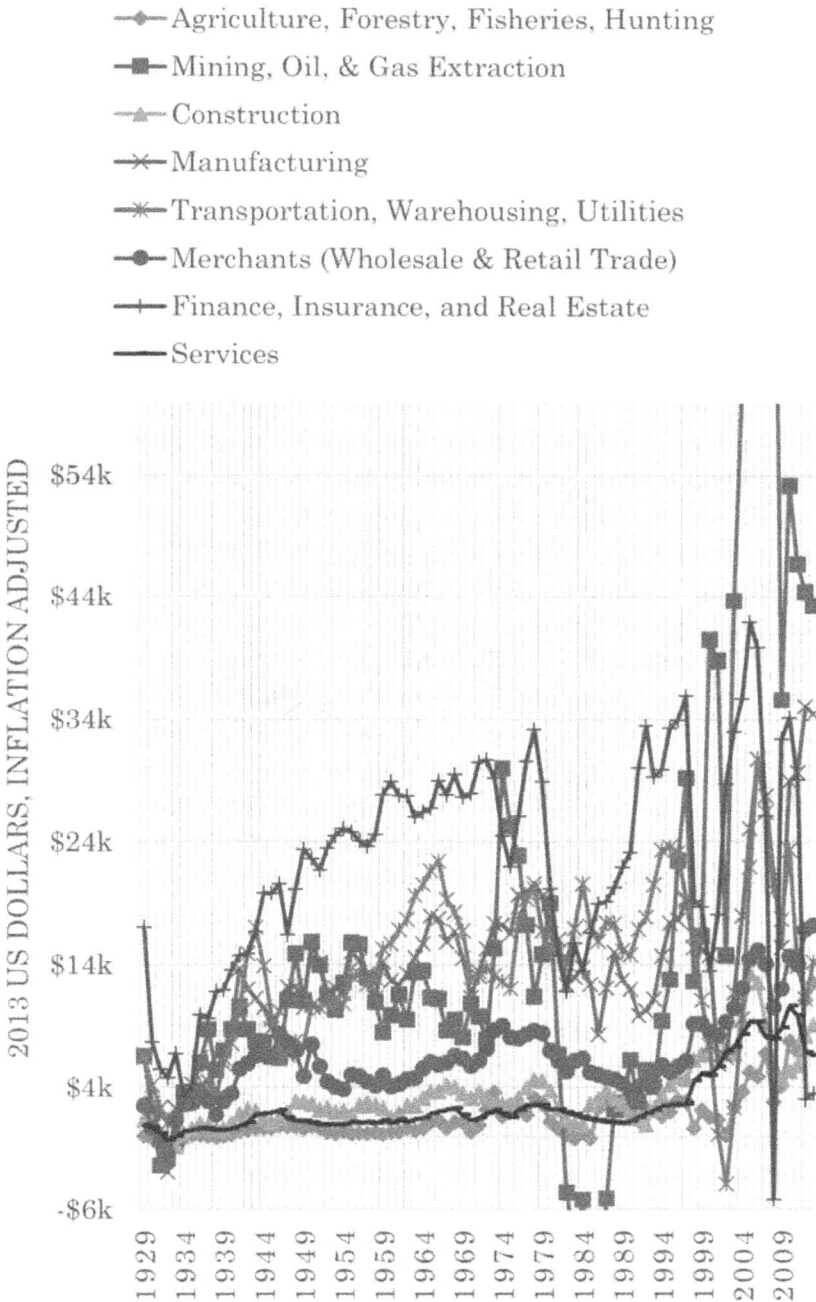

Figure 25: Profits per Worker

Legend:
- Agriculture, Forestry, Fisheries, Hunting
- Mining, Oil, & Gas Extraction
- Construction
- Manufacturing
- Transportation, Warehousing, Utilities
- Merchants (Wholesale & Retail Trade)
- Finance, Insurance, and Real Estate
- Services

Y-axis: 2013 US DOLLARS, INFLATION ADJUSTED
Values: -$6k, $4k, $14k, $24k, $34k, $44k, $54k

X-axis: 1929, 1934, 1939, 1944, 1949, 1954, 1959, 1964, 1969, 1974, 1979, 1984, 1989, 1994, 1999, 2004, 2009

Figure 26: Savings per Capita

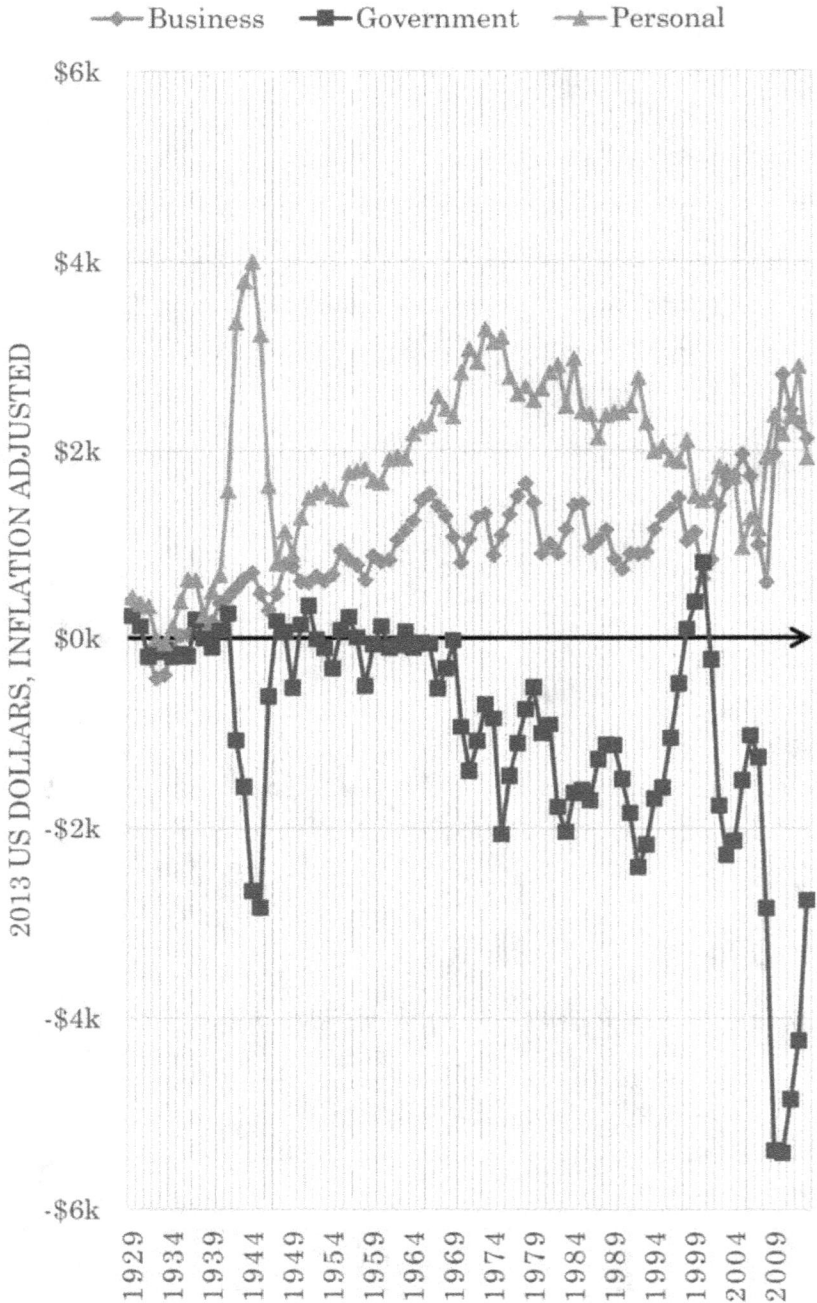

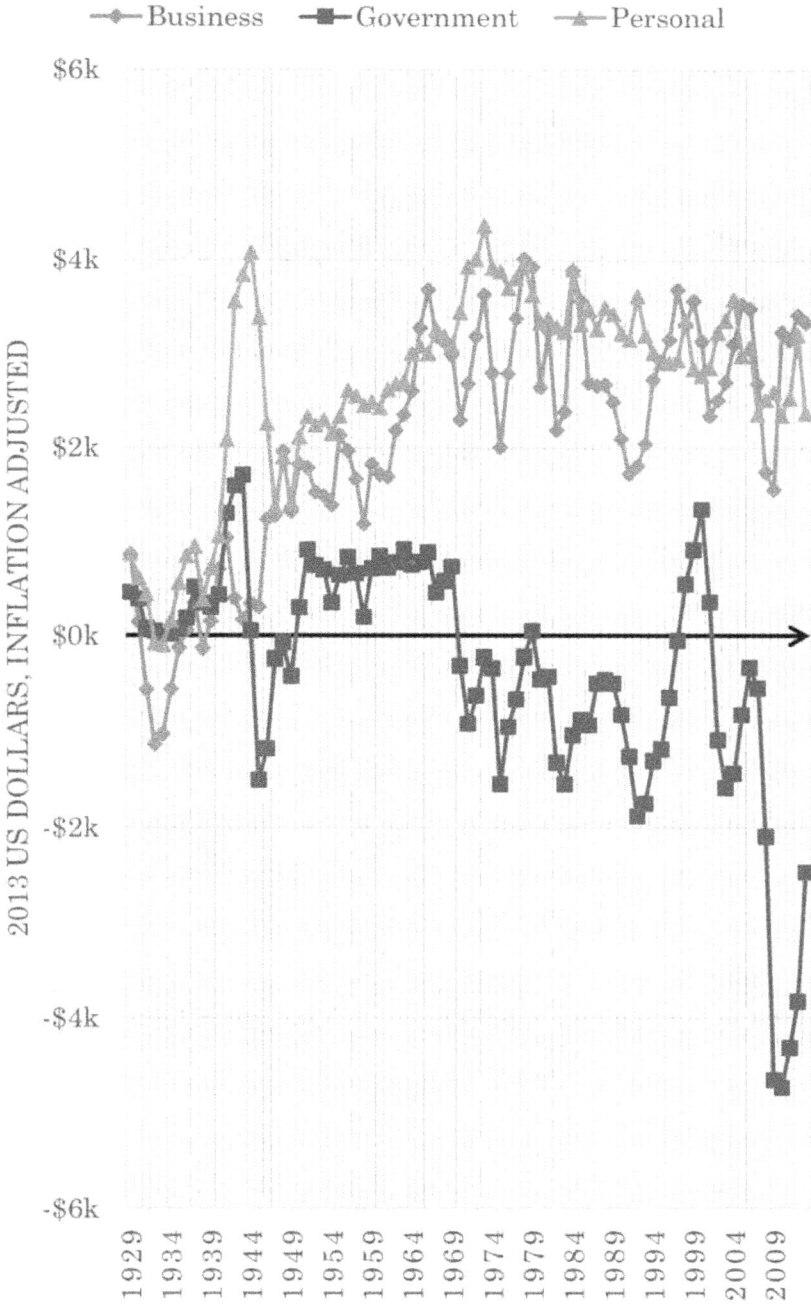

Figure 27: Surplus per Capita

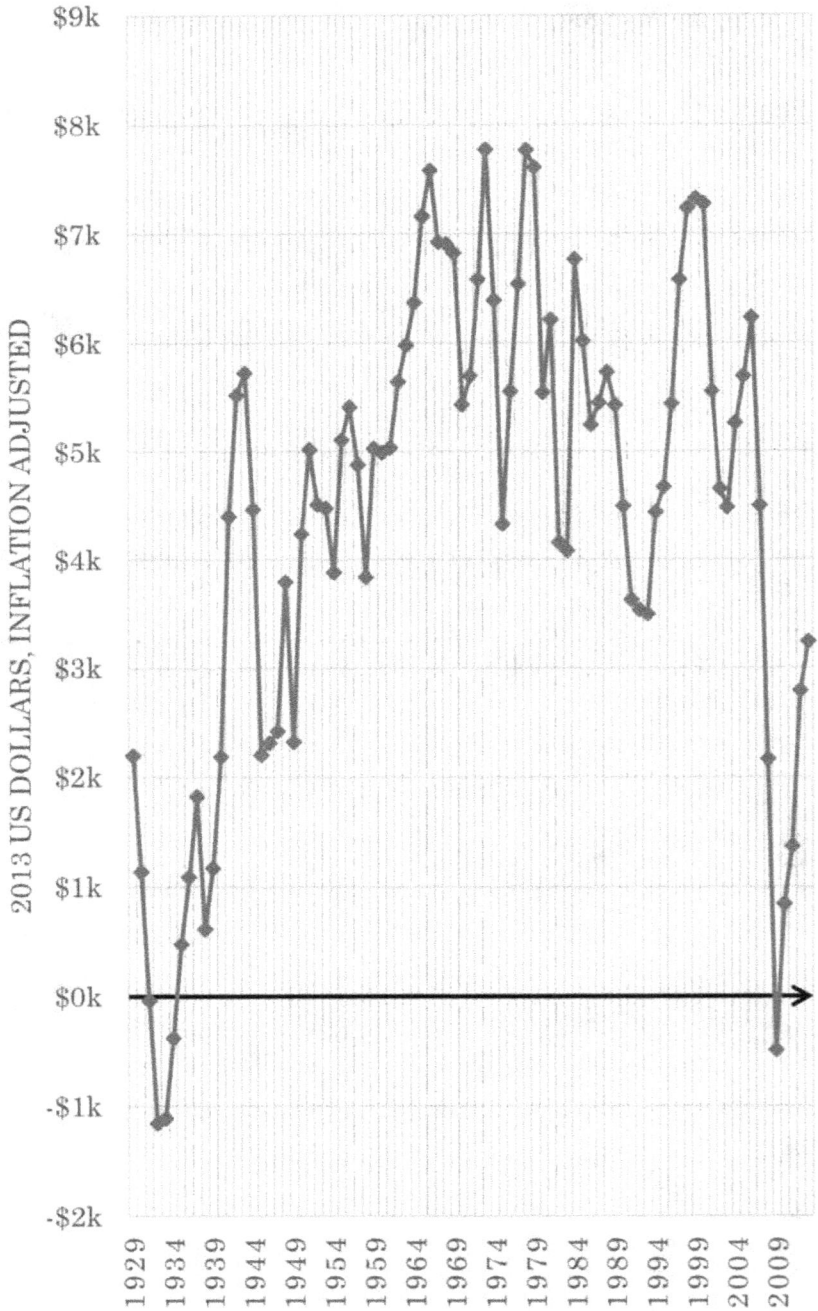

Appendix 1: Taxation, Income, Assets, Goods
Figure 28: Combined Surplus per Capita

Thomas E. Kurek

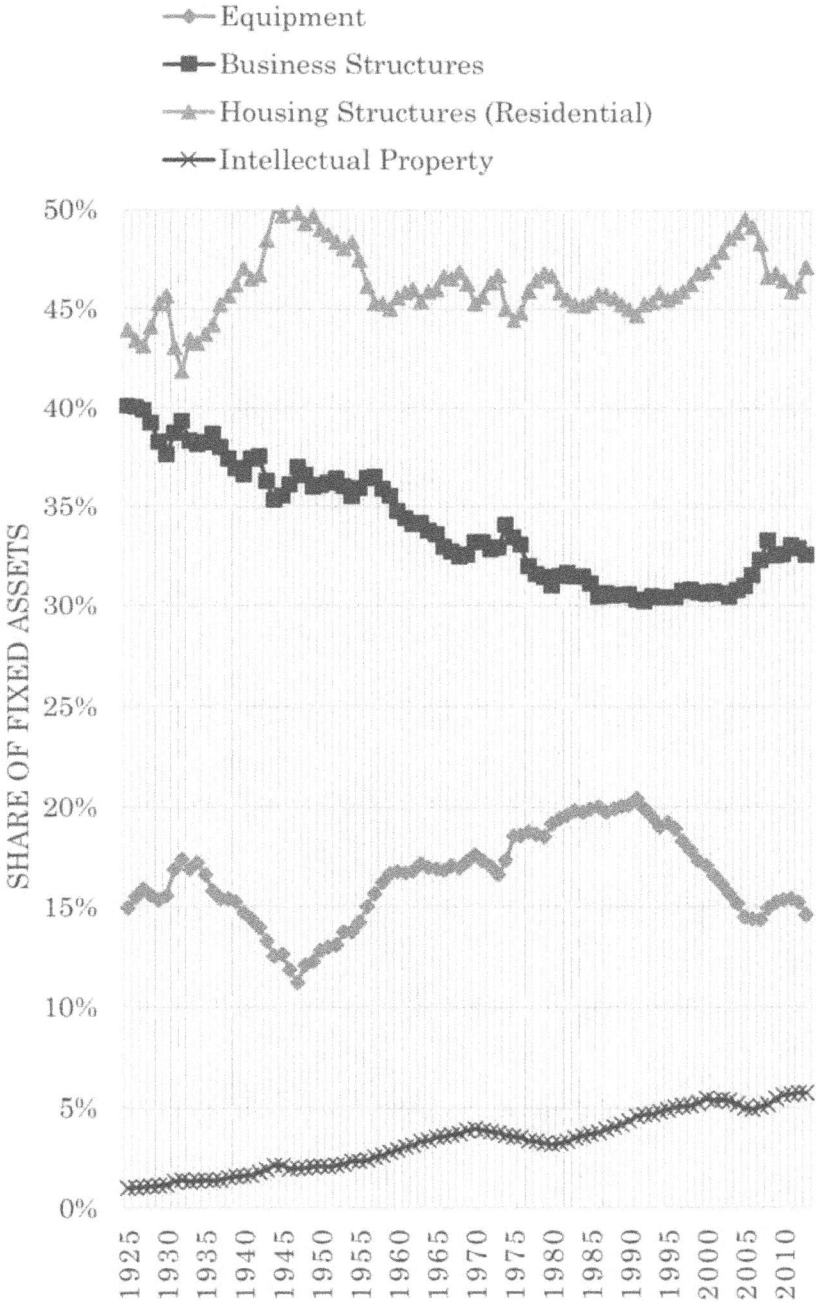

Figure 29: Share of Private Fixed Asset Value

Figure 30: Growth of Private Fixed Asset Value

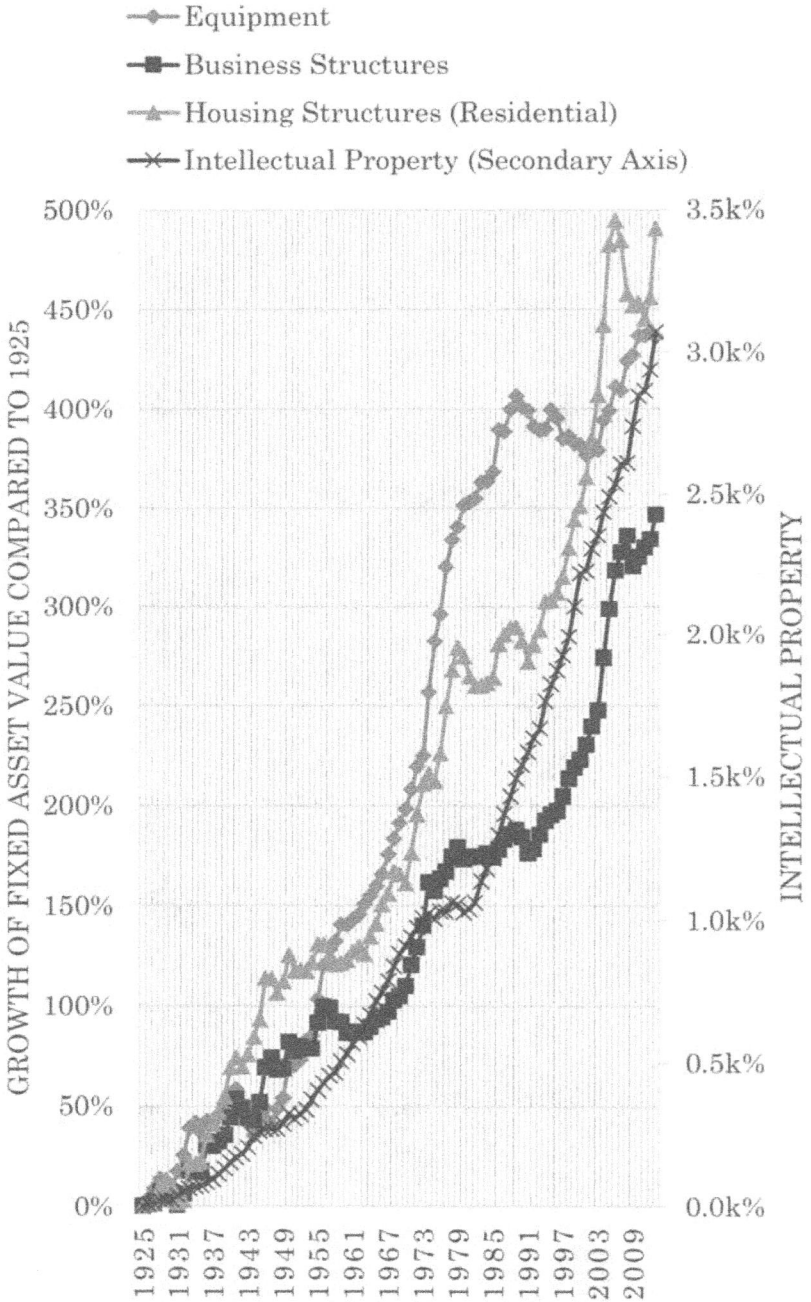

Legend:
- —◆— Equipment
- —■— Business Structures
- —▲— Housing Structures (Residential)
- —✕— Intellectual Property (Secondary Axis)

Thomas E. Kurek

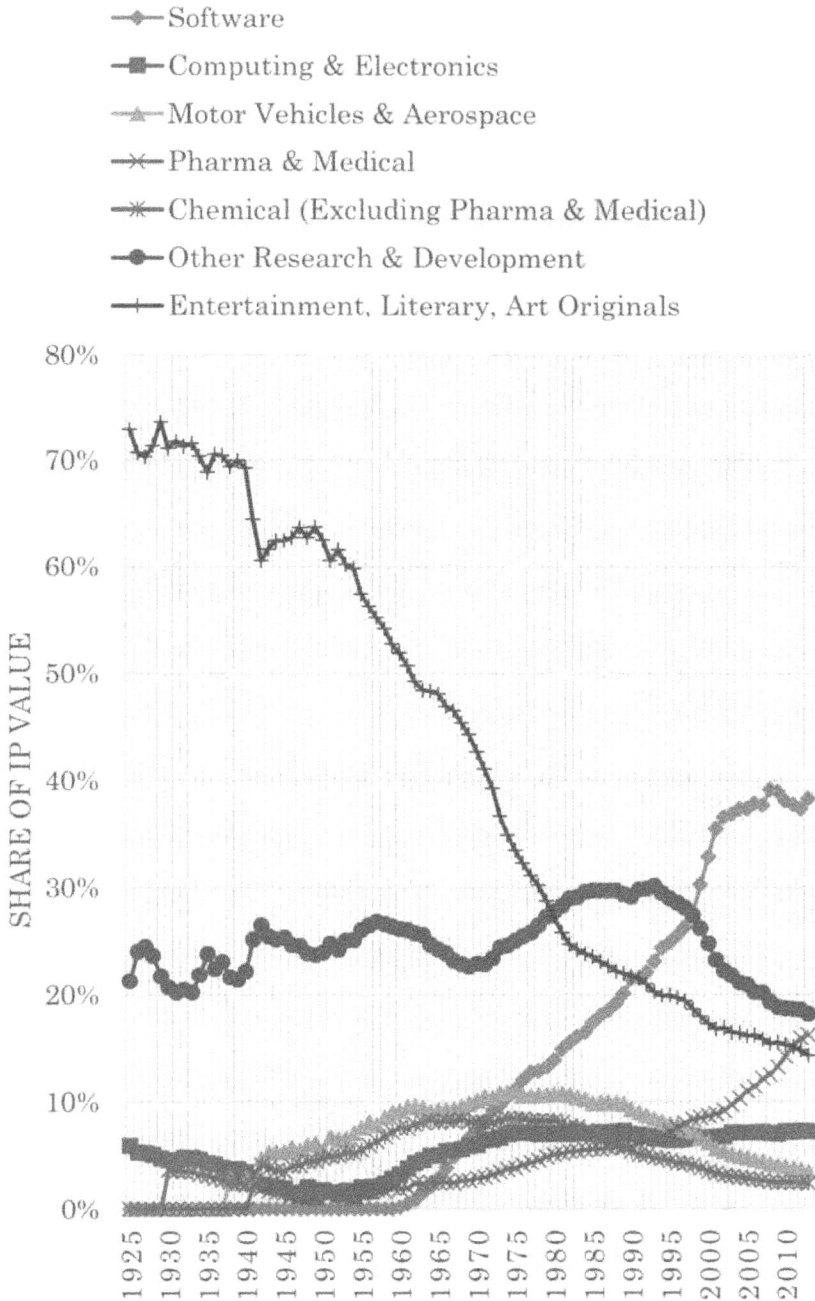

Figure 31: Share of Intellectual Property Value

Legend:
- Software
- Computing & Electronics
- Motor Vehicles & Aerospace
- Pharma & Medical
- Chemical (Excluding Pharma & Medical)
- Other Research & Development
- Entertainment, Literary, Art Originals

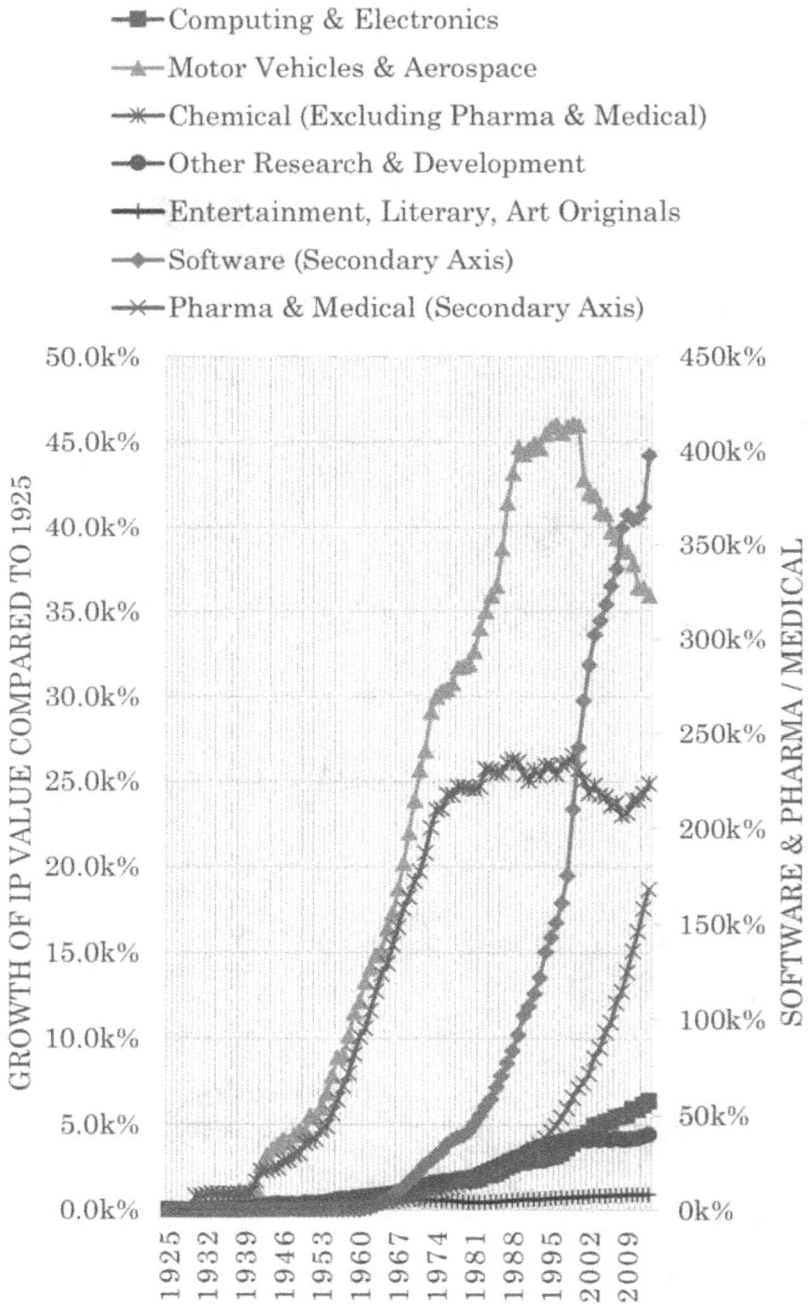

Appendix 1: Taxation, Income, Assets, Goods
Figure 32: Growth of Intellectual Property Value

—■— Computing & Electronics
—▲— Motor Vehicles & Aerospace
—✳— Chemical (Excluding Pharma & Medical)
—●— Other Research & Development
—+— Entertainment, Literary, Art Originals
—◆— Software (Secondary Axis)
—✕— Pharma & Medical (Secondary Axis)

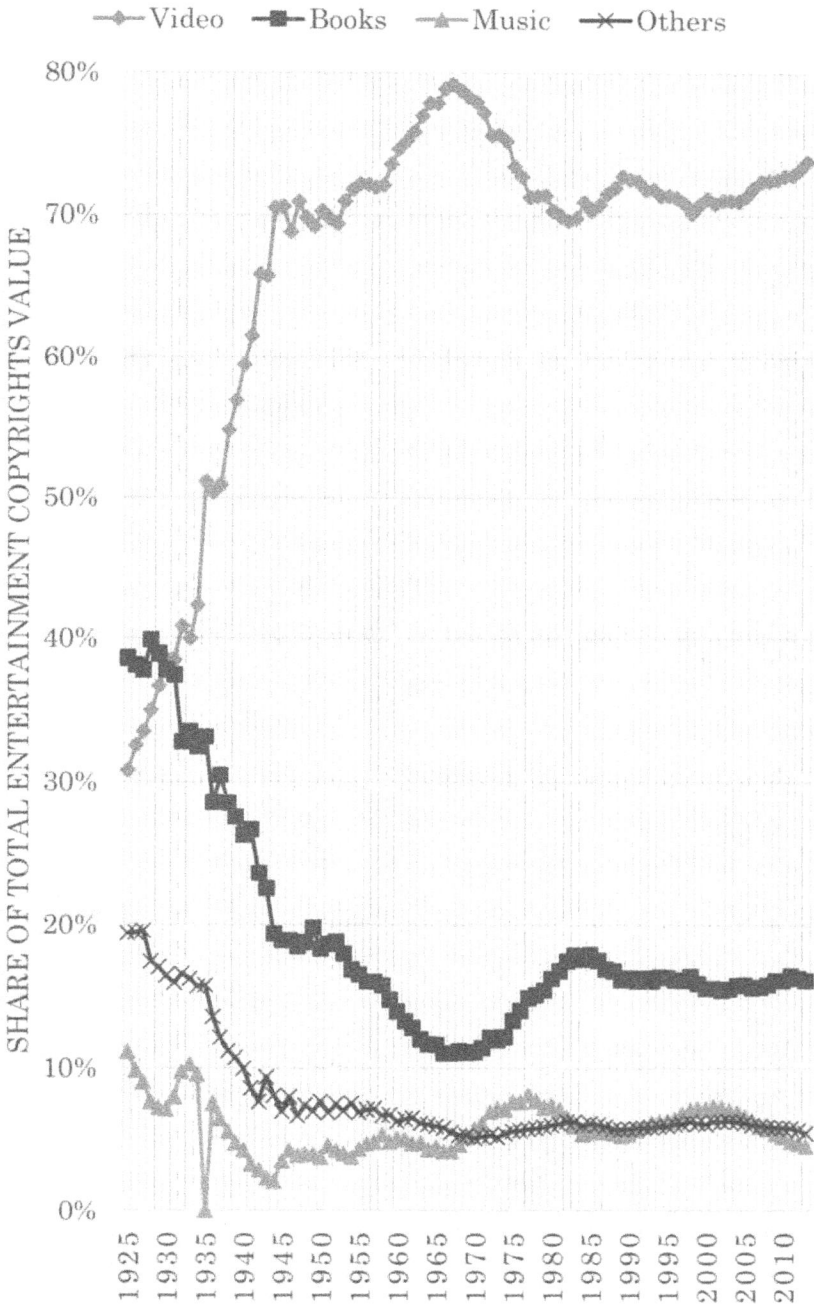

Figure 33: Share of Entertainment Copyrights Value

Figure 34: Growth of Entertainment Copyrights Value

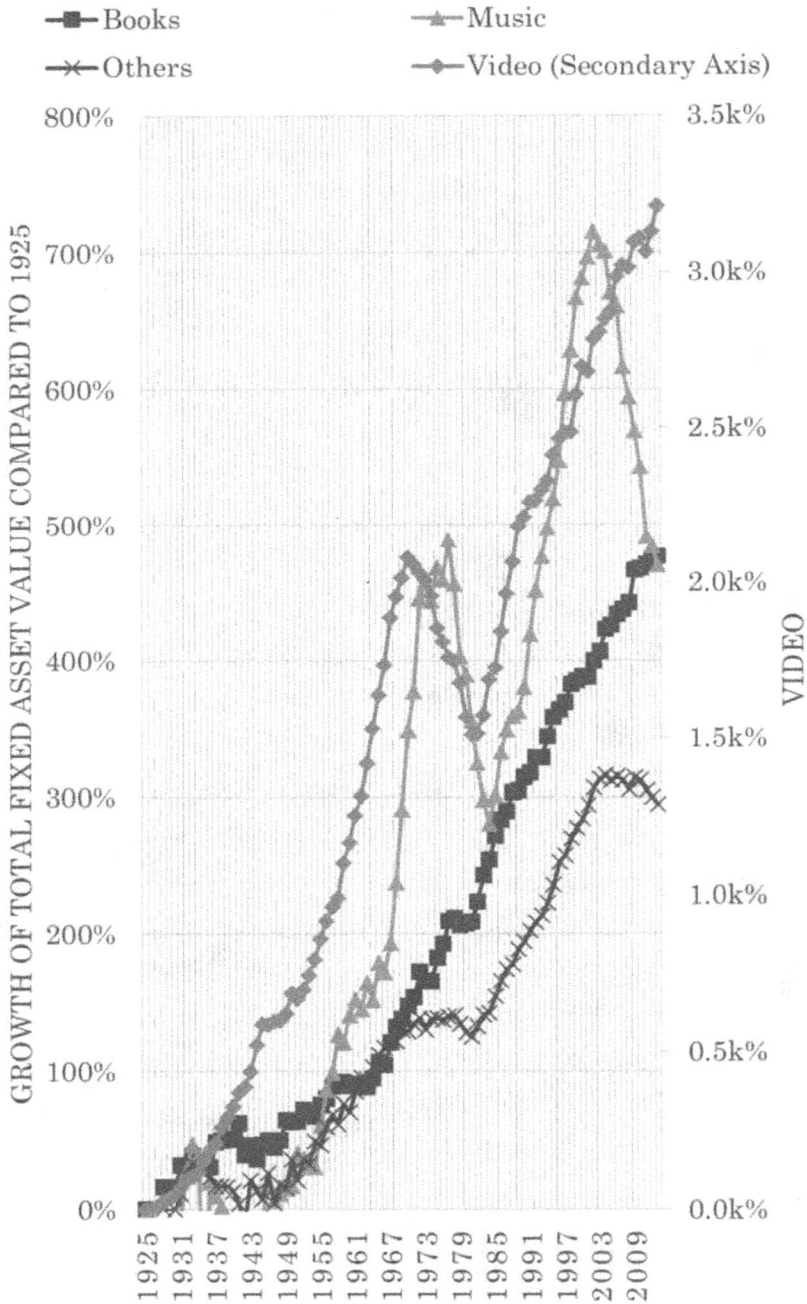

— Books — Music
— Others — Video (Secondary Axis)

GROWTH OF TOTAL FIXED ASSET VALUE COMPARED TO 1925

VIDEO

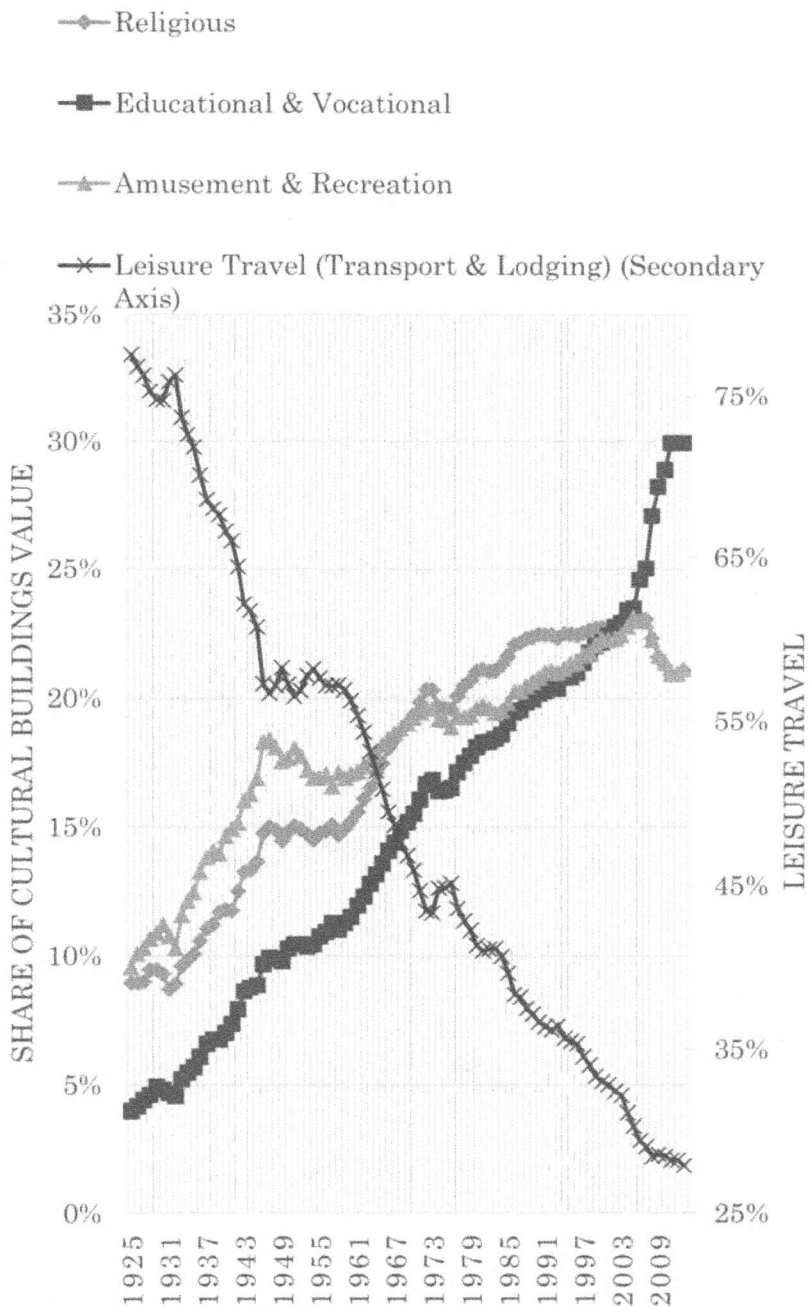

Figure 35: Share of Cultural Buildings Value

Legend:
- ——◆——Religious
- ——■——Educational & Vocational
- ——▲——Amusement & Recreation
- ——✕——Leisure Travel (Transport & Lodging) (Secondary Axis)

Y-axis (left): SHARE OF CULTURAL BUILDINGS VALUE — 0%, 5%, 10%, 15%, 20%, 25%, 30%, 35%

Y-axis (right): LEISURE TRAVEL — 25%, 35%, 45%, 55%, 65%, 75%

X-axis: 1925, 1931, 1937, 1943, 1949, 1955, 1961, 1967, 1973, 1979, 1985, 1991, 1997, 2003, 2009

Figure 36: Growth of Cultural Buildings Value

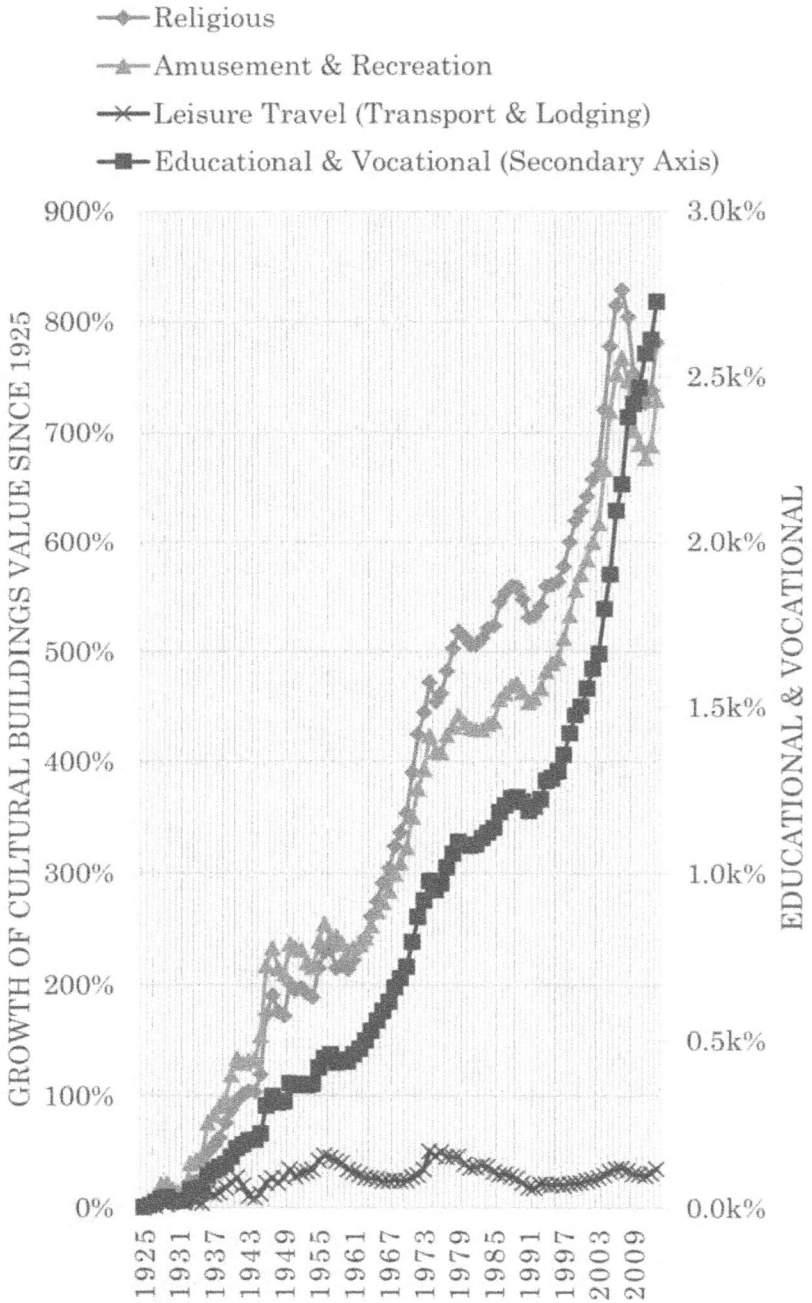

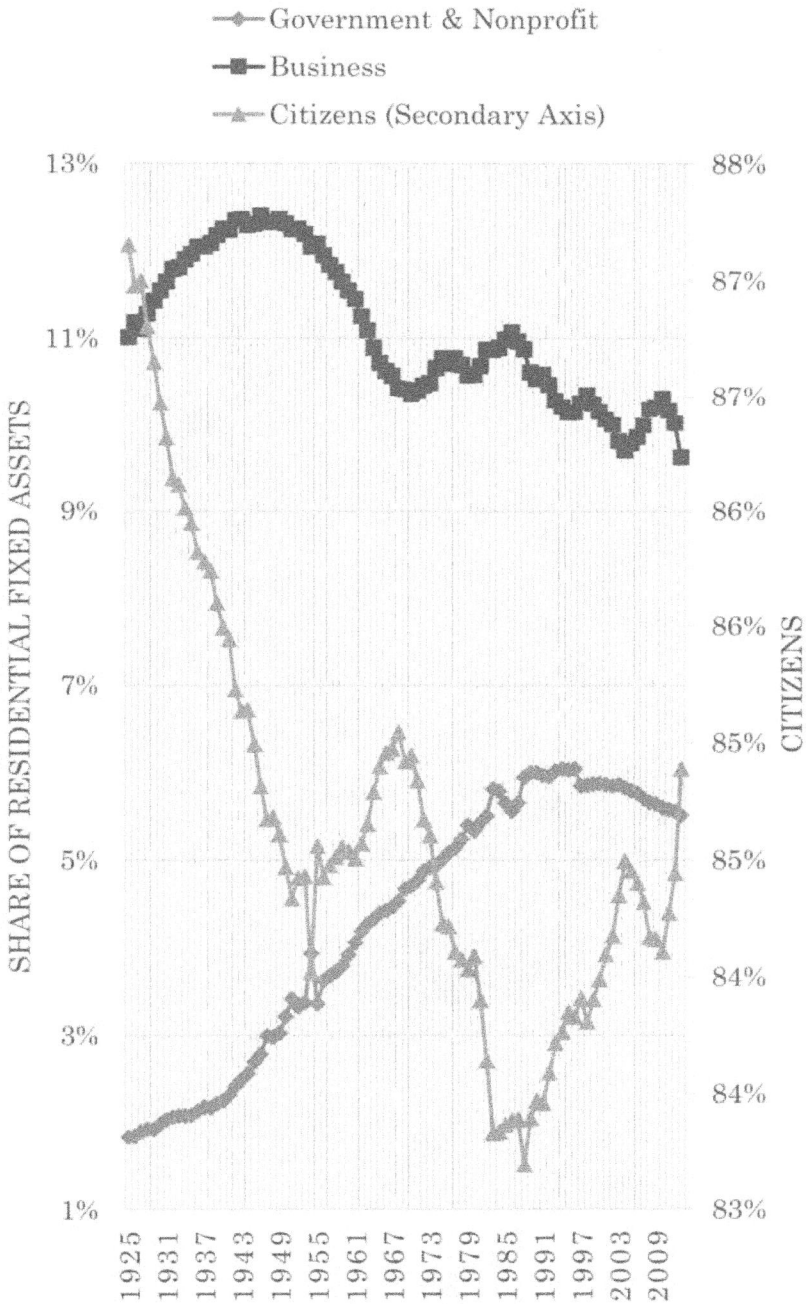

Figure 37: Share of Housing by Ownership

Figure 38: Growth of Housing by Ownership

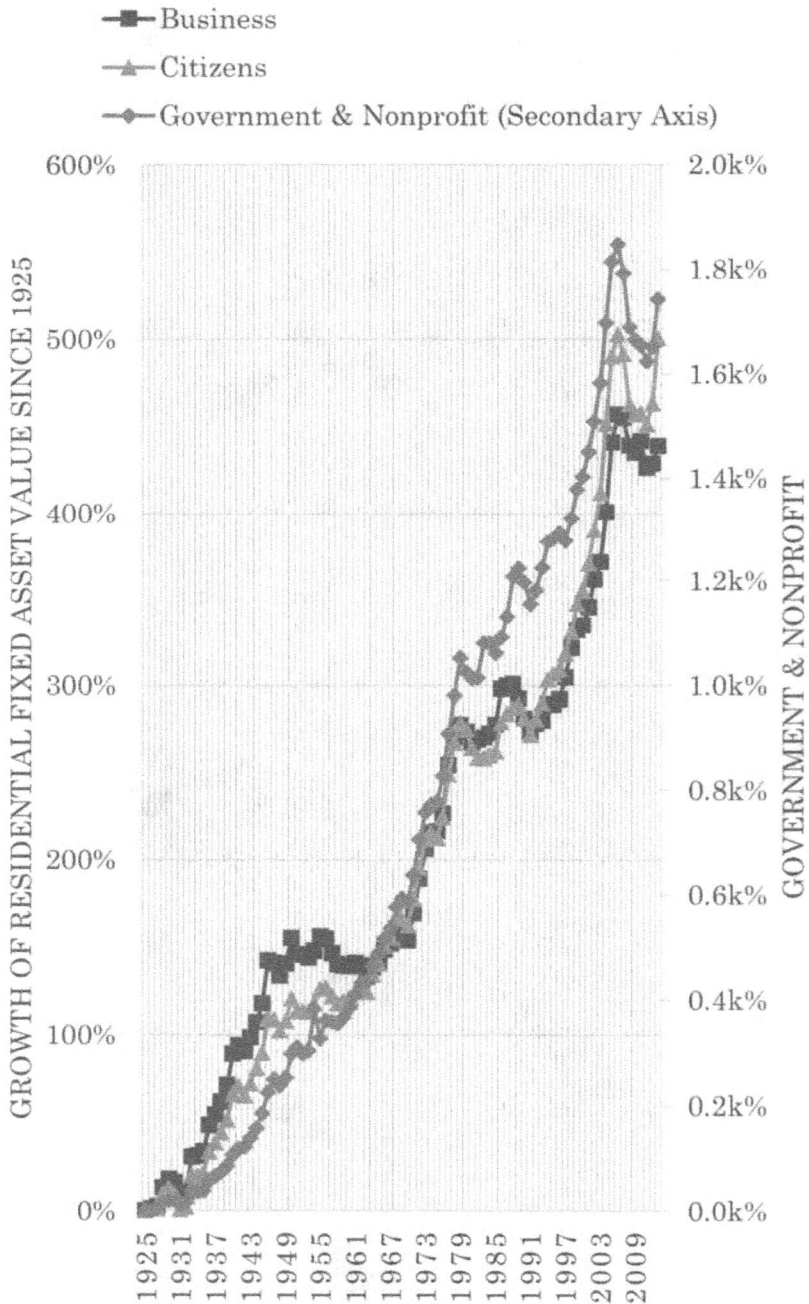

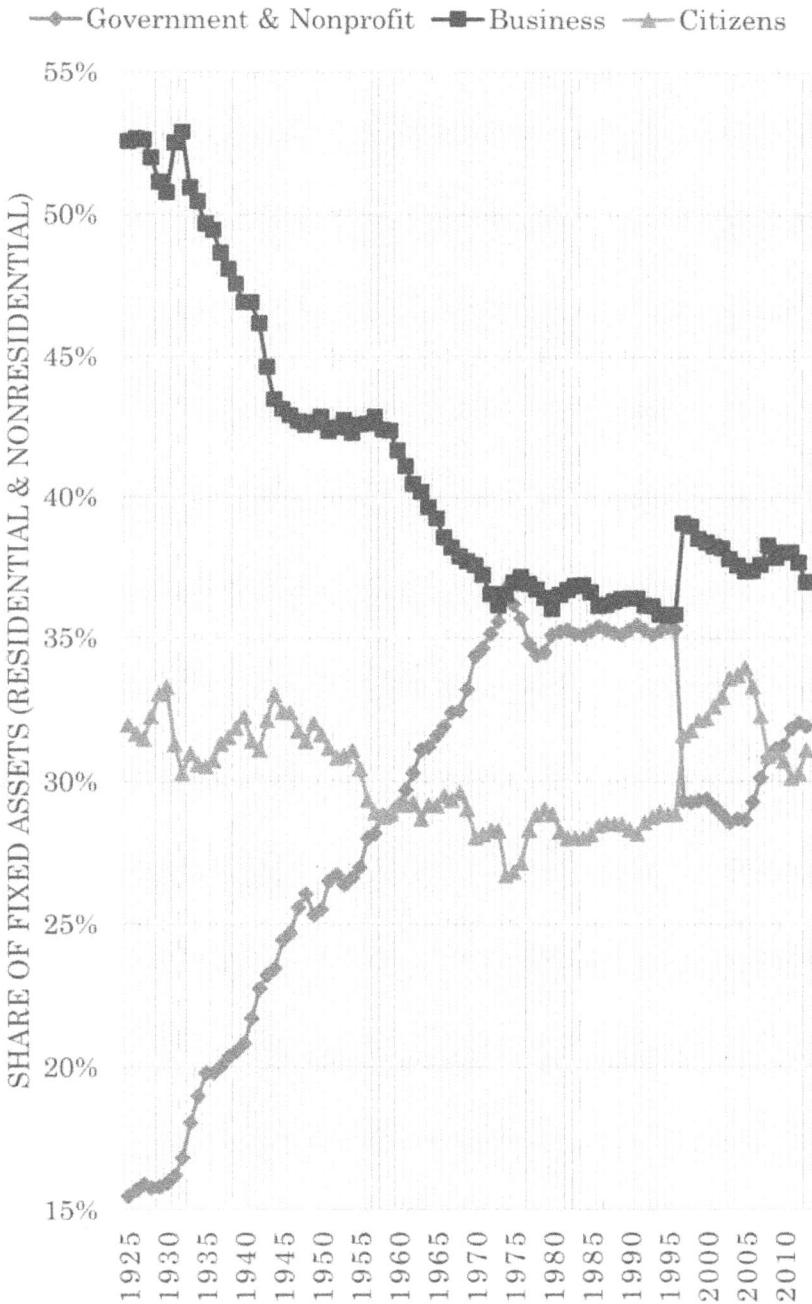

Figure 39: Share of Fixed Assets by Ownership

Appendix 1: Taxation, Income, Assets, Goods
Figure 40: Growth of Fixed Asset Value by Ownership

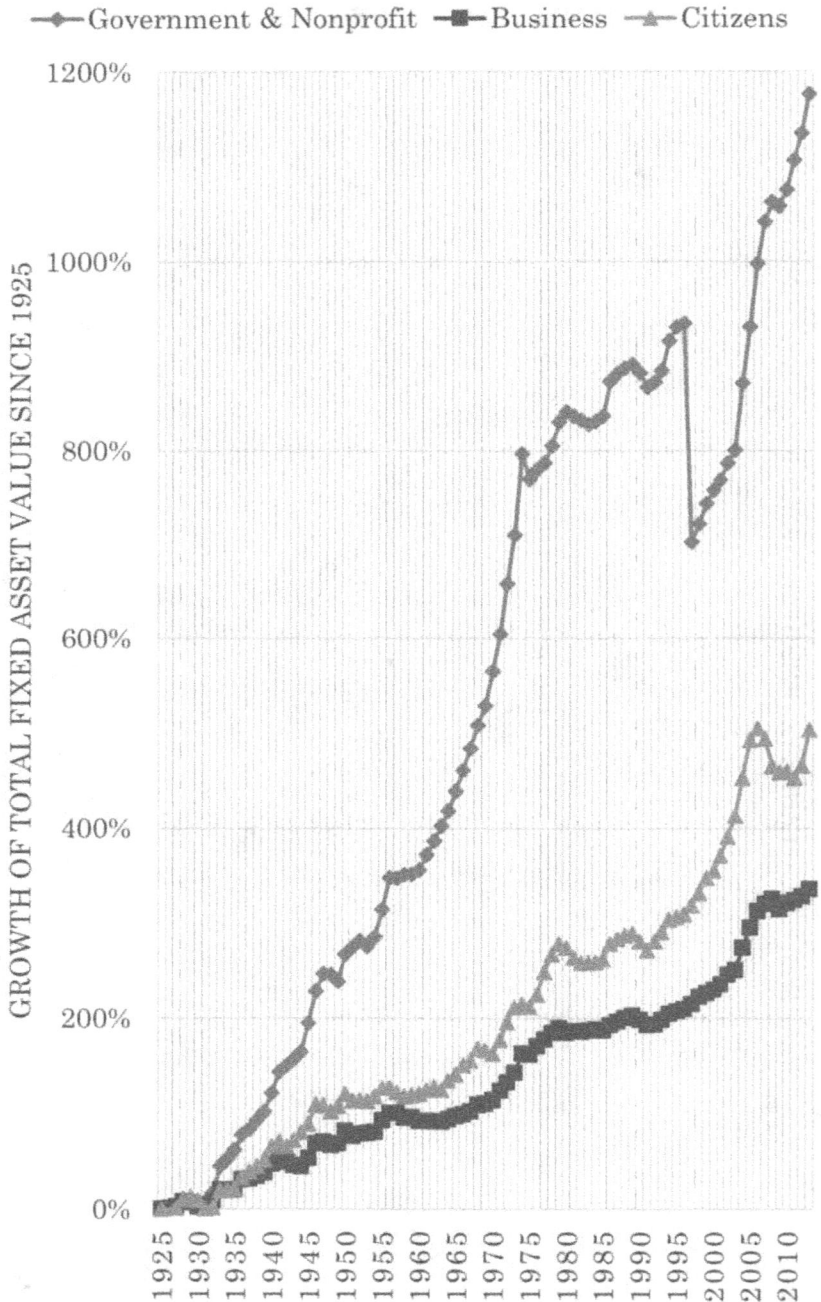

GROWTH OF TOTAL FIXED ASSET VALUE SINCE 1925

Legend: Government & Nonprofit — Business — Citizens

Thomas E. Kurek

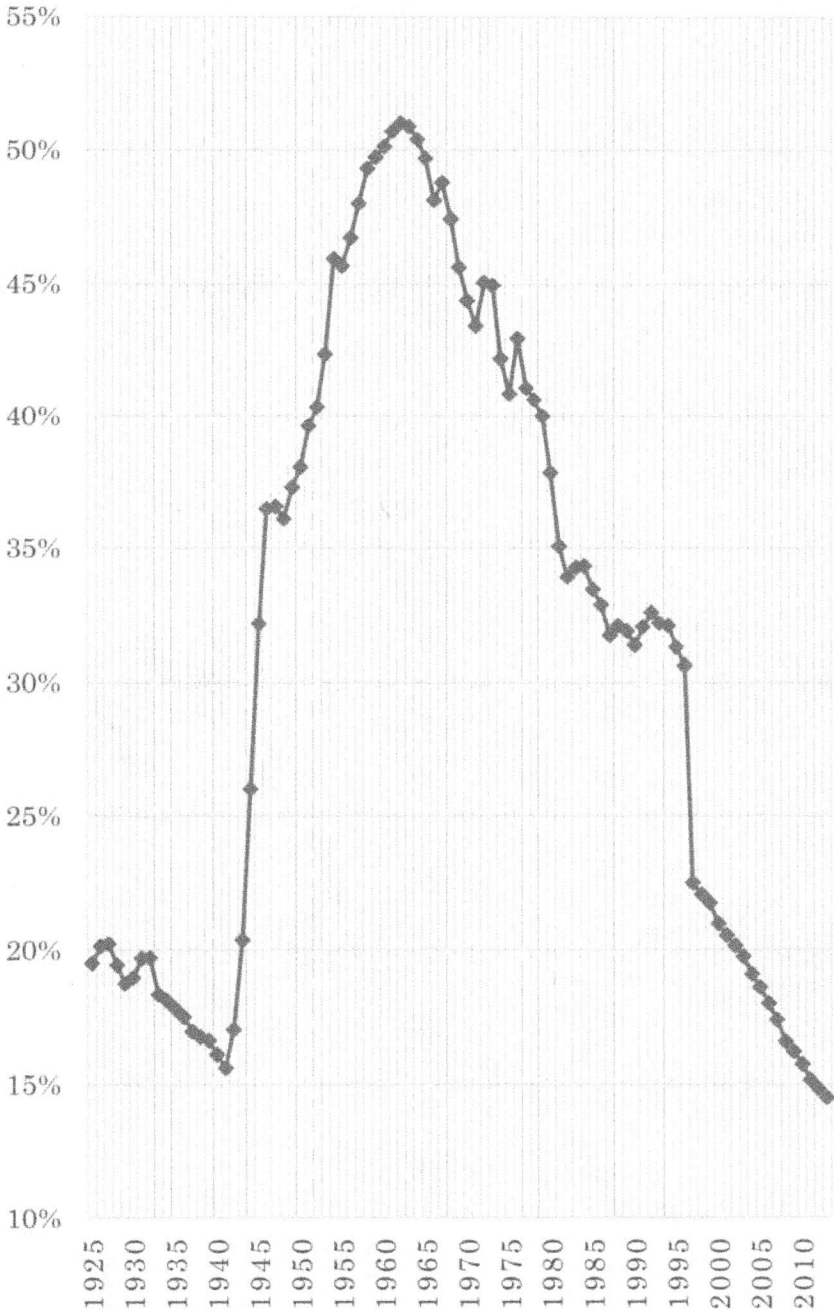

Figure 41: Defense-to-Non-Defense Fixed Asset Ratio

Figure 42: Growth of Government Fixed Assets by Defense Function

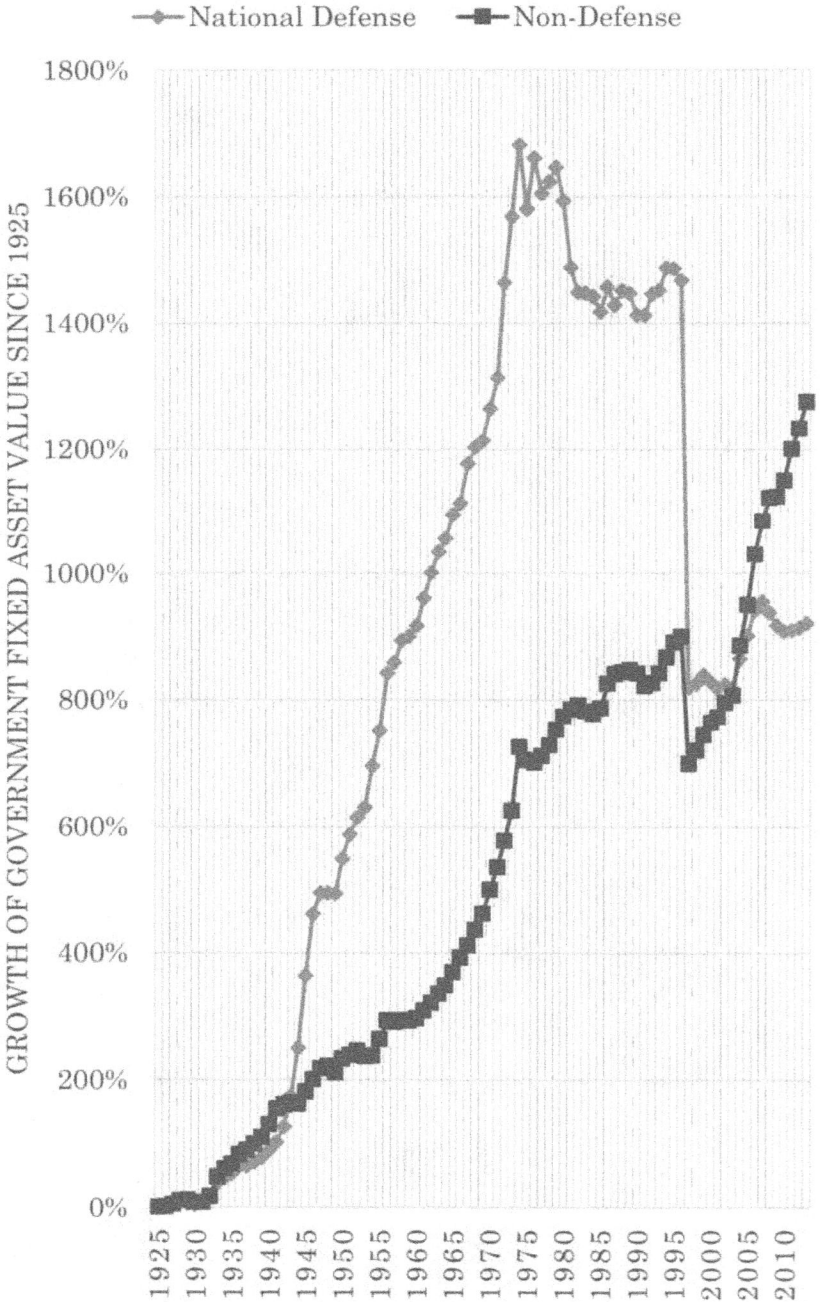

Thomas E. Kurek

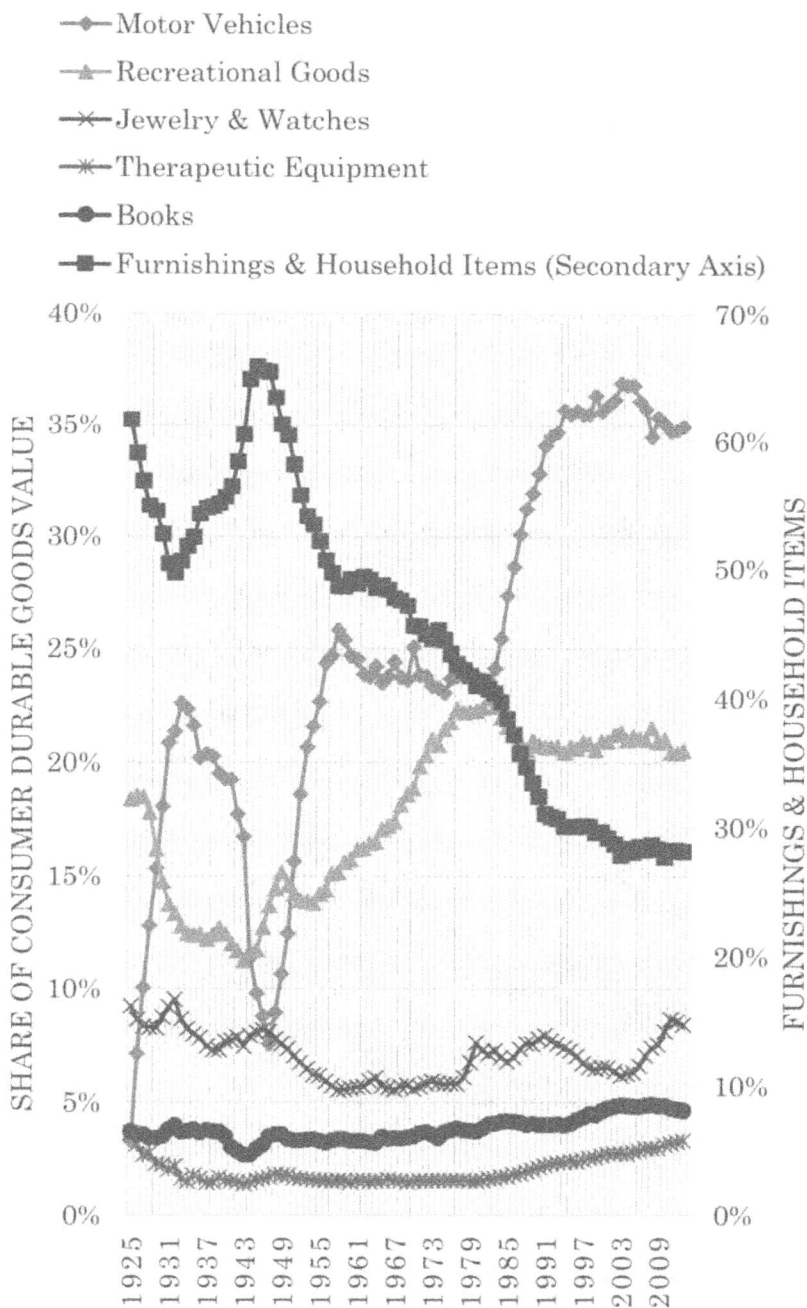

Figure 43: Share of Consumer Durable Goods Value

- Motor Vehicles
- Recreational Goods
- Jewelry & Watches
- Therapeutic Equipment
- Books
- Furnishings & Household Items (Secondary Axis)

Figure 44: Growth of Consumer Durable Goods Value

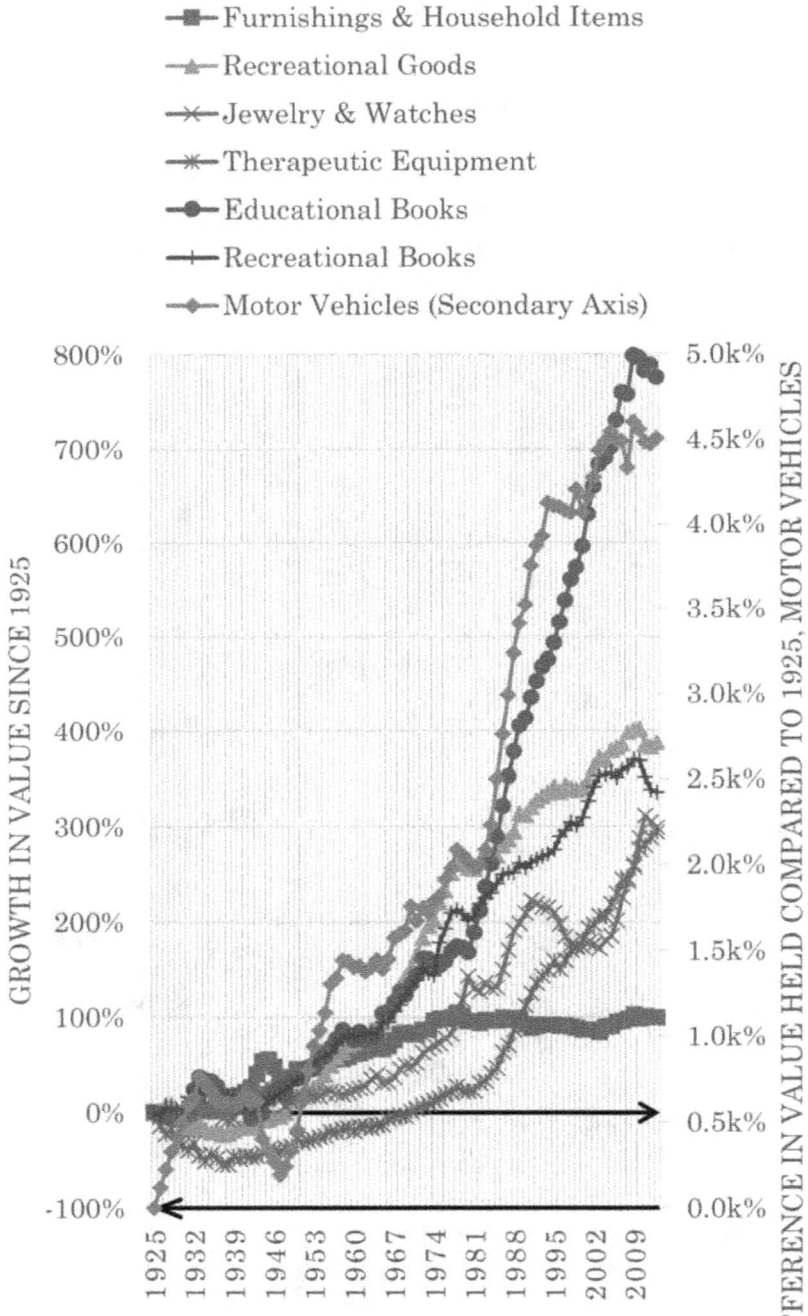

Legend:
- ■ Furnishings & Household Items
- ▲ Recreational Goods
- ✕ Jewelry & Watches
- ✳ Therapeutic Equipment
- ● Educational Books
- + Recreational Books
- ◆ Motor Vehicles (Secondary Axis)

GROWTH IN VALUE SINCE 1925

Left axis: -100%, 0%, 100%, 200%, 300%, 400%, 500%, 600%, 700%, 800%

Right axis: 0.0k%, 0.5k%, 1.0k%, 1.5k%, 2.0k%, 2.5k%, 3.0k%, 3.5k%, 4.0k%, 4.5k%, 5.0k%

DIFFERENCE IN VALUE HELD COMPARED TO 1925, MOTOR VEHICLES

Horizontal axis: 1925, 1932, 1939, 1946, 1953, 1960, 1967, 1974, 1981, 1988, 1995, 2002, 2009

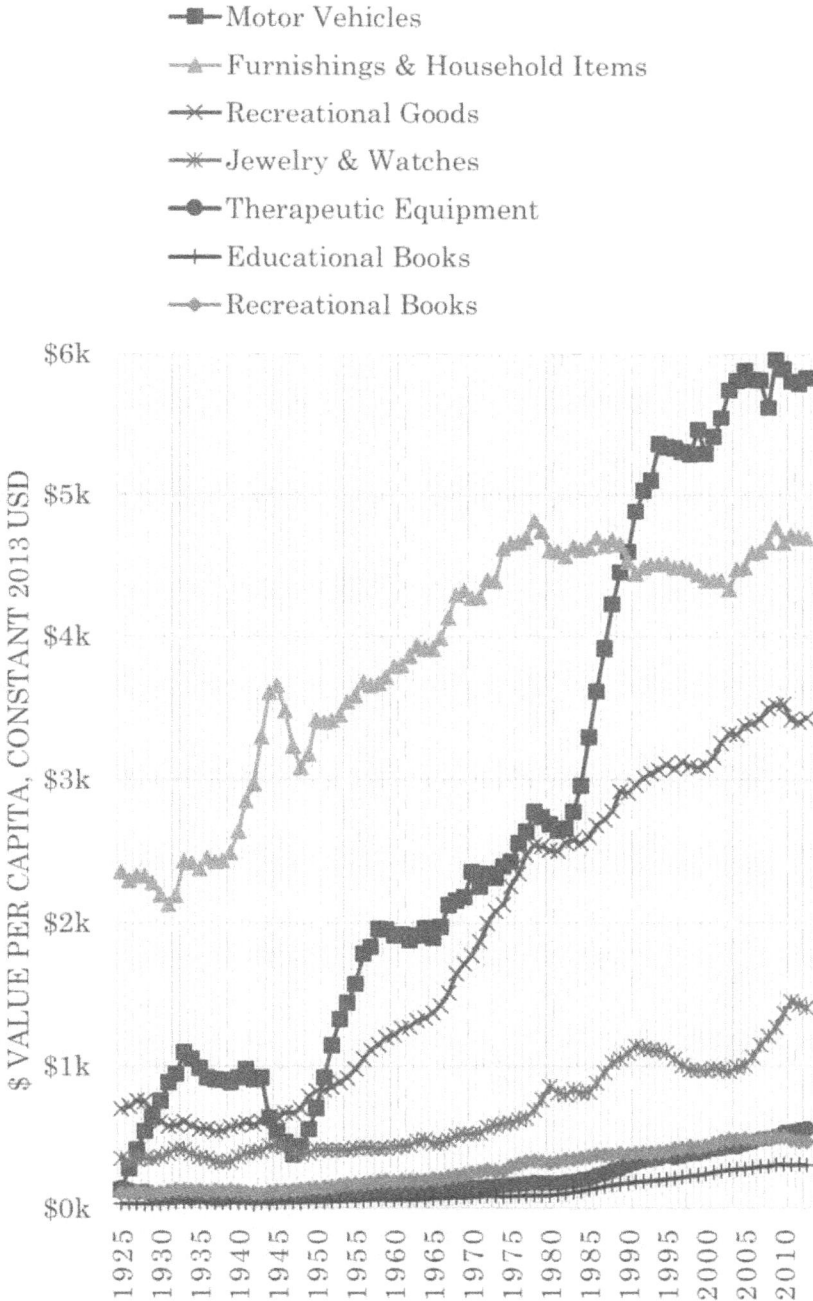

Figure 45: Consumer Durable Goods Value per Capita

Appendix 1: Taxation, Income, Assets, Goods
Figure 46: Net Worth of the Wealthy vs. Average Net Worth

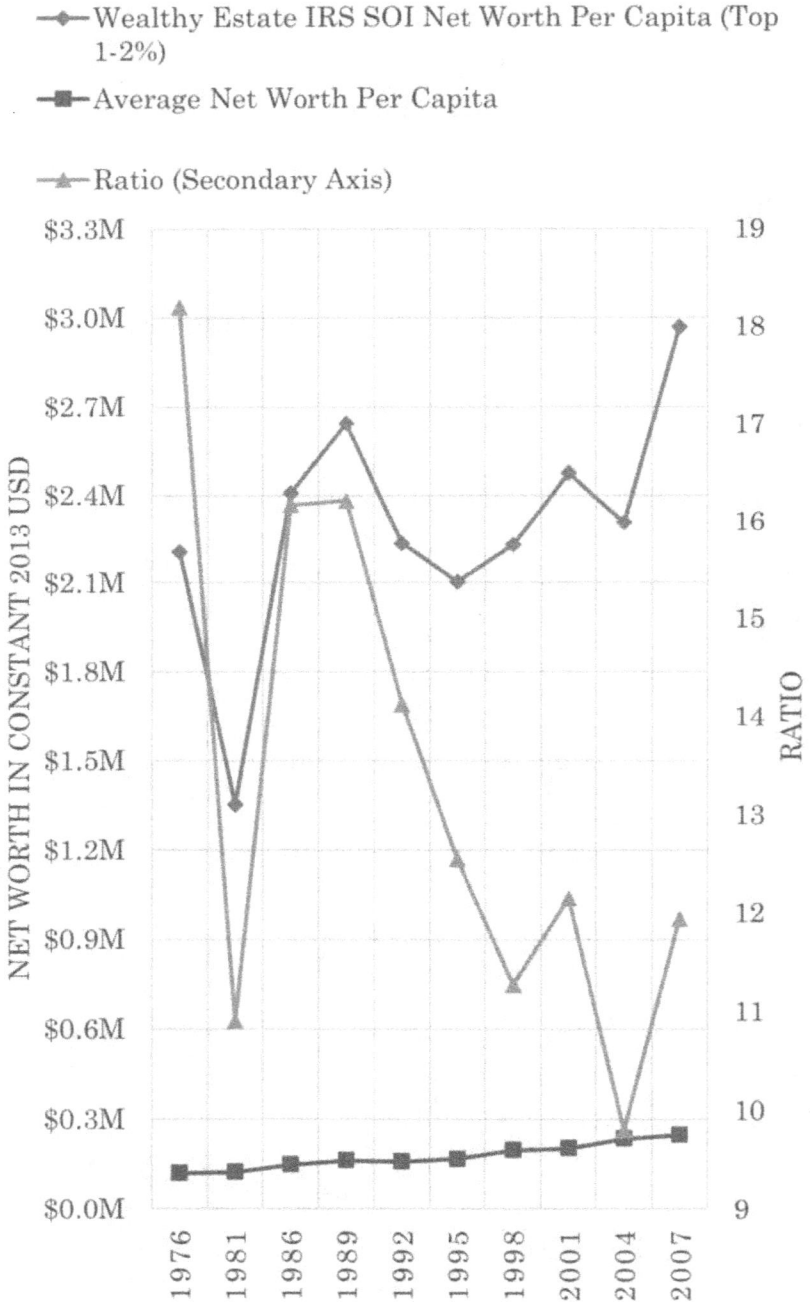

◆ Wealthy Estate IRS SOI Net Worth Per Capita (Top 1-2%)

■ Average Net Worth Per Capita

▲ Ratio (Secondary Axis)

Thomas E. Kurek

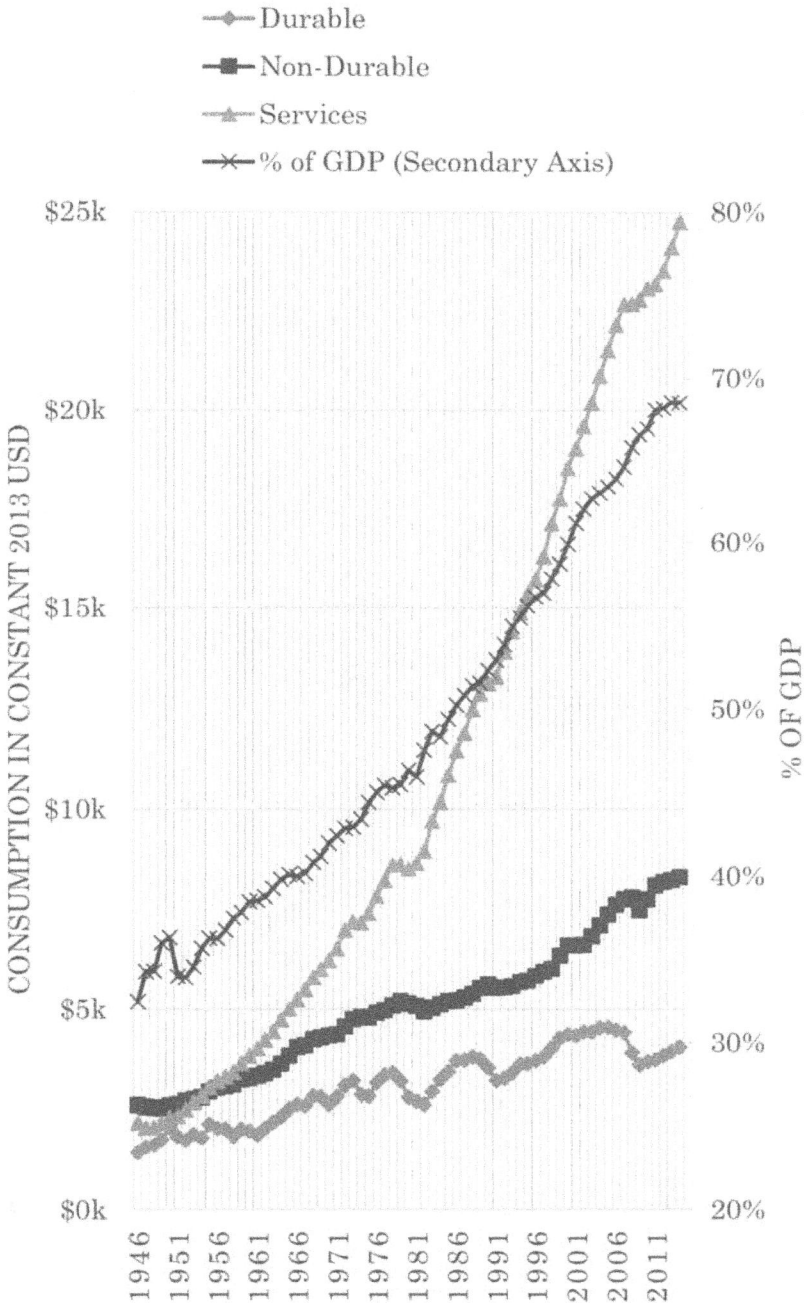

Figure 47: Consumption per Capita

◆ Durable
■ Non-Durable
▲ Services
✕ % of GDP (Secondary Axis)

Figure 48: Share of Personal Consumption

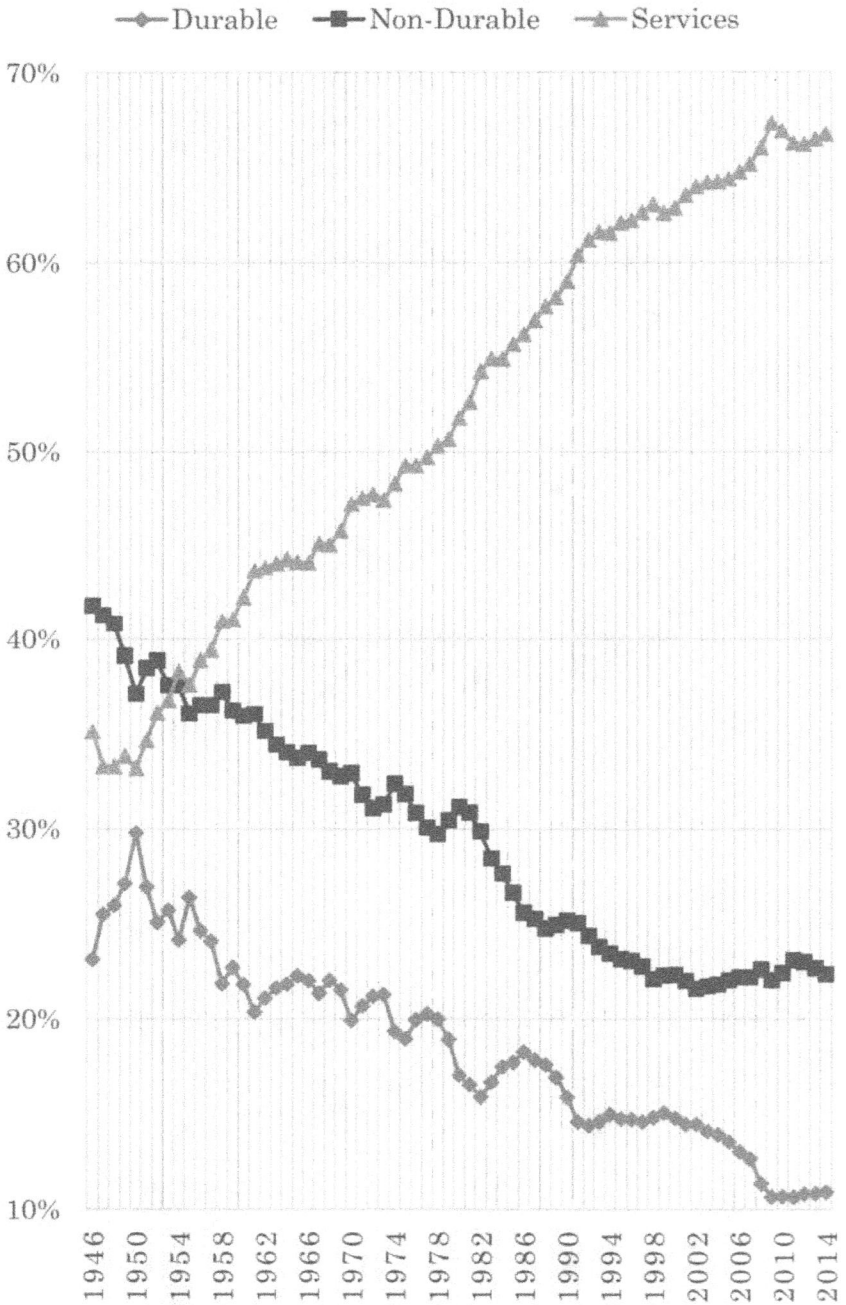

Appendix 2: Labor & Productivity

The following figures show an accurate picture of American productivity and encumbrance. Common and popular discussions about the productivity of the nation ignore the most significant factors. Those factors include: shifts in the population pyramid, workers over the age of 64 who choose to continue work, working age people who choose not to work, false categorization of part-time workers, and numerical presentations that do not respect population growth. This analysis corrects all of those errors, by synthesizing World Bank indicators:[278] Labor Force Participation Rate (LFPR)15+, LFPR 15-64, LFPR 65+, Unemployment Rate, Youth (0-14), Elderly (65+), and Working Age (15-64) demographics. The US Department of Labor data series, *"Unadjusted Employed, Usually Work Part Time,"* was used to determine part-time labor participation.[279] The annual averages from the series, *"Persons at work in agriculture and nonagricultural industries by hours of work,"* yielded a 55.9 percent average work week for part-time workers (22.4 hours).[280] That data was used to determine full-time work equivalence (FTE).

---

[278] (World Bank, 2014)
[279] (Bureau of Labor Statistics, 2014)
[280] (Bureau of Labor Statistics, 2014)

Figure 49: U.S. Labor by Aged Work Status

—◆—Unemployed (15-64)

—■—Part-Time Worker Unemployment Equivalent

—▲—Not Pursuing Work (15-64)

—✕—Retirees (65+)

—✳—Youth (0-14)

—●—Workers (15-64)

—+—Workers (65+)

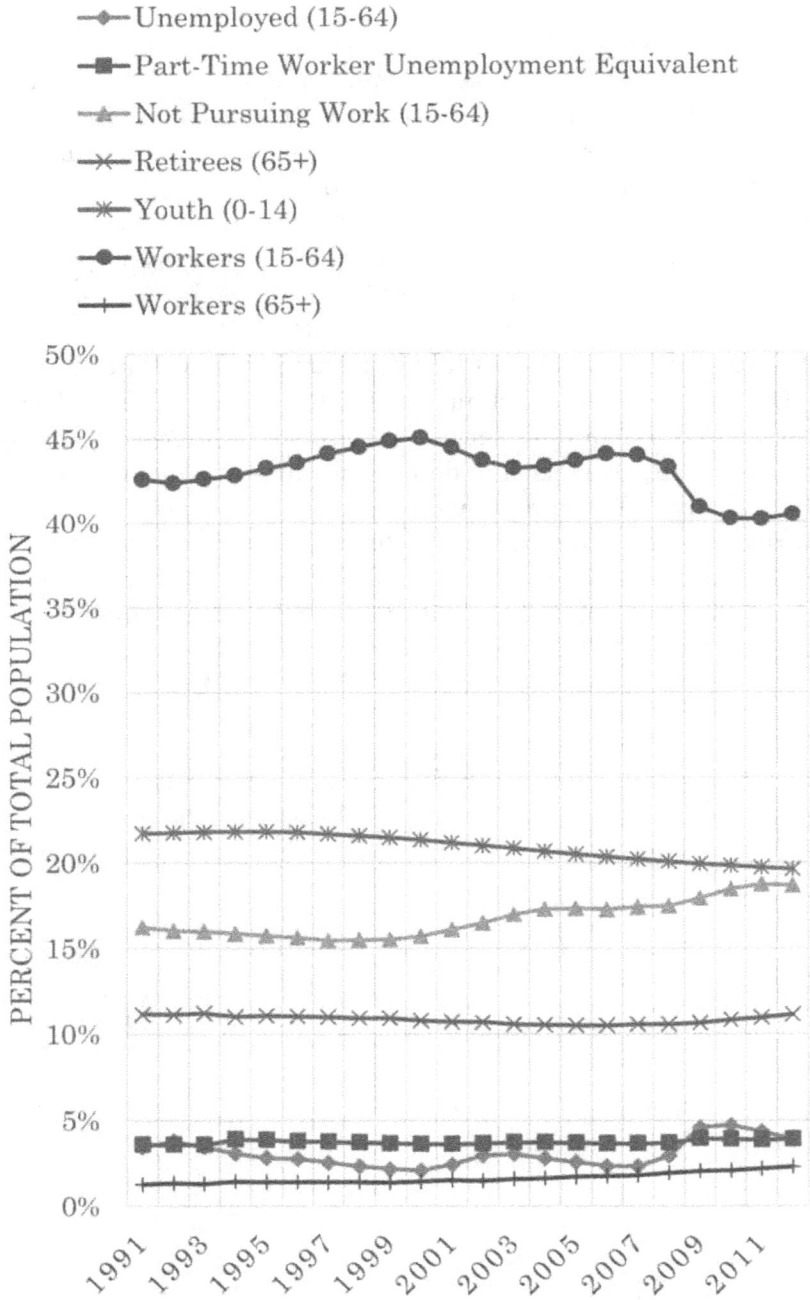

Thomas E. Kurek

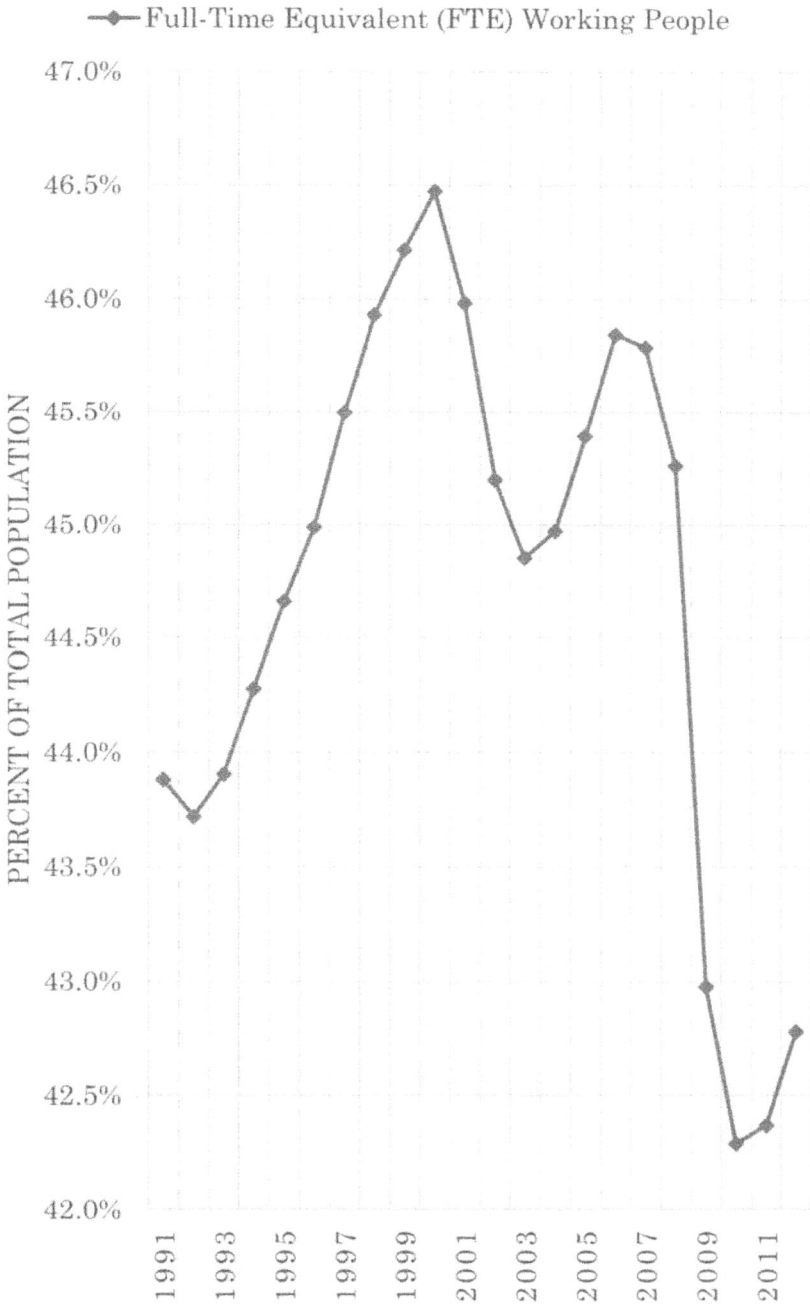

Figure 50: U.S. Labor Aggregate

Appendix 2: Labor & Productivity

Figure 51: U.S. Labor by Output

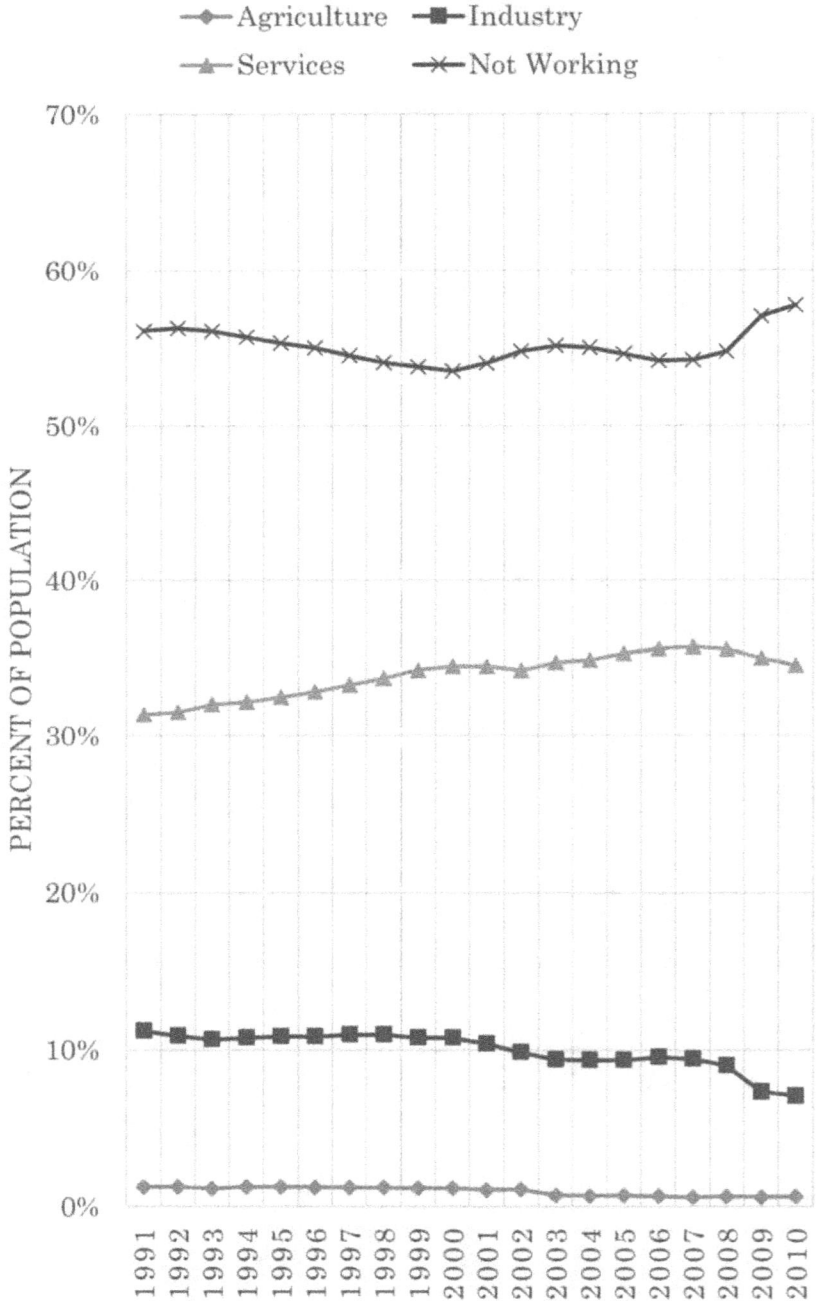

Thomas E. Kurek

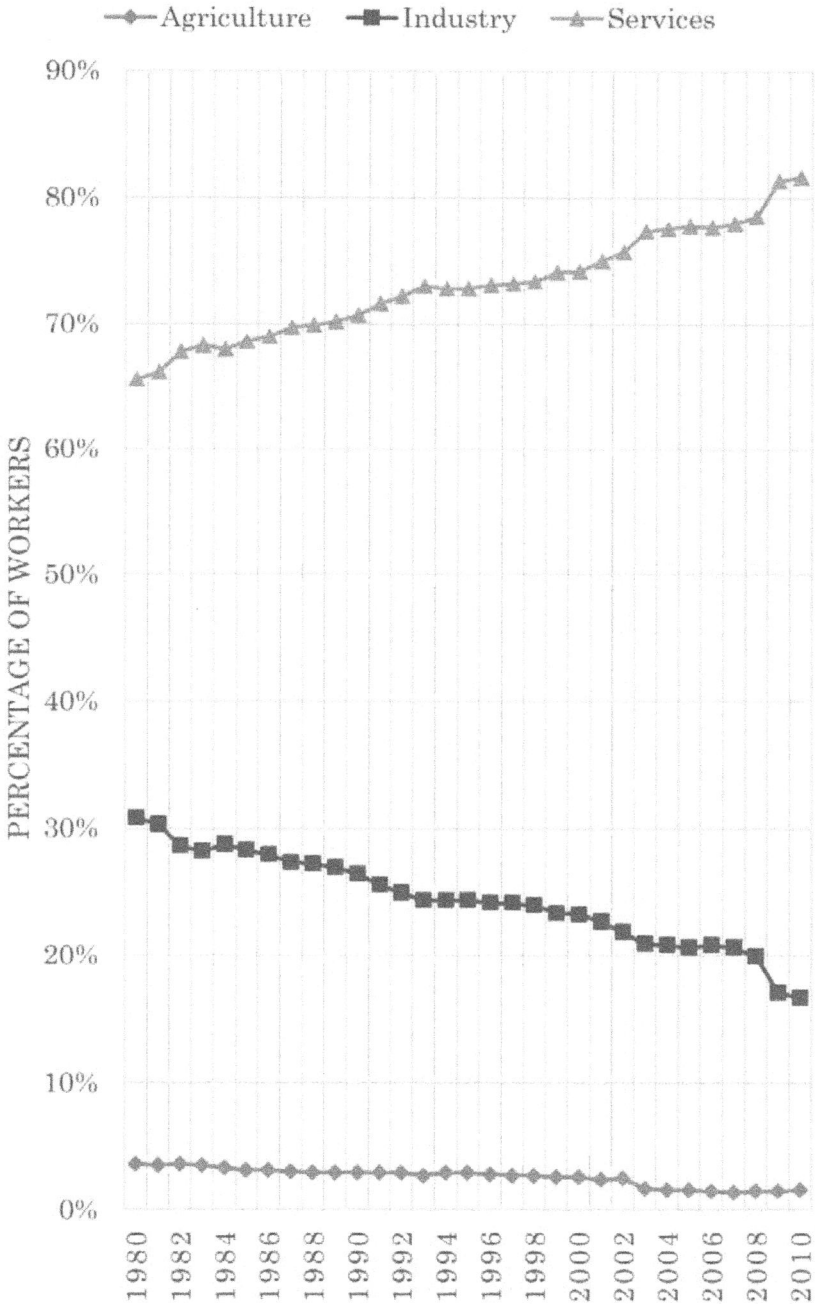

Figure 52: U.S. Labor Share by Output

Figure 53: *US-to-World Labor Output Ratios*

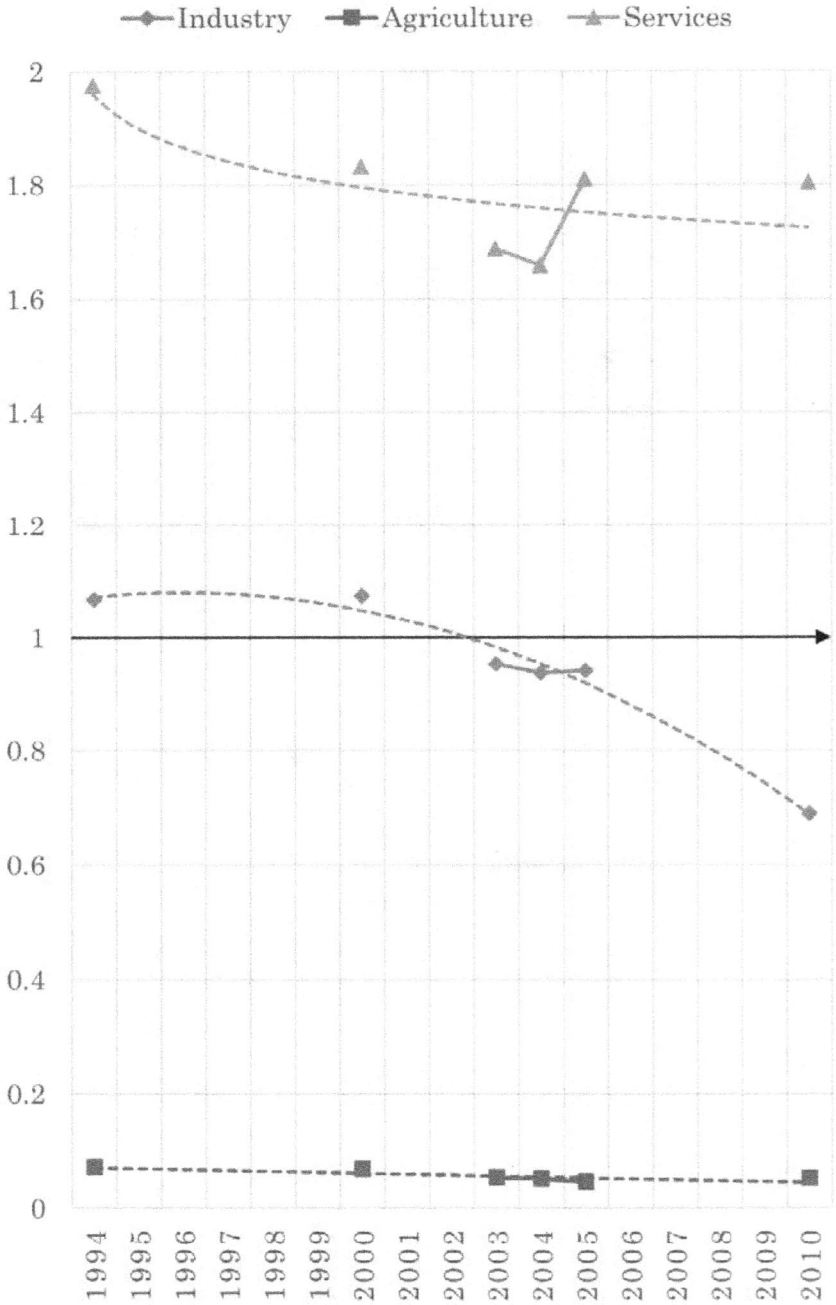

Figure 54: Gross Domestic Product Growth

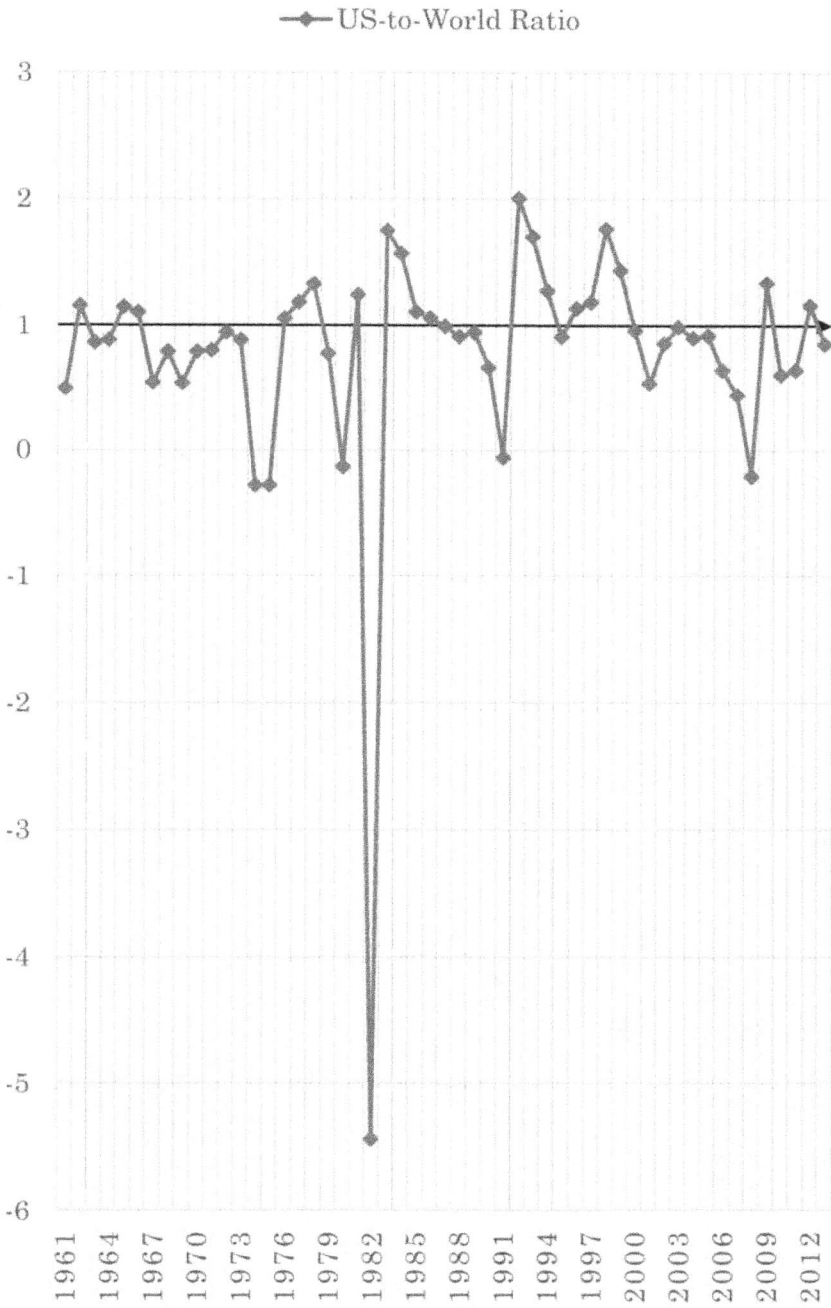

—◆— US-to-World Ratio

Appendix 2: Labor & Productivity
Figure 55: Gross Domestic Product per Capita

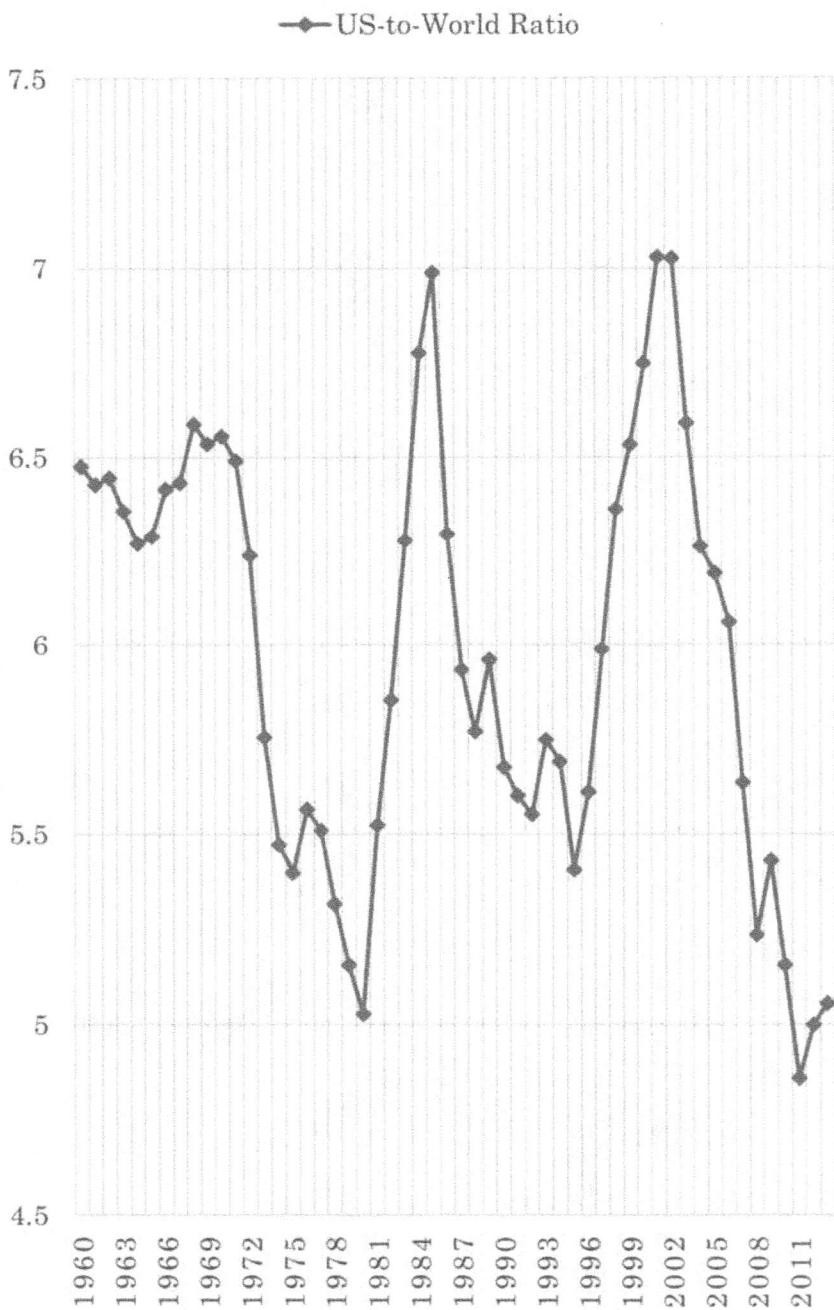

US-to-World Ratio

Thomas E. Kurek

Figure 56: GDP per Employee Ratio

US-to-World Ratio

Appendix 2: Labor & Productivity

Figure 57: Gross Domestic Product per Energy Use

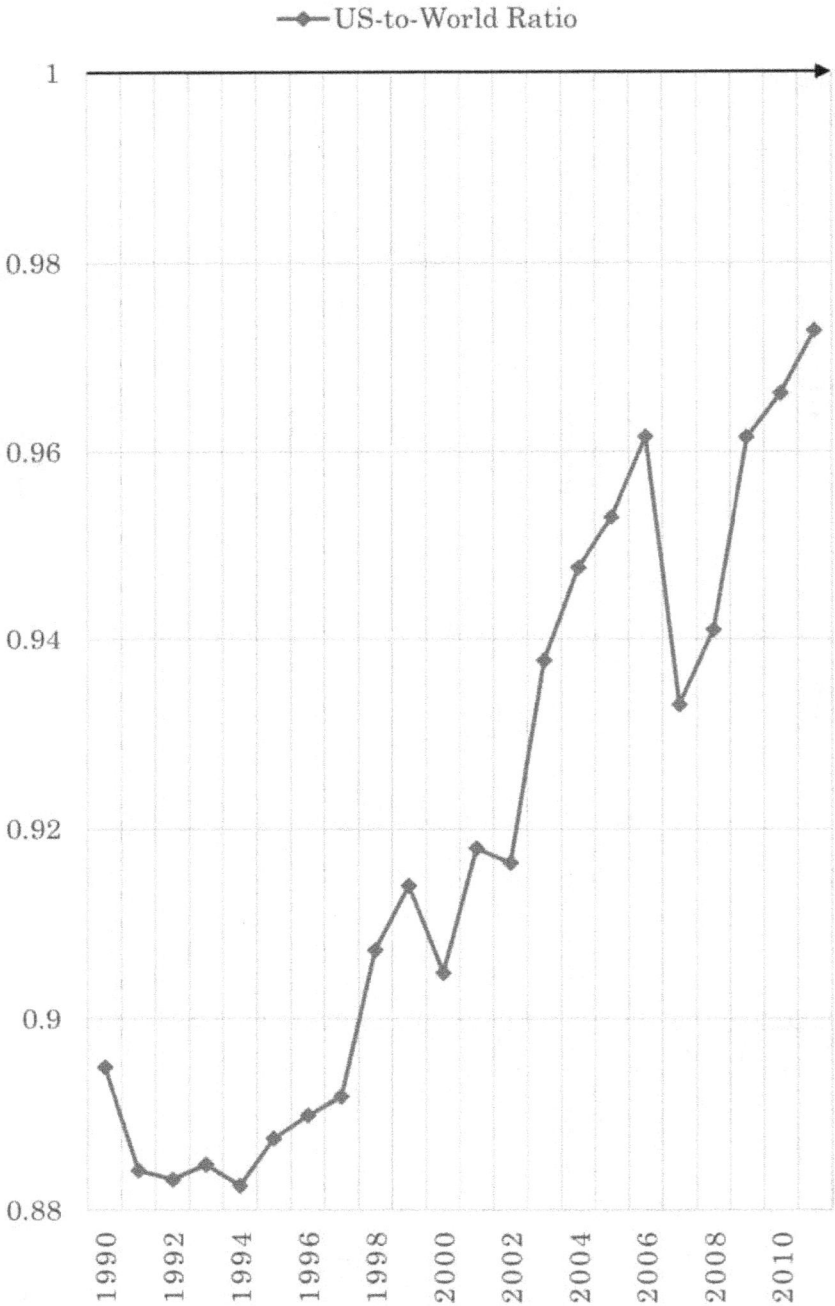

Thomas E. Kurek

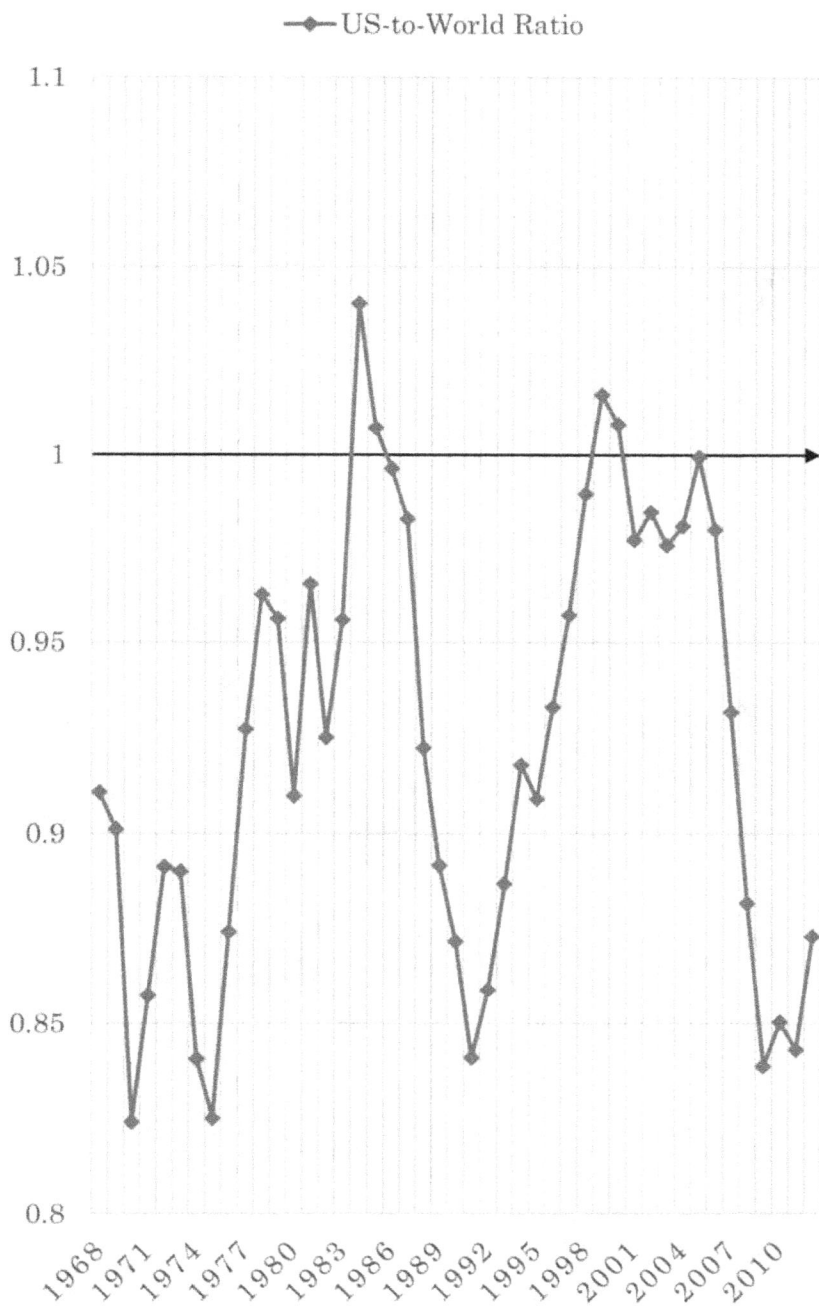

Figure 58: Gross Capital Formation

US-to-World Ratio

Figure 59: M2 Growth

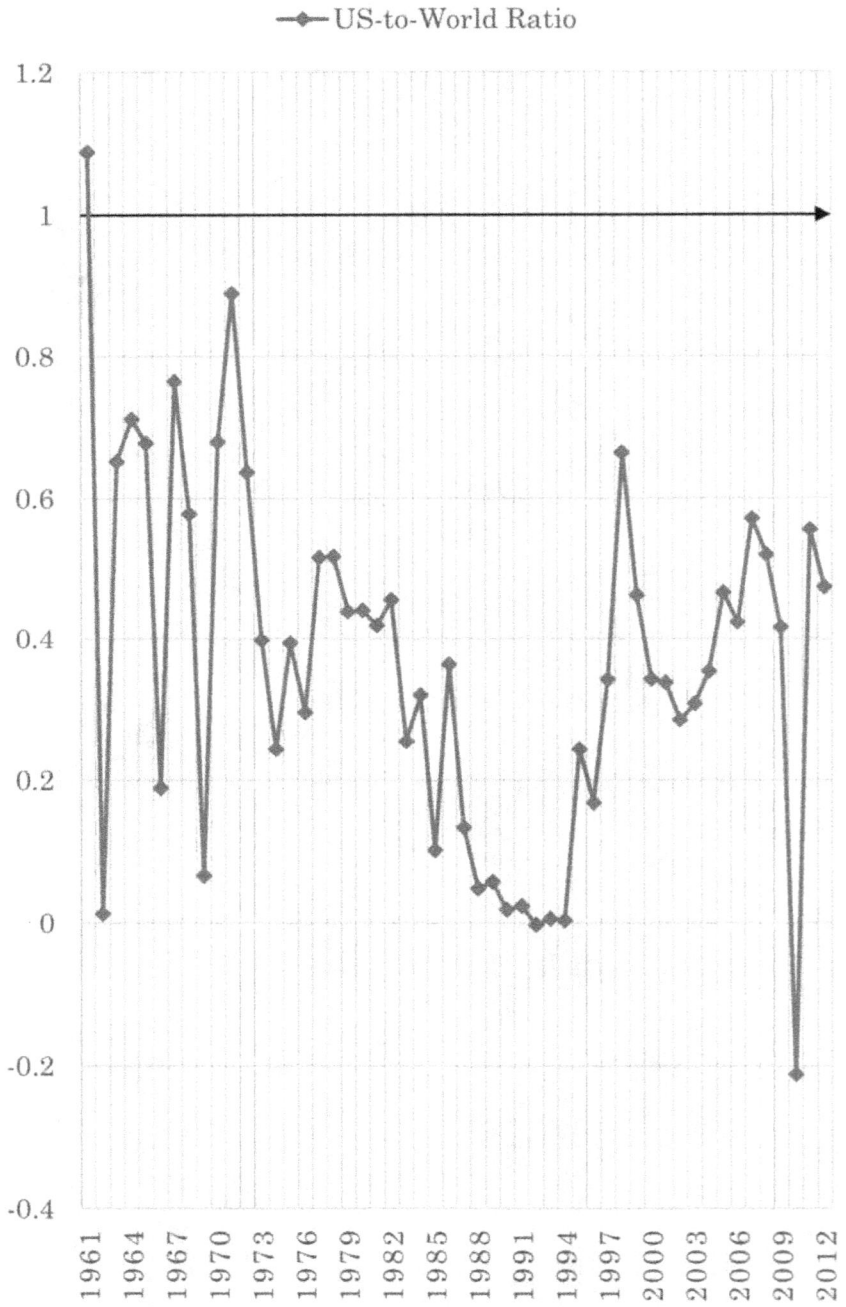

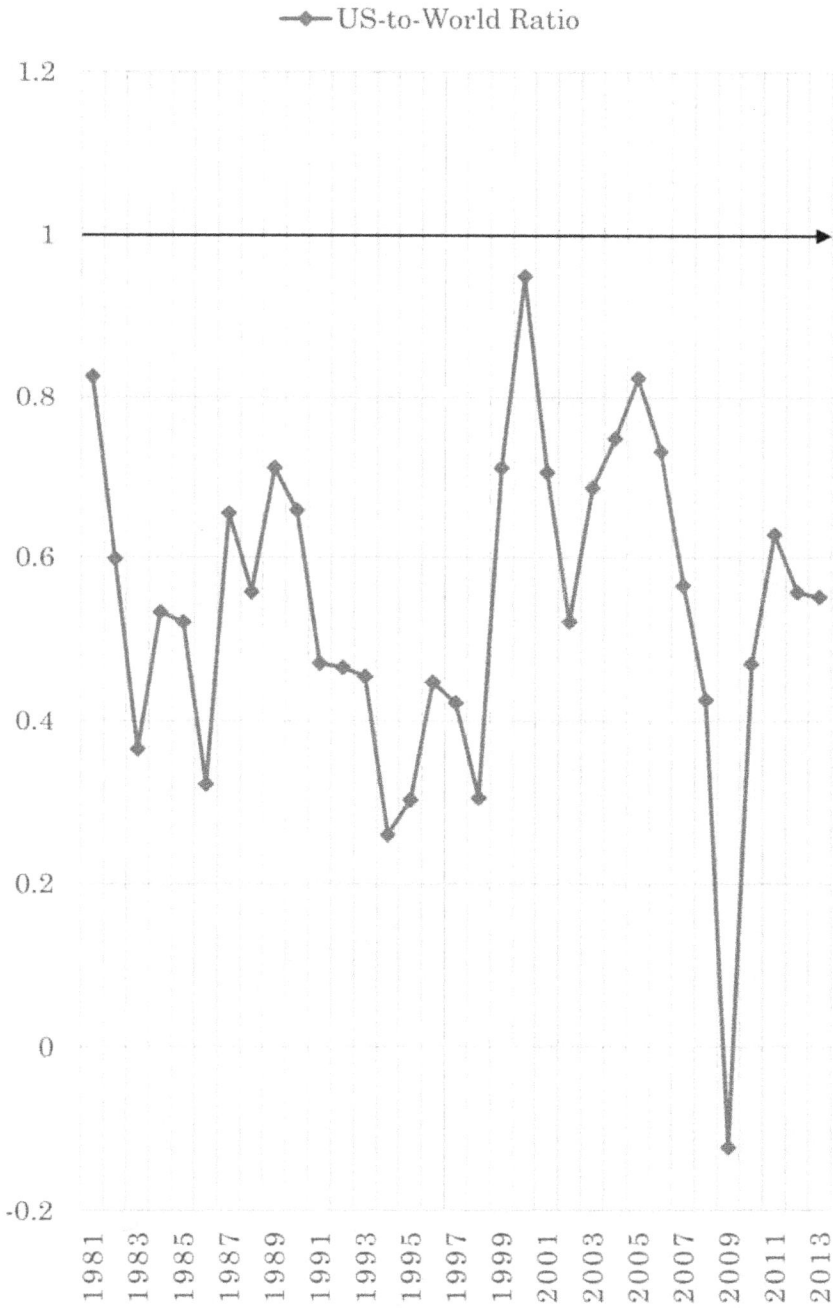

Figure 60: Consumer Price Inflation

Figure 61: Imports and Exports

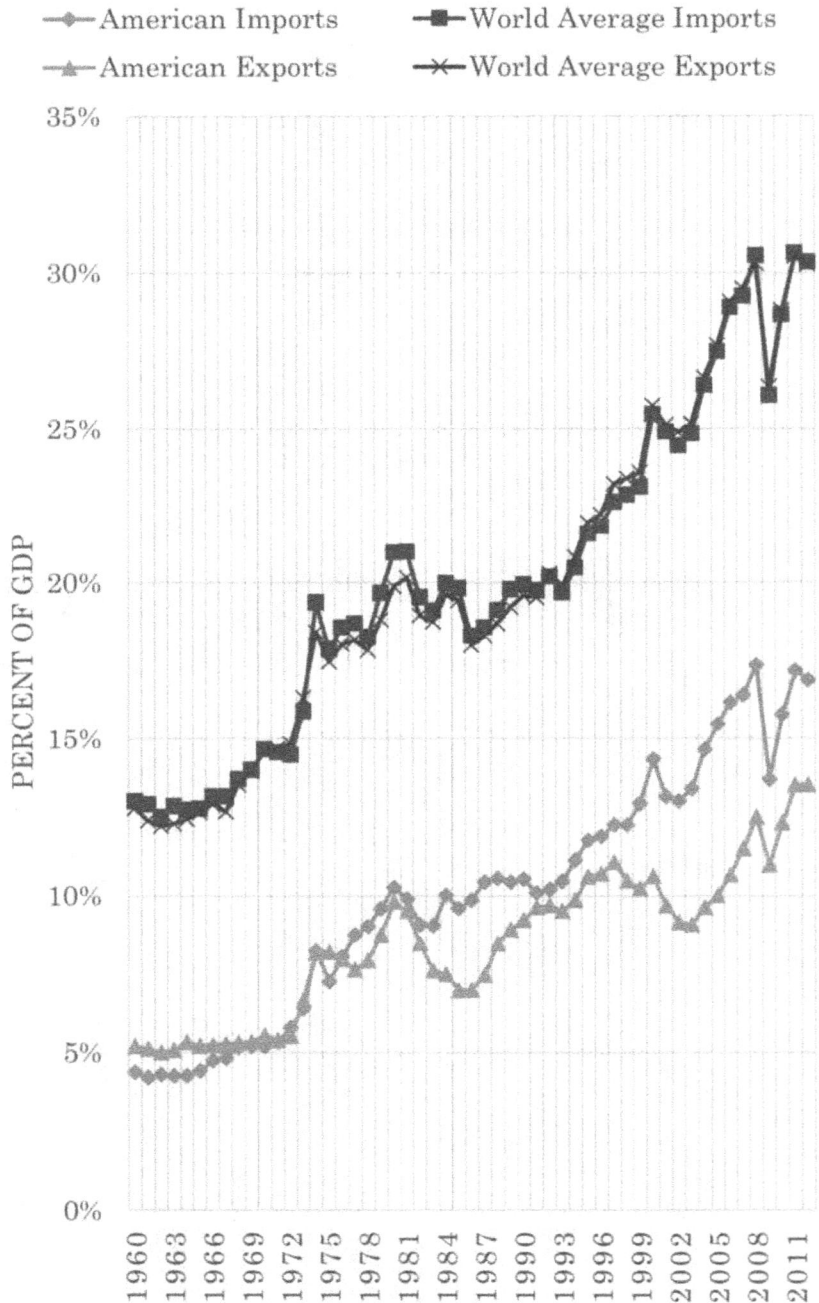

Thomas E. Kurek

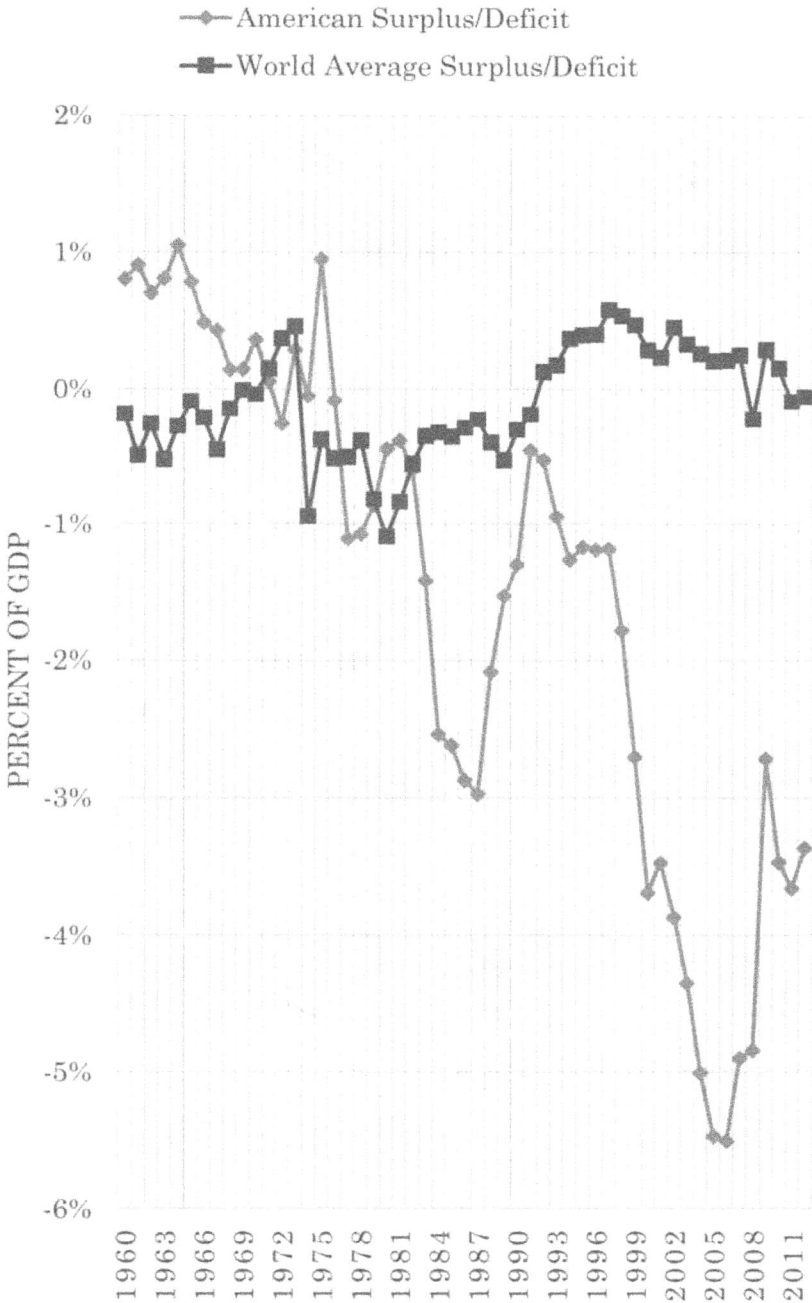

Figure 62: Trade Surplus / Deficit

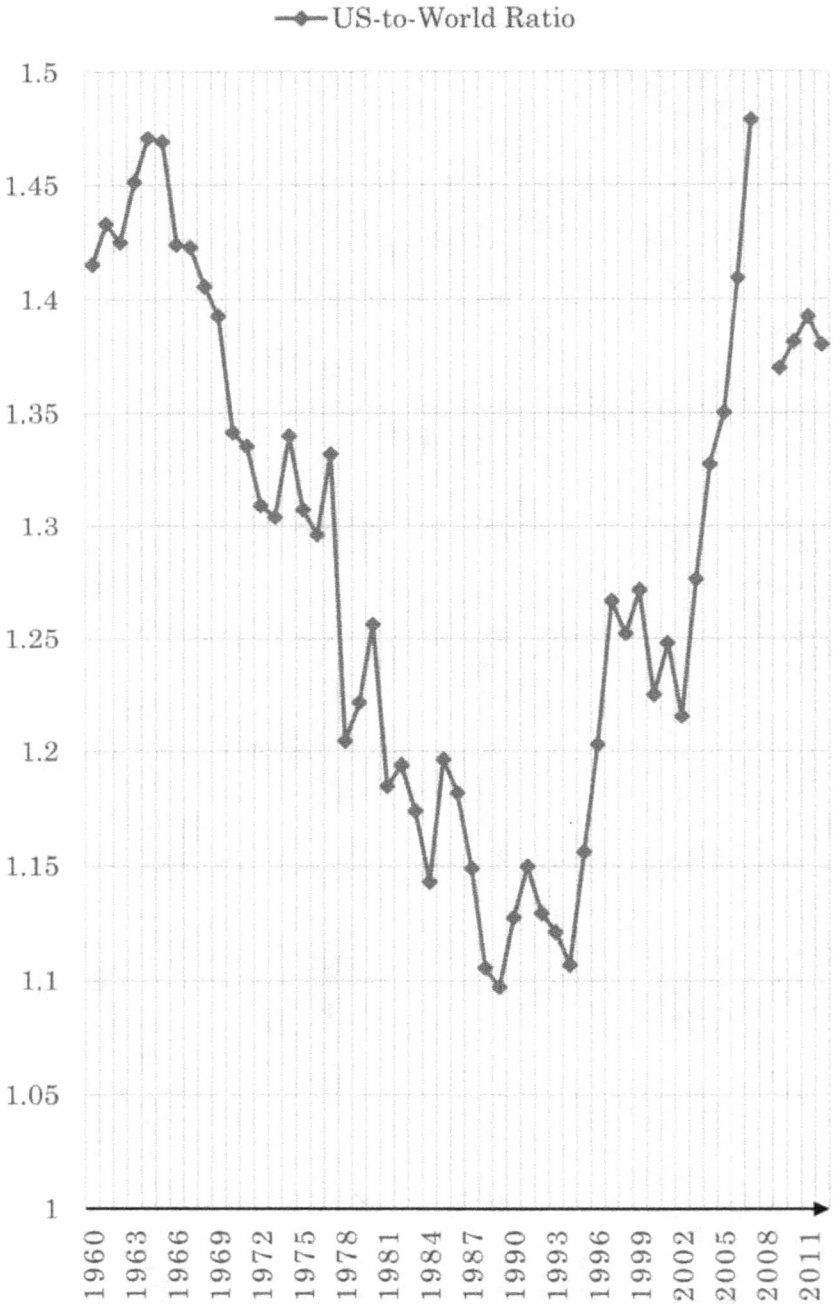

Appendix 2: Labor & Productivity
Figure 63: Financial-Sector-Provided Domestic Credit

Appendix 3: Invention, Science, & Technology

The following figures compare United States intellectual property, high technology production, and research and development to the rest of the world, by synthesizing World Bank indicators.[281]

---

[281] (World Bank, 2014)

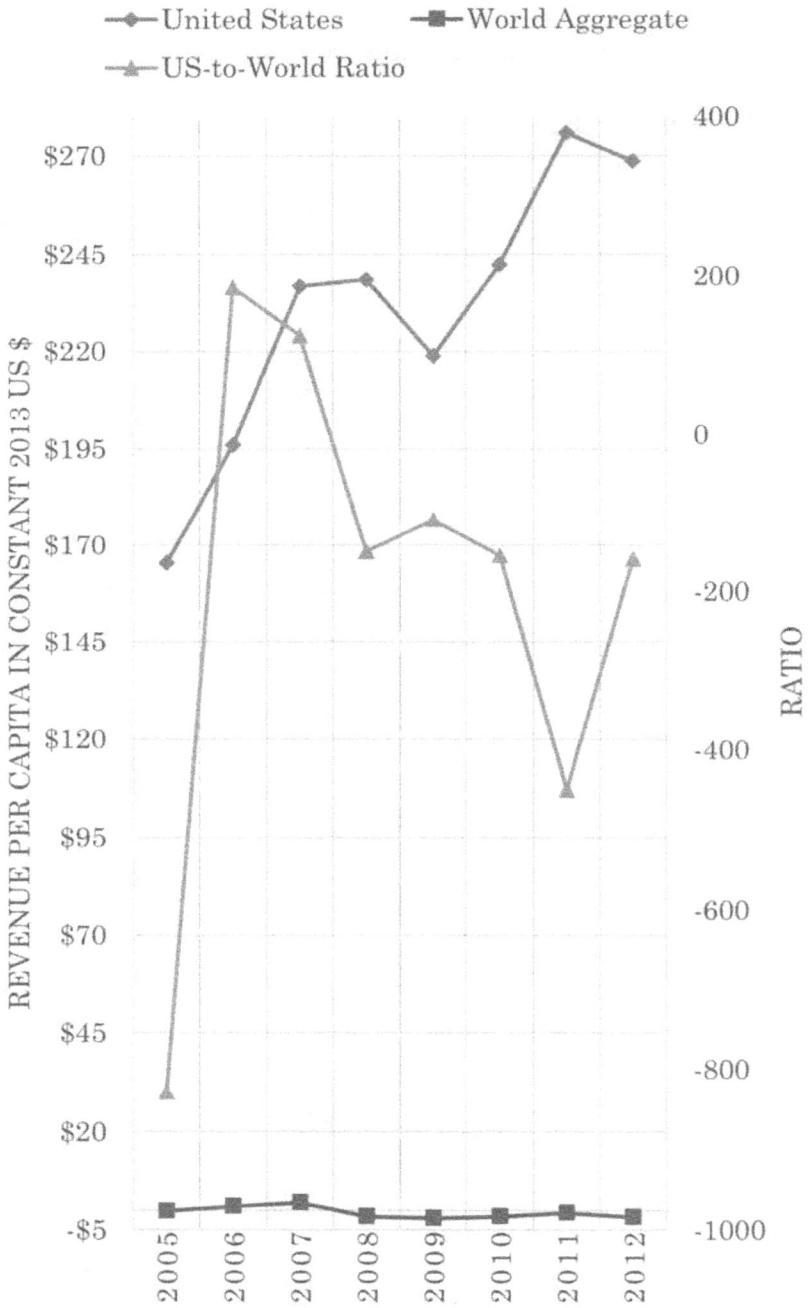

Appendix 3: Invention, Science, & Technology
Figure 64: Intellectual Property Revenue

Thomas E. Kurek

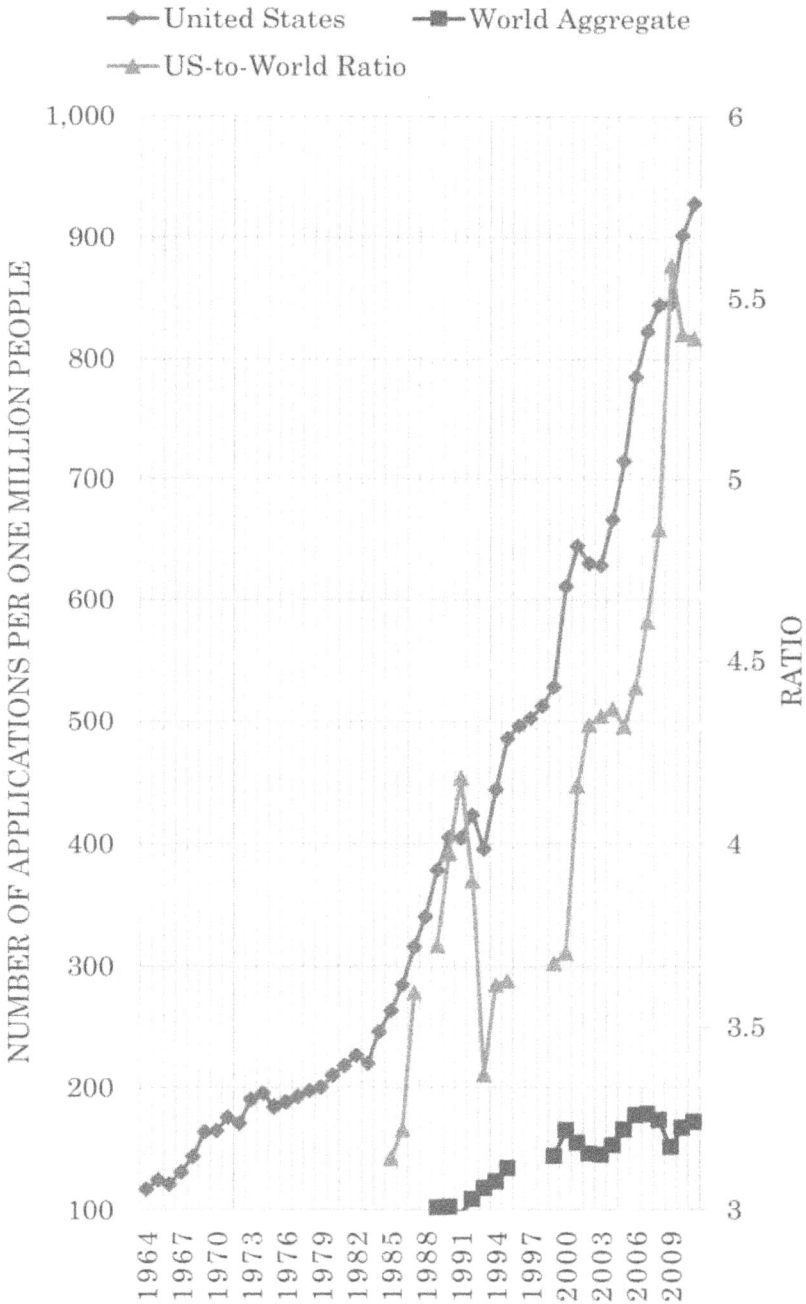

Figure 65: Non-Resident Patent and Trademark Applications

Figure 66: Resident Patent and Trademark Applications

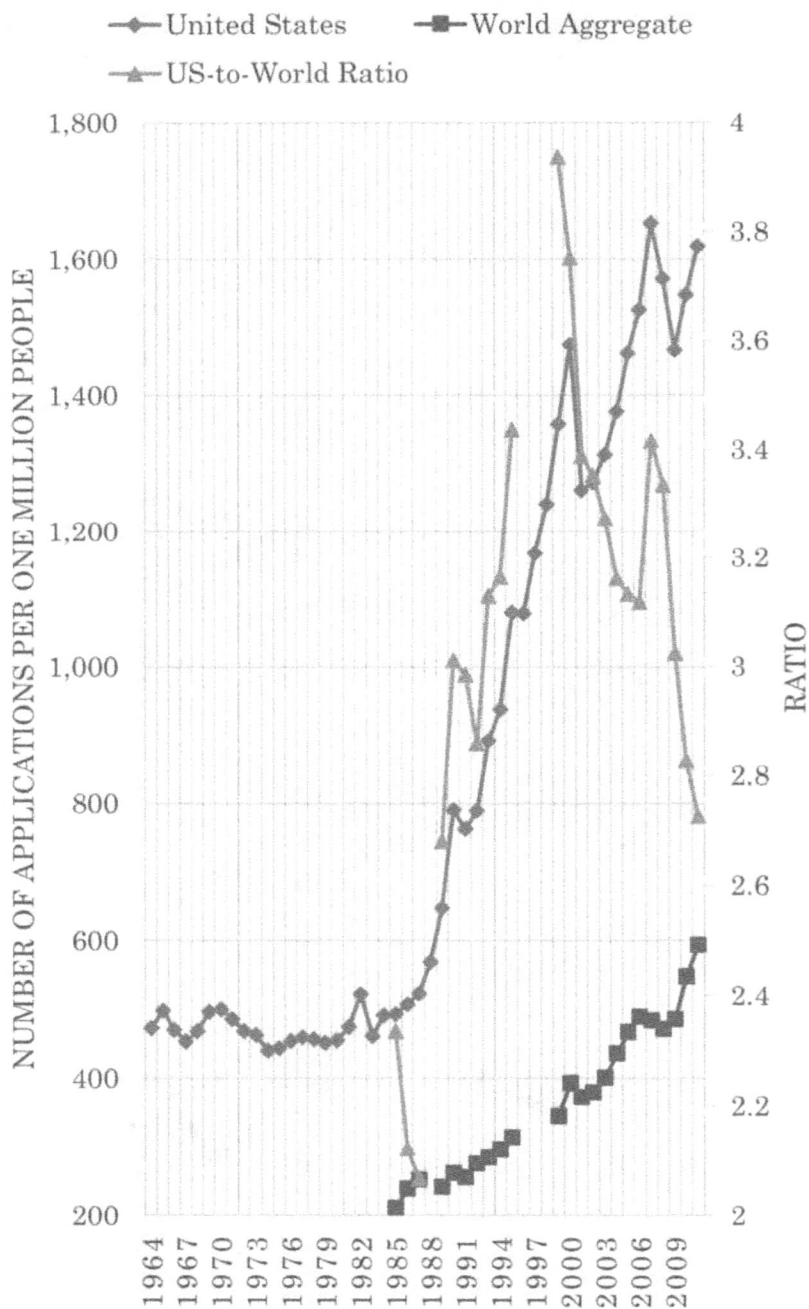

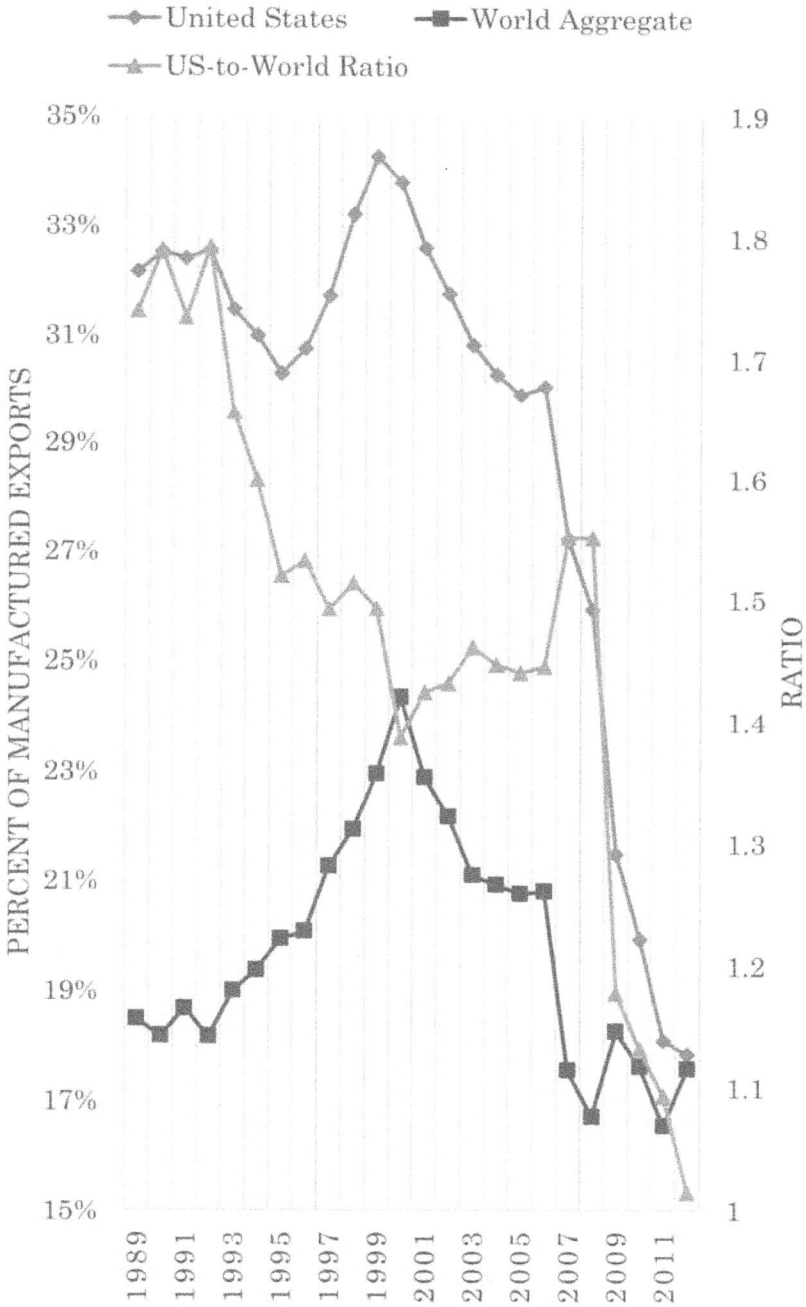

Figure 67: High-Tech Exports

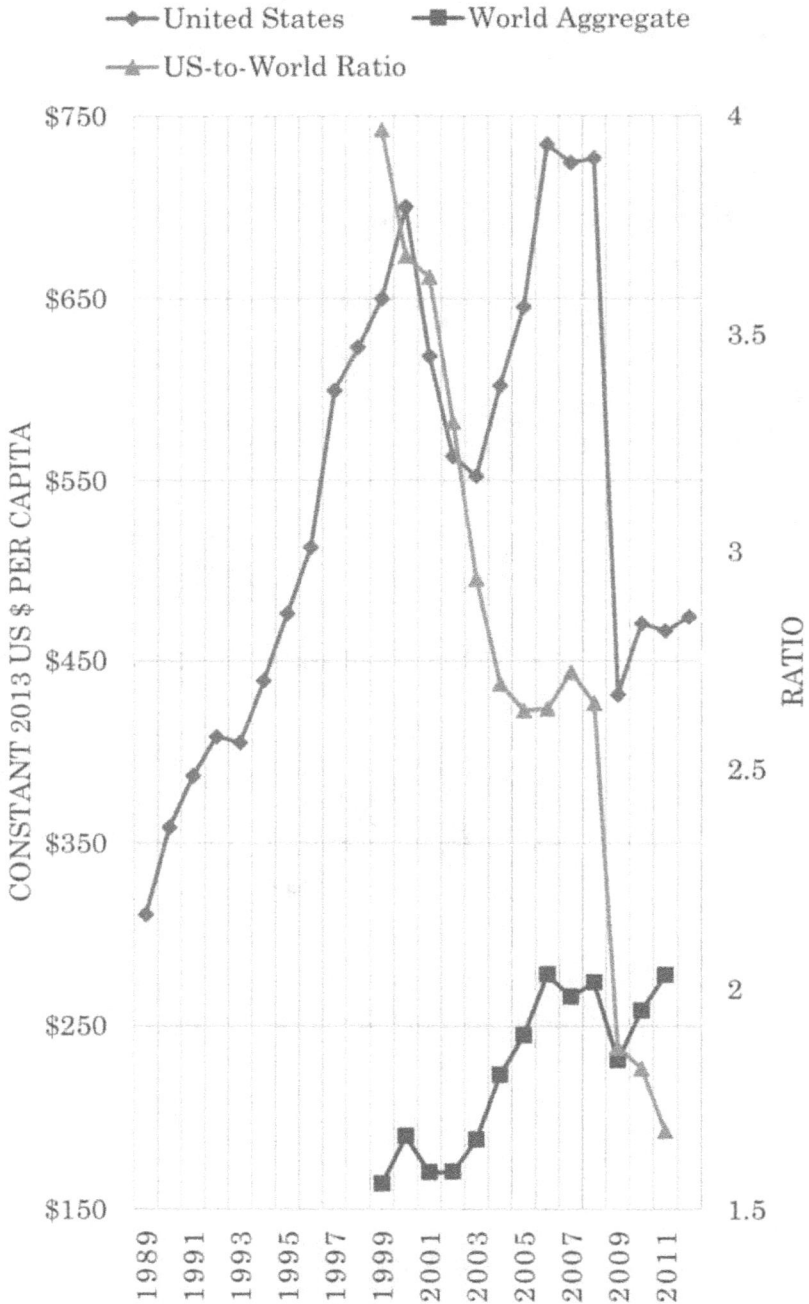

Appendix 3: Invention, Science, & Technology
Figure 68: High-Tech Export Value

Thomas E. Kurek

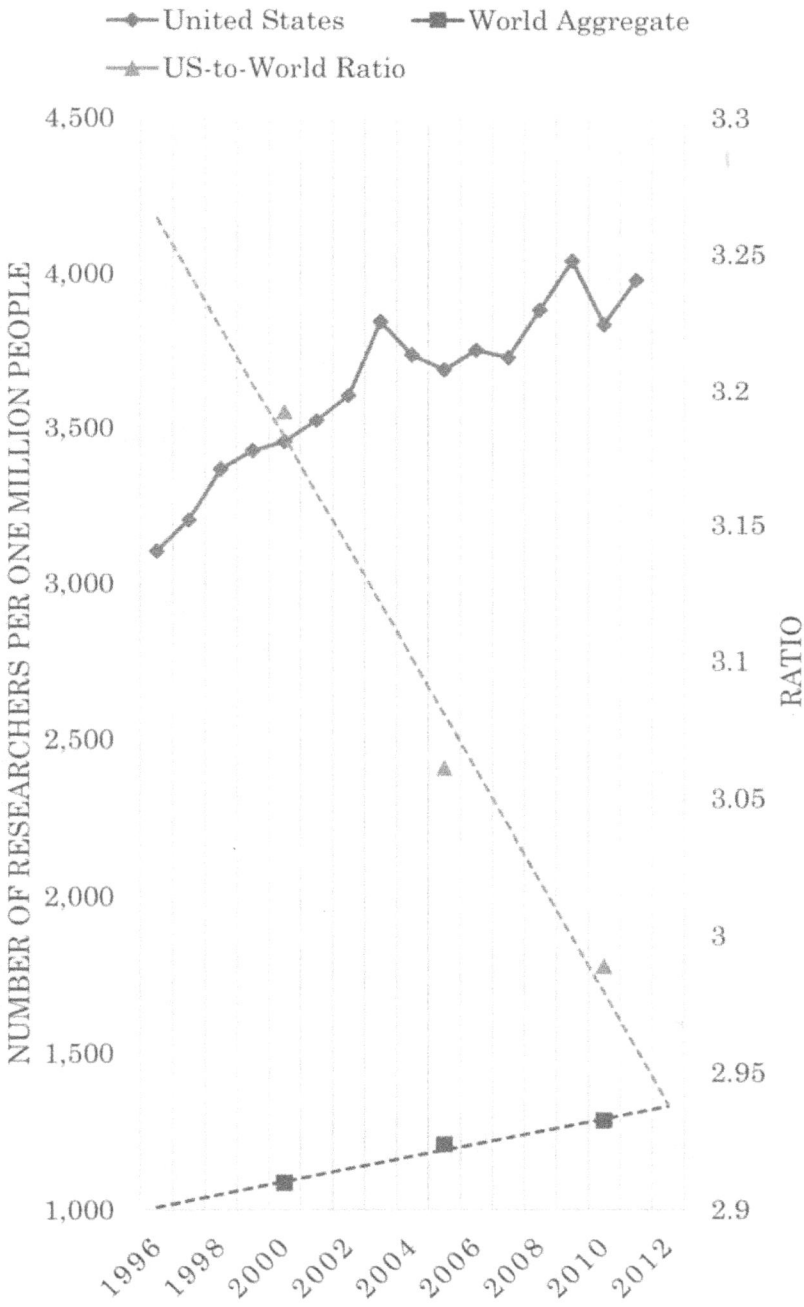

Figure 69: Research and Development Researchers

Figure 70: Research & Development Expenditure

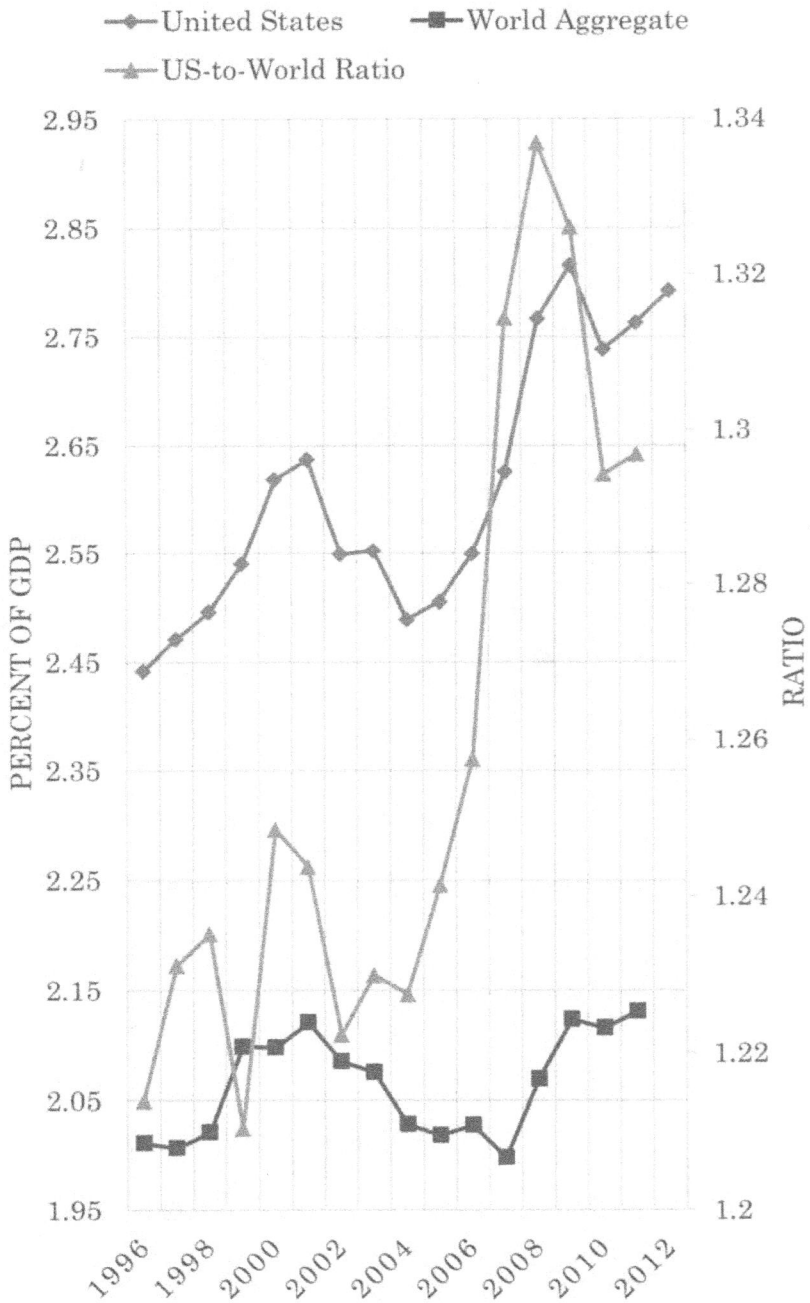

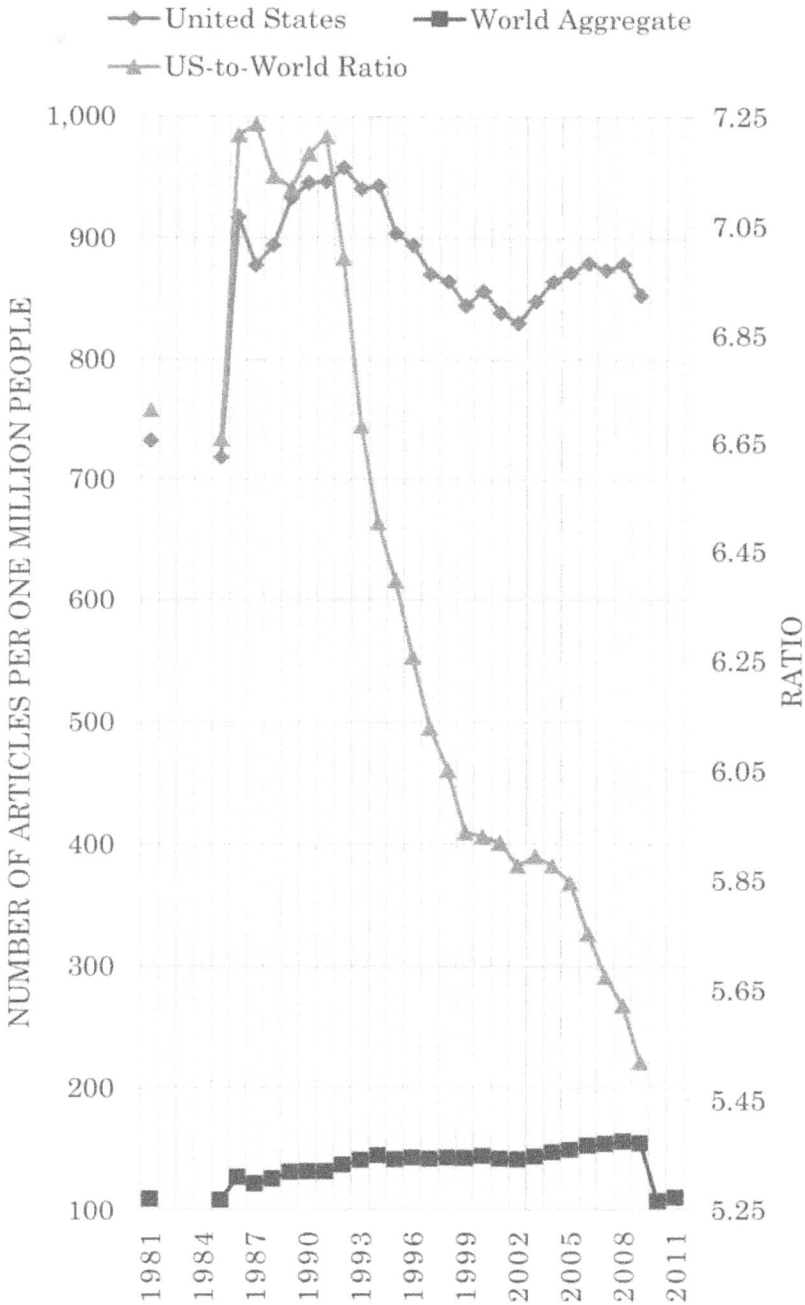

Figure 71: Scientific and Technical Journal Articles

Appendix 4: Energy & Transportation

The following figures compare United States energy use and transportation to the rest of the world, by synthesizing World Bank indicators.[282]

---

[282] (World Bank, 2014)

Thomas E. Kurek

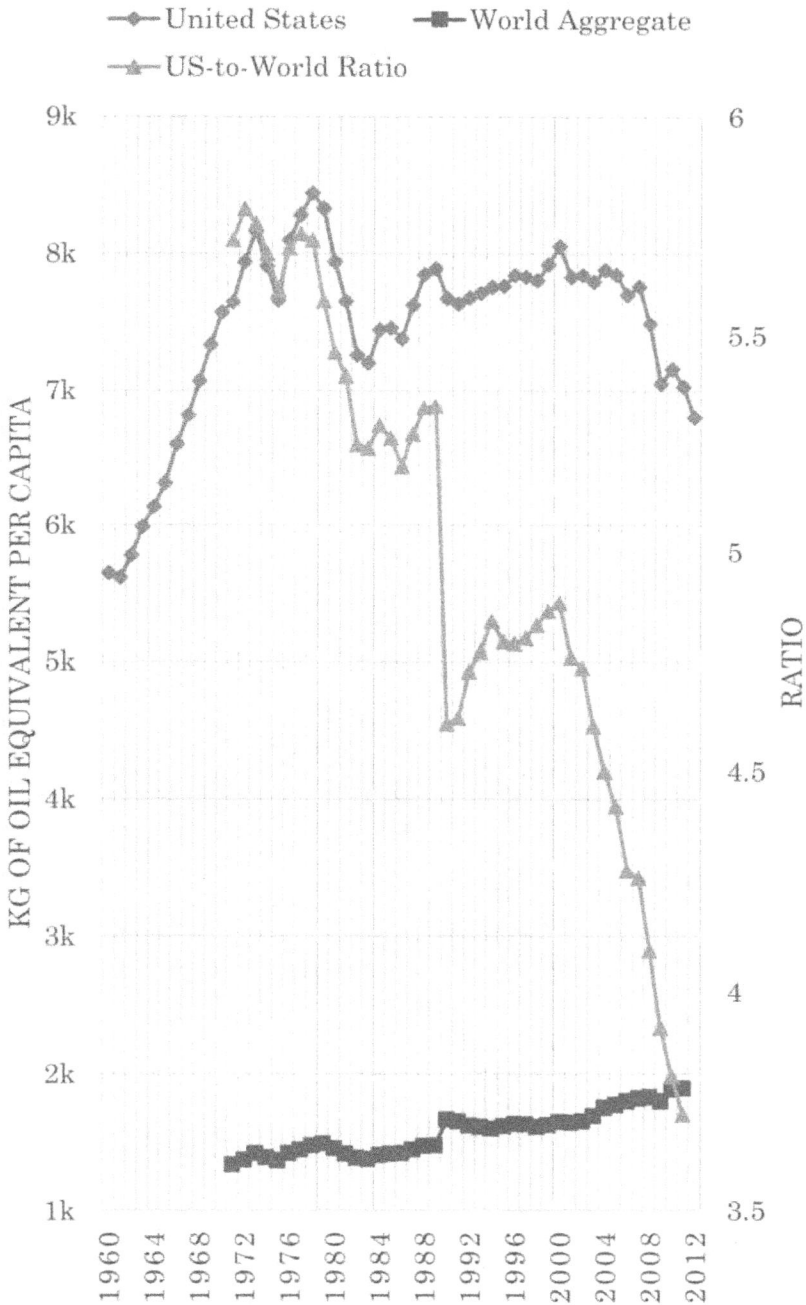

Figure 72: Energy Use

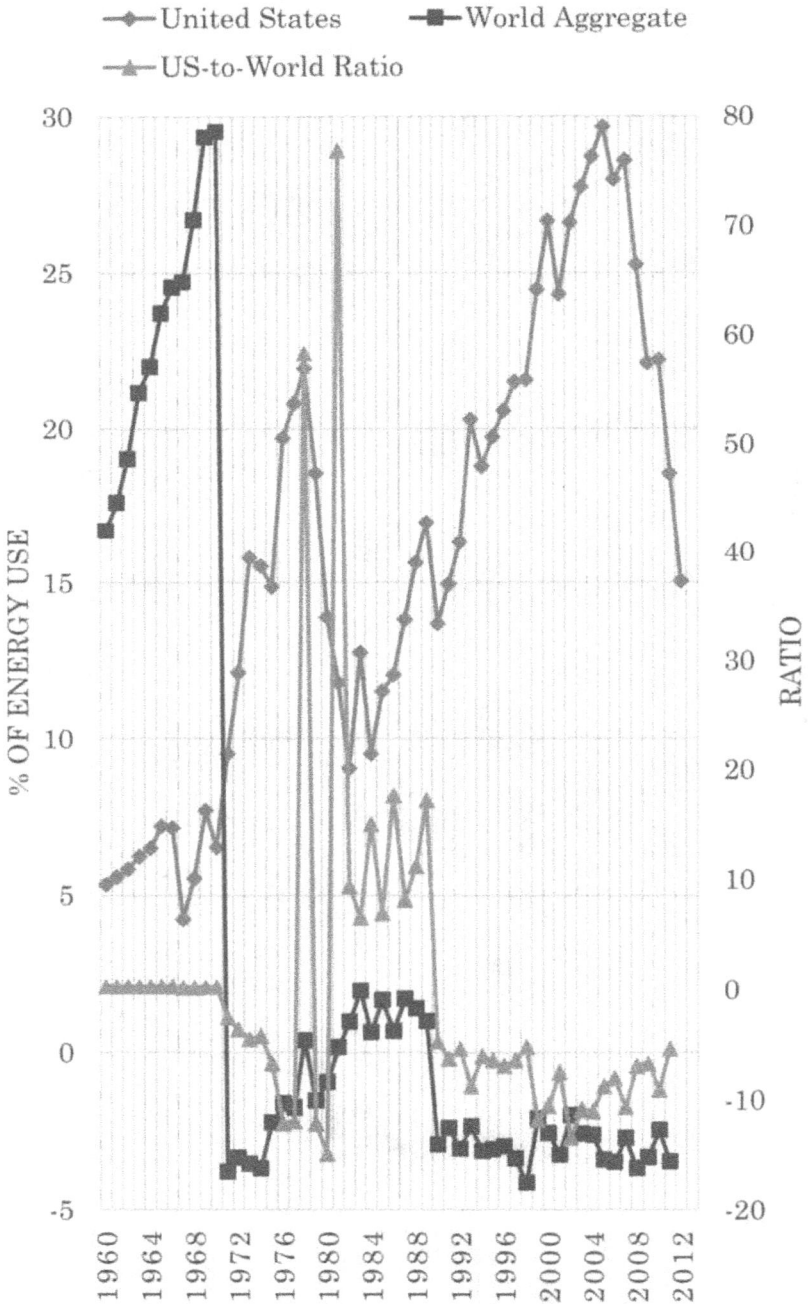

Appendix 4: Energy & Transportation
Figure 73: Net Energy Imports

Thomas E. Kurek

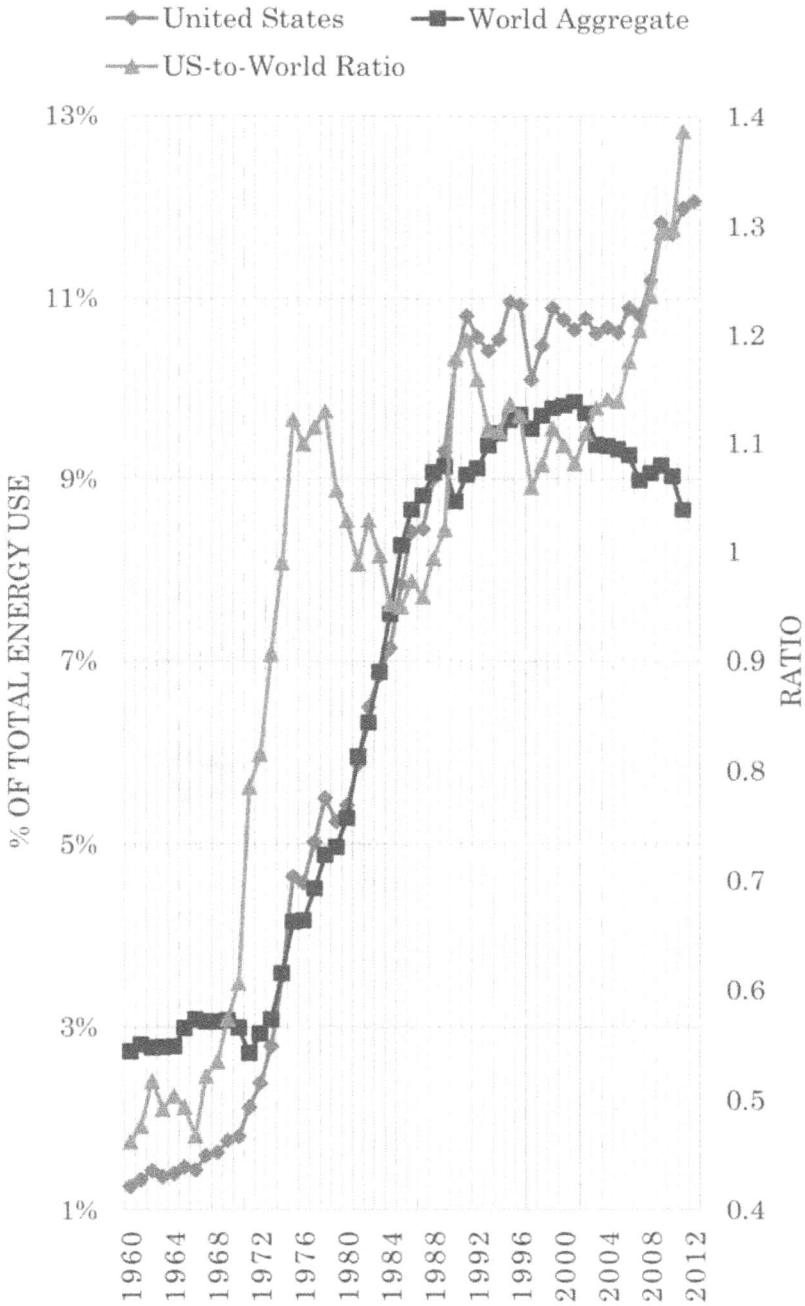

Figure 74: Alternative & Nuclear Energy

Figure 75: Fossil Fuel Energy

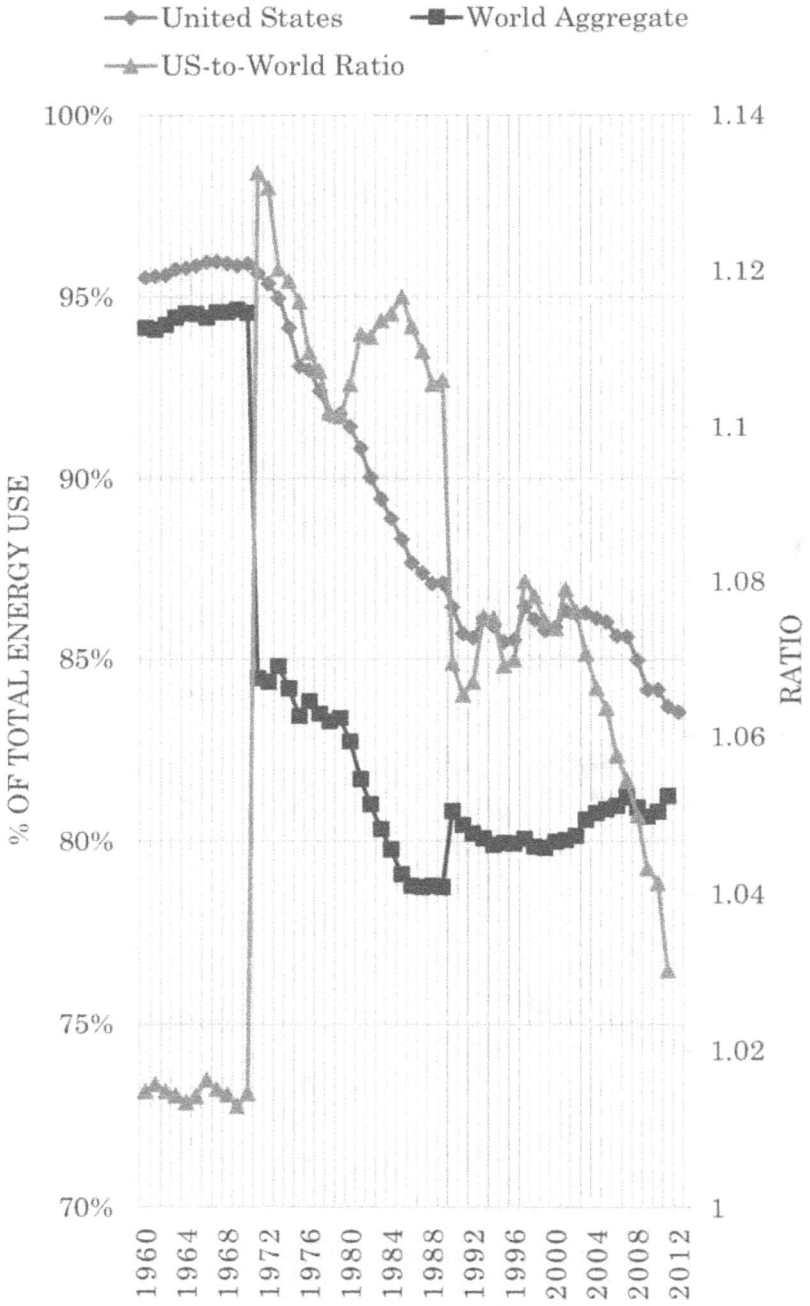

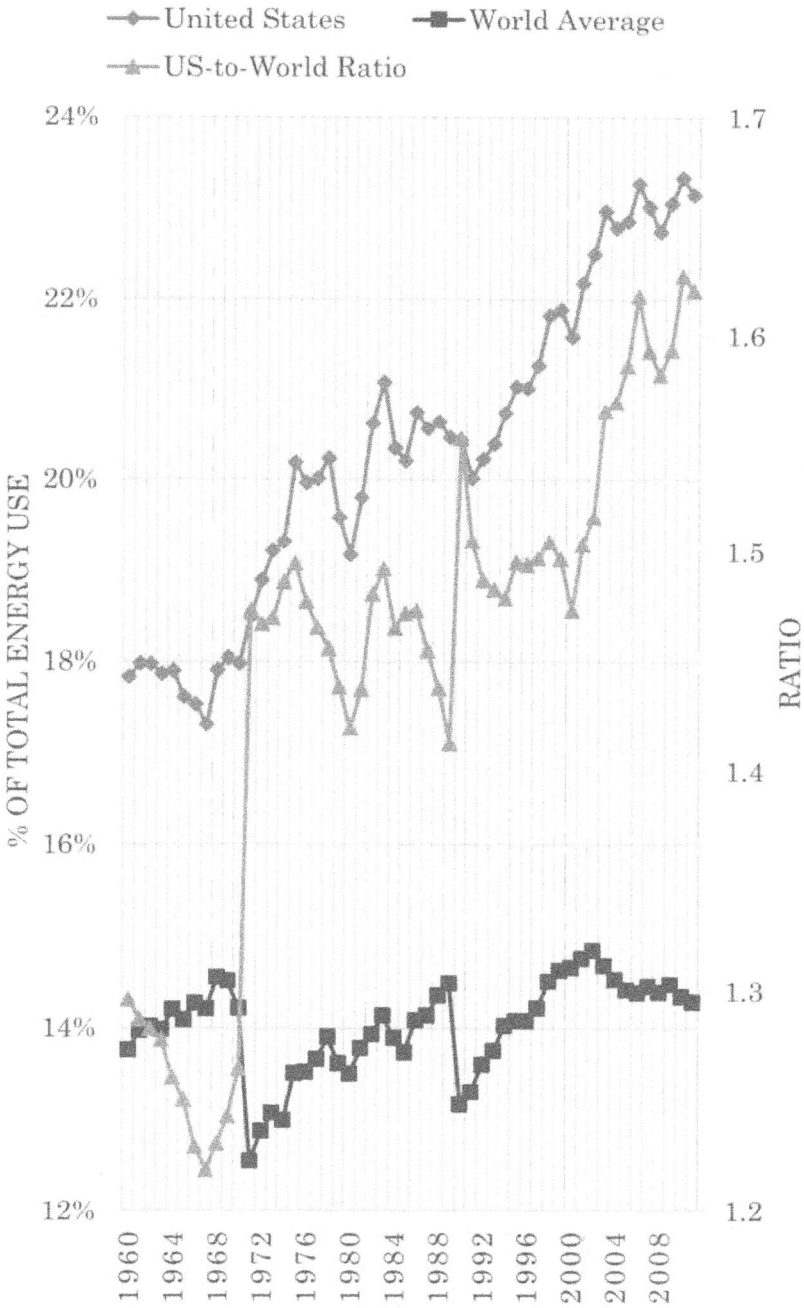

Figure 76: Road Sector Energy Use

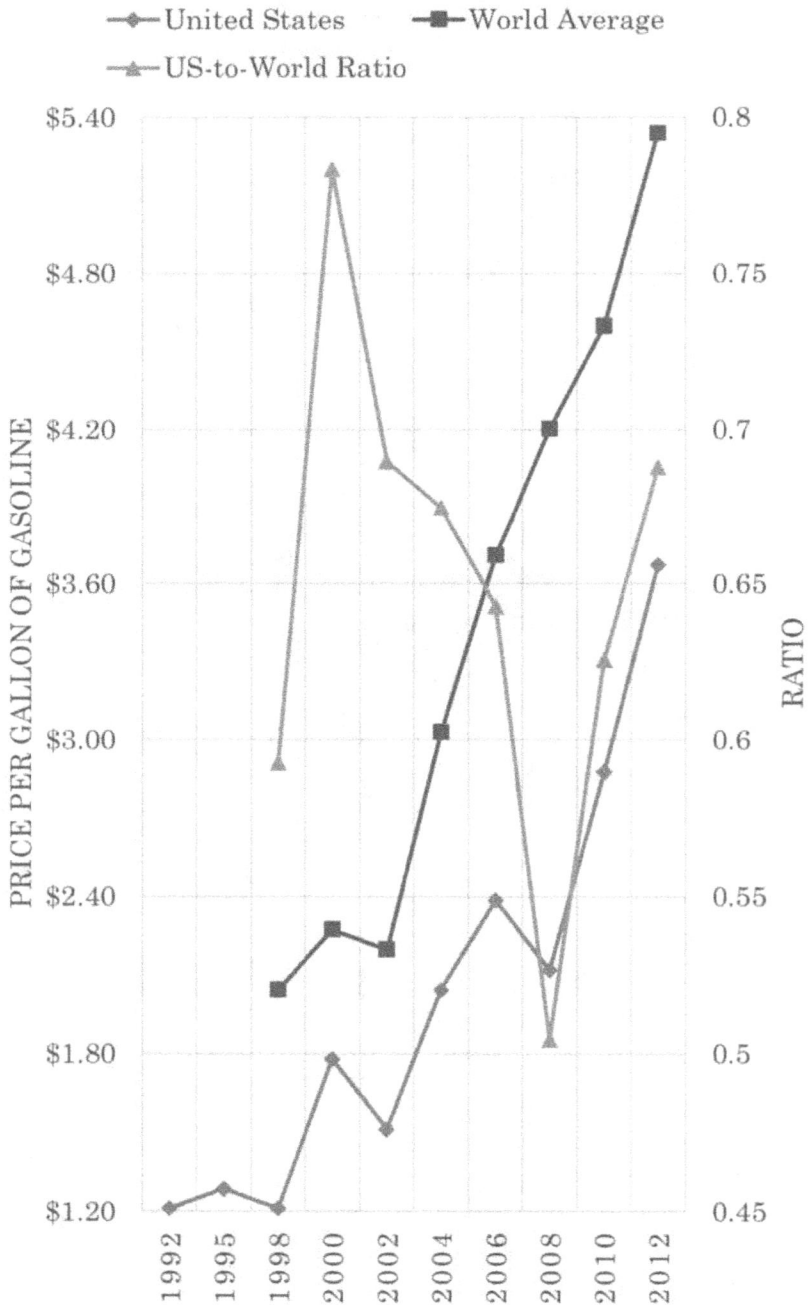

Appendix 4: Energy & Transportation
Figure 77: Gasoline Price

Thomas E. Kurek

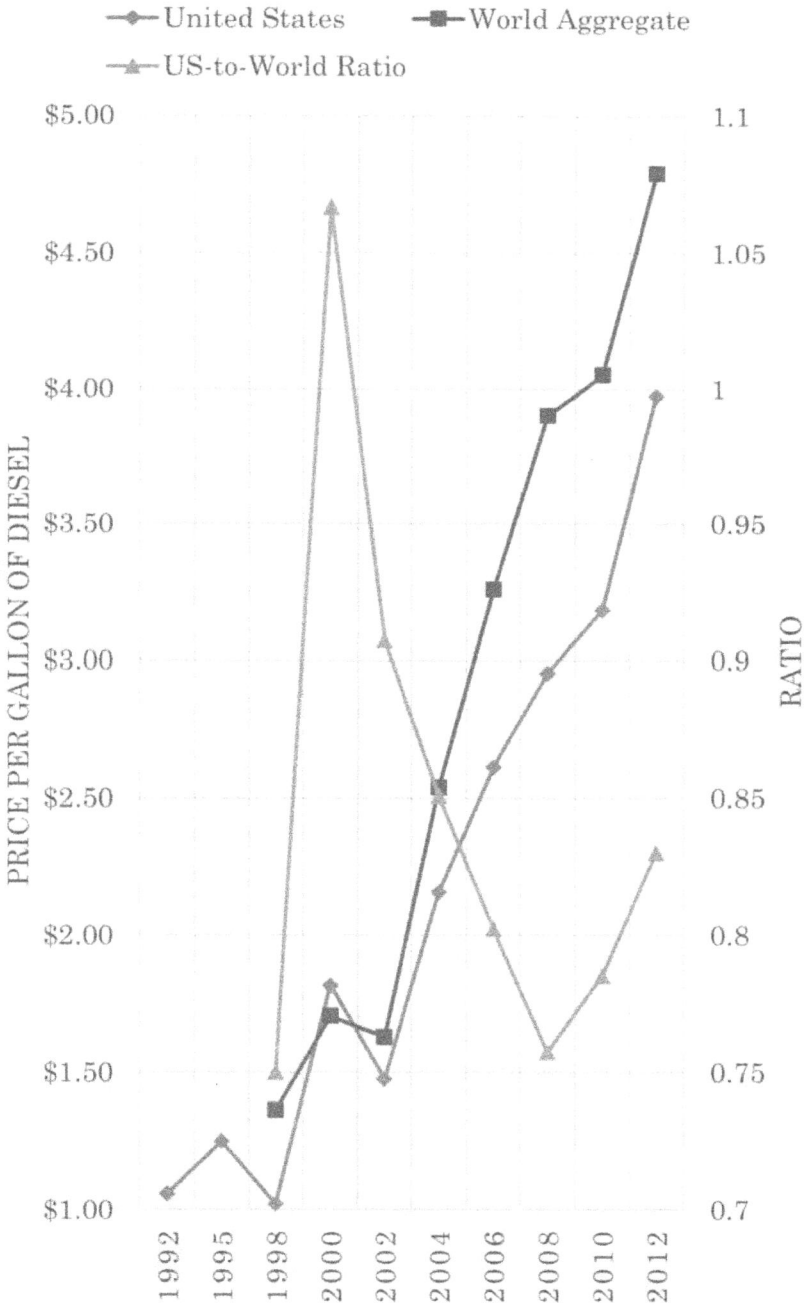

Figure 78: Diesel Price

Figure 79: Motor Vehicles

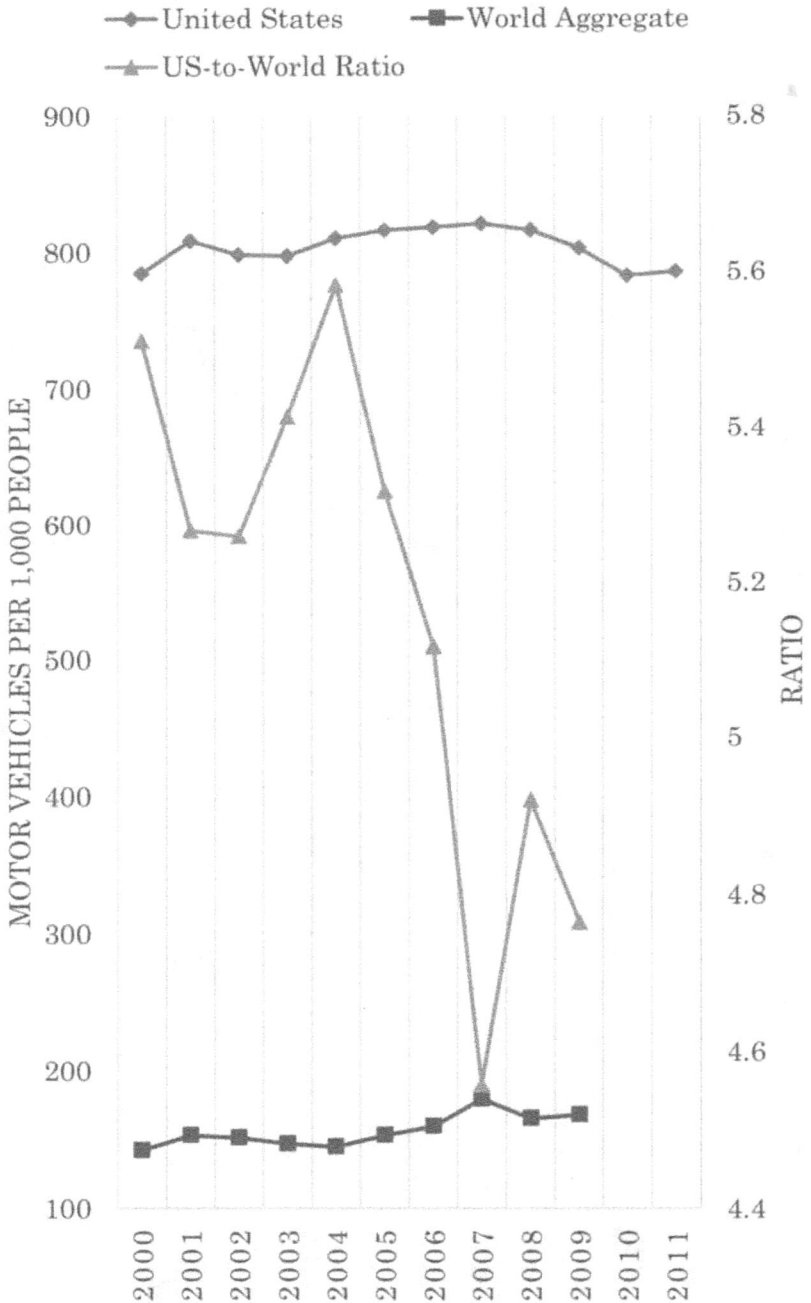

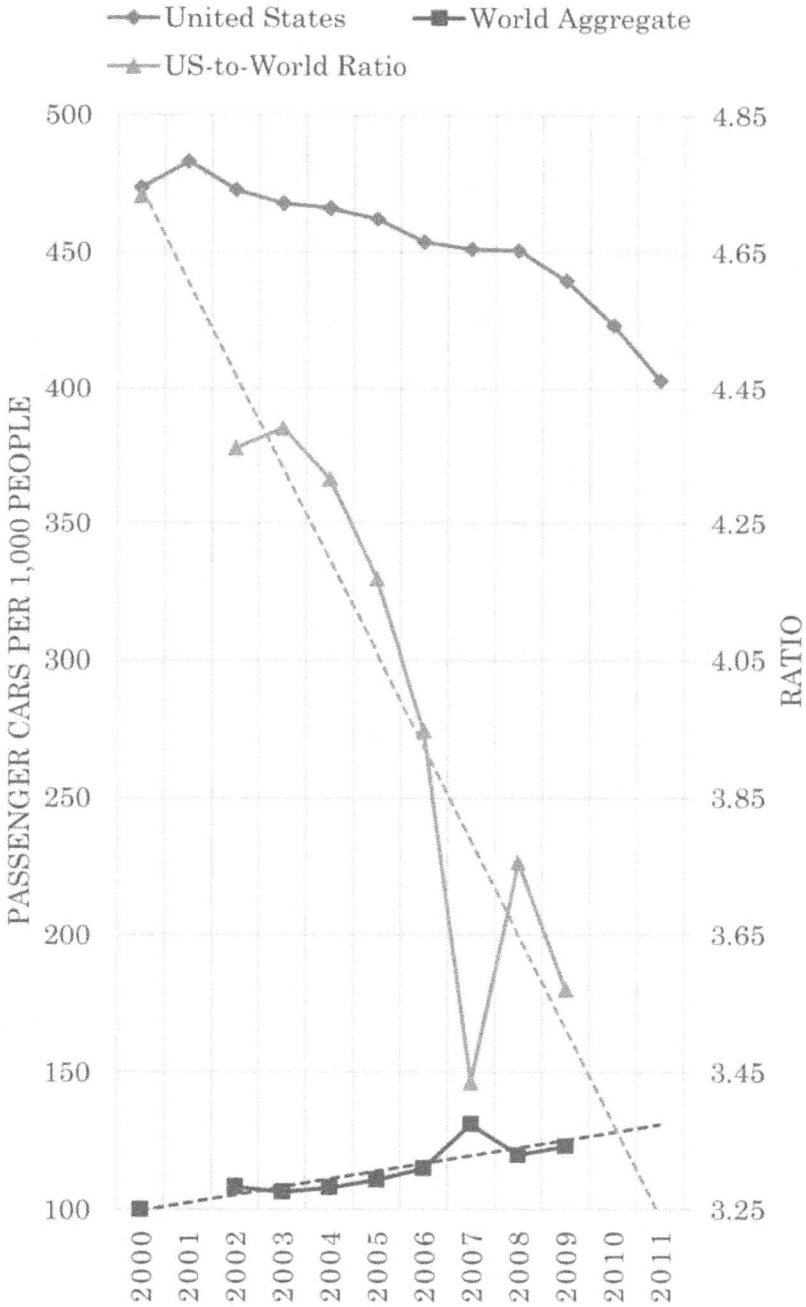

Figure 80: Passenger Cars

Appendix 4: Energy & Transportation
Figure 81: Road Density

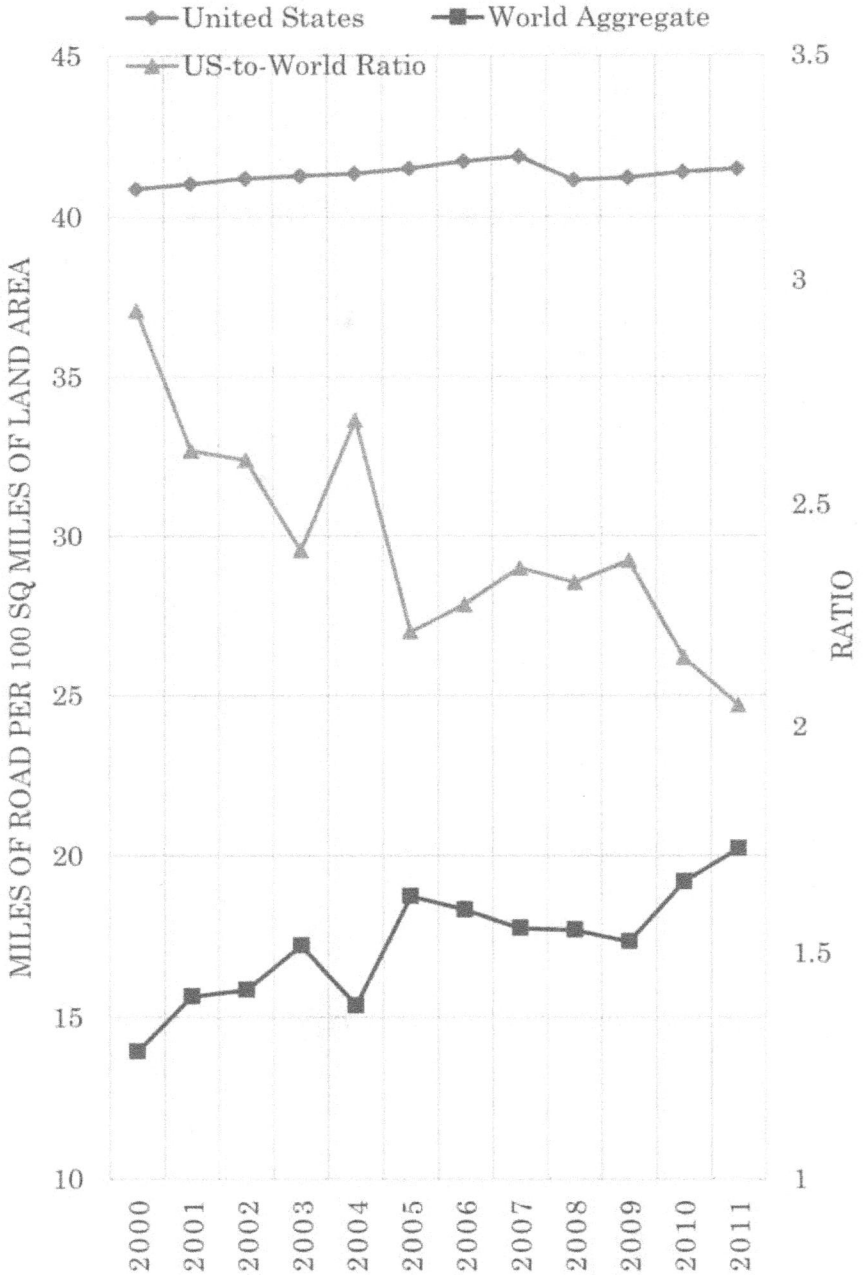

Appendix 5: Demographics, Natural Resources, Military

The following figures compare United States demographics, natural resources, and military to the rest of the world, by synthesizing World Bank indicators.[283] Racial demographics are synthesized from U.S. Census data and various researchers.[284] [285] [286] [287]

---

[283] (World Bank, 2014)
[284] (U.S. Bureau of the Census, 1975)
[285] (Gibson & Jung, 2002)
[286] (Gratton & Butmann, 2006)
[287] (Humes, Jones, & Ramirez, 2011)

Figure 82: Population, % of the World

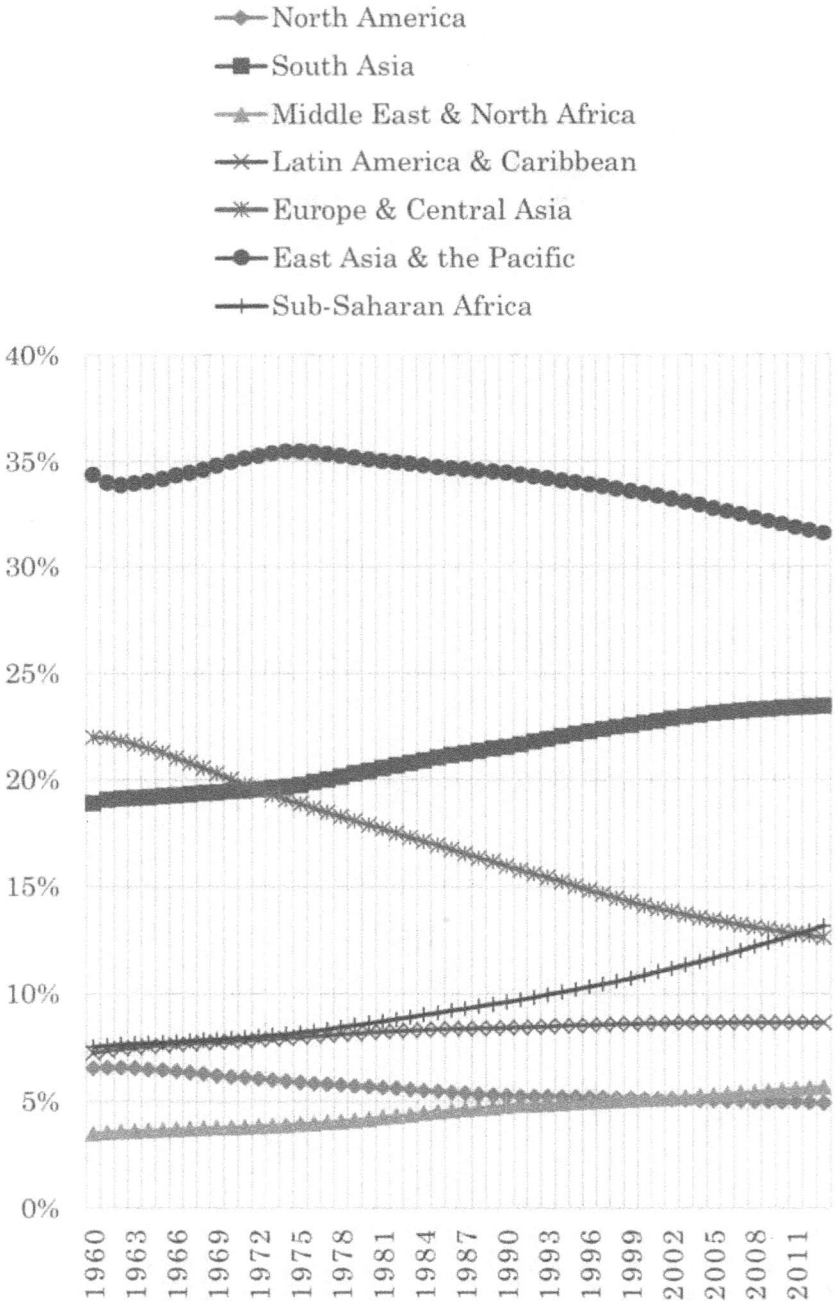

- North America
- South Asia
- Middle East & North Africa
- Latin America & Caribbean
- Europe & Central Asia
- East Asia & the Pacific
- Sub-Saharan Africa

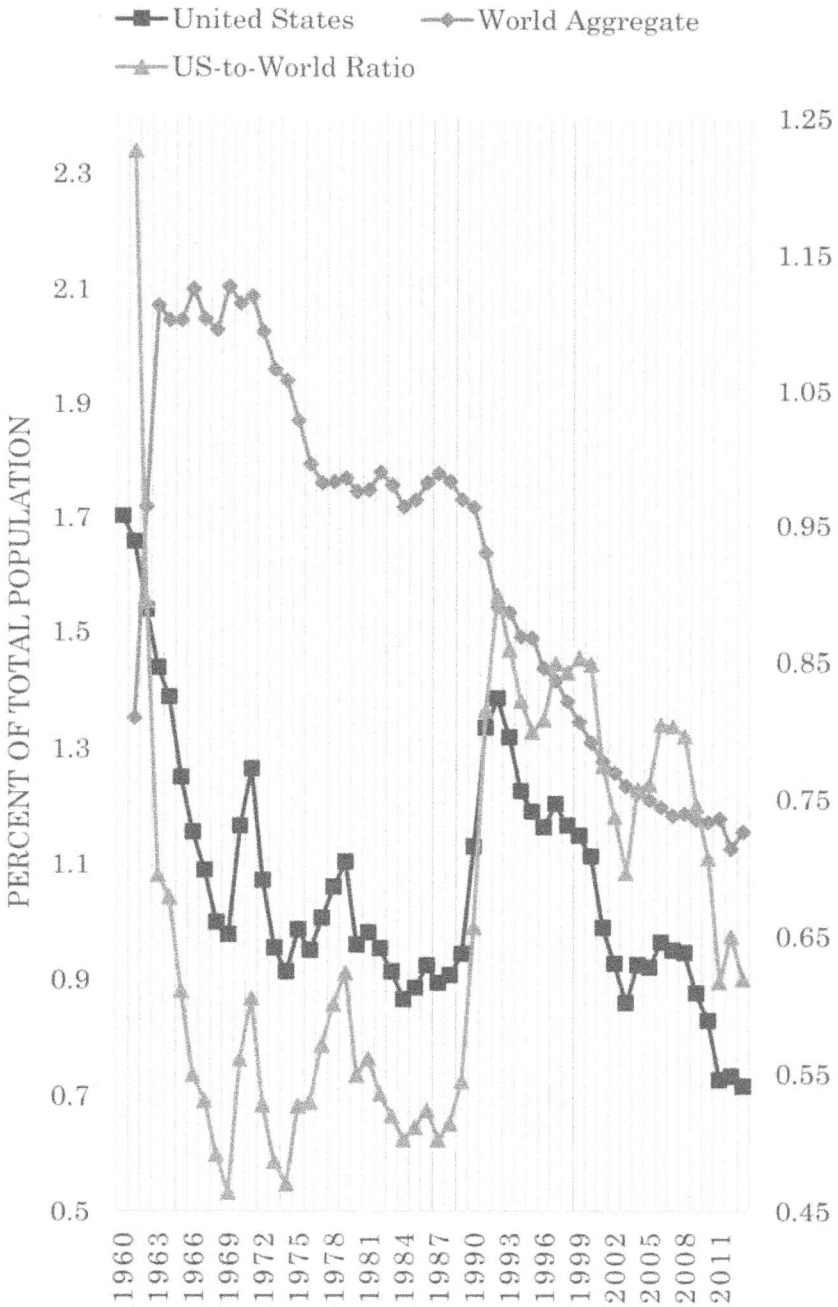

Figure 83: Population Growth, Annual %

Figure 84: Population Density

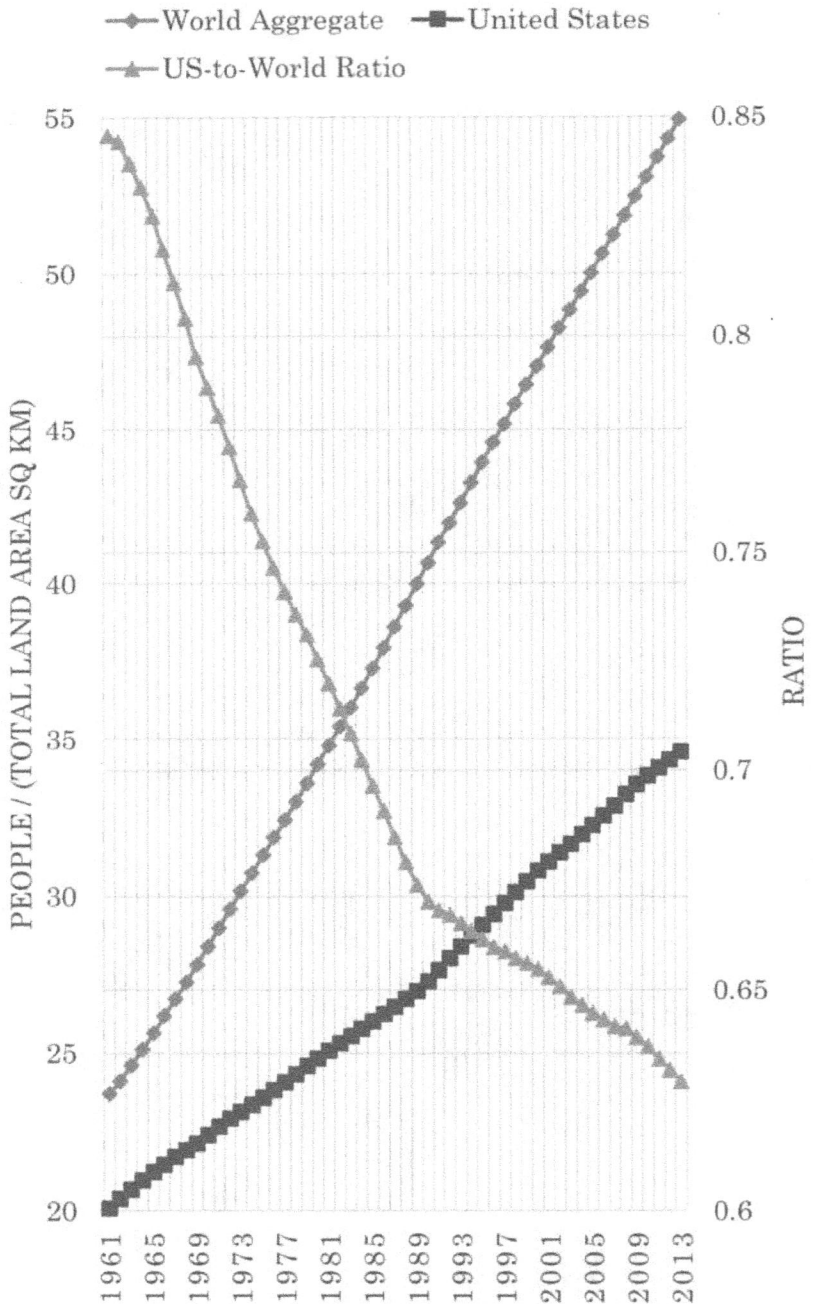

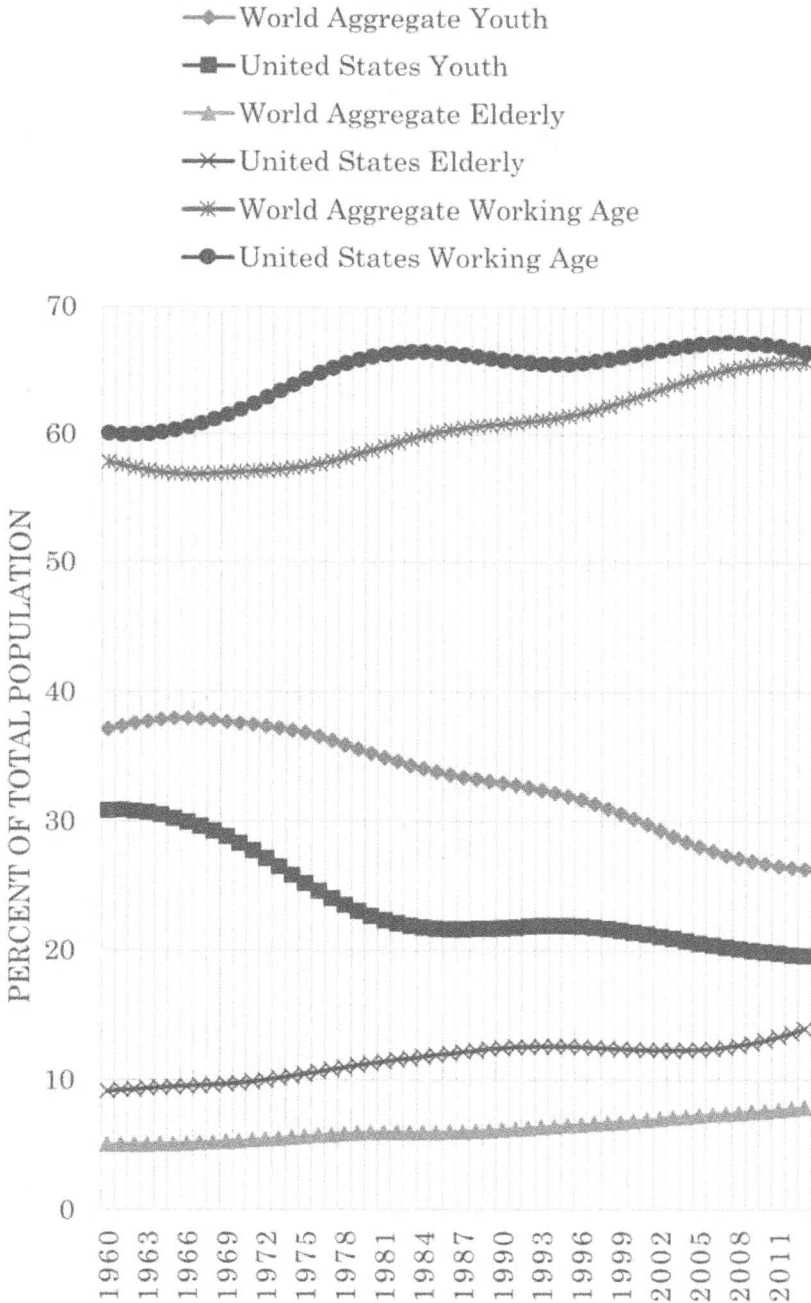

Figure 85: Age Demographics, % of Total Population

Legend:
—◆— World Aggregate Youth
—■— United States Youth
—▲— World Aggregate Elderly
—✕— United States Elderly
—✶— World Aggregate Working Age
—●— United States Working Age

Y-axis: PERCENT OF TOTAL POPULATION (0, 10, 20, 30, 40, 50, 60, 70)

X-axis: 1960, 1963, 1966, 1969, 1972, 1975, 1978, 1981, 1984, 1987, 1990, 1993, 1996, 1999, 2002, 2005, 2008, 2011

Figure 86: Age Demographics, US-to-World Ratio

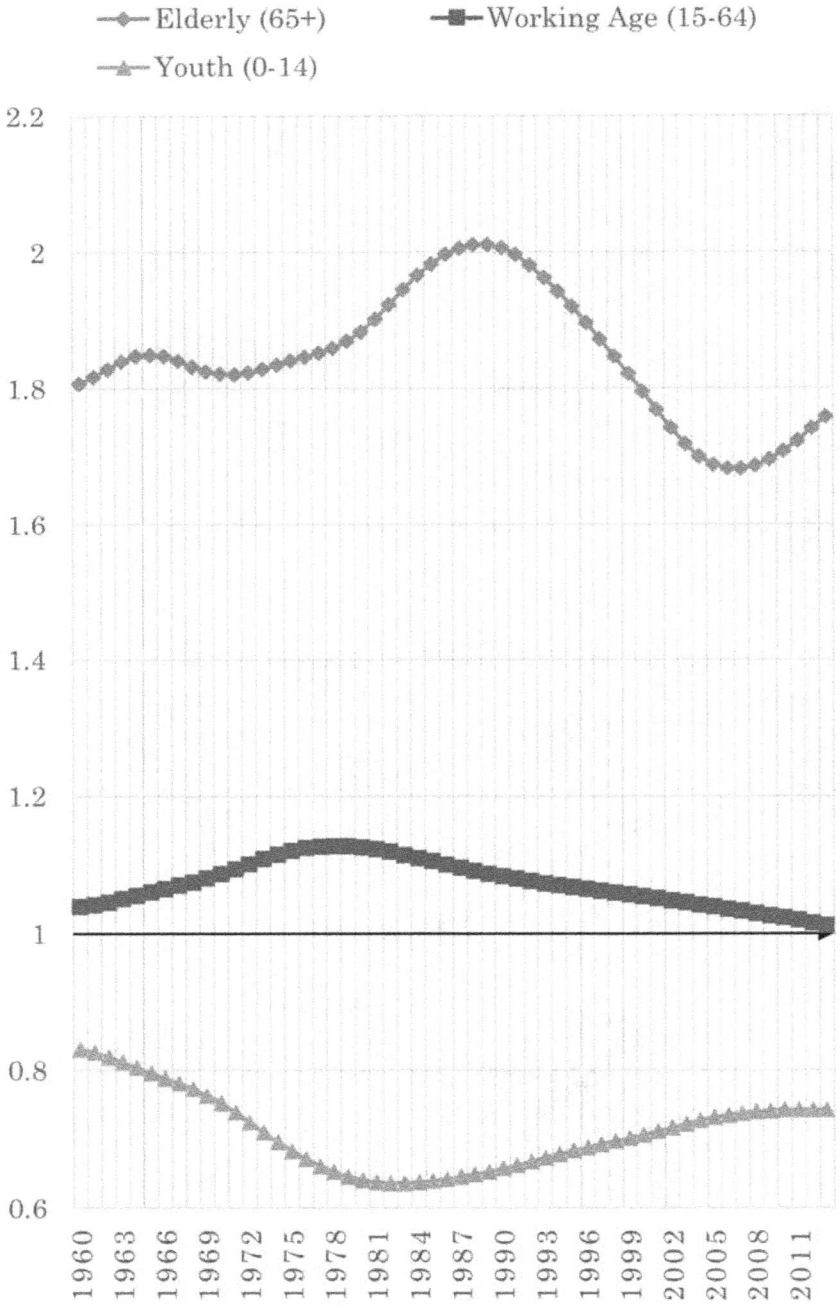

Thomas E. Kurek

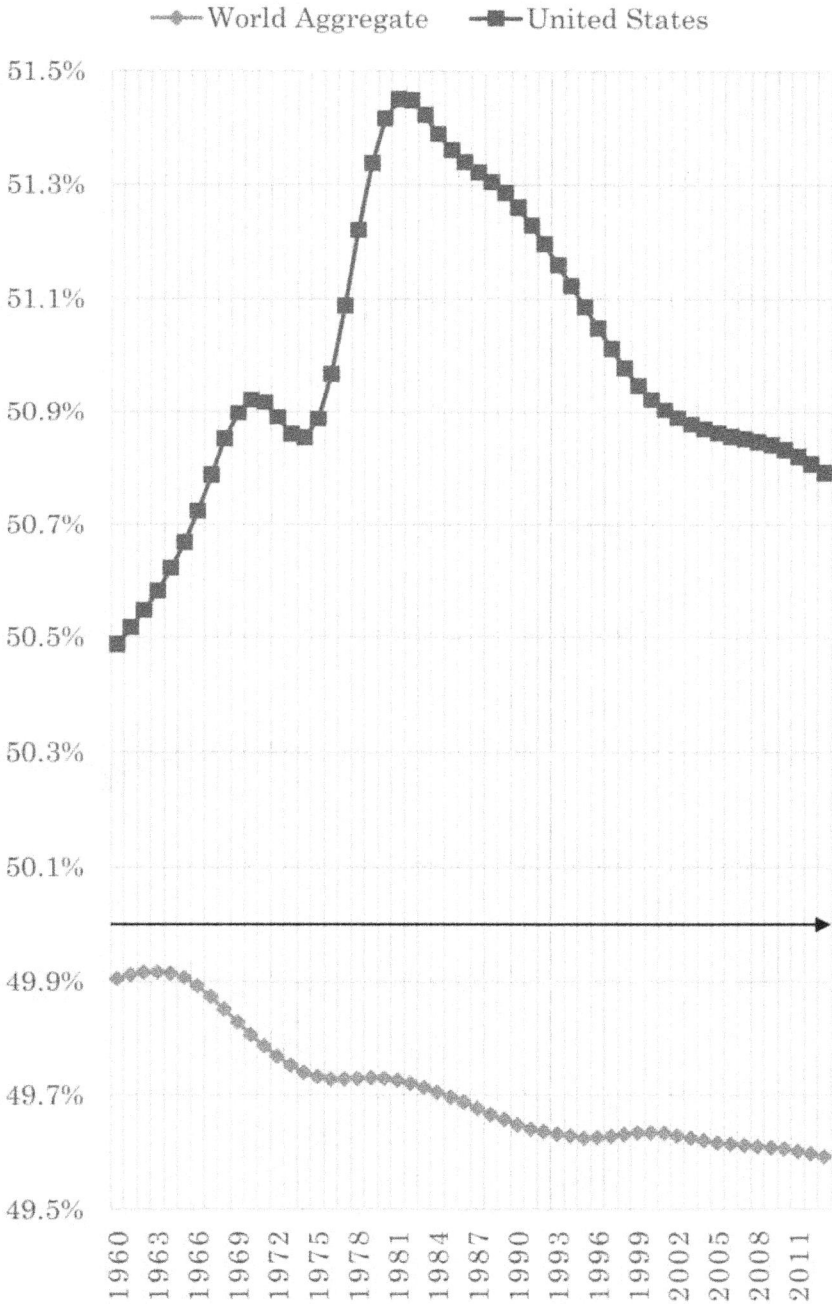

Figure 87: Females, % of Population

Figure 88: Immigrants

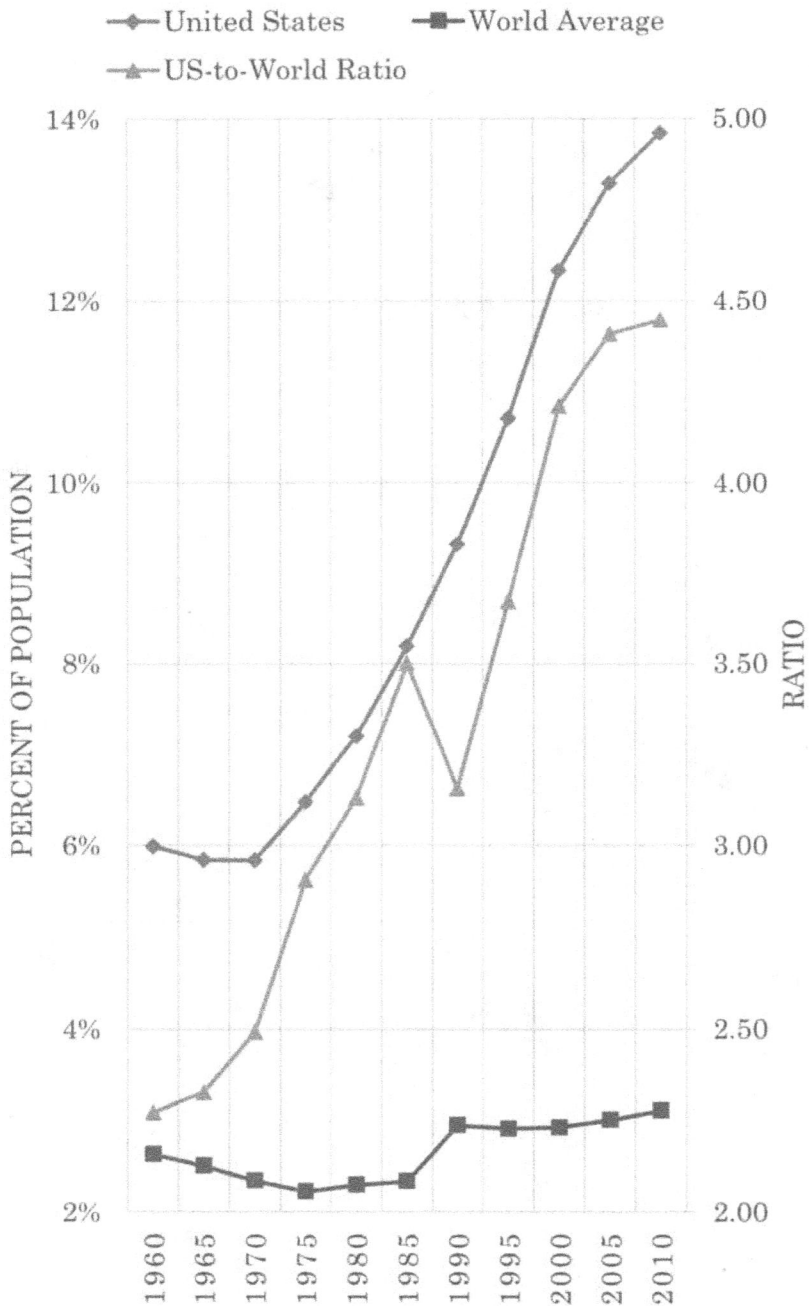

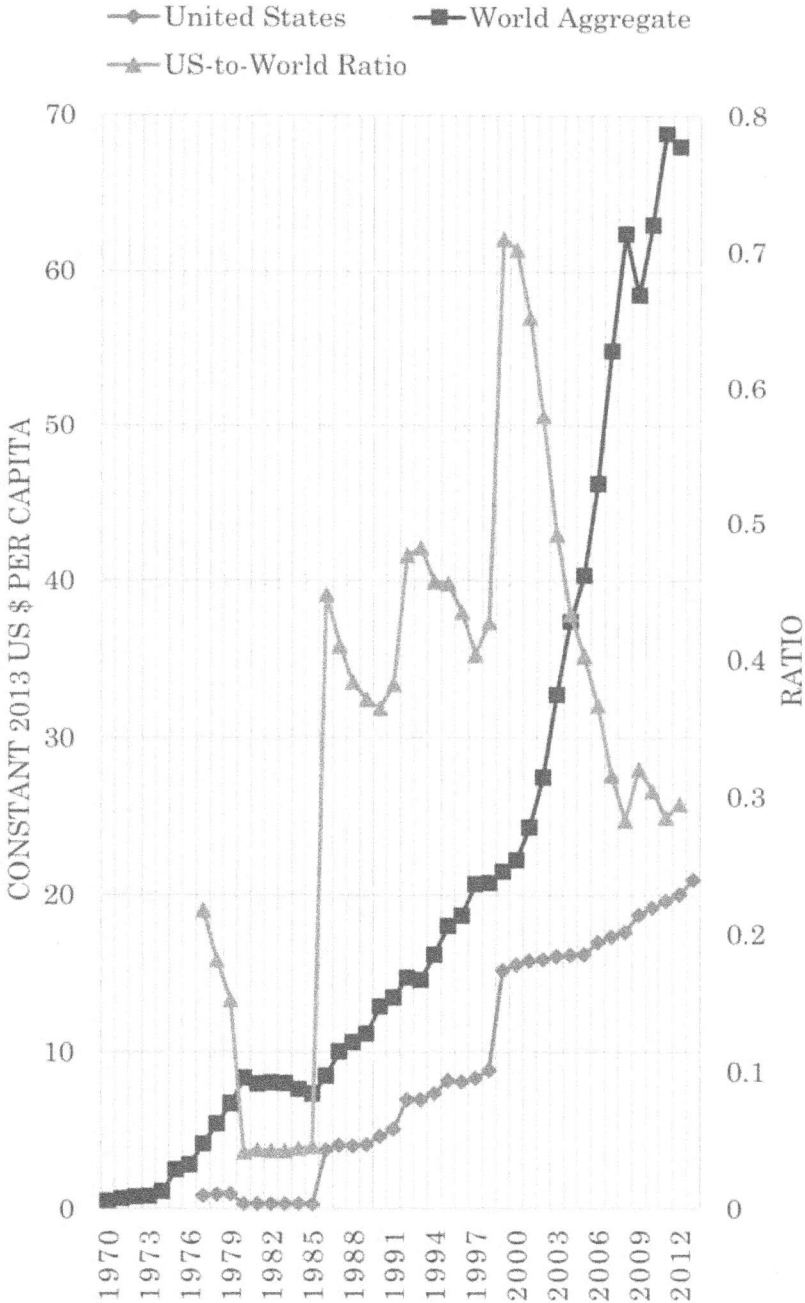

Figure 89: Personal Transfers (Cash & Kind between Foreign Nations)

Figure 90: Urbanization

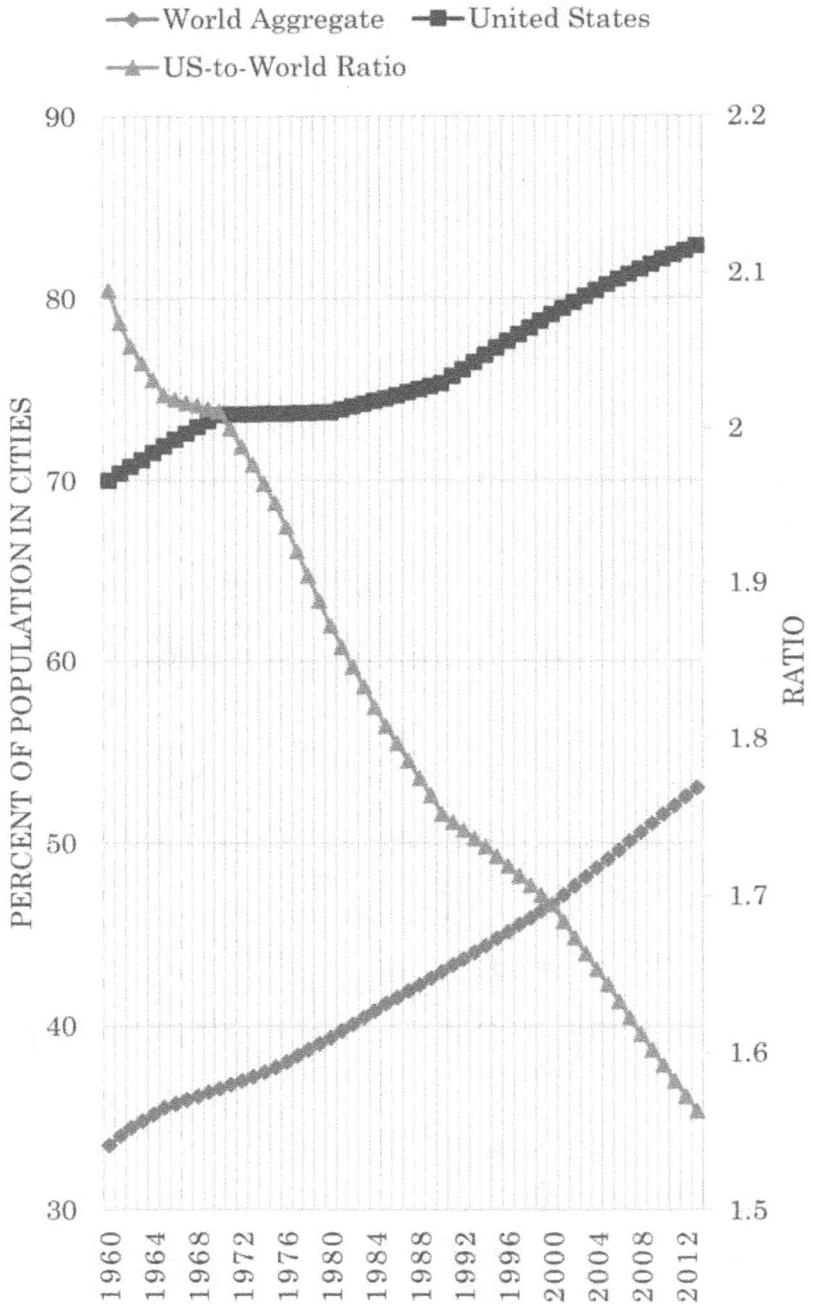

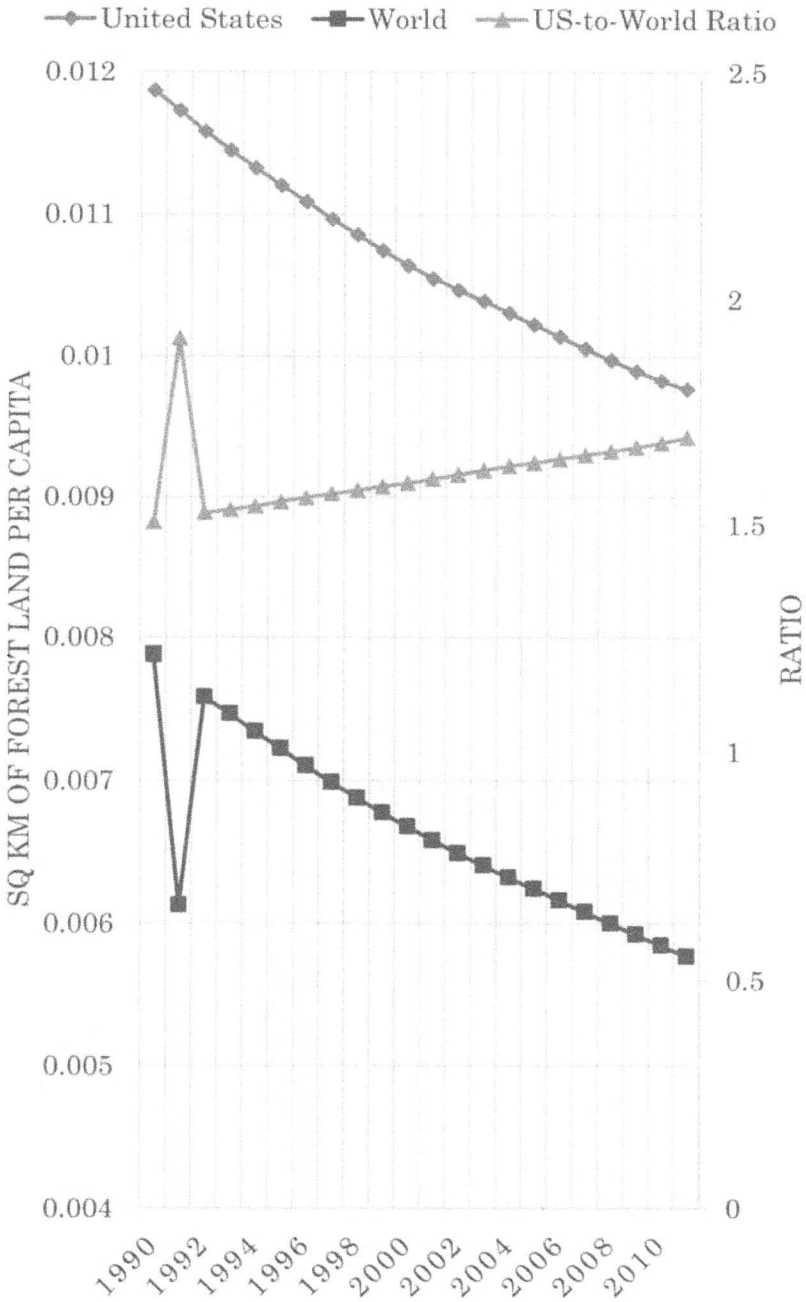

Figure 91: Forest Land per Capita

Figure 92: Agricultural Land per Capita

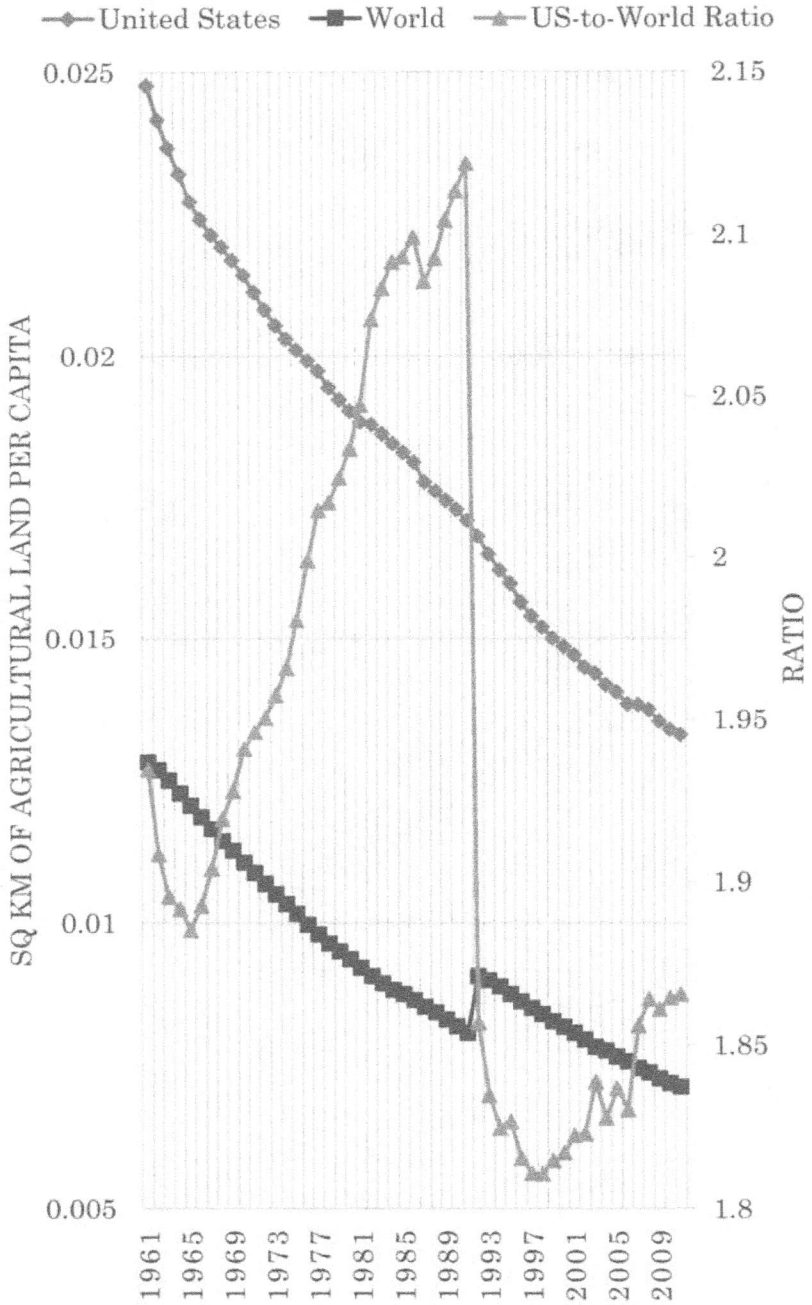

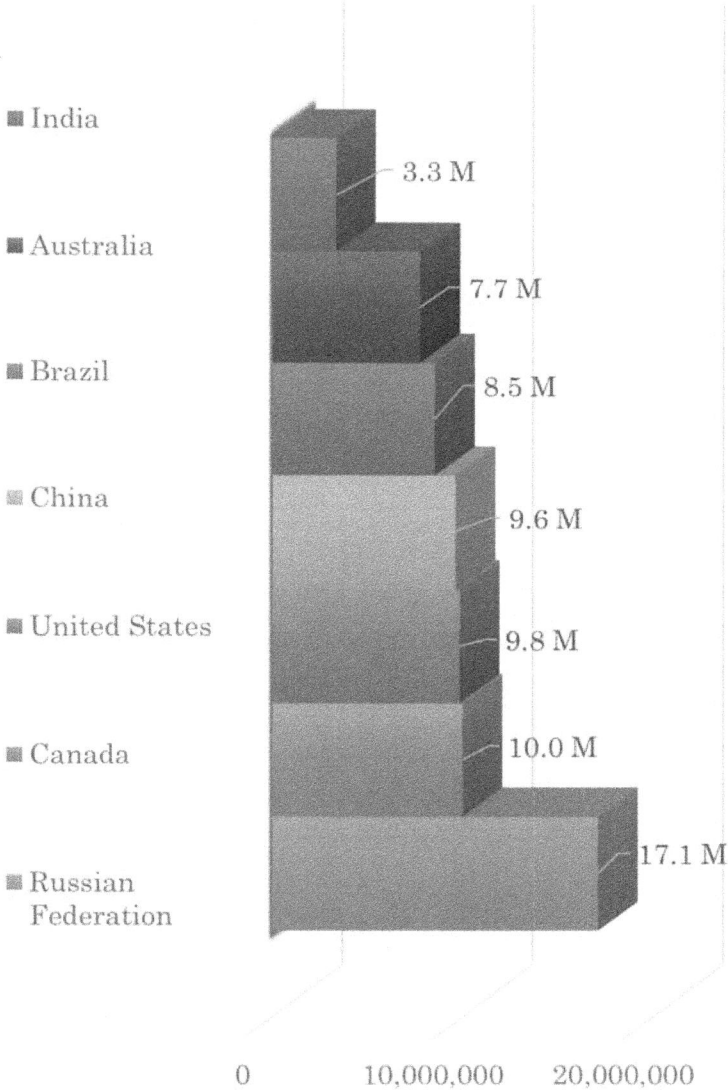

Figure 93: Surface Area (Land & Water), km²

India — 3.3 M

Australia — 7.7 M

Brazil — 8.5 M

China — 9.6 M

United States — 9.8 M

Canada — 10.0 M

Russian Federation — 17.1 M

0   10,000,000   20,000,000

Figure 94: Racial Demographics, 1690 – 2010

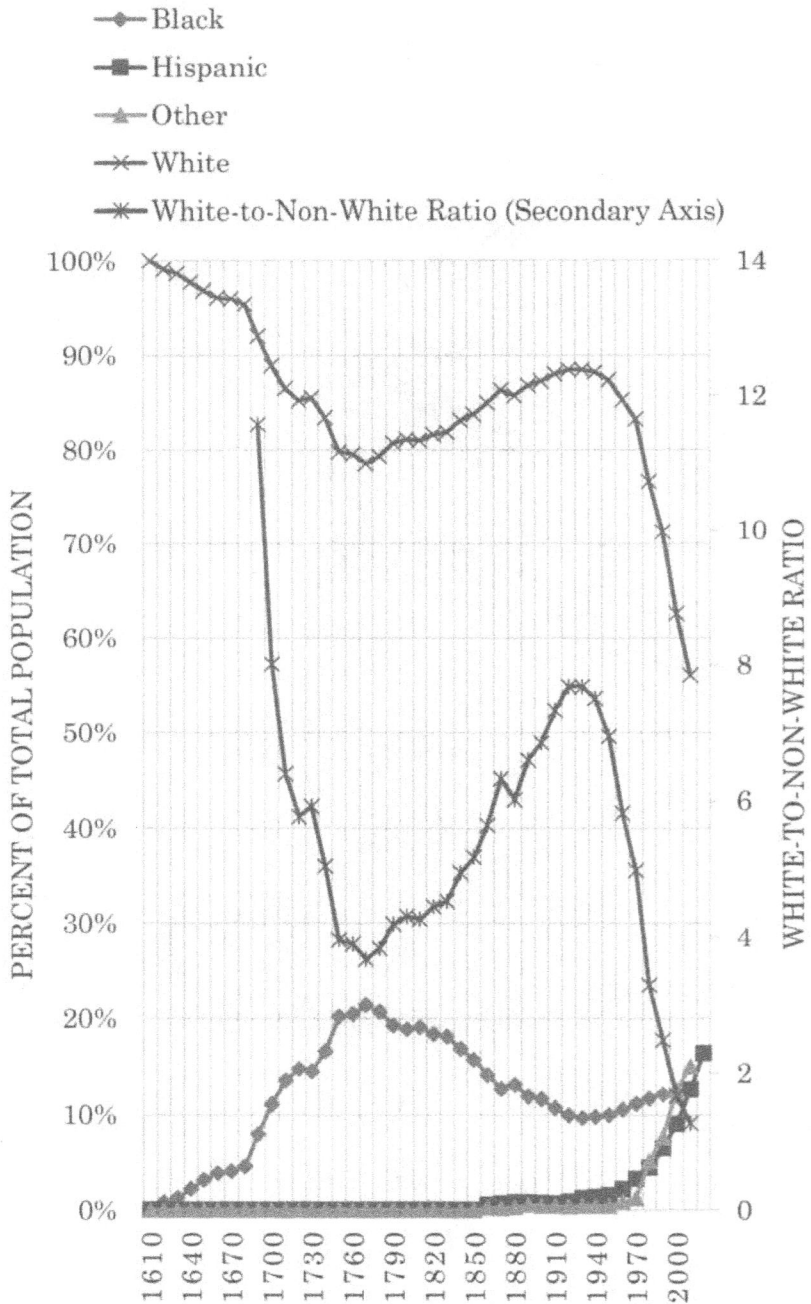

Thomas E. Kurek

Appendix 6: Labor, Wages, and Tax

Disutility of labor is taken from Ludwig von Mises' classic work.[288]

Lifetime compensation, education, training cost models based upon various industrial sources. Cost of living and head of household by age income are from U.S. BLS.

.

---

[288] (von Mises, Chapter IV, Section 2: The Disutilities and Satisfactions of Labour, 1922)

Figure 95: Disutility of Labor

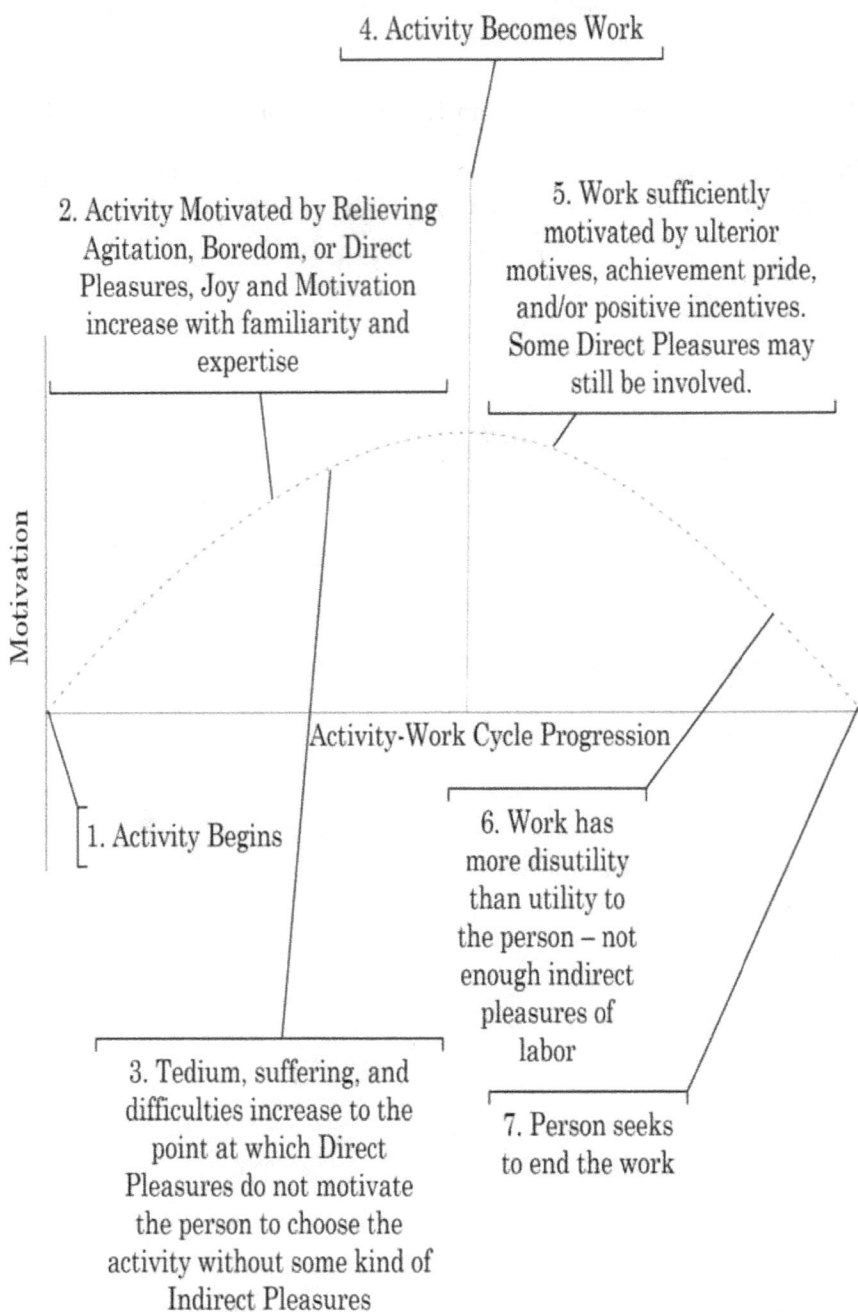

4. Activity Becomes Work

2. Activity Motivated by Relieving Agitation, Boredom, or Direct Pleasures, Joy and Motivation increase with familiarity and expertise

5. Work sufficiently motivated by ulterior motives, achievement pride, and/or positive incentives. Some Direct Pleasures may still be involved.

Motivation

Activity-Work Cycle Progression

1. Activity Begins

6. Work has more disutility than utility to the person – not enough indirect pleasures of labor

3. Tedium, suffering, and difficulties increase to the point at which Direct Pleasures do not motivate the person to choose the activity without some kind of Indirect Pleasures

7. Person seeks to end the work

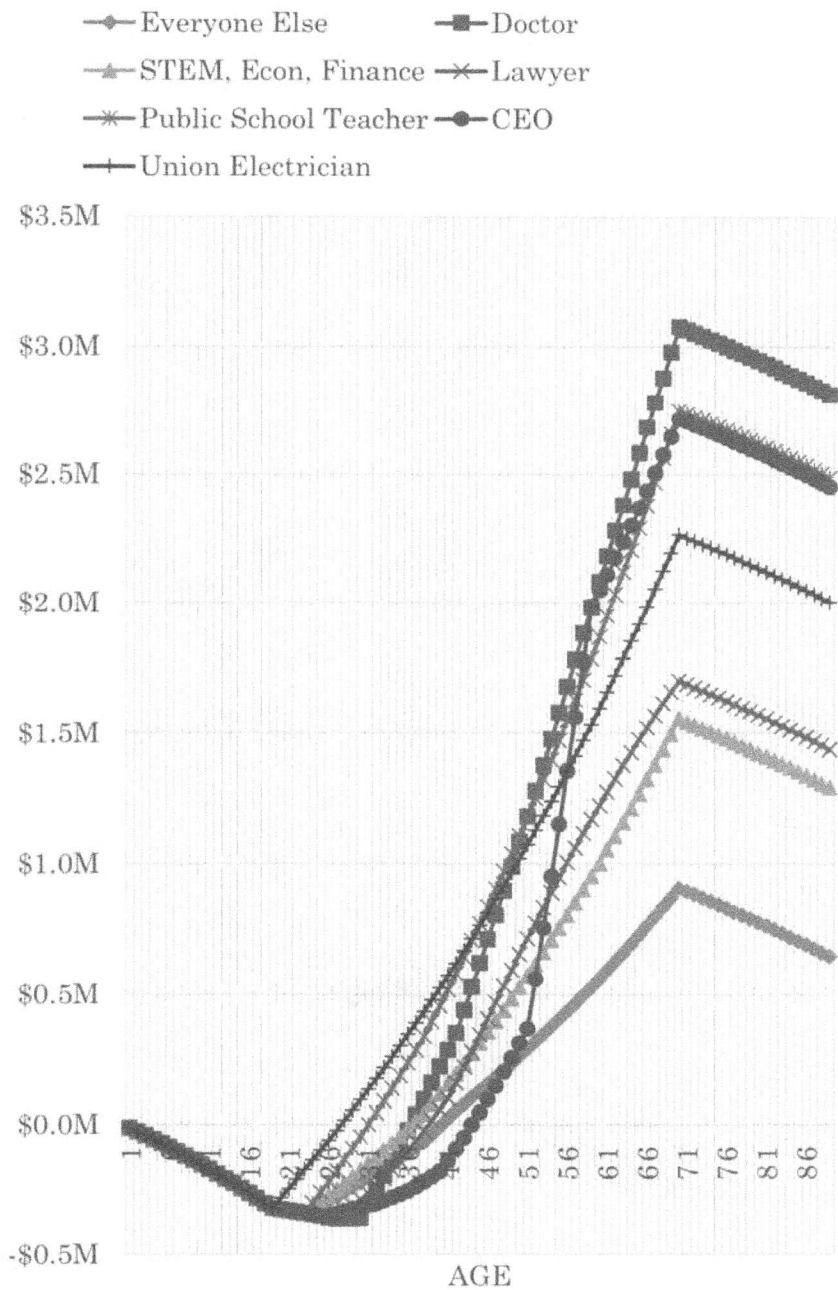

Figure 96: Lifetime Accrued Disposable Income

Figure 97: Lifetime Accrued Income-Related Tax

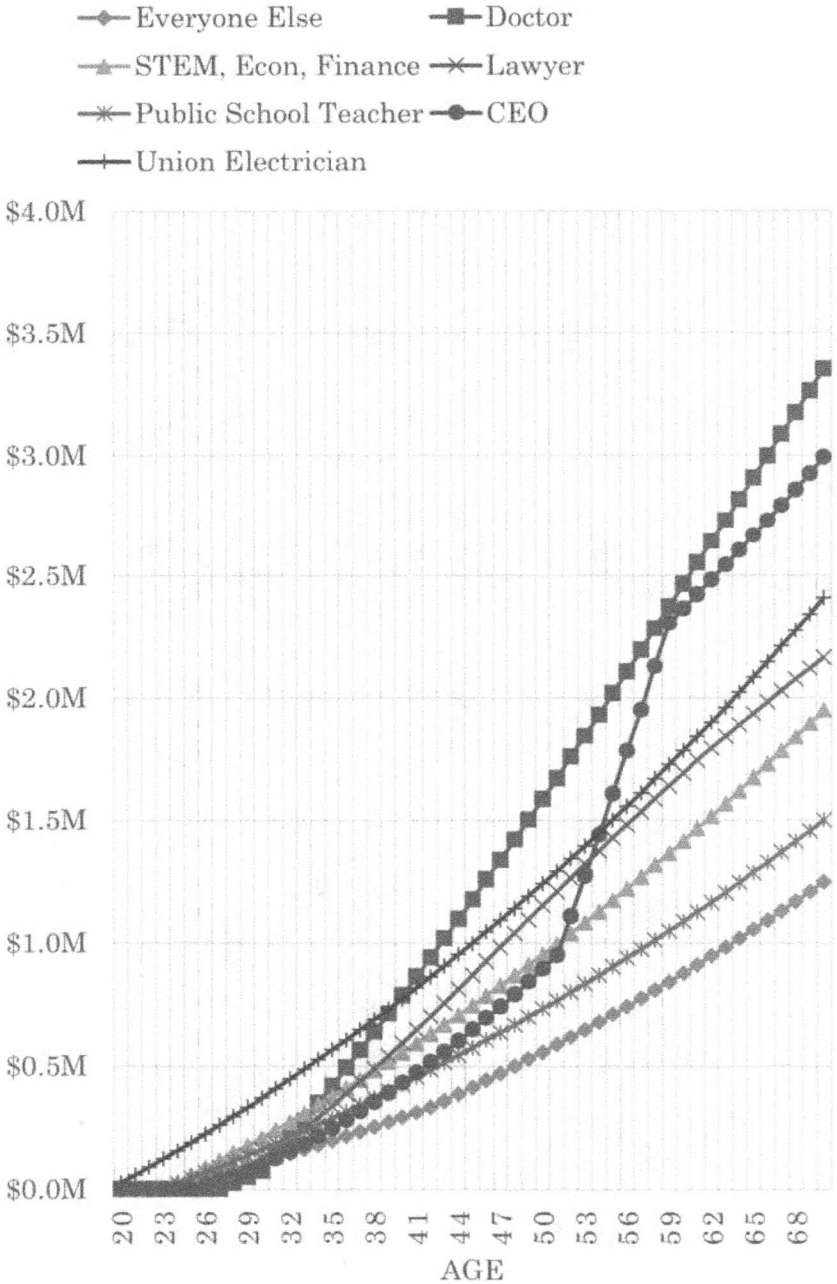

Legend:
- Everyone Else
- Doctor
- STEM, Econ, Finance
- Lawyer
- Public School Teacher
- CEO
- Union Electrician

AGE

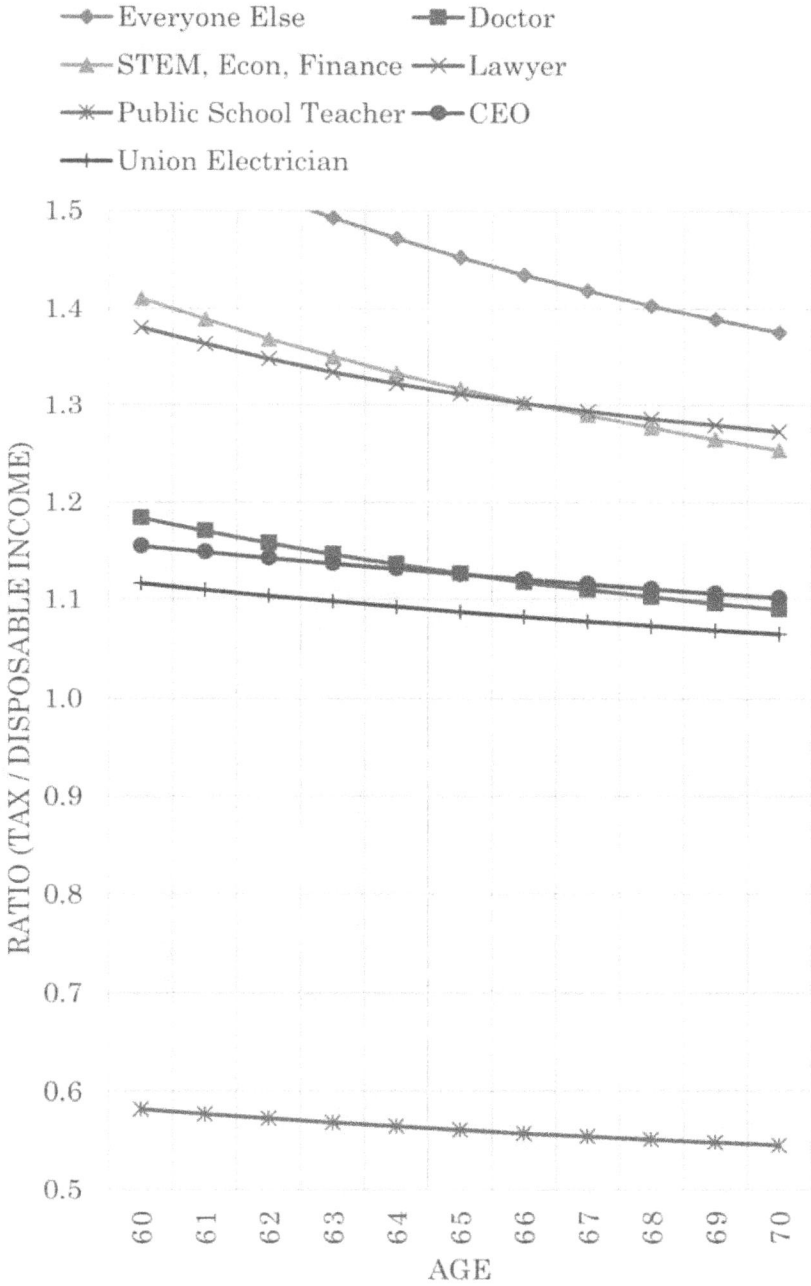

Figure 98: Accrued Tax-to-Income Ratio, End-of-Life Outcomes

Figure 99: Head of Household Median Income by Age

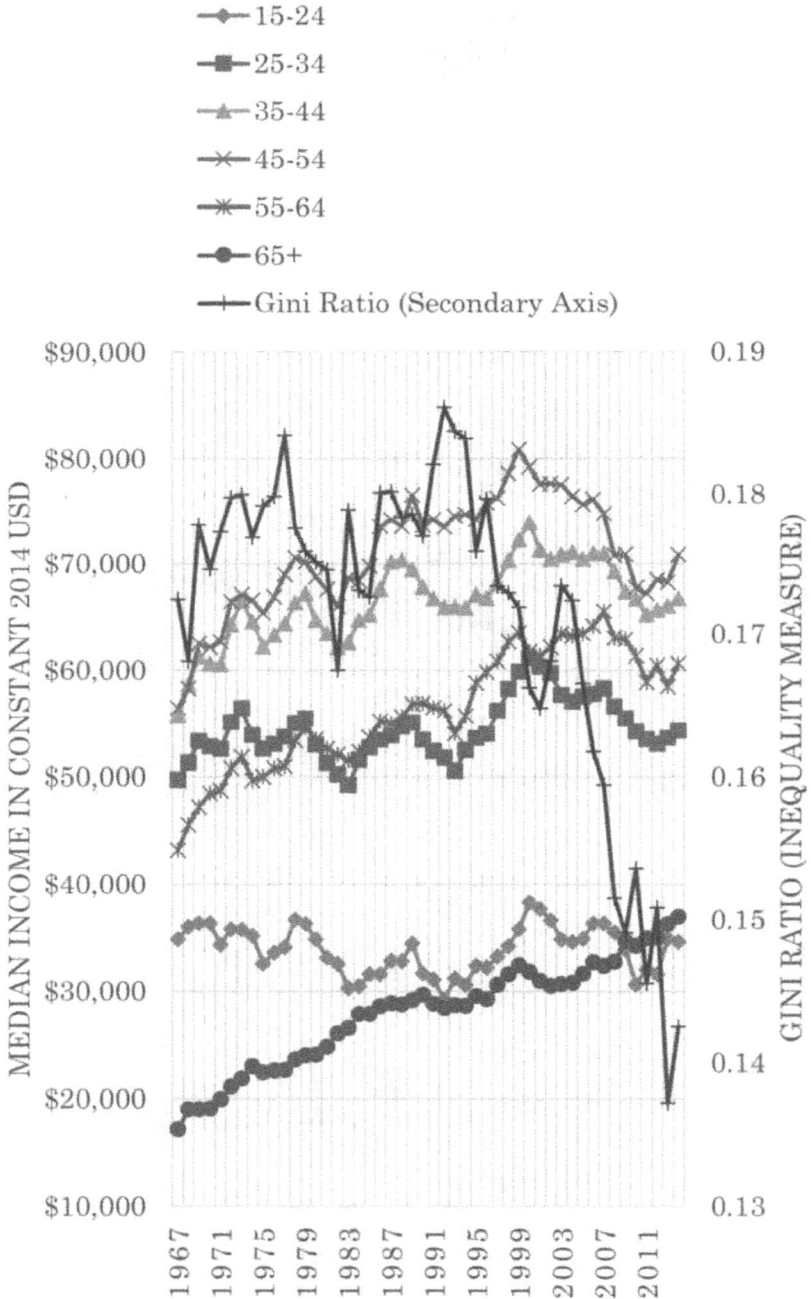

Legend:
- 15-24
- 25-34
- 35-44
- 45-54
- 55-64
- 65+
- Gini Ratio (Secondary Axis)

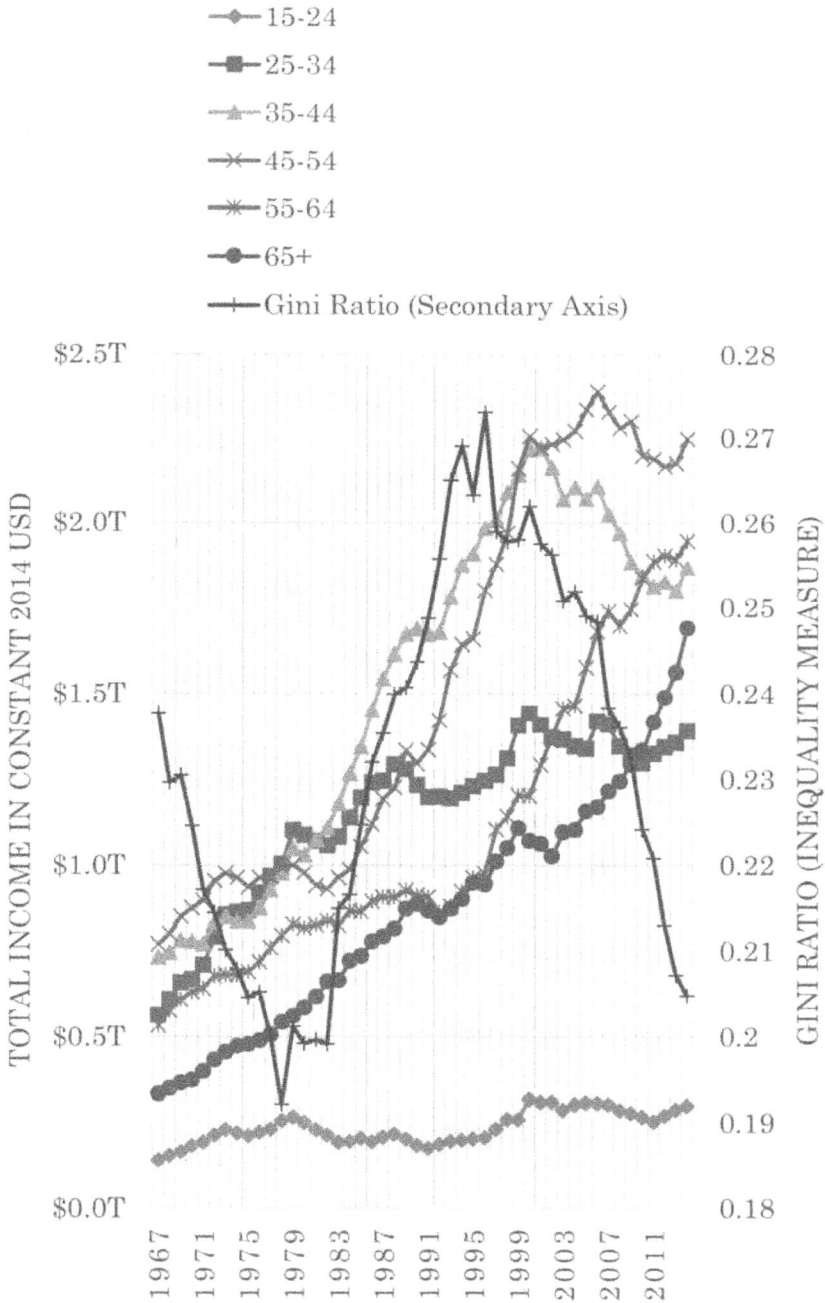

Figure 100: Head of Household Total Income by Age

Legend:
- 15-24
- 25-34
- 35-44
- 45-54
- 55-64
- 65+
- Gini Ratio (Secondary Axis)

Appendix 7: Tax & Income Tables

IR Tax Rate – Income-Related Tax Rate for wage and salary earners, %, a 2012 snapshot showing how income-related taxes are much heavier and progressive than typical income tax reports which only include payroll taxes.

Income-Related tax includes all taxes levied upon earning activity, for example: Federal Income Tax, Social Security Tax, Medicare & Medicaid Tax, Employer-Levied Social Security Tax, Employer-Levied Medicare & Medicaid Tax, Federal Unemployment Tax (FUTA), Worker's Comp Tax, State Income Tax, State Unemployment Tax (SUTA), Federal & State Gasoline Tax (charged upon a daily work commute of 15 miles, in a 22 mile-per-gallon vehicle, for 260 working days per year), tolls, phone, sales, car, and real estate tax related to work activities. Welfare policies currently redistribute around $1T to people earning under $50.5k per year (the welfare cliff).[289] That source of income is not included in this model, to better evaluate tax-burden on wages.

Income per Earner – median, $, 2012;[290] **% of Total Income** – percent of all household income in the US;[291] **Earners in Quintile** – millions; **No-Earner Homes** – percent, households with no earners (only receiving unearned income), total is percent of all households; **People in Quintile** – millions; **Non-Earners in Quintile** – millions;

Income quintiles adjusted to 2013 for population growth and inflation. Median income per earner derived from 2012 data.

---

[289] (Zerohedge, 2012)
[290] (Perry, Explaining income inequality by household demographics, 2014)
[291] (US Census Bureau, 2014)

Thomas E. Kurek

Table 1: Taxation & Income Quintiles, 2012

Category	IR Tax Rate	IR Tax per Earner	Net Income per Earner
Lowest	15.2	4,064	22,606
2nd	19.3	6,636	27,829
3rd	28.9	11,672	28,827
4th	39.9	19,987	30,163
Highest	44.4	41,346	51,795
Total	N/A	N/A	N/A

Table 2: Summary Wage Tax Table, 2012

Quintile of Earners	0-19th	20-39th	40-59th	60-79th	80-99th
Wage Taxes (%)	15.2	19.3	28.8	39.9	44.4
National Income (%)	3.2	8.3	14.4	23.0	51.0
Income / Household ($, k)	11.5	29.7	51.2	82.1	181.9
Income / Earner ($, k)	25.5	33.0	38.8	48.0	89.2
Earners / Household	0.45	0.9	1.32	1.71	2.04
Earners / Quintile (M)	10.8	21.6	31.9	41.2	49.2
Wage Taxes ($, B)	41.9	137	357	788	1,946

Table 3: Income Quintiles, 2012

Quintile	Income per Earner[292]	Earners per Home	% of Total Income [293]	Earners in Quintile	No-Earner Homes
Lowest	25,533	0.45	3.2	10.3	61
2nd	32,996	0.9	8.3	20.7	31.8
3rd	38,772	1.32	14.4	30.5	14.4
4th	48,011	1.71	23.0	39.4	6.6
Highest	89,169	2.04	51.0	47.1	3.0
Total	N/A	N/A	N/A	148.1	23.4

Quintile	People per Household	People in Quintile*	Non-Earners in Quintile
Lowest	1.7	39.0	31.8
2nd	2.3	52.9	36.4
3rd	2.6	60.2	34.4
4th	2.9	66.9	32.7
Highest	3.2	73.8	32.6
Total	N/A	316.1	168.0

---

[292] (Perry, Explaining income inequality by household demographics, 2014)
[293] (US Census Bureau, 2014)

Thomas E. Kurek

Works Cited

Ames, M. (2014, March 22). *Revealed: Apple and Google's wage-fixing cartel involved dozens more companies, over one million employees.* Retrieved from Pando: https://pando.com/2014/03/22/revealed-apple-and-googles-wage-fixing-cartel-involved-dozens-more-companies-over-one-million-employees/

Annett, A. F. (1999). *The Federal Government's Poor Management of America's Land Resources.* Washington D.C.: The Heritage Foundation.

Bamberger. (2012, November 16). *How Much Does The Average CEO Really Earn?* Retrieved from Chief Executive: http://chiefexecutive.net/how-much-does-the-average-ceo-really-earn/

Beach, W. W., Campbell Ph.D., K., Kreutzer Ph.D., D. W., Lieberman, B., & Loris, N. (2009). *The Economic Consequences of Waxman-Markey: An Analysis of the American Clean Energy and Security Act of 2009.* Washington D.C.: Heritage Foundation.

Bednar, R. (Director). (2009). *Earth 2100* [Motion Picture].

Bohannon, J. (2013). Who's Afraid of Peer Review? *Science, 342 (6154)*, 60-65.

Buckley, Jr., W. F. (2004, July 11). Questions for William F. Buckley: Conservatively Speaking. (The New York Times Magazine, Interviewer)

Bureau of Labor Statistics. (2014, July 15). *Databases, Tables & Calculators by Subject (LNU02600000).* Retrieved from BLS.gov: http://data.bls.gov/timeseries/LNU02600000

Bureau of Labor Statistics. (2014, July 15). *Labor Force Statistics from the Current Population Survey 19. Persons at work in agriculture and nonagricultural industries by hours of work.* Retrieved from BLS.gov: http://www.bls.gov/cps/cpsaat19.htm

Burnison, G. (2013, March 21). *The CEO Pay Circus of 2013.* Retrieved from Yahoo Finance:

http://finance.yahoo.com/blogs/the-exchange/ceo-pay-circus-2013-214028626.html

Chantrill, C. (2014, June 24). *Government Spending Totals, 2013*. Retrieved from USGovernmentSpending.com: http://www.usgovernmentspending.com/total_2013USrt_15rs5n

Chesterton, G. K. (1915). *All Things Considered*. London: Public Domain.

Clabaugh, J. (2015, May 19). *Does your college student expect support after graduation? They're not alone*. Retrieved from Washington Business Journal: http://www.bizjournals.com/washington/news/2015/05/19/does-your-college-grad-expect-support-after.html

Clarke, J. (2009, February 9). *Viewpoint: The end of the neo-cons?* Retrieved from BBC: http://news.bbc.co.uk/2/hi/americas/7825039.stm

Competitive Enterprise Institute. (2016, April 7). *CEI Fights Subpoena to Silence Debate on Climate Change*. Retrieved from CEI.org: https://cei.org/content/cei-fights-subpoena-silence-debate-climate-change

Corporation for National and Community Service. (2012). *Volunteering and Civic Live in America 2012*. Washington, DC: Corporation for National and Community Service.

Crews Jr., C. W. (2014). *An Annual Snapshot of the Federal Regulatory State*. Washington, D.C.: Competitive Enterprise Institute.

Crews Jr., C. W. (2014). *Ten Thousand Commandments - An Annual Snapshot of the Federal Regulatory State*. Washington, D.C.: Competitive Enterprise Institute.

Dickens, C. (1861). *Great Expectations*. London: Public Domain.

Dovere, E.-I. (2012, July 4). Obama: Historian-in-chief. *Politico*.

Dubay, C. S. (2005, February 2). *Stock Market Investing: Good Enough for Public Employee and Union Pension Funds*. Retrieved from The Tax Foundation:

http://taxfoundation.org/article/stock-market-investing-good-enough-public-employee-and-union-pension-funds

Dworkin, R. W. (2010). The Rise of the Caring Industry. *Hoover Institution: Policy Review.*

Eastwood, C. (Director). (2008). *Gran Torino* [Motion Picture].

Epstein, R. A. (2011). The Shortsighted Keynesians. *Hoover Institution: Defining Ideas.*

Evans-Pritchard, A. (2009, February 2). *Let banks fail, says Nobel economist Joseph Stiglitz.* Retrieved from The Telegraph: http://www.telegraph.co.uk/finance/newsbysector/banksandfinance/4424418/Let-banks-fail-says-Nobel-economist-Joseph-Stiglitz.html

Farrell, D., Jensen, E., Kocher, B., Lovegrove, N., Melhem, F., Mendonca, L., & Parish, B. (2008). *Accounting for the cost of US health care: A new look at why Americans spend more.* New York: McKinsey Global Institute.

Fincher, D. (Director). (1999). *Fight Club* [Motion Picture].

Friedman, M. (1962). Medical Licensure. In Friedman, Milton, *Capitalism and Freedom* (pp. 149-160). Chicago, IL: The University of Chicago Press.

Friedman, M. (2001, winter). How to Cure Healthcare. *The Public Interest, 142*, 3-30.

Gibson, C., & Jung, K. (2002). *Historical Census Statistics on Population Totals By Race, 1790 to 1990, and By Hispanic Origin, 1970 to 1990, For The United States, Regions, Divisions, and States. (Working Paper Series No. 56).* Washington, D.C.: Population Division, U.S. Census Bureau.

Godwin, W. (1793). Enquiry Concerning Political Justice. *II*, 129. London: Public Domain.

Gratton, B., & Butmann, M. (2006). Historical Statistics of the United States: Millennial Edition 1 (First Edition ed.). Cambridge, UK: Cambridge University Press.

Hamilton, A., Madison, J., & Jay, J. (1788). *The Federalist Papers.* New York: Public Domain.

Hayek, F. A. (1944). *The Road to Serfdom.* London: Routledge.

Hershbein, B. (2016, February 19). *A college degree is worth less if you are raised poor* . Retrieved from Brookings Institution: http://www.brookings.edu/blogs/social-mobility-memos/posts/2016/02/19-college-degree-worth-less-raised-poor-hershbein

Hitler, A. (1940, December 18). Speech at the Annual Rally of Young Officer Cadets. Berlin, Germany.

Humes, K., Jones, N., & Ramirez, R. (2011). *Overview of Race and Hispanic Origin: 2010, 2010 Census Briefs.* Washington, D.C.: U.S. Census Bureau.

Hyman, M. (2011, November 11). *Man vs. Beetle.* Retrieved from The American Spectator: http://spectator.org/articles/36653/man-vs-beetle

Ioannidis, J. P. (2005). Why Most Published Research Findings are False. *PLoS Medicine, 2(8).*

Jefferson, T. (1816, May 18). Extract from Thomas Jefferson's Addition to Note for Destutt de Tracy's Treatise on Political Economy. *Letter to Joseph Milligan.*

Kane, L. (2016, January 12). *Student loan debt in the US has topped $1.3 trillion.* Retrieved from Business Insider: http://www.businessinsider.com/student-loan-debt-state-of-the-union-2016-1

Katz, A. J. (2012). *Explaining Long-term Differences Between Census and BEA Measures of Household Income.* Washington, DC: Federal Committee on Statistical Methodology Research Conference.

Korte, G. (2014, December 17). *Obama issues 'executive orders by another name'.* Retrieved from USA Today: http://www.usatoday.com/story/news/politics/2014/12/16/obama-presidential-memoranda-executive-orders/20191805/

Kristol, I. (1995). American conservatism 1945-1995. *National Affairs: Fall (121)*.

Lavelle, K., Silverstone, Y., & Smith, D. (2015). *Are you the weakest link? Strengthening your talent supply chain*. Chicago, IL: Accenture.

Loris, N., & Dubay, C. S. (2011). *What's an Oil Subsidy?* Washington D.C.: The Heritage Foundation.

Ma, Y. (2010). *China's View of Climate Change*. Stanford, CA: Hoover Institution.

Marcus, A., & Oransky, I. (2014). *Crack Down on Scientific Fraudsters*. New York: New York Times.

Marr, C., & Huang, C.-C. (2012). *Misconceptions and Realities About Who Pays Taxes*. Washington, D.C.: Center on Budget and Policy Priorities.

Masunaga, S., & Lien, T. (2016, February 2). *Yahoo ex-employee sues, alleging manipulation of performance reviews and gender bias*. Retrieved from LA Times: http://www.latimes.com/business/technology/la-fi-tn-yahoo-lawsuit-20160202-story.html

Metcalf, G. E. (1997). *The National Sales Tax: Who Bears the Burden? (Cato Policy Analysis No. 289)*. Washington, D.C.: The Cato Institute.

Nash, C. (2016, February 2). *Former Yahoo Employee Sues over Alleged Discrimination Against Men*. Retrieved from Breitbart: http://www.breitbart.com/tech/2016/02/02/former-yahoo-employee-sues-for-bias-against-men/

National Center for Charitable Statistics. (2014, April 16). *NCCS All Registered Nonprofits Table Wizard*. Retrieved from National Center for Charitable Statistics: http://nccsweb.urban.org/tablewiz/bmf.php

Nosek, B. A. (2015). Estimating the Reproducibility of Psychological Science. *Science Magazine, 349 (6251)*.

Obama, B. H. (2001). Interview of Illinois Senator Barack Obama on Chicago Public Radio WBEZ Chicago 91.5 FM. (Moderator, Interviewer)

Obama, B. H. (2014, July 10). Remarks by the President on the Economy. Austin, TX, USA. Retrieved from https://www.whitehouse.gov/the-press-office/2014/07/10/remarks-president-economy-austin-tx

Obata, S. (2015, October 21). *O Wage Inflation, Where Art Thou?* Retrieved from Zero Hedge: http://www.zerohedge.com/news/2015-10-21/o-wage-inflation-where-art-thou

Paine, T. (1794). *The Age of Reason.* Luxembourg: Public Domain.

Perry, M. J. (2009, June 24). *The Medical Cartel: Why are MD Salaries So High?* Retrieved from Wall Street Pit: http://wallstreetpit.com/5769-the-medical-cartel-why-are-md-salaries-so-high/

Perry, M. J. (2011, May 12). *Oil Industry Profit Margin Ranks #114 out 215.* Retrieved from Carpe Diem - Professor Mark J. Perry's Blog for Economics and Finance: http://mjperry.blogspot.com/2011/05/oil-profit-margin-ranks-114-out-215.html

Perry, M. J. (2014, July 16). *Explaining income inequality by household demographics.* Retrieved from American Enterprise Institute: http://www.aei-ideas.org/2013/12/explaining-income-inequality-by-household-demographics/

Pew Research Center. (2013). *Pew Research Center tabulations of March Current Population Survey (CPS) Integrated Public Use Micro Samples.* Washington, D.C.: Pew Research.

Plato. (380 BC). *The Republic, Book III.* Athens: Public Domain.

Polybius, & Paton, W. R. (117 B.C.; Translation, 1922). *Polybius - The Histories.* London: William Heinemann.

Rector, R., & Sheffield, R. (2011). *Air Conditioning, Cable TV, and an Xbox: What is Poverty in the United States Today?* Washington, D.C.: The Heritage Foundation.

Rector, R., & Sheffield, R. (2014). *The War on Poverty After 50 Years.* Washington, D.C.: Heritage Foundation.

Reisman, G. (2015, April 9). *Freedom Of Opportunity, Not Equality Of Opportunity*. Retrieved from Amazon: http://www.amazon.com/dp/B00VW8RJ26

Ruser, J., Pilot, A., & Nelson, C. (2004). *Alternative Measures of Household Income.* Washington, DC: Federal Economic Statistics Advisory Committee.

Sahr, R. (2014). *Inflation Conversion Factors for years 1774 to estimated 2024*. Retrieved from Oregon State University: http://liberalarts.oregonstate.edu/spp/polisci/research/inflatio n-conversion-factors-convert-dollars-1774-estimated-2024-dollars-recent-year

Schumpeter, J. A. (1954). *History of Economic Analysis.* New York: Oxford University Press.

Service, R. (2000). *Lenin: A Biography.* New York: MacMillan.

Smith, R. (2010). Classical Peer Review: An Empty Gun. *Breast Cancer Research, 12 (Suppl 4):S13.*

Sowell, T. (1981, November 12). Firing Line: The Economic Lot of Minorities. (W. F. Buckley Jr., Interviewer)

Sowell, T. (1987). *A Conflict of Visions.* New York: William Morrow & Co.

Sowell, T. (2009). *Intellectuals and Society.* New York: Basic Books.

Sowell, T. (2009). *The Housing Boom and Bust.* New York: Basic Books.

Spiegel Staff. (2013, September 13). *Germany's Energy Poverty: How Electricity Became a Luxury Good*. Retrieved from Spiegel Online International: http://www.spiegel.de/international/germany/high-costs-and-errors-of-german-transition-to-renewable-energy-a-920288.html

Stewart, J., & O'Reilly, B. (2012, October 6). The Rumble 2012. (E. D. Hill, Interviewer)

The Heritage Foundation. (2016, February 5). *FDR's Second Bill of Rights*. Retrieved from The Heritage Foundation: http://www.heritage.org/initiatives/first-principles/primary-sources/fdrs-second-bill-of-rights

Thorpe, F. N. (1898). *A Constitutional History of the American People: 1776 - 1850*. London: Harper & Brothers.

U.S. Bureau of Economic Analysis. (2014, November 7). *Table 2.1. Personal Income and Its Disposition*. Retrieved from US BEA: http://www.bea.gov/iTable/index_nipa.cfm

U.S. Bureau of Economic Analysis. (2015, January 2). *Table 2.2A-B. Wages and Salaries by Industry*. Retrieved from US BEA: http://www.bea.gov/iTable/index_nipa.cfm

U.S. Bureau of Economic Analysis. (2015, January 2). *Table 5.1. Saving and Investment by Sector*. Retrieved from US BEA: http://www.bea.gov/iTable/index_nipa.cfm

U.S. Bureau of Economic Analysis. (2015, January 2). *Table 6.17A-D. Corporate Profits Before Tax by Industry*. Retrieved from US BEA: http://www.bea.gov/iTable/index_nipa.cfm

U.S. Bureau of Economic Analysis. (2015, January 2). *Table 6.19A-D. Corporate Profits After Tax by Industry*. Retrieved from US BEA: http://www.bea.gov/iTable/index_nipa.cfm

U.S. Bureau of Economic Analysis. (2015, January 15). *Table 6.2A-D. Compensation of Employees by Industry*. Retrieved from US BEA: http://www.bea.gov/iTable/index_nipa.cfm

U.S. Bureau of Economic Analysis. (2015, January 2). *Table 6.5A-D. Full-Time Equivalent Employees by Industry*. Retrieved from US BEA: http://www.bea.gov/iTable/index_nipa.cfm

U.S. Bureau of the Census. (1975). *Historical Statistics of the United States, Colonial Times to 1970, Bicentennial Edition, Part 2, Series Z 1–19*. Washington, D.C.: U.S. Bureau of the Census.

Thomas E. Kurek

U.S. Census Bureau. (2016, March 8). *Survey of Income and Program Participation - 2001 Panel Wave 08*. Retrieved from U.S. Census Bureau: http://www.census.gov/programs-surveys/sipp/data/2001-panel/wave-8.html

U.S. Department of Housing and Urban Development. (2010). *The 2009 Annual Homeless Assessment Report to Congress, June 2010*. Washington, D.C.: Office of Community Planning and Development.

U.S. Federal Bureau of Investigation - FBI. (2014). *Uniform Crime Reporting Program (Data Collected in Accordance with the Hate Crimes Statistics Act of 1990)*. Washington, D.C.: FBI.

U.S. General Services Administration. (2016, March 12). *FY 2016 Per Diem Rates for New York*. Retrieved from GSA: http://www.gsa.gov/portal/category/100120

US Census Bureau. (2014, July 16). *Shares of household income of quintiles in the United States from 1970 to 2012*. Retrieved from Statista: http://www.statista.com/statistics/203247/shares-of-household-income-of-quintiles-in-the-us/

von Mises, L. (1922). Chapter IV The Socialist Community under Stationary Conditions. In L. von Mises, *Socialism: An Economic and Sociological Analysis*. Vienna, Austria.

von Mises, L. (1922). Chapter IV, Section 2: The Disutilities and Satisfactions of Labour. In L. von Mises, *Socialism: An Economic and Sociological Analysis* (pp. 163-169). Vienna, Austria: Public Domain.

von Mises, L. (2015, October 15). *Socialism: An Economic and Sociological Analysis, Part V, Destructionism, Chapter 33*. Retrieved from Library of Economics and Liberty: http://www.econlib.org/library/Mises/msS12.html

von Spakovsky, H. A. (2015, October 30). *Shutting Down Debate on Climate Change*. Retrieved from The Heritage Foundation: http://www.heritage.org/research/commentary/2015/10/shutting-down-debate-on-climate-change

World Bank. (2014, July 15). *World Development Indicators.* Retrieved from The World Bank: http://data.worldbank.org/data-catalog/world-development-indicators

Zerohedge. (2012, November 27). *When Work Is Punished: The Tragedy Of America's Welfare State.* Retrieved from Zerohedge: http://www.zerohedge.com/news/2012-11-27/when-work-punished-tragedy-americas-welfare-state

ZeroHedge. (2014, September 24). *Household Net Worth Just Hit A Record High: Here Is Who Benefited.* Retrieved from ZeroHedge: http://www.zerohedge.com/news/2014-09-24/household-net-worth-just-hit-record-high-here-who-benefited

Zubrin, R. (2015). Germnay's Green-Power Program Crushes the Poor. *National Review.*

Index

        Thomas E. Kurek

Thomas E. Kurek

Thomas E. Kurek

About the Author

Thomas Kurek has designed, implemented, or managed eighteen enterprise information systems, including four for MYnstrel, Inc., a corporation that he founded and built from the ground up. His other technologies were commissioned by the State Department, global hospitality and tourism, ecommerce, healthcare, state government, FBI, and Department of Defense. As a biomechanics researcher, he produced prototypes for (1) improving the material properties of bioprosthetic heart valves, and (2) sports medicine compensatory mechanism diagnostics and correction. He developed the theory of *alvarism* over the course of a decade of cultural and economic research, presenting the results in briefings delivered across Washington D.C. and in the U.S. Senate, ultimately founding Alvarism LLC, a think tank for economic and sociological analysis based upon empirical, rational, and perennial knowledge paradigms. On one occasion, he saved the Department of Defense ten-million dollars per year with just one week of labor, Microsoft Excel, and access to billing records.

He holds a B.Sc. in Engineering Physics (ESM) with a concentration in Biomechanics over the course of 154 credit hours, from Virginia Tech – a program tied with Stanford. He completed three years of economics courses in one semester with alternative coursework that relied upon advanced mathematics. Programming, researching, and gainfully employed since age 15, he is also skilled in persuasive, expository, and descriptive non-fiction writing, entrepreneurship, leadership, philosophy, and cultural commerce and strategy. He enjoys deep interpersonal connections, community development, history, classic literature, culture and music festivals, live theater, weight lifting, running, and academic lectures.

Thomas E. Kurek